Story Frames
for Teaching Literacy

Story Frames
for Teaching Literacy
Enhancing Student Learning
Through the Power of Storytelling

by

Carolee Dean, M.S., CCC-SLP, CALT
Word Travel LLC
Denver, Colorado

with invited contributors

·P·A·U·L·H·
BROOKES
PUBLISHING Cº ®

Baltimore • London • Sydney

Paul H. Brookes Publishing Co.
Post Office Box 10624
Baltimore, Maryland 21285-0624
USA

www.brookespublishing.com

Typeset by Progressive Publishing Services, York, Pennsylvania.
Manufactured in the United States of America by
Sheridan Books, Inc., Chelsea, Michigan.

Case studies are real people or composites based on the authors' experiences. Real names and identifying
details are used by permission.

Stock photos and stock art © iStock.com and © AdobeStock.

Icons used in the Editor's Toolbox, Wh-Questions, Vocabulary Words With Images, and student worksheets are
used courtesy of The Noun Project (thenounproject.com).

Illustrations for the Twelve Elements were created by Christopher Jochens and are included courtesy
of Mr. Jochens. Used by permission.

Library of Congress Cataloging-in-Publication Data

Names: Dean, Carolee, author.
Title: Story frames for teaching literacy : enhancing student
    learning through the power of storytelling / by Carolee Dean;
    with invited contributors.
Description: Baltimore, Maryland : Paul H. Brookes Publishing Co., 2021. |
    Includes bibliographical references and index.
Identifiers: LCCN 2020044150 (print) | LCCN 2020044151 (ebook) |
    ISBN 9781681254548 (paperback) | ISBN 9781681254555 (epub) |
    ISBN 9781681254562 (pdf)
Subjects: LCSH: Storytelling. | Language arts (Elementary) |
    Language arts (Middle school)
Classification: LCC LB1042.D43 2021 (print) | LCC LB1042 (ebook) |
    DDC 372.6—dc23
LC record available at https://lccn.loc.gov/2020044150
LC ebook record available at https://lccn.loc.gov/2020044151

British Library Cataloguing in Publication data are available from the British Library.

2025   2024   2023   2022   2021

10   9   8   7   6   5   4   3   2   1

Contents

About the Downloads

Purchasers of this book may download, print, and/or photocopy handouts, worksheets, story analyses, and other provided classroom and professional development resources for their own educational use and the use of their school or professional practice. These materials may not be distributed at large.

To access the materials that come with this book:

1. Go to the Brookes Publishing Download Hub: http://downloads.brookespublishing.com

2. Register to create an account (or log in with an existing account)

3. Filter or search for your book title

About the Author

Carolee Dean, M.S., CCC-SLP, CALT, Speech-Language Pathologist and Certified Academic Language Therapist; Founder, Word Travel Literacy, Denver, Colorado

Carolee Dean, the founder of Word Travel Literacy (a division of Word Travel LLC), specializes in the treatment of dyslexia, other language-based learning differences, and autism. With more than 20 years of experience in the public schools, she now focuses on teletherapy, consultation, and resource development. She is a former president of the Southwest Branch of the International Dyslexia Association and an award-winning author of the young adult fiction titles *Comfort* (HMH Books for Young Readers, 2002), *Take Me There* (Simon Pulse, 2010), and *Forget Me Not* (Simon Pulse, 2012). She frequently combines her knowledge of story structure and learning differences to speak at national and international conferences on the subject of narrative intervention.

About the Contributors

Amy Miller, M.A., M.F.A., ICALP, Founder and Executive Director, May Center for Learning, Santa Fe, New Mexico

Amy Miller is the founder and executive director of May Center for Learning, a nonprofit school and outreach center for students with learning differences. She frequently presents to educators, focusing on best practices for students with learning differences, the science of teaching structured reading and writing, and the importance of structuring the learning environment to improve executive functioning skills. Amy successfully advocated for SB 398, a New Mexico state law that mandates universal screening for characteristics of dyslexia and science-based reading instruction for all students. Founder of Dyslexia Justice League, a community organization that connects students with dyslexia with adult mentors, Amy is also the author of *The Way I See It* (Azro Press, 2015), a play and book that celebrates unique points of view, developed in collaboration with students at May Center. *Where I Come From* (Azro Press, 2014), a book that Amy coauthored with May Center students, won the 2014 New Mexico/Arizona Young Adult Book of the Year.

Paula Moraine, M.Ed., Educational Consultant, The Attention Fix Educational Consulting, LLC, Bel Air, Maryland

Paula Moraine is an international teacher, tutor, speaker, and author. She is in private practice in Bel Air, Maryland, as an educational consultant, specializing in executive functions, attention-deficit/hyperactivity disorder, dyslexia, dysgraphia, dyscalculia, and autism. She is the author of *Helping Students Take Control of Everyday Executive Functions—The Attention Fix* (Jessica Kingsley Publishers, 2012) and *Autism and Everyday Executive Functions* (Jessica Kingsley Publishers, 2015).

Mary Jo O'Neill, M.Ed., Special Education Advocate, Hickman & Lowder Company, Cleveland, Ohio

As an educational advocate, Mary Jo O'Neill works with families of children with learning disabilities. Her background as a teacher and intervention specialist supports collaboration with teachers, administrators, and school systems to work together to create and implement the best systems and tools for successful learning. Always at the center of the work is the student, as she facilitates collaboration with parents, teachers, and administrators. Her expertise is ensuring all voices are heard, as the process moves forward, always in the best interest of the student.

Lesley Roessing, M.Ed., Former Director, Coastal Savannah Writing Project; Senior Lecturer (retired), College of Education, Armstrong State University, Savannah, Georgia

Lesley Roessing taught middle school language arts and humanities for more than 20 years. She served as Founding Director of the Coastal Savannah Writing Project and Senior Lecturer in the College of Education of Armstrong University in Savannah, Georgia (now Georgia Southern University), and as a Literacy Consultant with a K–8 school.

Lesley is the author of *The Write to Read: Response Journals That Increase Comprehension* (Corwin, 2009); *Comma Quest: The Rules They Followed—The Sentences They Saved* (Discover Writing, 2019); *No More "Us" and "Them": Classroom Lessons and Activities to Promote Peer Respect* (R&L Education, 2012); *Bridging the Gap: Reading Critically and Writing Meaningfully to Get to the Core* (Rowman & Littlefield Publishers, 2014); and *Talking Texts: A Teachers' Guide to Book Clubs Across the Curriculum* (Rowman & Littlefield Publishers, 2019). She has written articles on literacy for a variety of academic journals and has served as editor for *Connections*, the Georgia Council of Teachers of English–award winning peer-reviewed journal, and as a columnist for *AMLE Magazine*.

William Van Cleave, M.A., Educational Consultant and President, W.V.C.ED, Louisville, Kentucky

William Van Cleave is in private practice as an educational consultant and author whose specialties include morphology and written expression. An internationally recognized speaker with an interactive, hands-on presentation style, William has presented on effective teaching practices both in the United States and abroad since 1995. In his career, William has consulted with both private and public schools; participated in state multi-tiered system of supports (MTSS) writing standards committee work; implemented Trainer of Trainers projects; and written a number of articles and books, including *Writing Matters: Developing Sentence Skills in Students of All Ages* (W.V.C.ED, 2014). In addition, William has served as a classroom teacher, tutor, and administrator.

Carol Westby, Ph.D., Consultant, Bilingual Multicultural Services, Albuquerque, New Mexico

Carol Westby has published and presented nationally and internationally on play, theory of mind, language–literacy relationships, attention-deficit/hyperactivity disorder, narrative/expository development and facilitation, screen time, children and families who have experienced trauma, and issues in assessment and intervention with culturally/linguistically diverse populations. She has received the American Speech-Language-Hearing Association's Honors of the Association, The Kleffner Lifetime Achievement Award, and the award for Contributions to Multicultural Affairs. Carol is Board Certified in Child Language and Language Disorders and has received the Distinguished Alumnus Award from Geneva College and the University of Iowa's Department of Speech Pathology and Audiology.

Acknowledgments

I humbly and gratefully acknowledge the authors of the contributing chapters who have added so much variety to the richness and texture of this resource—Amy Miller, Paula Moraine, Mary Jo O'Neill, Lesley Roessing, William Van Cleave, and Carol Westby. The visual artists were vital in bringing my vision to life. Thanks to Christopher Jochens, illustrator; Tommye Leigh Dean, graphic designer; the contributors from The Noun Project (www.thenounproject.com), and Erin Geoghegan, Graphic Design Manager at Brookes Publishing. Mary Kristen Dean Wilkinson provided invaluable help as a research assistant, while my husband, Thomas, and son, Jonathon, have been important sounding boards for brainstorming the many ways stories have enriched our lives. My admiration goes out to the talented and diverse authors of children's books that have been highlighted throughout *Story Frames*. Your work inspires young people and adults alike.

The entire team at Brookes Publishing has my undying gratitude, especially the acquisitions editors, Liz Gildea and Astrid Pohl Zuckerman, who understood my vision for this project and were the first to champion my book, and their assistant, Savannah Neubert. A special thanks goes out to Developmental Editor Tess Hoffman, whose organizational skills far surpass my own. Your insights and sharp eye helped give *Story Frames* its form and shape. Thanks to Copyeditor Lisa Long and Project Manager Nicole Schmidl, who oversaw a thousand little details, and to the Marketing and Sales teams, who worked to get this resource out to teachers and therapists. It truly takes a village to publish a book!

Finally, this book would never have come into being without the inspiration of my students, whose perseverance and passion for stories compelled me to create a method by which struggling learners could find a voice to create their own narratives. Thanks to you all!

Introduction

Stories existed long before books. We use stories to connect, to learn, to persuade, and to teach. Storytelling is an essential human skill that most people understand on a superficial level. Some turn it into an art form, but others struggle with its application. Educators know the power of stories and use them often, not only in language arts but in science, history, mathematics, and sports. Educators do not always understand the deep structure of stories, though, nor the full potential of their application.

Story Frames provides a dynamic, engaging framework for educators to use to inspire students of all ages to engage in the storytelling process, by both analyzing the stories of published authors and creating their own original tales. These may range from basic oral narratives to complex written plots. They might focus on history or fantasy or may even explore personal experiences. *Story Frames* uses the same 12-element plot structure to discuss a variety of genres, including narrative nonfiction picture books, chapter books, and novels. It is geared toward students in Grades 1–8, though it can be adapted for both younger and older students, and it may be used to explore the structure of any story.

Today's educators often must address the needs of various learners in the same classroom—from students who are still struggling with fundamental skills to gifted students who crave more significant challenges. Resources that provide opportunities for implementing universal design for learning are crucial for the modern-day classroom filled with students with a wide span of ability levels. *Story Frames* fills that void by providing strategies for teaching narrative structure to students across a variety of age ranges and skill sets, all while using the same story. As students truly engage with stories, some for the very first time, teachers and speech-language pathologists (SLPs) develop a better understanding of how to inspire and support both struggling and advanced learners.

One of the primary objectives of *Story Frames* is to take traditional story grammar analysis (Duchan, 2004; Stein & Glenn, 1979) to the next level by teaching students to think about stories the way authors do. What makes *Story Frames* unique is that this analysis incorporates the methods and strategies used by professional authors and screenwriters (Marks, 2007; McKee, 1997; Snyder, 2005; Vogler, 2007; Wiesner, 2005). It is also the underlying structure found in the myths and fairy tales of cultures around the world, as described by Joseph Campbell (1949) in *The Hero With a Thousand Faces*.

Most of the professional plotting strategies discussed in *Story Frames* focus on screenwriting methods, but the applications have been used by many novelists as well. In fact, every November, thousands of writers—professionals, amateurs, and students alike—take part in National Novel Writing Month (NaNoWriMo) with the objective of completing the first draft of a novel by the end of the month. The program offers support throughout the year for adults as well as young writers under age 18 and their educators. Their web site (www.nanowrimo.org), recommends plotting resources like *Save the Cat! The Last Book On Screenwriting You'll Ever Need* (2005) by Blake Snyder (discussed in Chapter 2), which contain plot elements similar to those found in *Story Frames*. You can find a NaNoWriMo version of the *Save the Cat!* Beat Sheet (a tool for identifying the important beats or key elements of a story) at http://nanowrimo.org/nano-prep-101. Many of these resources focus on the structure of screenplays since scripts must follow a more highly structured format

> "Tell me the facts and I'll learn. Tell me the truth and I'll believe. But tell me a story and it will live in my heart forever."
>
> —Native American Proverb

than novels to meet the constraints of a 90- to 120-minute film. The three-act, beginning, middle, end architecture found in most (but not all) scripts is also present in three-act plays as well as many longer stories.

The term *frames* refers to the freeze-frame or still shot that appears when you pause a movie or video. When you hold an old-fashioned reel of a film up to the light, each frame is visible. These are the "frames" explored in *Story Frames*, the moments in a story where we get a glimpse of its deeper structure. When these frames play on a screen, they create a seamless whole, but we can stop at any point along the way, pause, and explore each one more deeply.

The 12-element structure in the *Story Frames* approach may seem complicated at first, but it is not difficult to understand. With some variations, most stories follow a structure that includes these elements: 1) Ordinary World, 2) Call and Response, 3) Mentors, Guides, and Gifts, 4) Crossing, 5) New World, 6) Problems, Prizes, and Plans, 7) Midpoint Attempt, 8) Downtime Response, 9) Chase and Escape, 10) Death and Transformation, 11) Climax: The Final Test, and 12) Final Reward.

Young children can grasp these concepts with ease. They are not within the child's conscious awareness at first, but once students understand the terminology and concepts, there is immediate understanding. They quickly draw associations and reorganize old information into the story schema. There is a sense of "Yes, I understand. These are things I have somehow always known." These concepts are not new. The process is merely about awakening an ancient understanding that we have not always had the words to describe.

HOW *STORY FRAMES* EVOLVED

The use of story grammar to improve comprehension has a long history. In 1979, Stein and Glenn introduced a story schema they created based on their study of children's stories and fables. They described their work as a " . . . first approximation in the attempt to delineate the distinctions people naturally use" (Stein & Glenn, 1979, p. 58) and admitted that their definitions might need modification over time. Indeed, several authors have expanded upon the story grammar first outlined by Stein and Glenn or have created new schemas for stories (Graves & Montague, 1991; Montgomery & Kahn, 2005). Maryellen Rooney Moreau, M.Ed., CCC-SLP, uses a set of icons organized sequentially on a Story Grammar Marker along with a doll called Braidy to teach narrative structure that is used by SLPs in many school districts. Students place three-dimensional objects representing the icons on the doll's braids as they retell a story. Find out more about her program at the MindWing Concepts web site (https://www.mindwingconcepts.com). English teachers often implement a somewhat different approach to story structure. They use Freitag's Pyramid (Noden, 1999, p. 143) to represent the rising action of the story.

Film analyst Christopher Vogler (2007) speaks about having sensed a foundational structure for stories that he did not fully understand until he learned of the Hero's Journey. He speaks of the universal nature of Campbell's (1949) work when he states, "In his study of world hero myths Campbell discovered that they are all basically the same story, retold endlessly in infinite variation" (Vogler, 1992, p. 14).

Table I.1 compares the story elements found in *Story Frames* to those outlined by Christopher Vogler. See his book for a more in-depth discussion of the elements of professional storytelling.

Several other professional story analysts have influenced the creation of the *Story Frames* approach (Marks, 2007; McKee, 1997; Snyder, 2005; Wiesner, 2005). As I incorporated their insights as well as the contributions of professionals in education and speech-language pathology, a story analysis emerged that young children could easily understand in the general education setting, as well as older students and those with severe learning

Table I.1. Comparison of *Story Frames* and *The Writer's Journey*

Story Frames	The Writer's Journey
Ordinary World	The Ordinary World
Call and Response	The Call to Adventure
	Refusal of the Call
Mentors, Guides, and Gifts	Meeting with the Mentor
Crossing	Crossing the First Threshold
New World	Tests, Allies and Enemies
Problems, Prizes, and Plans	Approach to the Innermost Cave
Midpoint Attempt	The Ordeal
Downtime Response	Reward
Chase and Escape	The Road Back
Death and Transformation	
Climax: The Final Test	The Resurrection
Final Reward	Return with the Elixir

Elements for *The Writer's Journey* from Vogler, C. (2007). *The writer's journey: Mythic structure for writers* (3rd ed.). Studio City, CA: Michael Wiese Productions, www.mwp.com; reprinted by permission.

disabilities and developmental concerns. Thus, *Story Frames* was born. What makes this method unique is that while accessible to students of all ages and ability levels, it still presents a challenging framework for older students and even adult professional writers to use in plotting more complicated endeavors. Using the method in *Story Frames*, readers and writers discuss and analyze stories by highlighting the following elements:

1. **Beginning:** Ordinary World; Call and Response; Mentors, Guides, and Gifts; Crossing

2. **Middle:** New World; Problems, Prizes, and Plans; Midpoint Challenge; Downtime Response

3. **End:** Chase and Escape; Death and Transformation; Climax: The Final Test; Final Reward

Different Approaches for Teaching Story Grammar

Though experts agree that understanding story structure is essential to student success, different types of professionals have traditionally taken different approaches for teaching story grammar.

Stein and Glenn (1979) summarize the SLP's view of story grammar as including *setting, initiating events, internal responses, internal plans, attempts, direct consequences,* and *reactions.* In *Image Grammar: Using Grammatical Structures to Teach Writing* (1999, pp. 142–143), Henry R. Noden noted that many reading teachers observe a six-element structure to define the elements of a story: *initiating event, internal response, attempts, outcomes, resolution,* and *reaction.* German writer and critic Gustav Freytag (1816–1895) observed a five-act structure in most of the plays of his time, which he described as *exposition, rising action, climax, falling action,* and *denouement.* Many educators as well as story analysts have expounded on Freytag's Pyramid; Figure I.1 shows a modification of it. Noden (1999, p. 143) uses slightly different terms for the pyramid to discuss the way English teachers typically approach story structure with their students: *setting, setup (initiating event), rising action (internal response, conflict, attempts), climax (outcome), falling action,* and *resolution (reactions).*

Story Frames takes the basic story elements already used by SLPs, reading teachers, and English teachers and expands them, making them more concrete and visual for students. It goes beyond story grammar to make stories come alive.

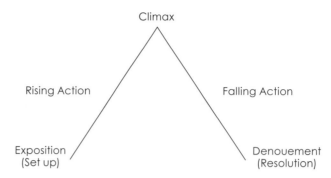

Figure I.1. Adaptation of Freitag's Pyramid. (*Source:* Noden, 1999.)

Story Frames and Literacy Skills

Since its inception, *Story Frames* has been used with students of all ages and ability levels as well as for teaching adult writing workshops for those aspiring to write professionally. The material has been presented to educators from a variety of disciplines, including general education teachers, special education teachers, SLPs, and librarians. Many have reported using the techniques with great success. I have personally used *Story Frames* with students in Grades K–12 in a variety of settings as well as to plot fiction novels written for teens. Paula Moraine, author of the chapter on executive functions as well as a book on the topic, has used *Story Frames* in one-to-one and small group settings to support the executive functions and comprehension of her students in Grades 4–12. At the university level, Jennifer Cervantes, children's literature instructor and best-selling author of the *Storm Runner* series, used *Story Frames* to teach her college students the structure of story. The wide range of disciplines impacted as well as the diverse population of students who benefit from this program make it a valuable tool for collaboration and differentiated instruction.

Narratives have become invaluable in the evaluation and treatment of students with language learning disabilities. Hoffman (2009) lists several reasons for using narratives in language intervention. Retelling stories provides an opportunity for a discourse-level analysis of spoken language and shows how well a student can organize ideas. Stories provide a meaningful context for addressing a wide range of language skills, and they provide a structure for communication.

SLPs are being called on more and more to help create and carry out reading interventions in response to intervention (RTI) programs (Justice, 2006). An increased understanding of story structure helps equip ancillary staff to support educators in this endeavor.

Skills that teachers, SLPs, or other professionals can address and improve using *Story Frames* include expressive and receptive vocabulary, oral language, storytelling, making story predictions, analyzing stories, sequencing, problem solving (e.g., making inferences), using pragmatic language (e.g., taking another's perspective), and written language.

WHO CAN USE THIS BOOK

Target users for the *Story Frames* approach include educators and specialists who work with students in Grades 1–12. This particular resource emphasizes Grades 1–8. The strategies may be facilitated one to one, in small group settings, in inclusion classes, and in general education classes. In addition, many strategies can be implemented during lessons or therapy sessions conducted virtually; see the Tips for Online Learning and Teletherapy sections included in many of the instructional chapters. Activities presented in this book include methods for differentiating instruction for both emerging and advanced readers and writers. The story analysis explored may be implemented by teachers, librarians, and SLPs, either in collaboration with other educators or when working alone.

HELPING STUDENTS GROW AS READERS AND WRITERS

Figure I.2 shows the 12 elements of *Story Frames* with pictures for younger students. These images represent the icons used with students of all ages. Figure I.3 shows the 12 elements with more elaborate illustrations that may be used when introducing the concepts to older students.

The 12 elements, when organized into rows designating the beginning, middle, and end of a story, provide a structure that is easy for students to understand and remember. When giving a summary, many students struggle with knowing what is essential to include. Using these categories provides a useful organizational framework. Students and teachers may not always agree on what should go where, and not all elements will always appear, but the process of applying these elements helps the student organize something complicated, like a story, into manageable and memorable parts.

As students grow in their ability to understand and analyze stories, the next step is to encourage them to write stories of their own. Writing requires the synthesis and integration of multiple skills and makes students more engaged in the learning process. Whereas reading can be a more passive process, writing is always active. A student must first make meaning out of ideas, information, and experiences and then create a written product reflecting that understanding (Santa, 1988).

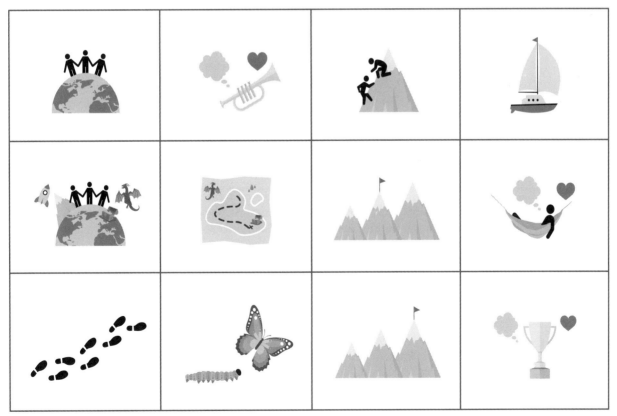

Figure I.2. *Story Frames* icons for the 12 elements, for use with all ages.

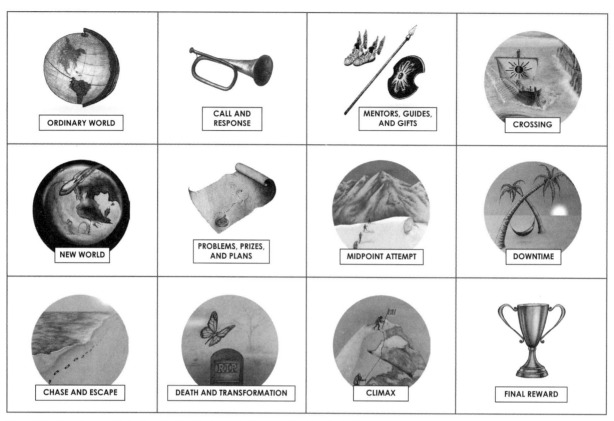

Figure I.3. *Story Frames* illustrations for the 12 elements, for use with older students.

Story Frames can be used to help students create written or oral narratives. Some well-known authors and poets, such as William Butler Yeats, have struggled with the mechanics of writing (Miner & Siegel, 1992). Yet even though a student struggles with the foundational skills required for writing, he or she may still have many creative ideas to express verbally. Students blossom with simple modifications such as dictation or speech-to-text tools provided as a bridge between their oral and written narratives.

HOW TO USE THIS BOOK

There are two approaches for handling the material presented in Section I of *Story Frames*. Those who want to jump into story analysis with their students or who may have little preparation time may use Chapter 1 to acquaint themselves with the approach, tools, and techniques, including use of storyboards and pictography, and then skip ahead to Chapter 3 ("Getting Started With Story Frames"). This chapter provides two options for introductory lessons, including sample scripts for each element. Chapter 2 explores the 12 story elements in depth and may be studied as time permits. The other option is to read the first three chapters in order, develop a deeper understanding of each of the story elements, and then use Chapter 3 to teach them to students.

Section II focuses on using *Story Frames* to build key skills. Chapter 4 explores how young children develop an understanding of narrative as oral language is emerging and discusses expectations for each stage of narrative development. Chapter 5 discusses how oral story retells can help students develop vocabulary, sequencing skills, and an understanding of grammar. Chapter 6 examines the use of stories and strategies to help students make the leap to writing sentences and paragraphs, summarizing stories, and ultimately to writing their own stories; this chapter includes the Common Core writing expectations for each grade. Though many states have created their own standards, the Common Core is still a useful tool for identifying skills for teaching and intervention that may be applied to other states' standards. Chapter 7 discusses how narrative can also be used to teach expository writing skills. Chapter 8 discusses building key skills in another area, reading comprehension, through the use of Wh-questions.

The final three chapters of Section II examine the use of narrative to develop a broader range of skills for literacy and learning: grammar and syntax (Chapter 9); connections to poetry and rhyme, alliteration, and phonological awareness (Chapter 10); and finally executive function skills (Chapter 11).

Section III explores writing several varieties of personal stories, including personal narratives (Chapter 12), memoir (Chapter 13), the creation of superheroes (Chapter 14), the family story (Chapter 15), and multicultural stories (Chapter 16). Specific strategies are outlined for teaching students, especially students with disabilities, how to create personal narratives as a means of self-reflection and self-empowerment.

The downloadable materials for this book, available online through the Brookes Publishing Download Hub, include a wealth of resources to help teachers and other educational professionals get started using *Story Frames* with students. Many are easily adaptable for online learning. These resources include two brief guides to using *Story Frames* with popular books, *Using* Story Frames *With Picture Books* and *Using* Story Frames *With Chapter Books and Novels*. Accompanying these guides are story analyses for 32 books. These books include the following:

- A wide range of popular nonfiction narrative picture books for Grades 1–5; the guide *Using* Story Frames *With Picture Books* includes suggestions for using picture books with middle school students.

- Fiction picture books, including fairy tales from various cultures as well as twists and retellings of familiar fairy tales.

- An assortment of books for Grades 3–8, ranging from chapter books to middle-grade and young adult novels to novels in verse.

The tables provided at the end of this Introduction provide a quick overview of the story analyses available with this book.

Also included with the downloadable resources are reproducible worksheets and graphic organizers for student use as well as PowerPoint activities to facilitate online learning. Overall, *Story Frames* includes more than three dozen lesson plans adaptable to almost any story that are found throughout the book.

As teachers become excited about the magic and power of stories, so will students. By using *Story Frames*, young people grow in their appreciation of stories so that they may find a voice to tell their own intriguing tales.

Get ready for an exciting adventure!

Story Frames
Analyses of Picture Books

Analyses of the picture books listed in Table I.2 are available with *Story Frames* through the Brookes Publishing Download Hub.

Table I.2. Selected picture books to use with *Story Frames*

Title, author, and illustrator	Genre	Grade	Lexile	Consider teaching with . . .
Adelita: A Mexican Cinderella Story (2002), written and illustrated by Tomie dePaola	Fairy tale	PreK–3	660L	*The Rough-Face Girl* (Martin, 1992)
Bad News for Outlaws: The Remarkable Life of Bass Reeves, Deputy Marshal (2009), written by Vaunda Micheaux Nelson with illustrations by Tyrone Geter	Nonfiction narrative	3 and up.	NA	*Let 'er Buck!: George Fletcher, the People's Champion* (Nelson, 2019)
Counting on Katherine: How Katherine Johnson Saved Apollo 13 (2018), written by Helaine Becker and illustrated by Dow Phumiruk	Nonfiction narrative	K–4	710L	*Hidden Figures: The True Story About Four Black Women and the Space Race* (Shetterley, 2018)
Curious George (1941/1969) by Hans Augusto Rey	Fiction	PreK–3	400L	*Margret & H.A. Rey's Curious George Goes to a Bookstore* (Bartynski, 2014); other books in the Curious George series
Margret & H.A. Rey's Curious George Goes to a Bookstore (2014), written by Julie M. Bartynski and illustrated by Mary O'Keefe Young	Fiction	PreK–3	NA	*Curious George* (Rey, 1941/1969); other books in the series
Emmanuel's Dream: The True Story of Emmanuel Ofosu Yeboah (2015), written by Laurie Ann Thompson and illustrated by Sean Qualls	Nonfiction narrative	PreK–3	AD 770L	*Six Dots: A Story of Young Louis Braille* (Bryant, 2016); *Thank You, Mr. Falker* (Polacco, 1998)
Finding Winnie: The True Story of the World's Most Famous Bear (2015), written by Lindsay Mattick and illustrated by Sophie Blackall	Nonfiction narrative	PreK–3	AD 590L	A.A. Milne's *Winnie the Pooh* stories
The Frog Prince, Continued (1994), written by Jon Scieszcka and illustrated by Steve Johnson	Spoof	PreK	AD 600L	*The True Story of the Three Little Pigs* (Scieszcka, 1989/1996)
Gingerbread for Liberty: How a German Baker Helped Win the American Revolution (2015a), written by Mara Rockliff and illustrated by Vincent X. Kirsch	Nonfiction narrative	1 and up	AD 590L	*When Washington Crossed the Delaware* (Cheney, 2004); other texts about the Revolutionary War
The Little Match Girl (2001), written by Hans Christian Anderson and illustrated by Rachel Isadora	Fairy tale	PreK–3	800L	Other fairy tales

Title, author, and illustrator	Genre	Grade	Lexile	Consider teaching with . . .
Lon Po-Po: A Red Riding Hood Story from China (1996), written and illustrated by Ed Young	Fairy tale	PreK–3	670L	*Little Red Riding Hood;* other fairy tales from different cultures
Mesmerized: How Ben Franklin Solved a Mystery That Baffled All of France (2015b), written by Mara Rockliff and illustrated by Iacopo Bruno	Nonfiction narrative	1–4	NA	*Gingerbread for Liberty: How a German Baker Helped Win the American Revolution* (Rockliff, 2015a); other texts about the Revolutionary War
Mr. Ferris and His Wheel (2014), written by Kathryn Gibbs Davis and illustrated by Gilbert Ford	Nonfiction narrative	K–3	900L	Any of the many picture books about George Ferris
A Race Around the World: The True Story of Nellie Bly and Elizabeth Bisland (2019), written by Caroline Starr Rose and illustrated by Alexandra Bye	Nonfiction narrative	K–2	NA	Other books in the *She Made History* series
The Rough-Face Girl (1992), written by Rafe Martin with illustrations by David Shannon	Fairy tale	3 and up	AD540L	*Adelita: A Mexican Cinderella Story* (dePaola, 2002)
Sadako (1993), written by Eleanor Coerr with illustrations by Ed Young	Nonfiction narrative	PreK–3	AD660L	Informational texts about World War II, Hiroshima, and the atomic bomb.
Six Dots: The Story of Young Louis Braille (2016), written by Jen Bryant and illustrated by Boris Kulikov	Nonfiction narrative	PreK–4	590L	*Emmanuel's Dream: The True Story of Emmanuel Ofosu Yeboah* (Thompson, 2015); *Thank You, Mr. Falker* (Polacco, 1998)
Thank You, Mr. Falker (1998), written and illustrated by Patricia Polacco	Nonfiction narrative	K–3	AD650L	*Fish in a Tree* (Hunt, 2015) or *May B.* (Rose, 2014); *Emmanuel's Dream: The True Story of Emmanuel Ofosu Yeboah* (Thompson, 2015); *Six Dots: A Story of Young Louis Braille* (Bryant, 2016)
The True Story of the Three Little Pigs (1989/1996), written by Jon Scieszka and illustrated by Lane Smith	Spoof	K–3	AD510L	*The Frog Prince, Continued* (Scieszka, 1994)
When Washington Crossed the Delaware (2004), written by Lynne Cheney and illustrated by Peter M. Fiore	Nonfiction narrative	K–4	860	*Sadako* (Coerr,1993)
Magic Ramen: The Story of Momofuko Ando (2019), written by Andrea Wang and illustrated by Kana Urbanowitcz	Nonfiction narrative	PreK–3	590L	*Gingerbread for Liberty: How a German Baker Helped Win the American Revolution* (Rockliff, 2015a); other texts about the Revolutionary War
An Inconvenient Alphabet: Ben Franklin and Noah Webster's Spelling Revolution (2018), written by Beth Anderson and illustrated by Elizabeth Baddeley	Nonfiction Narrative	PreK–3	680L	*Mesmerized: How Ben Franklin Solved a Mystery That Baffled All of France* (Rockliff, 2015b)

Story Frames
Analyses of Chapter Books and Novels

Analyses of the chapter books and novels listed in Table I.3 are available with *Story Frames* through the Brookes Publishing Download Hub.

Table I.3. Selected chapter books and novels to use with *Story Frames*

Title, author, and illustrator	Genre	Grade	Lexile	Summary
Comfort (2002), by Carolee Dean	YA novel	7–9	670L	Kenny wants out of Comfort, Texas, away from his crazy, workaholic mother and his ex-convict, alcoholic father. He finds his escape through a statewide poetry competition. *Comfort* contains mature themes of teen pregnancy, family violence, and addiction.
The Crossover (2014), by Kwame Alexander	Novel in verse	5–7	750L	This novel in verse is about twin brothers who are junior high basketball stars. Their father is a former basketball player who had to retire because of his health. He helps train them while their mother, an assistant principal, keeps everyone in line.
Fish in a Tree (2015), by Lynda Mullally Hunt	Middle-grade/YA novel	5–9	550L	Every time Ally Nickerson moves to a new school, she hides the fact that she cannot read by creating diversions and disruptions—that is, until a caring new teacher sees through her act and begins to help her overcome her challenges.
Home of the Brave (2008), by Katherine Applegate	Novel in verse	5–9	NA	Kek, one of the lost boys of the Sudan, saw his father and brother killed in Africa and then came to America to live with his aunt. The spare verse is accessible for students ages 10 and up, yet the themes of relocation, ostracism, and political oppression make this book appropriate for high school students as well, especially struggling readers. It fits well with African units and study themes.
Island of the Blue Dolphins (1960), by Scott O'Dell	Novel	2–5	1000L	This Newbery Award–winning novel is based on the true story of The Lost Woman of San Nicolas, a Native American woman who lived alone on an island off the coast of California from 1835 to 1853.

Title, author, and illustrator	Genre	Grade	Lexile	Summary
Love That Dog (2001), by Sharon Creech	Novel in verse	3–7	1010L	As Jack's teacher, Miss Stretchberry, continues to give poetry writing assignments and post Jack's poems on the wall, Jack discovers he might just be a poet—especially as he tells the story of his beloved dog, Sky.
May B. (2014), by Caroline Starr Rose	Middle-grade novel	3–7	680L	Mavis Elizabeth Betterly, May B., is sent to a neighbor's house to help out until Christmas but finds herself in a fight for her life when she is left all alone in the sod house on the Kansas prairie during the harsh winter.
Sarah, Plain and Tall (1985/2015), by Patricia MacLachlan	Chapter book	1–5	650L	This is the first in a series of five books about the Witting family, who live on the prairie in the late nineteenth century. In it, Sarah comes from Maine after answering an advertisement in the newspaper for a wife and mother. The story is written from Anna Witting's point of view.
Steal Away Home (1994), by Lois Ruby	Middle-grade novel	3–7	890L	Twelve-year-old Dana Shannon discovers a skeleton sealed away in a closet in the wall of a house her family has purchased—along with the diary of Millicent Weaver, a previous owner. It tells the story of Lizbet Charles and her participation in the Underground Railroad. All of the characters are fictitious, but the story centers on historical events.
The Whipping Boy (1986), written by Sid Fleischman and illustrated by Peter Sis	Illustrated middle-grade novel	3–8	570L	Prince Horace is such a spoiled child that everyone calls him Prince Brat. No one can spank him because he is a prince, so Jemmy, an orphan, is brought to the castle from the streets to be his "whipping boy."

To the storyteller in all of us

Your *Story Frames* Toolbox

Section I provides the foundational understandings and essential tools you'll need to begin using *Story Frames*. Chapter 1 introduces the goals of the *Story Frames* approach and provides an overview of the 12 story elements and the use of storyboarding and Quick Draws in instruction. This chapter also introduces the Complete Storyboard based on the 12 elements, as well as a simplified Basic Storyboard that is appropriate for some stories and some learners. Chapter 2 explores in depth the 12 story elements and the connections among them, with examples from a diverse range of texts written for children, teenagers, and adults. (We'll revisit some of these texts throughout the book.) Chapter 3 presents two different lesson approaches for introducing *Story Frames* to students; sample scripting is included.

If you're pressed for time and eager to get started with *Story Frames*, you may choose to skim or skip Chapter 2 initially. Chapters 1 and 3 provide sufficient overview and practical tools for you to begin. Do plan to come back to Chapter 2, though, for a richer understanding of the inner workings of stories.

The *Story Frames* Approach

Introduction and Tools

Narratives not only touch our hearts and minds, but can also be used to address a wide variety of literacy skills. After reviewing the research on story grammar, Lehr (1987) concludes that developing a structure for understanding stories is one of the best ways to encourage the development of reading comprehension and writing organization. Marzola (2018) reports that students who understand story structure not only have a more effective framework for retelling stories, they are also better at both asking and answering questions about a narrative. Although students will encounter a variety of text structures throughout their school years, Marzola reminds us that most of the texts they will read in elementary school are narratives. Yet reading remains a daunting task for many.

A considerable number of students struggle with achieving reading proficiency. The 2019 Nation's Report Cards for math and reading (Grades 4 and 8), released in October 2019 and based on National Assessment of Educational Progress (NAEP) data, showed that reading scores were lower in 2019 than in 2017. The percentage of students at or above proficiency was 35% for fourth graders (down three percentage points from 2017) and 34% for eighth graders (down two percentage points from 2017). (See https://nces.ed.gov /nationsreportcard.)

Writing also poses difficulties for students. Students with expressive language deficits often struggle with writing, but even students in the general education population have difficulty with this highly complex task. Most children can create simple narratives by age 6. Students with language disorders often continue to have difficulty with both oral and written narratives in their teens. Students with communication challenges need "explicit, systematic instruction" to learn to write narratives, even more so than their peers (Montgomery & Kahn, 2005, pp. 5–6). Writing is a painful and challenging task for these students. Without intervention, their writing skills do not improve. As time passes, their deficits only become more glaring (Roth, 2000).

In regard to dyslexia, writing difficulties often persist into adulthood with continuing deficits in spelling. Even adults with dyslexia who have developed accurate spelling often have challenges with writing speed that can affect tasks like note-taking, essential for success in higher education courses. Struggles with reading and writing can ultimately lead to both social and emotional disadvantages, such as increased anxiety, depression, and low self-esteem (Moojen et al., 2020). Moojen et al.'s study found that adult subjects both with and without dyslexia benefitted from using text structure to organize recall of what they had read. They determined that understanding text structure helped adults with dyslexia compensate for persisting core deficits in phonological awareness, pseudoword reading, reading fluency, and writing.

Story grammar can be a useful tool to teach writing skills as well as comprehension because it represents the internal structure of a story. It provides guidelines for each part

DOWNLOADABLE RESOURCES

Keep these core instructional resources on hand to use with Story Frames: Complete Storyboard, Basic Storyboard, Blank Storyboard template (Complete), Blank Storyboard template (Basic), Story Element Rubric (Complete), and Story Element Rubric (Basic).

of the story and explains how these story units fit together (Stein & Glenn, 1979). This structure is sometimes referred to as *story schema*. It enables students to make abstract concepts more concrete and understandable. They are then able to compare old ideas with new ones. Adults use metaphors and symbols to help aid their understanding of abstract or unfamiliar concepts. Schemas often work in the same way to help students interpret not only stories, but also experiences and the world around them (Duchan, 2004).

Oral language forms the foundation for written language. By developing tools to *talk* about stories, students lay the groundwork for *writing* about the stories they read and for ultimately creating their own original narratives.

With the increasing prominence of the inclusion model, teachers are seeing more and more students in the general education classroom who have learning difficulties. As related service providers and special education teachers are challenged to provide support within the general education setting, narratives provide an excellent framework for collaboration between various professionals. Narratives are also excellent vehicles for practicing differentiated instruction so that the more advanced students are not left behind while teachers address more fundamental skills with students who struggle. Also, the increasing number of narrative nonfiction books provide excellent teaching resources and opportunities to explore the Common Core State Standards' (CCSS) focus on nonfiction at the same time students learn narrative structure.

USING *STORY FRAMES*

As described in the Introduction, the *Story Frames* approach can be applied to a wide range of narrative genres, with students of varied ages and ability levels, and used to teach and improve both reading and writing skills.

Goals

Specific objectives for the use of *Story Frames* appear throughout this resource. Some general areas include those that follow, which will be discussed in more detail in later chapters.

- Increasing expressive and receptive vocabulary

- Increasing oral language and storytelling abilities

- Improving the ability to make story predictions and analyze stories

- Improving sequencing abilities

- Improving problem-solving abilities such as making inferences, drawing conclusions, identifying problems, and generating solutions

- Improving critical thinking skills

- Improving pragmatic language skills such as taking a listener's/reader's perspective and adapting a message to make it concise and to the point

- Improving written language skills in the areas of sentences, paragraphs, and essays

Your Tools

Fundamental to the *Story Frames* approach are two powerful instructional tools:

1. A 12-element story structure that is quickly grasped by students and applicable to a broad range of fiction and nonfiction narratives

2. Use of Quick Draws and storyboarding to represent this narrative structure visually

The sections that follow provide an overview of each of these instructional tools and how to introduce Quick Draws and storyboarding to students. Chapter 2 will explore each of the 12 elements in depth, and Chapter 3 will present two lesson options for fully introducing students to *Story Frames*.

OVERVIEW: THE TWELVE ELEMENTS

The 12 story elements outlined as follows form the basis of *Story Frames*. These elements are rooted in traditional story grammar analysis as well as the types of story plotting outlines professional authors use. Not all stories follow a Hero's Journey structure, but most will still contain many of the same elements; therefore, this analysis is applicable to almost any narrative. Exceptions include picture books that are more sequential, such as *Brown Bear, Brown Bear* by Bill Martin (1967) with illustrations by Eric Carle or *If You Give a Mouse a Cookie* by Laura Numeroff (1985), and nonfiction texts that focus primarily on conveying facts and information. See the downloadable resources "Using *Story Frames* With Picture Books" and "Using *Story Frames* With Chapter Books and Novels" for examples of *Story Frames'* application to specific picture books and chapter books.

A variety of resources inspired the creation of *Story Frames*, but the most influential was the work of Christopher Vogler, author of *The Writer's Journey: Mythic Structure for Writers* (2007). Vogler's work was based on *The Hero With a Thousand Faces* by Joseph Campbell (1949), who studied the myths and fairy tales of many cultures looking for their similar themes. Joseph Campbell received much of his inspiration from the work of psychologist Carl Jung and his exploration of archetypes.

A Hero's Journey is not just about an epic quest of danger and fortune. Heroes come in all shapes and sizes. The problems they solve and the prizes they seek are as diverse as the stars in the sky. For that reason, the terms *hero, protagonist,* and *main character (MC)* are interchangeable.

The 12 elements found in *Story Frames* are described briefly here, but are explored in greater detail in later chapters. Whenever *he or she* appears generically, these terms should be considered as gender-neutral references.

1. **Ordinary World:** The MC appears in his everyday world.

2. **Call and Response:** Something alerts the MC that things are about to change. She may quickly embark on the story journey, or a period of reflection, argument, and defiance may follow.

3. **Mentors, Guides, and Gifts:** Someone comes along to help the MC get started. This story element often involves gifts or information that will help the hero on his journey and motivate him to begin.

4. **Crossing:** The MC crosses over from the Ordinary World to the New World.

5. **New World:** The MC may travel to an entirely new location or his current world may be changed by the arrival of someone or something new. Whatever happens, a new situation will arise.

6. **Problems, Prizes, and Plans:** A clear story goal emerges. It will start with either a Problem to be solved or a Prize to attain. The MC then makes Plans to attain the Prize or solve the Problem.

7. **Midpoint Attempt: Going for the Prize:** This represents a major attempt to achieve a goal and the consequence of that effort. It occurs midway through the story.

8. **Downtime Response:** The MC responds to whatever happened at the Midpoint. It may be a time of celebration or reflection. New Plans may need to be made. Some twist usually sends the action off in a new direction.

9. **Chase and Escape:** The MC pursues her goal or, sometimes, she is pursued by an adversary.

10. **Death and Transformation:** The MC's life or happiness may be in peril, someone close to him might die, or what he holds most dear may be threatened. As a result, he goes through an inner Transformation.

11. **Climax: The Final Test:** The MC must face his ultimate challenge and prove that the changes he has made are real and not just temporary. It is the Final Test.

12. **Final Reward:** The MC gets what she has earned. There is often a celebration and reflection on what has happened.

Figure 1.1 shows a Complete Storyboard illustrating these elements. See the section on Storyboards and Quick Draws for more information on the use and importance of storyboarding within *Story Frames.*

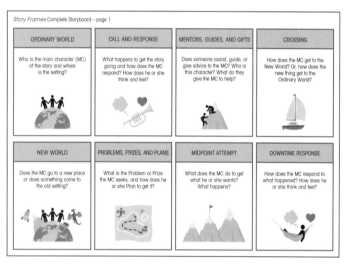

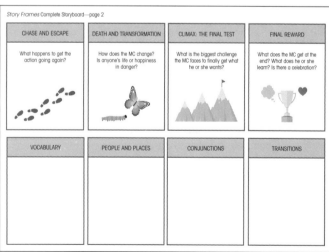

Figure 1.1. The Complete Storyboard.

TEACHING SIMPLER STORIES

Some very simple stories for young children, such as *Little Red Hen,* are characterized by repeating events and don't include all of the nuances of more complicated stories. For these stories, it may be more appropriate to analyze them in terms of the following simplified, eight-element structure: 1) Ordinary World, 2) Call and Response, 3) Problem and Prize, 4) Plan, 5) Attempt, 6) Attempt, 7) Climax, and 8) Reward. Figure 1.2 shows a Basic Storyboard illustrating these elements. Full-size versions of both the Complete and Basic Storyboards are available with the downloadable resources for this book. (The materials are available through the Brookes Publishing Download Hub; for how to access them, see this book's "About the Downloads" page.)

STORYBOARDS AND QUICK DRAWS

Although the structure shown in the previous section may seem complex, students grasp it fairly quickly and intuitively. Use of visuals supports this. Central to the *Story Frames* approach is the use of Quick Draws depicting story events, and storyboards organizing these events into frames for each of the elements.

What the Evidence Says

Storyboards are a type of graphic organizer implemented frequently throughout *Story Frames,* along with simple pictures (Quick Draws) that depict the elements of the plot. In the film and movie industry,

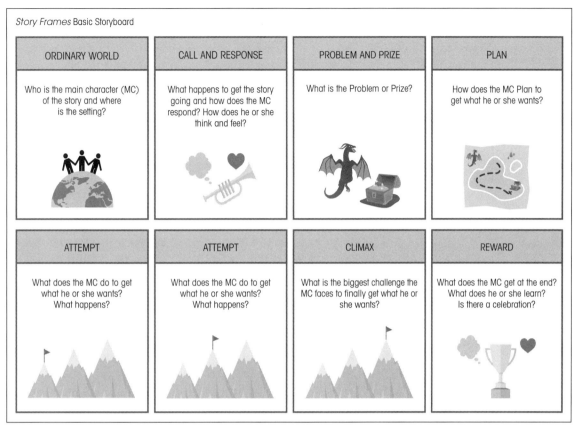

Figure 1.2. The Basic Storyboard.

storyboard artists use storyboards to create a map of what a movie will become. The artist comes up with images resembling cartoon strips that contain rough sketches of each scene. The production team then uses the storyboard to plan what is needed for lighting, costumes, set design, and special effects. (To learn more about the use of storyboards in films, see *Movie Storyboards: The Art of Visualizing Screenplays* [2013] by Fionnuala Halligan.)

When educators use storyboards with students, they learn to create Quick Draws, stick figures organized left to right to represent the story action graphically. This strategy provides a visual aid that helps with memory, sequencing, and organization. Green and Klecan-Aker (2012) examined several practical approaches for improving a student's understanding of narrative structure. One of the most straightforward and accessible to implement was pictography.

Pictography or "Stickwriting": The Foundation for Quick Draws Ukrainetz (1998) first described pictography or "picture writing" in case studies of 8- to 10-year-olds with specific language learning challenges to use for both understanding stories and brainstorming their own written narratives. Pictography was effective in improving time concepts and sequencing, as well as the content quality and structure of stories. With the burden of spelling, punctuation, and sentence construction removed during the planning stage, students were more able to focus on content and overall organization. Many did initiate using keywords, dialogue, and short phrases, but this was not a requirement and they did not get bogged down with punctuation and spelling the way they did with a more traditional first draft.

The term *Stickwriting* was coined by Ukrainetz to describe this approach and she made several helpful observations about its use. She warned that students should not be allowed to turn these sketches into an art project. She often used the term "quick and easy" to remind them to keep their sketches simple. She also instructed students to use arrows moving left to right between pictures to show the forward motion of a story.

Ukrainetz did not recommend *Stickwriting* with students younger than second grade, even if they are using traditional drawing as a prewriting strategy in the general education classroom. She found that younger children often have difficulty with the concept of "quick and easy." She did point out that even preschool students and kindergarteners can retell a story from an adult's sketches and recommended using the pictography of an adult until the student could effectively draw stick figures to represents the parts of a story on their own.

She also observed that "drawing" a narrative can become counterproductive for older elementary students, who may create detailed illustrations and then write about the art and fail to elaborate on information not directly represented in their pictures. Stick drawing is preferred to traditional drawing for this reason because the simple symbols function like notes to represent more significant pieces of information. In addition to using *Stickwriting* to work on narrative structure, she found it productive for addressing broader goal areas such as sequencing, vocabulary, sentence structure, and listening comprehension.

Ukrainetz (2019) subsequently used her *Stickwriting* strategy as an expository intervention she called Sketch and Speak, which involved consolidating ideas from science articles into pictographic representations as well as bulleted notes that were later used for creating both oral and written reports.

Improving Understanding of Syntax

Although Ukrainetz did not elaborate on specific strategies for using *Stickwriting* to improve syntax, any teacher may quickly and easily sketch stick figures on a whiteboard to demonstrate to students the concrete meaning of complex sentences.

Eberhardt (2019) discussed the importance of understanding complex sentence structures for both reading comprehension and writing. She outlined several strategies, including asking Wh-questions (who, what, where, when, and why) to determine what is going on in a sentence. This strategy is discussed in detail in Chapter 8 on reading comprehension. The purpose is to make complex ideas more concrete, which is also a strength of pictography. Though it is not a strategy she suggested, it is still useful for creating a graphic representation of abstract or confusing ideas.

Identifying the subject of a sentence and even the action can be challenging for many children, especially those with language-related disabilities. This is especially true if additional information is interjected between the subject and the predicate. When temporal terms (*when, after, before, while*) are used in a sentence, drawing sketches showing the sequence of the action can be helpful.

Sometimes information is missing and inferencing is required. Consider this sequence of events from *Six Dots: A Story of Young Louis Braille* (2016), written by Jen Bryant and illustrated by Boris Kulikov. Page 14 shows an illustration of a noble lady holding a letter that she is about to send to the Royal School for the Blind requesting that they allow Louis to study there. The next illustration, on page 15, shows Louis' family reading a letter. The text mentions the woman sending the letter to the school and Louis' family receiving a reply.

Who sent the letter to Louis? For many children, the identity of this unnamed character is a great mystery. Elementary school students with language impairments assume it was the noble lady. Adding to this confusion is the fact that the first illustration shows the

Marquise holding an envelope, and the very next illustration shows Louis's family reading a letter. Most children without language impairments can easily visualize the missing scene where the letter arrives at the school, some unnamed person reads it, and then that person sends a subsequent letter to Louis's family, but many children will benefit from a Quick Draw depicting the missing scene.

Six Dots is a narrative nonfiction picture book that involves real people and historical events. The plot is outlined in the downloadable resources accompanying this book, along with the plots of many other stories. The focus is on the big ideas, not each sentence, but Quick Draws can be quickly implemented whenever students appear to be struggling with any aspect of the story. Because of the books' subject matter and complexity, they are appropriate for older students as well as young ones.

Improving Understanding of Story Grammar   *Story Frames* combines the use of pictography, storyboards, and icons representing each story element to help students make sense out of the major events in a narrative. Gillam, Olszewski, Fargo, & Gillam (2014) used these three strategies, as well. They conducted a study with two first-grade classrooms (an experimental group and a control group) at a Title 1 school, using a storyboard with icons representing the various story grammar elements (character, setting, initiating event, internal response, plans, attempts, consequences). Students were given the *Test of Narrative Language* (Gillam & Pearson, 2004) before starting the intervention and were considered to be high-risk if they scored in the 25th percentile or lower. Students in the experimental classroom first learned the story grammar elements and then used them to listen to and tell simple stories. Eventually, they learned to create their own stories by drawing stick figures in each square of a storyboard to go with the icon representing that particular story element. Students then told stories using their picture sequences. Target vocabulary related to general story concepts, specific story content, and story elements was presented each week. Students also learned visualization strategies.

The class receiving the intervention was compared to a control group. Both the high-risk and low-risk students in the experimental classroom improved significantly more than the control group, but the high-risk students made much more significant gains and even caught up to their low-risk peers in terms of the complexity of their stories. The researchers focused on teaching cause and effect while discussing story elements. They felt this helped the overall story production of students in the experimental group. Instruction included much discussion of feelings, motivations, plans, and the reasons for those plans.

Vocabulary skills in the experimental group also improved, but high-risk students did not make nearly the gains that low-risk students did. The implications were that all students benefit from group narrative instruction in the general classroom, but students with extra challenges will need more intensive and targeted instruction for vocabulary.

Gillam et al. (2018) point out that many narrative interventions focus on the "macrostructure" of a story (the overarching plot and the story elements) but do not address the "microstructure" (vocabulary, complex sentence structure, causal/temporal words, cohesive ties, clarity). These are the essential building blocks of a story. In their study, they incorporated elements of both macrostructure and microstructure as well as editing, answering questions about stories, evaluating, comparing, and contrasting. They used a program called Supporting Knowledge in Language and Literacy (SKILL; Gillam, Gillam, & Laing-Rogers, 2014), which incorporated storyboards as well as story elements represented by icons in a methodology similar to *Story Frames*. All four children receiving the narrative intervention showed improvement in the length and complexity of their narratives as well as in the variety of the vocabulary used while telling stories.

Using Storyboards With Students

The *Story Frames* Complete Storyboard includes a total of 12 frames divided into three rows for the beginning, middle, and end of the story, with four frames in each row. In the bottom right-hand corner of each frame appears an icon representing that story element. The same graphic organizer used for understanding the structure of the narrative will be used later for summary writing at the sentence, paragraph, and essay level, and for creating original stories.

To introduce students to the use of this storyboard, follow the steps given here. These steps can be modified based on the age of the students. Start by introducing students to the 12 story elements (see Chapter 3, "Getting Started With *Story Frames*"), then:

1. Briefly review the 12 story elements.

2. Give each student an 8½″ × 11″ piece of blank printer paper. Instruct them to draw simple stick figures of people, places, and key events with arrows in between each picture as they listen to a story.

3. Read the story and model how to draw stick figures to represent important information.

4. When the story is completed, use the questions from the Story Element Rubric to discuss the story elements. Decide which stick figures go with which story element.

5. Copy stick figures onto the Blank Storyboard. You may use either the Complete Storyboard (12 elements) or the Basic Storyboard (8 elements). Students may need to add, delete, or refine their drawings.

6. Use the storyboard to retell stories or write story summaries.

Introduce students to the concept of using storyboards by first telling them a simple story that can be shared in one session. (See Chapter 3 for step-by-step directions.) Picture books are short and work well for all ages for discussing plot structure and story elements. This book's downloadable resources include many examples, including the one previously mentioned.

Present the Story as Students Listen and Draw   The first time through the story students may want to just listen, or you may want to have them start sketching events from the plot right away. Students with attention deficits often become much more focused when drawing in response to what they are hearing. On the other hand, young students and students with fine motor challenges may be more distracted by the challenges of drawing and may just listen and watch the teacher sketch. If students ask to write words instead of drawing pictures or in combination with drawing, allow this.

Model Quick Draws   While presenting the story, it is helpful to model drawing simple pictures (stick figures) for each section of the story. Remember, these sketches are meant to be a visualization tool, not an art assignment. Refer to Ukrainetz (1998) for specific strategies using pictography.

Discuss Story Elements   Students may find it difficult to determine the key elements until you have reached the end of the story. It may take some reflection and discussion to know how the parts fit with the whole. When you finish with reading and drawing the preliminary stick figures, go back through the students' pictures and talk about each element. It may be useful to ask the questions on the Story Element Rubric to decide if all of the elements appear in the story. This may be as far as you want to go. These simple drawings can be used for a story retell.

Create a Storyboard   Alternatively, you may want to transfer the information onto a blank storyboard if you plan to use it as a graphic organizer for summary writing; a blank storyboard template is provided as a downloadable resource for this book. The storyboard is helpful for students who have difficulty determining paragraph boundaries because the 12 pictures are grouped into a beginning, middle, end paragraph structure that easily lends itself to summary writing. (See more on this subject in Chapter 6, "From Speaking to Writing: Sentences, Paragraphs, and Stories.")

When it comes to deciding what information should go in which frame, it's important to remember that there is no right or wrong answer if a student can give a reason for why he or she has included information under one story element or another. The emphasis is on creating a schema, learning a structure, and stimulating a discussion. That said, the group may decide after discussion to put the information into a different part of the story.

Discussion Questions for Complete Storyboard

The following discussion questions may be found in the Story Element Rubric, available as a downloadable resource, and go with the Complete Storyboard. These questions are helpful for analyzing the stories of professional authors as well as for analyzing the student story summaries, story retells, and original stories.

Beginning

1. Who is the main character (MC)? What is the setting at the beginning of the story? (Ordinary World)
2. What happens to get the story going? How does the MC respond? (Call and Response)
3. Does the MC have any special helpers? Does she give him any special gifts or advice? (Mentors, Guides, and Gifts)
4. Does the MC go somewhere new? If so, how does he get there? (Crossing)

Middle

5. Is there another setting in the story? Where is it? If there is not a new setting, does something happen that changes the first setting? (New World)
6. Is there a clear problem? Is there something the MC wants or needs? What is the plan for solving the problem or getting the desired prize? (Problems, Prizes, and Plans)
7. What does the MC do to solve the problem or get the prize? What happens? (Midpoint Attempt)
8. Was the MC successful? How does she react to what happened at the Midpoint? What does she think? How does she feel? (Downtime)

End

9. Does something happen to get the action moving again? Is there a surprise or a twist? (Chase and Escape)
10. Is something or someone in danger? (Death and Transformation)
11. What is the final attempt to get a prize or solve a problem? (Climax: The Final Test)
12. What is the result of the MC's actions and how does the MC feel about what happened? Is there a celebration or reward of some kind? (Final Reward)

Discussion Questions for Basic Storyboard

The following questions go with the Basic Storyboard and may be useful for younger children.

1. Who is the main character (MC)? What is the setting at the beginning of the story? (Ordinary World)
2. What happens to get the story going? How does the MC respond? (Call and Response)
3. Is there a problem? Is there something the MC wants or needs? (Problem and Prize)
4. What is the plan for solving the problem or getting the desired prize? (Plan)
5. What does the MC do to solve the problem or get the prize? (Attempt)
6. What does the MC do next? (Attempt)
7. What is the final attempt to get a prize or solve a problem? (Climax)
8. What is the result and how does the MC feel about it? Is there a celebration or reward of some kind? (Reward)

Utilizing storyboards and pictography gives students a visual foundation for the events of a story, while using the underlying structure found in story grammar analysis helps them create schemas for narratives. The organizational strategies provided in this chapter help with the executive function skills needed for both prewriting and editing, explored in Chapters 6 and 7, along with focusing attention, forming mental images, and organizing thoughts/feelings discussed in Chapter 11 by Paula Moraine, all while improving perspective-taking and social communication.

Now that the storyboard is complete, the same story is used as the context for building additional key skills that are discussed in Section 2. Stories represent virtual gold mines when it comes to the many different ways they may be used to help students become better readers, writers, problem solvers, and communicators.

USING THE STORY ELEMENTS IN THE CLASSROOM

Strategies for incorporating *Story Frames* in the classroom will be provided in subsequent chapters and will include the ideas that follow explored in more detail.

1. *Use picture books with students of all ages to discuss the plot.* Several picture book examples appear with this book's downloadable resources. They are short, and the entire story may be told and analyzed in one session. Spoofs on fairy tales such as *The Frog Prince, Continued* are fun because they demonstrate how an old story may be twisted and changed to make a new story.

2. *Encourage students to use the story elements to discuss movies they have seen.* The ability to talk with peers about movies is an essential interpersonal skill. Movie clubs may be organized around this idea and movie reviews may be written or filmed. Students with social communication issues may benefit from watching these video reviews and discussing both their verbal and nonverbal communication behavior.

3. *Explore story downtime.* Students are typically good at creating action in their original stories and identifying these high points in the stories of others, but much can be gained from exploring what happens during the quieter moments in a story. These downtimes are when planning, reflection, and internal responses occur—the evidence of higher cognitive processes. Entire discussions may be focused on describing the downtime of a story. By using concrete examples with students, they may more easily understand these abstract concepts.

4. *Generate story ideas.* Oral language precedes written language and provides a foundation for writing (American Speech-Language-Hearing Association, 2001), so get students talking about story ideas before you ask them to put their thoughts down on paper. Provide activities to generate a large number of ideas before you ask a student to pick one to write about.

5. *Help students who are "stuck" in their narrative writing.* When students say they do not know what to write, have them refer back to the 12 story elements. Ask them to identify where they are in their own story and offer suggestions for what might come next.

6. *Create a collaborative story.* Students often benefit from writing a collaborative story before attempting to write a story on their own. This is accomplished with the teacher guiding the story writing process. See a description of this in Chapter 6: "From Speaking to Writing: Sentences, Paragraphs, and Stories."

Comparing and contrasting story elements helps to bring them into sharper relief. Sometimes it is easier to talk about how things are different than to talk about how they are the same. Explore these contrasts with students through discussions, Venn diagrams, and compare/contrast essays exploring the Ordinary World versus the New World, the Problem versus the Prize, or the character flaws introduced at the beginning of the story versus the character strengths found after the Transformation.

TIPS FOR ONLINE LEARNING AND TELETHERAPY

1. *Utilize online whiteboards to demonstrate pictography.* Many online platforms such as Zoom include a whiteboard feature that can be shown to students via screen sharing. A mouse or track pad may be used to draw the type of simple stick figures found in pictography. The instructor can give a student remote control so he or she can draw on the same whiteboard (but beware that the student may not want to relinquish control or may take over your device). It may be easiest to simply instruct the student to draw on unlined paper or on graphic organizers that you have emailed to the home or school. Other online whiteboard options are available that allow both teacher and student to access a file remotely.

2. *Share graphic organizers.* Any of the downloadable *Story Frames* worksheets and graphic organizers may be shown to students using the screen share feature of Zoom. The annotation feature may be used to draw stick figures directly on the worksheets.

CONCLUSION: THE *STORY FRAMES* APPROACH AND TOOLS

Story Frames provides a structure for understanding stories that may be used to develop key skills for students of any ability level. The use of pictography strategies, storyboards, and icons representing the various story elements helps to make abstract concepts concrete and accessible. Narratives provide a meaningful context for exploring both the macrostructure of stories and the microstructure of the underlying skills needed for school and the world beyond.

The Twelve Elements in Depth

2

Chapter 1 explored the traditional story grammar elements used by teachers and speech-language pathologists (SLPs), as well as the evidence base for using story icons to represent the various parts of a story. This chapter focuses on story analysis as seen through the lens of professional writers. The combination of these two viewpoints is one of the features that makes *Story Frames* unique. This perspective provides a glimpse into the richness and depth with which authors plot stories and gives students a wealth of visual images and examples to use to solidify abstract concepts.

Robert McKee, author of *Story: Substance, Structure, Style, and the Principles of Screenwriting* (1997), teaches writing seminars around the world. He discusses the importance of stories in our daily lives and describes how most of our time includes stories of one kind or another. Video games contain characters, settings, goals, and plans. Besides the now endless supply of shows and movies available via television and the Internet, there are 24-hour news channels, YouTube channels, and music apps, not to mention the everyday stories we hear from neighbors, friends, and coworkers. Gossip, bragging, secret telling, sales pitches, and pep-talks all contain elements of the story. Much of our self-talk comes in the form of a narrative. The stories we tell ourselves shape our thoughts and beliefs. McKee explains why stories play such a vital role in our lives. Besides bringing structure to the confusion all around us, he says they answer Aristotle's fundamental question, "How should a human being lead his life?" (p. 11).

Dara Marks, author of *Inside Story: The Power of the Transformational Arc* (2007), says a truly great story is one that helps us find meaning in our life experiences. Not all stories do this, but those that have this power stay in our hearts and minds. Christopher Vogler, author of *The Writer's Journey: Mythic Structure for Writers* (2007), provides a set of plotting elements for writers found in the Hero's Journey. Vogler says the principles in the Hero's Journey are not just observations of the structure of stories, but also a guide for how to be fully human.

Stories are much more than an escape from life; stories prepare us for life. Educators who use stories merely to test a student's ability to recall details, write summaries, and understand new vocabulary are doing the student a great disservice. *Story Frames* provides many useful tips for building those academic skills and many more. Yet we should never forget that the higher value of stories is in teaching young people about the things that cannot be measured but have the power to change our lives: clearly seeing our motives and others' motives, appreciating people who are different, building empathy, overcoming prejudice, understanding how an action leads to a reaction, and more. The list goes on and on.

Looking at a story as a Hero's Journey, as Joseph Campbell described it in *The Hero With a Thousand Faces* (1949), we see that all stories give us an up-close and personal

DOWNLOADABLE RESOURCES

There are no downloads specific to Chapter 2, but to see additional examples of the 12 elements in children's and young adult literature, check out these resources online: Using *Story Frames* With Picture Books and Using *Story Frames* With Chapter Books and Novels.

look into one character's unique struggles. Those struggles have a universal pattern; the pattern that exists within the structure of the story. The particular *one in a thousand* face found in any individual protagonist may be that of a warrior, a school mouse, a princess, or a slave. The struggle might be something monumental like saving the world, or small and personal like getting a hot meal to a sick grandmother or saving the life of a beloved pig.

That universal story pattern is what is explored in *Story Frames*. The reason so much time is spent investigating it is that for stories to have any lasting impact on children's lives, they need a framework for remembering and understanding narratives. They also need a basic framework for creating their own stories, whether short or long, real or imagined.

The *Story Frames* plot analysis is broken down into 12 memorable and straightforward elements. The level of detail provided here does not have to be shared with students in its entirety, especially with very young students. Some of the movie examples are for adult reference only. Chapter 1 introduced these elements and Chapter 3 will discuss how educators may concisely share them with students. If you're eager to get started with *Story Frames*, feel free to skip ahead to Chapter 3 for the condensed, student-friendly explanation, but plan to return to this chapter. The in-depth discussion here provides the background knowledge to be able to talk about story structure with confidence to students and adults of all ages and ability levels.

OVERVIEW: BEGINNING, MIDDLE, AND END

Let's begin by looking at an overview of the beginning, middle, and end of the story, and then discussing each of the 12 elements more thoroughly.

Beginning

The beginning is the setup for what is to come. It may be very short or quite lengthy. The protagonist's history and backstory may appear here or may weave throughout the story. This is the section where serious questions arise. Will the hero succeed? What will he find out? What is lacking in his Ordinary World? The beginning includes four elements: 1) Ordinary World; 2) Call and Response; 2) Mentors, Guides, and Gifts; and 4) Crossing.

Middle

The middle is by far the most extended section of the story. It includes the next four elements: 5) New World; 6) Problems, Prizes, and Plans; 7) Midpoint Attempt; and 8) Downtime Response. It is called the initiation phase by Joseph Campbell because the hero is learning how to get along in the New World and prove himself as he faces a series of increasingly difficult challenges. Some questions will get answered, but more perplexing questions may arise. The middle section is all about building complications. What makes it longer than either the beginning or the end is a repetition of the Plan, Attempt/Consequence, and Response sequence, which can go on indefinitely for hundreds of pages.

End

It may seem as if the story is over after the Midpoint Attempt and the subsequent Downtime, especially if the protagonist seems to have acquired what he was after. However, the Downtime is typically followed by a turning point and often a twist that signifies the beginning of the end and propels him in another direction. He may even be back with his friends, thinking he is safe and enjoying a victory, but the ultimate challenge is about to happen. In this section of the story, everything is wrapped up and all (or most) of the questions will get answered. Sometimes a book will end on a cliffhanger where a brand-new question arises, suggesting that there might be a sequel, but the end should still have a sense of resolution. The end section includes: 9) Chase and Escape; 10) Death and Transformation; 11) Climax: The Final Test; and 12) Final Reward.

Now, let's take a look at each of these 12 parts of the story in depth.

BEGINNING

The beginning section of the story is the setup for what is to come.

1. Ordinary World

This section describes the main character (MC) and the setting in detail. The setting includes not only the place where the story begins, but also the time, customs, costumes, traditions, social norms, and so forth. The story may begin in a fantasy world, a real world with magical elements, or a past, present, or future location. Novelists may spend many pages creating a sense of place. An entire chapter may be devoted to establishing the setting in an adult novel. Children's books, especially fantasies, spend much time establishing the setting as well, as exemplified in the colorful descriptions in the *Harry Potter* series.

A picture book does not usually go into detailed descriptions of places but rather depicts the setting primarily through the artwork. When using a picture book for story retells with students, it is essential to point out the story elements that appear in the illustrations so students do not miss or forget them. The visual images convey vital information, and illustrations must be shared with care. Projecting an e-book on a smartboard or using a document camera to show the pages of the print version are two ways to emphasize the meaning of the illustrations to larger groups and classrooms.

Genre conventions can give information about setting, too. For example, a story may begin, "Once upon a time . . .," which indicates it is probably a fairy tale. The reader knows right away that it may include fantasy or magical elements, perhaps animals with human characteristics, and that the setting will feel like a place from long ago.

The Flaws of the Ordinary World The Ordinary World is often a dreary place in comparison to the new, magical, exciting world the hero is about to enter. If the hero stayed in the Ordinary World, forging ahead on the same path, there would be no rising action, no conflict, and no story. He would continue indefinitely in his present condition.

His situation is not perfect, however. In longer works that delve more deeply into character development, the hero will most likely have flaws or personal struggles to overcome, such as insecurity, challenges with interpersonal skills, bad habits, or difficulty standing up to bullies. In *Save the Cat! The Last Book on Screenwriting You'll Ever Need* (2005), Blake Snyder calls these flaws "the six things that need fixing" and suggests coming up with several at the very beginning for movie-length stories. These flaws will be in high contrast to the Transformation that comes at the end. Even if the Ordinary World seems ideal at first, the MC typically goes through growth opportunities and challenges that reveal there may have been unrecognized trouble in paradise.

An example of this phenomenon appears in Sid Fleischman's Newbery Award-winning novel, *The Whipping Boy* (1986). At first, Prince Horace is such a terrible rascal that everyone calls him Prince Brat. No one can spank him because he is a prince, so Jemmy, an orphan, is brought to the castle from the streets to be his "whipping boy." Prince Brat does not pay any attention to his lessons and cannot even spell his name, but the keen and observant Jemmy, sitting in on lessons in case the prince needs a whipping, learns to read, write, and do math early in the story. Both characters have Problems to overcome and a Transformation to undergo.

Key Contrast: The Ordinary World and the New World   Nearly all stories show the MC growing and changing as a result of people or experiences encountered in the New World. The middle section will discuss this phenomenon more fully, but it is helpful to introduce the concept of the New World at the beginning of *Story Frames* instruction so that students understand the importance of the contrast. One way *Story Frames* differs from other story analysis methods is its emphasis on the importance of comparing and contrasting the various story elements.

The hero begins in his everyday world with what is commonplace or status quo for him, even if it is quite different and extraordinary to the reader. This is especially true for historical and fantasy settings. Even the boring, day-to-day routines of these places will feel new to children, but these places are about to become even more exciting.

Something about the Ordinary World changes to turn it upside down, or else the hero embarks on an adventure to an entirely new locale. Dorothy starts her story on a farm in Kansas but ends up in the colorful world of Oz. In George Lucas's *Star Wars* movies, Luke Skywalker leaves the dry, dusty planet of Tatooine to join the rebel forces trying to destroy the Death Star. Cinderella leaves her life of servitude for a night at the ball. In *Harry Potter and the Sorcerer's Stone* (originally entitled *Harry Potter and the Philosopher's Stone*, Rowling, 1997), Harry leaves Privet Drive to journey to Hogwarts School of Witchcraft and Wizardry. In *Twilight* (Meyer, 2005), Bella leaves Arizona to go live with her father in Forks, Washington, only to enter an even more unique world of teenage vampires.

In many stories for children and young adults, the MC never leaves town, but a new person arrives in the Ordinary World and becomes a friend, enemy, or love interest. Nothing is ever the same again. In *Bridge to Terabithia* by Katherine Paterson (1977), Jess Aarons's world changes forever when Leslie Burke, the girl who moves in next door, helps him build a secret world called Terabithia in the woods near his home. Even quiet stories contain many of the elements of *Story Frames*. In Patricia MacLachlan's Newbery Award–winning novel, *Sarah, Plain and Tall* (1985/2015), Anna and her younger brother, Caleb, live in a simple house on the prairie with their father, a farmer, who used to sing every day but hasn't done so since his wife died shortly after Caleb's birth. Their lives are sad and bleak until Sarah Wheaton arrives and changes everything.

Each of these stories shows a character growing and changing as a result of a new or transformed setting. Anyone who has undergone a significant change in their living situation understands just what an impact a new place can have. Adults have all had to start over at one time or another. It is both frightening and exciting. Stories show us how other characters cope with that change. Students who have moved or experienced changes due to death or divorce understand this impact. On the other hand, many young people may have never ventured very far from the town where they were born and may have difficulty with the concept of setting because of this lack of contrast. Stories open up new worlds to all.

2. Call and Response

Here, something happens to alert us that things are about to change. In story grammar language, this is often referred to as the initiating event, though some have called it the inciting incident. The hero may receive a threat, a dare, or an invitation, and must then decide whether to accept the challenge. A period of debate (Snyder, 2005) often follows that may be short or quite long as he decides how to respond. Vogler (2007) divides the *call to adventure* and the *refusal of the call* into two different story elements. Marks (2007) talks separately about the *inciting incident* and the *call to action*. In *Story Frames*, all of these appear in the Call and Response.

The Call   The Call may arrive in a variety of ways—a letter, a phone call, a verbal confrontation. In olden times a king sent a herald with a bugle to call everyone to the town square to make important announcements, such as calling the young men to war or informing the young ladies of a palace ball. In the Disney movie *Mulan* (Cook, 1998), based on the Chinese legend of Hua Mulan, her father receives a notice that one man from each family must go help fight the invading Huns.

In *Sarah, Plain and Tall*, Anna's father informs her and her brother that he has put an advertisement in several newspapers for a wife. In *The Whipping Boy*, Prince Brat tells his whipping boy, Jemmy, that he is running away and taking Jemmy with him. In Suzanne Collins's dystopian young adult novel, *The Hunger Games* (2008), everyone from District 12 is called to the town square for the "reaping," in which two names are drawn in a lottery whose "winners" will participate in a fight to the death with tributes from the other districts. When Primrose Everdeen's name is picked, her sister, Katniss, must decide how to respond.

The Response   The Response to this Call has two parts—the emotional response and the action one decides to take. For instance, Katniss responds to the Call by instantly offering to take her sister's place. Mulan responds to the Call to war by disguising herself as a male so that her aging father will not have to go. Such decisive actions, however, are typically preceded by an emotional response.

A character may go through a wide range of emotions before deciding on a course of action. It is an excellent time to explore the story grammar concept of an inner response—what he is feeling and what he is thinking. The images of a heart and thought bubble used throughout *Story Frames* remind students to talk about the inner thoughts and feelings of characters.

The Reluctant Hero   Protagonists often appear reluctant at first to leave their comfortable homes and the things that are familiar to them to journey into dangerous and unknown territory. They may feel afraid, unprepared, or unworthy. They may hide, run away, argue, or refuse to accept the challenge. For instance, in *The Hunger Games* the "debate" actually occurs before the reaping when Katniss's best friend, Gale, suggests they run away to avoid the selection. They ultimately decide this would have devastating consequences for their families and decide to stay.

The Reluctant Hero is an archetype frequently found in fiction. The greater the potential danger, the more reluctant a character may be to commit to the journey. Jemmy is certain nothing terrible will happen to Prince Brat when the king catches up with his son, but his whipping boy will surely be punished severely and might even get the noose.

For a more thorough discussion of the Refusal of the Call, read *The Writer's Journey: Mythic Structure for Writers* by Christopher Vogler (2007). To learn more about the "debate" that precedes the entry into the New World, read *Save the Cat!* by Blake Snyder (2005).

Examples of the Call and the Refusal abound in children's literature. Harry Potter receives his Call in the form of letters from Hogwarts, but even the great boy wizard is reluctant at first to journey there, thinking there has been a mistake. He does not believe he could be a wizard. It is not until his mentor, Hagrid, asks if he was ever able to make things happen when he was frightened or angry, that Harry has any idea he might have magical powers. Hagrid then takes him to Diagon Alley, where Harry receives numerous magical gifts, including a wand and a cauldron. Sometimes the Call comes from inside a person in the form of an attraction—often the case in romances, such as *Twilight*, in which Bella is interested in the porcelain-white vampire guy in the cafeteria but then decides he is a snob and tries to forget about him.

It is no small coincidence that when a person feels an inner stirring to pursue a vocation or profession this is often referred to as a *calling*. A strong impulse or desire, whether or not it is related to an occupation, is also sometimes referred to as an *inner calling*.

3. Mentors, Guides, and Gifts

Mentors are hero helpers such as teachers, coaches, guides, Jedi warriors, fairy godmothers, gods, or goddesses. The Mentor offers help, advice, assistance, and often a special gift such as an invisibility cloak or a lightsaber. Any character (a sidekick or other helper, even the villain) might serve as a temporary Mentor, giving the hero advice or knowledge valuable to his or her quest. The Mentor often helps the reluctant hero overcome the fear of the adventure and start on the journey. She may reappear at crucial times when the hero seems to stall out or give up.

Greek myths abound with gods and goddesses who serve as Mentors to lowly mortals, giving them a wide variety of gifts. Athena gives Odysseus the idea for the Trojan Horse, which he builds and then uses to sneak into Troy with Greek soldiers hiding inside. The conflict between Greece and Troy also begins with a gift—the Golden Apple of Discord. Some gifts, such as shoes, recur across many different stories: Dorothy receives ruby red slippers from the Good Witch Glenda, while Cinderella receives glass ones from her fairy godmother. When Perseus goes looking for Medusa, Hermes lends him his winged sandals. In Louis Sachar's award-winning novel *Holes* (1998), a judge sends Stanley Yelnats to Camp Green Lake after the boy allegedly steals a pair of sneakers belonging to the famous baseball star Clyde "Sweet Feet" Livingston—setting in motion the events that will drive the rest of the plot.

Mentors provide some of the most memorable personalities in fiction. They remind us that help often comes from the most unusual places.

4. Crossing

The Crossing occurs when the MC, often encouraged by a Mentor, decides to take action and get moving. Sometimes she makes this decision after a time of soul searching; sometimes she concedes reluctantly after being forced on the journey. She takes off toward the New World by boat, plane, time-traveling DeLorean, pumpkin carriage, a secret passage in a wardrobe closet, or even on foot. She may step through a portal or fall through a looking glass.

Usually the MC has a specific goal or intention, such as rescuing a princess, marrying a prince, winning a tournament, or stopping an evil wizard from taking over Middle Earth. For instance, Mulan travels by horseback to the army camp and pretends to be a boy so she can fight in her father's place. However, if the hero enters the New World against her will, her goals may not be apparent at first. Either way, this is a time of change and the protagonist may face opposition as she sets off on a new course.

Threshold Guardians   As anyone who has ever tried to make a significant transition knows, the people closest to us are not always supportive. Sometimes friends try to keep us from embarking on a journey, be it physical, emotional, or spiritual, because they think it is too dangerous. Sometimes the enemy has evil minions who try to prevent us from entering the New World. These types of characters may be Threshold Guardians (Vogler, 2007), people who prevent our entrance and test our commitment to the journey. *The Whipping Boy*'s Prince Brat and Jemmy ride off together into the forest on a horse from the royal stable and encounter two cutthroats who kidnap them. Cinderella's evil stepmother tells her she cannot go to the ball unless she finishes an insurmountable list of chores. Sometimes the protagonist must answer a riddle or perform a task before being allowed to enter the New World. For a more in-depth discussion of Threshold Guardians, read Vogler (2007) or Campbell (1949).

The Journeyless Crossing   This phase of the story does not always involve traveling to a new location. Sometimes the hero stays in the Ordinary World, but something new arrives to change that world.

In *Sarah, Plain and Tall*, Sarah Wheaton takes a train from her home by the sea in Maine to the prairie, but the children never leave home. In Scott O'Dell's *Island of the Blue Dolphins* (1960), a young girl, Karana, has her world turned upside down when a group of Aleutians comes to her island to hunt sea otters, setting into motion a chain of events that ultimately lead to Karana and her little brother, Ramo, being left alone on the island to fend for themselves. Karana does not leave the island; her Crossing occurs when her Ordinary World changes drastically.

MIDDLE

The middle section of the story is all about complications. The protagonist sets goals, makes plans, and carries out attempts, while those who oppose him undermine his efforts.

5. New World

In the New World phase, the hero arrives at a new setting or encounters a new situation. He may meet a host of new people. Some will prove allies and, some, enemies. There will be trials, obstacles, and challenges through which the hero will gain power, strength, and information while identifying and drawing closer to his ultimate goal. These painful trials and obstacles are nothing compared to the significant challenges to be faced later. At this point, the hero may have his first encounter with the antagonist. Additional allies may appear. It may be unclear who is a friend and who is a foe.

Initiations   Joseph Campbell (1949) compared this stage to an *Initiation* where new members of a society must go through a series of tests to prove themselves worthy of belonging in the New World.

Early in Rowling's *Harry Potter* series, Harry Potter travels to Hogwarts School of Witchcraft and Wizardry and meets his classmates. On the Hogwarts Express, he first encounters his friends Hermione and Ron, as well as Draco Malfoy, who will cause Harry trouble throughout the entire series. When Harry arrives at the school, he meets several adults who will serve as additional Mentors and helpers, such as Albus Dumbledore and Professor McGonagall, and potions master, Severus Snape, who torments him through several books. One of the first things Harry must do is learn how to pass Snape's class when it seems the professor is out to get him. He also must learn the general rules of the school, find his way around the place, and figure out how to ride a broomstick. Similarly, in *The Hunger Games* Katniss Everdeen meets her opponents, as well as the adults assigned to help her prepare for battle, and learns how to use a variety of weapons. Once inside the actual Hunger Games Arena, Katniss Everdeen faces increasing challenges. In the classic movie version of *The Wizard of Oz* (Fleming, 1939), based on the novel, *The Wonderful Wizard of Oz* by Baum (1900), Dorothy befriends the Scarecrow, the Tin Man, and the Lion and has her first, but not last, serious conflict with the Wicked Witch of the West.

Blake Snyder (2005) referred to this period as "fun and games." These fun or life-threatening scenes often appear in movie previews.

Fish Out of Water   This metaphor refers to someone who is out of his or her element. All stories contain a bit of this influence because they involve one person entering a strange New World; some stories' entire premise relies on this theme. Many comedies center on it, such as Mary Rodgers's (1972/2003) book, *Freaky Friday*, in which a teenage girl who dreams of being an adult wakes up in her mother's body. In the movie version (Nelson, 1976), the two trade places and both are fish out of water.

Many other stories feature two characters who switch places, and the story unfolds from both points of view: the stockbroker and the homeless con artist in the movie

Trading Places (Landis, 1983); the title characters in Mark Twain's (1882) *The Prince and the Pauper*. When a person arrives in a New World for which they are entirely unsuited, there are unlimited opportunities for hilarity as well as danger.

6. Problems, Prizes, and Plans

Some stories start with a Problem to solve. In these, the Prize is achieving some aim, such as rescuing a princess, destroying a monster, or defeating a villain. Other stories start with a Prize to obtain, such as winning a sporting event; the Problems arise as obstacles to the hero's attempts.

The hero may know from the beginning what he wants or spend a good deal of time in the New World before a clear need or goal emerges. The Prize may be anything significant to the hero: treasure, gold, medicine, a ship, a car, love, knowledge, information, an important clue, self-respect, epiphany, a new rank, or knighthood.

Once a clear story goal emerges, the protagonist makes Plans for attaining it. Some stories spend much time on Plans and preparations. Others may only imply, through the protagonist's actions, that they have been made—especially picture books, which do not always delve into character intentions or motivations.

Blueprints, maps, and game plans appear at this stage. The stage may include a series of scenes showing the hero and his allies preparing for a big event by running drills, working out, practicing routines, or rehearsing. New skills learned previously are now shaped and utilized for a specific purpose. For example, *Harry Potter's* Hermione often researches spells in the library before emerging with a Plan to help Harry. The hero may face more obstacles and setbacks as he approaches the Midpoint Attempt—or approach it with very little forethought and even stumble toward danger unknowingly.

The Challenges of Identifying a Central Problem   Many story grammar aids teach students to identify the central Problem. This seems straightforward enough. Even simple stories contain major Problems. In "Goldilocks and the Three Bears," the bears experience a home invasion by a fair-haired stranger. "Little Red Riding Hood" and "The Three Little Pigs" both feature a wolf who wants to eat the MCs for dinner. Hansel and Gretel wander homeless in the forest.

However, identifying a central Problem is not always so straightforward. Not all stories center on a Problem; some focus on attaining a very coveted Prize, such as the state football championship that the Permian High School Panthers strive to win in Peter Berg's 2004 movie, *Friday Night Lights* (based upon H.G. Bissinger's *Friday Night Lights: A Town, a Team, and a Dream* [1990]). In *Sarah, Plain and Tall*, the Prize is getting a new mother. In both stories, Problems arise but the story centers on attaining the Prize.

Another reason students have difficulty identifying the central Problem is that the objective often changes. Dorothy's central Problem is that she has landed in Oz and needs to get back home, but in the middle of the story the wizard tells her to go confront a witch and steal her broomstick. This Problem (confronting the witch) and the Prize (getting the broomstick) seem to have nothing to do with the central Problem (needing to get back home), except that this task is assigned to Dorothy as a prerequisite for attaining the wizard's help. In truth, the confrontation with the witch is key to Dorothy's growth.

Although the concept of a story Problem seems fairly simple to teachers, breakdowns happen when students are asked to generate a Problem for an original story. Many balk at the idea; they are used to staying out of trouble, not intentionally getting into it. In addition, struggling students tend to want to rush through the writing process, and creating Problems for a character to solve only seems to complicate it. In truth, the middle section of the story centers on just these sorts of complications. Many struggling students, especially teens, have perfected the art of avoiding this in their writing. They must learn that the joy of creating a compelling story outweighs the struggle of getting thoughts down on paper. It is often helpful to share stories of authors who have struggled with the written word, such as Patricia Palacco's picture book, *Thank You, Mr. Falker* (1998), which outlines the author/illustrator's struggles with dyslexia.

Key Contrasts: Problems and Prizes   Young people benefit from contrasting Problems with Prizes. For stories that start with a Problem, a Prize later emerges. Rescuing the princess or finding the sorcerer's stone before Voldemort gets it becomes the central goal. For stories that start with a Prize, such as capturing the attention of the cute boy in the cafeteria, Problems will inevitably arise. As soon as a protagonist sets a goal or aim, obstacles appear to block her path: Oops, the cute boy is a vampire. That certainly complicates matters.

In *The Whipping Boy*, the hoodlums who kidnap Prince Brat and Jemmy (Problem) order the prince to write a ransom note to the king, but the prince cannot even spell his name (another Problem). Jemmy formulates a Plan. He offers to write the letter knowing the outlaws will think he is the prince. He plans to trick the hoodlums into sending Prince Brat back to the castle with the note while Jemmy slips away and ditches both the pesky royal (his original Problem) and the kidnappers (his more recent Problem).

In summary, some stories start with a Problem, and the hero soon identifies a Prize to be attained that will help to overcome the Problem. Other stories start with a Prize, and obstacles (or Problems) arise to prevent the hero from attaining the Prize. Also, sometimes the Prize the hero is pursuing at the Midpoint is not the same Prize he seeks at the end. It may merely be a preliminary reward needed to advance him, or what the hero wants may change as he grows.

Intense opposition and resistance will almost always arise. Without it, the goal would be easily achieved, and the story would be over. Most young writers have difficulty understanding this complication. Once they set up a goal, they want to see their character achieve it quickly, and creating obstacles often seems like a contrivance, which, of course, it is. It is vital, however, to point out that without a Problem or conflict, there is no story. Even the personal stories people retell typically involve something going very wrong—the camping trip where the bear tried to break into the camper, the wedding where the maid of honor fell in the swimming pool. Conflict is what keeps us reading.

The critical thing to remember is that as we identify with the hero of the story attaining his goal against insurmountable odds, we start to believe that maybe we can face our own Problems and come away with a Prize worthy of our efforts.

7. Midpoint Attempt: Going for the Prize

The obstacles and challenges previously encountered are small in comparison to what is coming, but they have prepared the hero for the more significant Midpoint challenge. A Prize is at stake—treasure, medicine, love, information, or simply relief at having survived this particular challenge. The Prize may represent the ultimate story goal or merely something needed to attain it, such as information, getting past a dangerous obstacle, or winning a preliminary competition.

At the Midpoint, the hero may attain the Prize, or it may elude him. He takes action, and there is a consequence, positive or negative. If he does get what he is after, he may soon lose it, have to fight to keep it, or discover that something else of even greater importance still needs to be won. The stakes are high, and often it looks like the hero is about to die or suffer irreparable defeat. If the central character does not achieve his goal, he may have to form a new strategy to do so. A twist or turning point will occur at the Midpoint, the Downtime, or both.

Structural Variations on the Midpoint   Some short stories, fairy tales, and picture books may not have both a Midpoint and a Climax; these elements may combine into one quickly resolved attempt. Having a series of attempts (usually three) to meet a goal is also popular. Goldilocks tries three times to find a comfortable bed, and the Wolf attempts to blow down three houses. In these types of stories, rather than discussing a Midpoint, it might be helpful to talk in terms of the first attempt to meet the goal. Then the second. Then the third. The attempts still grow in size and difficulty, but perhaps without many moments of reflecting and planning in between. In stories with this structure, the Basic Storyboard may be more appropriate for analysis.

Vogler (2007) calls what happens at the Midpoint the *Ordeal*, a time when the hero faces his greatest challenge so far. He explains how some stories have a "central crisis" that occurs halfway through a story, and others a "delayed crisis" nearer to the end—in which case no event at the halfway point may seem particularly noteworthy. For our story analysis purposes with students, pick an important event near the middle to describe as the Midpoint.

Inner and Outer Changes   The Midpoint may represent an inner change or a new understanding. In more character-driven stories, the Midpoint usually focuses on an internal shift. In her book *Inside Story: The Power of the Transformational Arc* (2007), Dara Marks talks extensively about the Midpoint and what she calls the *Moment of Enlightenment*. It marks a change of perception or viewpoint that allows the hero and the story to move toward a resolution. Jemmy makes such an internal shift when he starts to act more royal than the real prince as he drafts a ransom note. When Sarah Wheaton misses the sea, the family tries to cheer her up by finding ways the prairie resembles Sarah's home in Maine. Papa leans a ladder against a pile of hay so they can all climb up, and then they take turns sliding down, pretending it is a sand dune.

Changes may also be external—or external and internal changes may both occur. A vital clue may appear at this time that sheds light on a mystery, a team may lose a key player on their way to the state championship and be forced to come up with a new strategy, or the hero may discover that friends or enemies are not quite whom they seem to be.

Cinderella dances with the prince. Beowulf slays the monster, Grendel. Romeo marries Juliet. In O. Henry's short story, "The Gift of the Magi," Della cuts off her hair at the Midpoint to buy a chain for her husband Jim's pocket watch for Christmas. The Climax occurs later when she must face him, hoping that he will still find her beautiful with her shorn hair. His shocked reaction surprises her until he reveals he sold his pocket watch to purchase combs for her hair. (There is a picture book version of the story, illustrated by Lisbeth Zwerger, which was published by Aladdin Paperbacks in 1997.)

The Agent of Action   The typical rule in stories is that the hero should be the one acting, planning, and making attempts to solve Problems; it is these actions that lead to or at least affect what happens at the Midpoint. However, in children's stories, someone else may be the agent of action. In *Charlie and the Chocolate Factory* (Dahl, 1964), Willie Wonka drives the action. Charlie does not even know until the end of the book that his Prize will be getting to run the entire Chocolate Factory. Is Snow White the heroine of her story? The queen/witch is the person with the explicit goals and all the evil plans. Snow White falls asleep and awaits rescue. The Prince thwarts the queen's plans, but it is not his story.

The protagonist is usually the central character or hero, but a true protagonist is the one driving the action, the story, and the plot forward. He may not be a hero at all or even a point-of-view character. Sometimes the villain is the protagonist driving the action, and the hero is the antagonist who blocks that action.

When working with younger students, these ideas are useful for understanding why the MC does not always seem to be the person making or carrying out the Plans in a story. A protagonist who is *not* a hero is a more appropriate subject for a high school or college level analysis. (The same is true for the concept of an anti-hero, which is outside the scope of the *Story Frames* analysis.) Just as important as discussing how a plot fits into the structure of *Story Frames* (or any other analysis) is understanding when it does not.

8. Downtime Response

The hero has survived the Midpoint Attempt (with or without attaining his initial goal). If he has been successful, this will be a time of celebration. If not, this may be a time for reflection and regrouping. The heart and thought bubble icons remind students to take time to explore the protagonist's emotional responses. How the various characters react at this juncture in the story reveals a lot about them.

Quieter Moments   Students sometimes have difficulty defining what is going on during these quieter moments because the action of the plot subdues as more subtle elements of character appear. People may be sitting around talking. It does not appear that much is happening, but the reader is learning about their interior lives and past experiences. Someone may reveal a secret or answer a nagging question. An essential piece of a puzzle may fall into place. These quieter moments may include character reflections or seemingly minor plot events whose significance may not become apparent until later. In movies and TV shows, anytime there is a close-up shown of an object, character, or facial expression, you can bet it will have significance later on. These camera shots are purposefully set up by directors to foreshadow what is coming.

In "The Gift of the Magi," Jim is late getting home, giving Della time to consider whether it was such a good idea to cut off all of her beautiful hair. In *Sarah, Plain and Tall*, Sarah Wheaton swims with the children in the cow pond, and Caleb makes waves to resemble the sea. Sarah is happy, and the children are content, but then a neighbor woman gives Sarah the idea that she should learn to drive the wagon so that she can go to town.

Downtime may include a time of revitalization and hope that Dara Marks (2007) refers to as a *Period of Grace*. It might involve a series of scenes showing what life would look like if a relationship, dream, or goal worked out. This occurs in the aforementioned scene at the cow pond, when Anna and Caleb get a glimpse of what life would be like with Sarah as a mother. However, the story is far from over.

New Twists and Obstacles   Often during Downtime it seems as if the story is wrapping up, and in some short stories this may be true, but even in short stories and picture books there is often a new and more significant obstacle to overcome. A twist or turning point of some kind will inevitably send the action off in a new direction. The goal or objective may change completely, and new Plans may develop. For instance, in *The Whipping Boy*, Jemmy reveals his Plan to Prince Brat for how they will escape the villains who have captured them, but Prince Brat states that he has no intention of returning to the castle just yet. Jemmy will need a new Plan.

During Downtime, the villain may take possession of the Prize, or if the hero destroys a monster, its evil minions (or mother) may come after the hero. Beowulf and his men celebrate victory, and King Hrothgar gives him many gifts, but as the men are sleeping, Grendel's mother comes to wreak vengeance. In a love story, a piece of information may appear that puts the relationship in jeopardy. Cinderella goes out on the balcony to talk to the prince; the story takes a turn when the clock strikes midnight and she must hurry home to her old life. After marrying, Romeo and Juliet plan to meet that night to consummate their wedding vows, but on his way home, Romeo walks into a conflict between Juliet's cousin, Tybalt, and Romeo's friend, Mercutio. Tybalt kills Mercutio, and Romeo kills Tybalt, causing his exile from Verona and the subsequent events that lead to Romeo and Juliet's deaths.

Repetition Within the Middle of the Story   The Downtime Response brings the middle section or second act to a close. The complications occurring in the middle make it much longer than the beginning section or the end. Any story element may reappear. Numerous new characters and settings may be introduced along the way. What makes the middle section longer in some novels is a repetition of the Plan, Attempt/Consequence, and Response sequence, which can go on indefinitely for hundreds of pages.

In *First Draft in 30 Days: A Novel Writer's System for Building a Complete and Cohesive Manuscript* (2005), Karen S. Wiesner describes the middle of the story as a series of actions and reactions that involve making plans, carrying out attempts, reacting to consequences, and then starting the cycle over again by setting new goals in response to ever-increasing threats and challenges. This cycle continues until a period of what she calls *Downtime*, during which there is a deeper reflection on events. Her analysis focuses on the blocking of attempts, but Downtime may also be a time of celebration if the hero is victorious at the Midpoint.

Wiesner's book is for professional authors, so her method is beyond the scope of working with children, but it helps students understand how stories can be short or long but still follow the same basic narrative structure. Analyzing every subplot and Plan, Attempt/Consequence, Response cycle is not the purpose of *Story Frames*. We are looking for big ideas and significant turning points.

END

The end section of the story is a time to wrap up the action and tie up loose ends. Here we see a character's complete arc and discover whether changes are lasting or temporary.

9. Chase and Escape

After the turning point occurring before or during the Downtime, the story spins off in a new direction. A sense of *pursuit* is the dominating motion; there was a consequence right after the Midpoint Attempt. Either the protagonist got what he was after, or he did not. The Chase and Escape is another consequence, perhaps a delayed reaction, to what happened at the Midpoint.

This juncture often includes a chase scene if the villain realizes the hero has made off with the goods. The antagonist may retaliate and may even temporarily gain possession of the Prize. This section may be very brief, or quite long with a detailed sequence of scenes. Car chases often occur. The hero may be chasing the villain, chasing down clues, or merely continuing to chase the dream. In a love story, the girl may be chasing the boy or vice versa.

In *The Whipping Boy*, Jemmy convinces one of the hoodlums to stick the ransom note in a sack and attach it to the royal horse's saddle. Jemmy then escapes with Prince Brat chasing behind. Cinderella flees from the castle. The prince pursues her and then sends his men out looking for her. Beowulf pursues Grendel's mother. Romeo must flee Verona; the priest sends a messenger to chase him down and give him Juliet's message.

In picture books, the Chase and Escape may not be obvious, or it may represent another, but slightly different, attempt to meet a goal. Whatever the focus, there is a feeling of movement, pursuit, and new direction.

At this point, the hero may feel that he has lost everything and may have to renew his commitment to the adventure to continue. Blake Snyder (2005) calls this *beat* in the story *Bad Guys Close In*, though the conflict is not always with the villain. There may be division within the ranks. Friends may go their separate ways for a while.

10. Death and Transformation

The Transformation of the protagonist is similar to the metamorphosis happening when a caterpillar enters a chrysalis to become a butterfly. The Prize is just within reach, and yet it seems as if the protagonist will fail in his quest. Whatever is most important to him is at stake. A Mentor may reappear to offer advice or assistance.

There is often an internal Death and rebirth, signifying a major internal shift. A change of heart and a change in thinking often characterize this stage. The Transformation may occur during one intense dramatic scene or over a series of smaller scenes. The intensity of the scene is not as important as the internal Transformation that results. External changes that have occurred up until this point (new clothing, stronger physical stature, fancy shoes) will pale in comparison to the internal character growth. Often this Transformation will take place during, or just before, the story Climax. This pattern is exemplified in *The Whipping Boy* when Jemmy learns there is a bounty on his head. Water, a symbol of rebirth, is often found in this stage.

During this part of the story, the MC seems to die to her old self and is reborn as a new person. Dara Marks (2007) refers to this pivotal change as the *Transformational Moment*. Christopher Vogler (2007) describes it as a more lengthy transition that begins during the Midpoint *Ordeal* and an encounter with Death. This inner change gains intensity during *The Road Back* and completes at what he calls the *Resurrection* or *Climax* of the story. Blake Snyder (2005) describes a period when it feels like *All Is Lost* followed by the *Dark Night of the Soul.*

Whether the change is sudden or slow, the new person emerges when the protagonist makes an internal decision to shed the old persona and claim a new identity. This alteration may appear in external signs, such as changes in appearance, but the *real* shift is something internal such as overcoming fear, learning to speak up for oneself, or conquering inadequacy.

This character Transformation even happens in short stories and picture books, though often to a lesser degree. The young wife, Della, in "The Gift of the Magi" starts out feeling sad because she has no money to buy her husband a Christmas gift. She cuts her hair in a major outward Transformation, but the real change occurs when they both realize that their love has made them rich. In Jon Scieszka's picture book, *The Frog Prince, Continued* (1994), the prince and his princess wife begin the story disgruntled; the prince runs off looking for a witch to change him back into a frog and suffers a near-death experience. When he finally returns, he and his wife have a newfound appreciation for each other, kiss, and are both transformed into frogs. In *Emmanuel's Dream: The True Story of Emmanuel Ofosu Yeboah* (Thompson, 2015), Emmanuel's mother dies. He bicycles 400 miles around Ghana to prove that people with disabilities are still capable people, a lesson she taught him. In the process, he transforms an entire society's perception of disability.

Transformation is often painful. It is that awkward change from caterpillar to butterfly and typically involves a Death experience, much like the chrysalis phase where the caterpillar melts into goo before being reborn as a monarch. There is no real change without this Death of the old and birth of the new, but it is human nature to avoid it, to hold onto what is comfortable and familiar. The one exception may be adolescence when teens are eager to throw off the bonds of childhood to embrace the "freedom" of adulthood. It is not until they are midstream through the river of reformation that they realize just how treacherous those waters can be.

Remember, this character Transformation may occur as a sudden change of heart at the Climax, a traumatic shift of perspective at the Midpoint, a series of smaller changes that lead to a gradual paradigm shift, or a combination of these. Some stories abound with Death experiences, and even fairy tales often include the threat of Death by a hungry wolf or jealous witch.

Death experiences come in many forms and may include the actual physical Death of a character, the threat of Death, or merely the loss of a way of life. Sarah Wheaton takes the wagon into town, and the children fear she is leaving them to catch a train back to Maine. They are overjoyed when she returns. Sarah admits that she misses her old home, but assures them that if she went back, she would miss them more. Sarah soon transforms into their new mother.

At this point in the narrative, whatever is most important to the protagonist is threatened, and attainment of the story goal seems impossible. In order to succeed, the hero will have to face what seem to be insurmountable obstacles.

The Final Test, occurring at the Climax, will involve demonstrating that the Transformation is real and permanent rather than a temporary reaction to adversity. The more clearly the character's defects are described at the beginning, the harder it will be to attain the Transformation, resulting in a stronger impact on the reader when the change finally occurs and we see the contrast from the old person he left behind to the new person the hero has become.

11. Climax: The Final Test

At the Climax, the protagonist faces his most difficult challenge, and the stakes are at their highest, often life and Death. The Climax may be a battle, shootout, duel, debate, contest, final court testimony, or a potentially relationship-ending argument—but it is not necessarily action-packed. The Climax of the story is the point of the highest emotional *tension*. This emotional response may or may not represent a rise in *action*. When students think about this part of the story only in terms of *rising action*, some quieter stories may confuse them.

The hero's prior Transformations have prepared him for this moment. The Final Test proves if the changes are internal and real or only external and temporary. The protagonist might now tackle a person or situation he could never have handled at the beginning. Moreover, even if the central character has had friends accompany him on a long and treacherous journey, at the Climax he often must act alone. The Climax is the point where the reader's/viewer's heart is pounding as he wonders if the hero will attain his Prize or fail. For example, in *The Whipping Boy*, when Jemmy hears there is a bounty on his head, he tries to leave Prince Brat behind and heads for the sewers (a symbol of watery Death), but the prince follows him. There they encounter the hoodlums who have caused them trouble throughout the story. Jemmy is familiar with the tunnels, so he and the Prince are able to evade the vagabonds and escape while a swarm of rats attack the bad guys.

Dara Marks (2007) refers to what happens at the Climax as a *Moment of Decision* that proves whether or not the MC has made a life-changing Transformation. Christopher Vogler (2007) calls this stage of the story the *Resurrection*, when there is one last brush with Death and where the hero emerges changed forever. He also describes it as a *Showdown* with the hero and the villain facing off for a final confrontation.

Most teens can relate to a person claiming he or she has changed but not meeting the challenge when it comes to a real test of character. On the positive side, the character arc found in the Hero's Journey reminds us that all people have the potential to transform.

12. Final Reward

The end of a story is a time to tie up loose ends and answer any remaining questions. The protagonist returns with a Prize that he may share with the group, such as an elixir, talisman, balm, treasure, or victory—something that restores peace and happiness to the land. Sometimes this "group" is merely the MC and the reader. The Prize (love, money, medicine, success) may be what the hero has sought all along, or something altogether different.

Sometimes a previously attained Prize has been lost, and the real Final Reward is knowledge, self-awareness, or merely a good story. There is often a celebration—a marriage ceremony in which the hero shares his love with family and friends, a parade sharing a victory, or, if the hero dies, a funeral or celebration of his life. Sometimes it is those who are left behind who learn the important lesson if the central character has died or failed due to foolish decisions.

Everyone gets their just deserts. If the MC has continued to act foolishly, the story may end tragically, with the character dying because of these foolish decisions. The picture book, *The Spider and the Fly* (2002), based on the cautionary tale by Mary Howitt and retold with eerie black-and-white illustrations by Tony DiTerlizzi, is an excellent example. The sinister images make the book work well for all ages. If the hero successfully makes his Transformation but dies during the Climax, then the Final Reward might be his departing to be with the souls of loved ones. There may also be a funeral or a brief gathering celebrating the hero's accomplishments and his final sacrifice. This is rare in children's literature. The movies *Braveheart* (Gibson, 1995) and *Gladiator* (Scott, 2000) are examples of adult stories where the hero dies at the end, but his Death brings victory and resolution to longstanding conflicts.

This stage may also be called the *denouement*, which means to *untie the knot* in Old French. Some stories have a quick or surprise ending without a denouement. Some writers give lengthy explanations tying up every loose end. Shakespeare often does this in his comedies. Other authors intentionally leave questions forever unanswered. In *The Lord of the Flies* (1954) by William Golding, Ralph hides in the forest while the other boys hunt him, starting a fire to drive him out. A naval ship sees the fire and comes to rescue the boys. When a British naval officer suddenly appears on the beach and sees the evidence of the boys' savagery, he asks them how nice British lads could resort to such behavior. The boys weep and the story ends abruptly, leaving many questions for the reader to ponder and answer on his own.

CONCLUSION: THE TWELVE ELEMENTS IN DEPTH

The 12 elements found in *Story Frames* provide a way to analyze and remember the plot of almost any story. Even if a story does not contain all of the plot elements, the discussion of those elements and how a story differs will still create a powerful framework for understanding the sequence of events. It should be noted that these elements may be naturally occurring, meaning that even when an author does not intentionally set out to include them, they will still often appear in the narrative. These authors (Pantsers) often claim to write "by the seat of their pants" without much planning. Some authors (Plotters) do intentionally plot their stories using a framework like *Story Frames*.

Getting Started With *Story Frames*

3

This chapter includes a script educators may use to begin teaching the *Story Frames* concepts immediately. It starts with an overview of the 12 story elements, discusses each part individually, then looks at the whole once again. This strategy of looking at the whole, then the parts, then the whole will be used often with students as they build story schemas for various narratives. Later chapters and downloadable resources provide sample stories for analysis and writing as well as directions for creating original narratives.

The format of *Story Frames* allows an educator to jump into action, using the strategies while continuing to build foundational knowledge. In time, the original script may be replaced with a more personal one as understanding and appreciation of stories and their underlying structure grows.

An instructor may get started with *Story Frames* having little background knowledge of story analysis by using the examples in this chapter. Additional chapters will go into more detail. For a deeper understanding of story structure, plan to read Chapter 2, "The Twelve Elements in Depth," if you have not done so already.

Because story structure is a topic that will often reoccur, begin with either the A or B option when you introduce *Story Frames* to students.

- *Introductory Lesson A:* Read a specific example story from the downloadable resources and discuss that story using the 12 elements, THEN discuss the 12 elements in depth. (This works best for students with limited exposure to stories who may have difficulty relating to examples).

- *Introductory Lesson B:* Discuss the 12 elements in depth, THEN apply the analysis to a specific story.

These two approaches are described in detail in the following sections.

LESSON PLAN FOR OPTION A: START WITH A PICTURE BOOK

For this option, you will start with a picture book. Read the story to the class, then go back and talk about each story element as it arises. *Emmanuel's Dream: The True Story of Emmanuel Ofosu Yeboah* (Thompson, 2015)

DOWNLOADABLE RESOURCES

Keep these resources on hand for teaching the Chapter 3 lessons and activities.

- Introductory Lesson 3A, Blank Storyboard template (Complete); Complete Storyboard; illustration and icon for each of the 12 elements

- Introductory Lesson 3B, Complete Storyboard; Twelve Elements Story Icons PowerPoint slide deck OR illustration and icon for each of the 12 elements

- Lesson 3C, Memory for Pictures: Complete Storyboard; Memory for Pictures baseline data collection sheet (sequencing)

- Other: Basic Storyboard and Blank Storyboard template (Basic). Consider using with very simple stories or when teaching young children, those with significant memory impairments, and/or second-language learners.

or *Six Dots: A Story of Young Louis Braille* (Bryant, 2016) are both excellent examples of picture books with a solid story structure, but other examples provided in later chapters would also work well. The picture books discussed in the downloadable resources are appropriate for most ages for story analysis purposes. See the sample lesson plan that follows.

ACTIVITY

INTRODUCTORY LESSON 3A: PICTURE BOOK DISCUSSION INTRODUCING *STORY FRAMES*

Objective:
Improve understanding of story structure

Time:
90 minutes (two 45-minute sessions or three 30-minute sessions)

Grade Level:
Grades 1–3

Directions: Day One

1. Read the story one time through for enjoyment and to get the big ideas. Talk through it a second time and encourage students to use the pictography strategies described in Chapter 1 to make stick figure drawings of what is happening in the story on a blank piece of 8½″ × 11″ paper. This may be done the first time through the book if it does not interrupt the flow of the story. The teacher/therapist should model stick figure drawings on the board.

2. Give each student either a blank storyboard (Grades 1–2) or one that has keywords and vocabulary from the selected story (Grades 3 and up). If these are not readily accessible, have students divide a piece of 8½″ × 11″ paper into 12 sections and create a word wall for vocabulary terms on the back. Storyboard graphic organizers suitable for copying are provided in the downloadable resources.

3. Briefly introduce and describe each plot element. Use the icons from Option B (in next section).

4. Ask students to use their stick drawings and help them decide which images go with which section of the story. They may cut their original stick drawing into individual pieces and glue the pieces in the appropriate frame, or they may create new stick figures for each section. They may also write words if they prefer. Young children might merely visualize what goes in each section or use copies of the teacher's stick drawings. Keep it simple.

Directions: Day Two

1. Go back through the storyboards created by the students while talking about each story element and the examples from the current narrative. Have them point to each section as you discuss it to help them keep their place in the story.

2. Show students the image of the storyboard with all 12 story elements from Option B (in the next section) and briefly review each element. Discuss how Row 1 represents the beginning of the story, Row 2 the middle, and Row 3 the end.

3. Go through each icon and discuss examples from other stories. Talk about age-appropriate books or movies with similar elements. Ask students to give examples.

Option A works well with young children and second language learners who may not have much experience with stories and may have difficulty either relating to movie examples or coming up with connections to books. Typically, around age 7, students will have enough background knowledge to share at least a few examples.

LESSON PLAN FOR OPTION B: START WITH THE TWELVE ELEMENTS

Begin with a conversation about the 12 story elements using the *Story Frame* icons and illustrations found in the figures in this chapter. The Story Icon PowerPoint in the downloadable resources is a useful tool for sharing these images. See the sample lesson plan and script that follow.

INTRODUCTORY LESSON 3B:
INTRODUCTION OF THE 12 ELEMENTS OF *STORY FRAMES*

Directions

1. Photocopy the pictures (icons and illustrations) found in the downloadable resources, or use the PowerPoint slide deck.

2. Discuss each plot element, giving examples from movies or books familiar to the students. (See lesson script that follows.)

3. Ask students for additional examples.

Objective:
Improve understanding of story structure

Time:
45 minutes

Grade Level:
Grades 3–8. Adjust story examples to fit the needs of students.

LESSON SCRIPT

See the sections that follow for a script that may be read verbatim to students or modified.

Before you begin discussing each story element in depth, you may want to enlarge and cut out the story icons individually so you can put them on the board as the story builds. Using a pocket display or laminating the images and using magnets so they adhere to a white board is helpful, or you can display them via PowerPoint on a SmartBoard. You may also want to create smaller versions for your students to color while you explain the elements and have them put the pictures in order as you talk. This often helps to keep them engaged. Give older students a larger version of the pictures and ask them to write examples from stories beside the pictures.

Introduction

1. *Display Figure 3.1, which shows the Complete Storyboard. Say:* Today I'm going to share with you secrets about the way many professional authors write stories and analyze stories that other authors write. This structure has 12 elements.

2. *Point to the pictures as you name each element:* The beginning: This includes the Ordinary World; Call and Response; Mentors, Guides, and Gifts; and Crossing. The middle: This includes New World; Problems, Prizes, and Plans; Midpoint Attempt; and Downtime Response. The end: This includes Chase and Escape; Death and Transformation; Climax: The Final Test; and Final Reward.

3. *Explain:* That is a lot of detail, but learning to chunk information will make it easier to remember. The pictures also help.

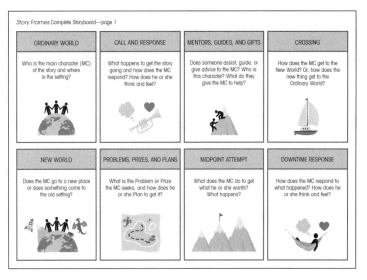

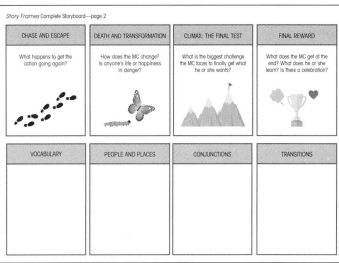

Figure 3.1. Complete Storyboard.

Not all stories will contain all of these elements, and they will not always be in precisely this order, but when you know what to look for, you will start to remember examples from movies and books.

You will easily recognize a lot of these elements once I explain them. I'll bet you can even give me examples from movies you've seen and books you've read. Be ready because I will be asking you for examples. You know a lot more about stories than you think you do.

We will learn how to put what you already know into words so we have a structure we can use to talk about stories. Once you understand these secrets, you'll start noticing them more and more in movies and books. Then you'll know how to build your own exciting stories.

Ordinary World

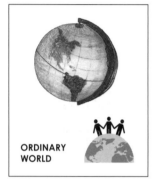

Figure 3.2. Ordinary World.

1. *Display Figure 3.2, which shows the Ordinary World. Say:* All stories begin in the hero's Ordinary World. It is often a boring place compared to the exciting New World the main character will soon enter. Charlie Bucket from *Charlie and the Chocolate Factory* (Dahl, 1964) starts out in the shabby house where he lives with his parents and grandparents and goes to Willie Wonka's Chocolate Factory. Dorothy leaves Kansas and travels to Oz. Wilbur, the pig in *Charlotte's Web* (White, 1952), leaves the Arable Farm to go live on the farm of Homer Zuckerman.

   Sometimes the hero stays in his Ordinary World, but something comes to him that changes his world. This often happens in romances, where a new girl or boy comes to town, and the hero's world turns upside down. In the movie *Transformers* (Bay, 2007), Sam Witwicky stays in the same town, but cars and trucks start coming to life. Karana in *Island of the Blue Dolphins* (O'Dell, 1960) stays behind on the island with her brother as everyone else leaves.

2. *To get students started on thinking of examples, ask students to respond to prompts such as:* Do you know the name of the boy who starts out on Privet Drive and then goes to Hogwarts School of Magic and Wizardry? (Harry Potter) Who is the girl who is forced to work day and night to take care of the house while her evil stepsisters do nothing? Where does she go? (Cinderella; to a ball at the Prince's castle)

3. *Next, ask:* What are other examples of the contrast between the Ordinary World and the New World from books you have read or movies you have seen? *Guide students in generating their own examples. Be prepared to add age-appropriate examples familiar to your students and remind them of the example story if you read one to them.*

Call and Response

Figure 3.3. Call and Response.

1. *Display Figure 3.3, which shows Call and Response. Say:* Soon after the story begins in the Ordinary World, we get a big hint that things are about to change. Sometimes the Call follows an inciting incident and sometimes it IS the inciting incident. It is what gets the action rolling. In olden times a king sent a herald with a bugle to call everyone to the town square to make important announcements. Similarly, the hero may receive an important threat, challenge, or invitation. It may arrive in a variety of ways—a letter, a phone call, an announcement about a contest, a request, a verbal confrontation, or in the form of an internal feeling or desire.

Heroes are often reluctant to set off on the adventure. They usually have strong thoughts and feelings about it. The image of the heart and the thought bubble remind us to consider what the hero is thinking and feeling.

Cinderella receives an invitation to a ball but is worried because she does not have anything to wear. Charlie finds a golden ticket but thinks he should sell it because his family is poor and needs the money. Harry Potter receives letters inviting him to attend Hogwarts. At first, he does not believe he could be a wizard.

2. *To get students started on thinking of additional examples, ask students to respond to prompts such as:* What are some of the ways secret agents receive information about a new mission? What are some other examples of the Call and Response? (Answers will vary.)

3. *Guide students in generating their own examples. Be prepared to add age-appropriate examples familiar to your students. Remind students of the example story if you read one.*

Mentors, Guides, and Gifts

1. *Display Figure 3.4, which shows Mentors, Guides, and Gifts. Say:* A Mentor, Guide, or helper often appears to give the hero what he or she needs to get started on the journey and often reappears to offer help whenever it is needed. Mentors are hero helpers that may include teachers, coaches, guides, Jedi warriors, fairy godmothers, gods, or goddesses. The Mentor often helps the reluctant hero overcome the fear of the adventure.

Figure 3.4. Mentors, Guides, and Gifts.

The Mentor also offers help, advice, assistance, and often a special gift such as glass slippers or a lightsaber. Greek gods and goddesses gave mortals gifts like flying shoes, shields, and expandable bags. Wilbur's friend, Charlotte, spins a special message in a web so that Zuckerman will think he is special and keep him alive.

2. *To help students identify examples, ask students to respond to prompts such as:* Who were some of Harry Potter's mentors? (Hagrid, Dumbledore, Lupin, Sirius, McGonagall) Who gave Charlie money to buy a chocolate bar? (His grandfather) Who gave Cinderella her glass slippers? (Her fairy godmother)

3. *To help students generate additional examples, ask:* Can you think of other Mentors and the types of gifts they gave to heroes? *Guide students in generating their own examples. Be prepared to add age-appropriate examples familiar to your students. Remind students of the example story if you read one to them.*

Crossing

1. *Display Figure 3.5, which shows the Crossing. Say:* This is the point in the story where the main character makes a decision to act and gets moving. Sometimes the hero jumps into action. Sometimes this takes longer, and she may need a mentor or friend to convince her to get going. Sometimes she is forced to go. Dorothy gets whisked away to Oz in a tornado. Cinderella goes to the ball in a pumpkin coach. The children in *The Lion, the Witch, and the Wardrobe* (Lewis, 1950) enter the land of Narnia through a wardrobe closet.

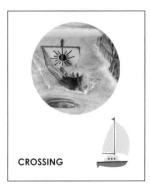

Figure 3.5. Crossing.

If the hero has stayed in his Ordinary World, that world will drastically change. Sometimes something unusual comes to him, like the cars that turn into robot fighting machines in *Transformers*, or important people may leave, as they do in *Island of the Blue Dolphins*.

2. *To help students identify examples, ask students to respond to prompts such as:* How does Harry Potter get to Hogwarts? (The Hogwarts Express) How does Alice get to Wonderland? (through a looking glass)

3. *To help students generate additional examples, ask:* Can you think of other ways heroes have traveled to a New World? What about boats, planes, or time machines? Can you tell me the title of a story that uses one of those? *Guide students in generating their own examples. Be prepared to add age-appropriate examples familiar to your students. Remind students of the example story if you read one to them.*

Review of the Beginning Section

1. *Display Figure 3.6, which shows a review of the beginning section. Say:* Let's review what happens in the beginning section of the story. It is a setup that prepares us for what will happen in the rest of the story. The main character starts out in his Ordinary World. He receives a Call to adventure. Often, he is reluctant to accept the challenge. There is often a Mentor, Guide, or sidekick who gives the protagonist encouragement, companionship, advice, or a specific gift that will help him in the New World. Then there is a Crossing into the New World. If the hero has stayed in his Ordinary World, something or someone may cross into his world, or someone important may cross out of it.

2. *Next, introduce the concept of plot twists and turns:* Major plot points occur when there is a twist in the story. This happens at the end of the beginning and middle sections and at the story Climax. The hero takes off to a new place, turns and goes in a new direction, or receives a piece of information that changes his thinking on a subject. There is usually some kind of surprise.

Now, let's examine what happens in the middle of a story after the hero has crossed over into the New World.

New World

1. *Display Figure 3.7, which shows the New World. Say:* When the hero arrives in the New World, he will meet new characters. Some will turn out to be friends and some will be enemies. As the hero gets used to the New World, there will be small trials, obstacles,

Figure 3.6.   Review of the beginning section: Ordinary World; Call and Response; Mentors, Guides, and Gifts; and Crossing.

and challenges. These challenges are nothing compared to what will come later, but they are helping to build the hero's character. Dorothy starts down the yellow brick road and befriends the Scarecrow, the Tin Man, and the Lion. Cinderella arrives at the palace. Wilbur realizes that it will be harder to make friends when he moves to Zuckerman's farm. Charlie is fascinated by the Oompa Loompas and rivers of chocolate inside the chocolate factory.

2. *To help students identify examples, ask students to respond to prompts such as:* What were some of the challenges Harry Potter faced when he first arrived at Hogwarts? (learning his schedule, figuring out how to fly a broom, avoiding Snape)

3. *To help students generate additional examples, ask:* What are other examples of small challenges that a hero faced in the New World? *Guide students in generating their own examples. Add age-appropriate examples familiar to your students. Remind students of the example story if you read one to them.*

Figure 3.7. The New World.

Problems, Prizes, and Plans

1. *Display Figure 3.8, which shows Problems, Prizes, and Plans. Explain:* Some stories begin focused on a Problem to be solved, and a Prize results from what the hero will gain by solving the Problem. Other stories start with a Prize the hero wants to obtain, and Problems arise as obstacles to the Prize appear.

   In the movie *Shrek* (Adamson, 2001), the Problem is that a princess is kidnapped, and Shrek must rescue her. Other stories that begin focused on a Prize might involve winning a sports championship or other contest. Whether a story begins with the Problem or begins with the Prize, stories usually contain both. If the Problem is the missing princess, then the Prize might be finding her. If the Prize is a sports championship, then the Problem might be that the team isn't very good, or maybe they have lost a coach or a key player.

   The Prize may be anything important to the hero: treasure, gold, medicine, a ship, a car, love, knowledge, information, an important clue, self-respect, a new rank, or knighthood. Once a goal is established, Plans are made for attaining the Prize and/or solving the problem. Blueprints and maps might be drawn or a game plan may be written on the chalkboard. Sometimes planning is implied. It may occur again later in the story as new Plans must be made.

Figure 3.8. Problems, Prizes, and Plans.

2. *To help students identify examples, ask students to respond to prompts such as:* How did Cinderella plan for the ball? (She asked her family for permission to go; she completed her chores in time; she got help from a fairy godmother to get a pretty gown and a carriage.)

3. *To help students generate additional examples, ask:* Who can give examples of the Problem, the Prize, or the Plan in other movies or books? *Guide students in generating their own examples. Add age-appropriate examples familiar to your students. Remind students of the sample story if you read one to them.*

Midpoint Attempt: Going for the Prize

1. *Display Figure 3.9, which shows the Midpoint Attempt. Say:* This stage represents a significant attempt to achieve a goal or gain a Prize. The Plan is carried out, and a consequence follows. The challenges faced up to this point are small compared to what is coming. The Prize at this stage may represent the ultimate goal, or just something

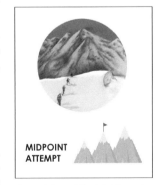

Figure 3.9. Midpoint Attempt: Going for the Prize.

needed to attain that goal, such as information, getting past a dangerous obstacle, or winning the first round of a contest or competition. For example, the team must win the regional championship before they advance to the state competition.

At the Midpoint, the hero may succeed in getting what he is after, or he may fail. If the main character does get the Prize, he may soon lose it, have to fight to keep it, or discover that there is something greater still to be won. In *Charlotte's Web*, Charlotte saves Wilbur from becoming Christmas dinner, but the real test of survival will come much later at the fair.

2. *To help students identify examples, ask students to respond to prompts such as:* In what story does a girl go to a ball to meet a handsome prince? (Cinderella) When she meets the prince and dances with him, do they immediately fall in love and get married and live happily ever after? (No, she has to leave; he has to find her but he doesn't know who she is or where she lives.)

   Explain: Cinderella carried out her Plan and met the prince, and they are falling in love, but she won't keep her Prize for long because she must leave at midnight. What else might prevent their living happily ever after? (He might not want to marry her if he finds out she is her stepfamily's housemaid; he might mistakenly marry someone else whose foot fits her slipper.)

3. *To help students generate additional examples, ask:* What are other goals or challenges you've seen characters go for at this stage of the story? *Guide students in generating examples. Add age-appropriate examples familiar to them. Remind students of the sample story if you read one.*

Downtime Response

Figure 3.10. Downtime Response.

1. *Display Figure 3.10, which shows the Downtime Response. Say:* This is where we see the hero's Response to what happened at the Midpoint. The heart and thought bubble remind us to consider what the main character is thinking and feeling. Maybe she has obtained what she is after, or maybe not. If the hero has obtained a Prize during the Midpoint challenge, Downtime may be a time for relaxation and celebration. If not, this may be a time to regroup and make a new Plan.

   It may appear that the story is over, but a twist or other turning point will soon send the hero off in a new direction. The villain may come back and steal the Prize from the hero. In a story of love or friendship, a piece of information may slip out that puts the relationship in jeopardy. Cinderella has a quiet moment with the prince on the balcony, but then the clock strikes midnight and she must leave.

   These quiet times are when we get to know who people are. It is an excellent time to talk about characters' thoughts, feelings, and emotional responses.

2. *To help students identify examples, ask students to respond to prompts such as:* In the movie *Shrek*, Shrek rescues princess Fiona and later learns a secret about her. Does anyone know what that secret is? (She is actually a monster too.)

3. *Ask:* Can you think of more examples? *Guide students in generating their own examples. Add age-appropriate examples familiar to them. Remind students of the sample story if you read one.*

Review of the Middle Section

1. *Display Figure 3.11, which shows a review of the middle section. Say:* Let's review what happens during the middle section of the story. The beginning starts with the Ordinary World, while the middle starts with the New World. It is right under the Ordinary World

Figure 3.11. Review of the middle section: New World; Problems, Prizes, and Plans; Midpoint Attempt; and Downtime Response.

as we look at the two rows of pictures. This will make it easy to remember where they go in the sequence.

The Crossing comes right before the New World because this is how the hero gets to the new setting. After the protagonist spends some time getting used to the New World, he then makes Plans and preparations to address a Problem or attain a Prize. Then comes the Midpoint Attempt where the hero takes action to get that Prize or solve that Problem. We also see the consequence of that attempt and whether the hero was successful. This consequence is followed by a period of Downtime Response that shows how the hero reacts to what happened at the Midpoint.

2. *Next, review twists and turns:* Recall that major plot points occur when there is a twist in the story. In the middle section this may happen during the Midpoint Attempt, after a period of Downtime, or both.

3. *You should now have two rows of pictures on the board if you have been displaying them during the lesson. Now, display Figure 3.12, which shows the Plan, Attempt/Consequence, Response Cycle. Put it after the other pictures in the middle row.*

    Explain: It appears that the middle section is equal in length to the beginning and end sections, but this can be very misleading. The middle is usually much longer. What makes it longer is repetitions of the Plan, Attempt/Consequence, Response cycle that can go on for quite a while. Other story elements may also be repeated at this time. There may be a new Call that sends the movement of the story in a different direction. Other Mentors may appear. There may be a Crossing over into yet another New World. This is how novels can be 800 pages long and still follow the basic story structure of much shorter stories.

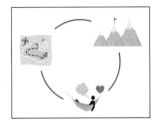

Figure 3.12. Plan, Attempt/ Consequence, Response Cycle.

Now, let's look closely at what happens at the end of the story. Once the middle of the story has given us another plot twist, and Downtime is over, the action starts up again.

Chase and Escape

1. *Display Figure 3.13, which shows the Chase and Escape. Say:* After the twist or turning point, the action takes off in a new direction. This is the stage where you might see a car chase, a horse chase, or some other kind of intense pursuit. If the hero has the Prize, then the villain may chase him. If the villain has the Prize, then the hero may chase him. The girl may chase the boy, or the boy may chase the girl. In a mystery, a detective might be "chasing" clues. In a sports story, the team may run drills to prepare for the final match.

    In the movie *Mulan* (Cook, 1998), the heroine races to the Imperial City to warn everyone that the Huns are coming. In *Charlie and the Chocolate Factory*, the parents of the naughty children run off to find their kids. In *Sarah, Plain and Tall* (MacLachlan,

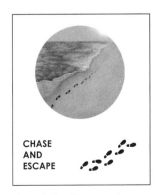

Figure 3.13. Chase and Escape.

1985/2015), Sarah heads to town in a wagon and the children fear she is trying to escape them and the farm.

2. *To help students identify examples, ask students to respond to prompts such as:* Who chases Cinderella after the clock strikes midnight? (the prince)

3. *Next, invite students to generate more examples. Say:* Can you think of more examples? What are some of your favorite chase scenes? *Guide students in generating examples. Add age-appropriate examples familiar to your students. Remind students of the sample story if you read one.*

Death and Transformation

Figure 3.14. Death and Transformation.

1. *Display Figure 3.14, which shows Death and Transformation. Say:* Following the Chase and Escape, the hero experiences a Death and Transformation. Death represents the hero losing what is most important to him (a friend, a dream, an important possession), but sometimes a real death takes place.

   For example, from the first page of *Charlotte's Web*, Wilbur's life is in danger. Later in the story, Charlotte dies after saving him, while Wilbur transforms into a prized pig. In *Charlie and the Chocolate Factory*, bad things happen to the naughty children, and they are physically changed. One is sucked into a tube and disappears. Another one shrinks. One turns into a giant blueberry.

   These Transformations are physical. However, outer changes to the main character, such as new clothing or a stronger body, will seem small compared to the changes experienced on the inside. The real Transformation might be learning to speak up for oneself or to appreciate other people.

   This stage is similar to a caterpillar going through the process of becoming a butterfly. It seems as if the insect has died, but then it reappears as something new and unusual. For example, the naughty children in *Charlie and the Chocolate Factory* are not only physically transformed, but also transformed on the inside. In the end, they learn not to be so selfish.

2. *To help students identify examples of Death, ask students to respond to prompts such as:* Think of examples of characters dying, or being in danger of dying, in fairy tales. How do Hansel and Gretel find themselves in danger at the gingerbread house? (They discover that the witch plans to cook and eat them.)

3. *To help students identify examples of Transformation, ask students to respond to prompts such as:* In fairy tales, main characters may undergo Transformation in a moment of danger that forces them to be braver, stronger, or smarter than ever before. For instance, what does Gretel do when the witch is getting ready to eat her and her brother? (Gretel tricks the witch so she can shut her in the oven and escape with Hansel.)

4. *To help students generate examples of Death and Transformation, ask them to respond to prompts such as:* Can you name someone important who has died at this stage in a movie or book? What are some major Transformations you've seen characters make? *Guide students in generating examples. Add age-appropriate examples familiar to your students. Remind students of the sample story if you read one.*

Climax: The Final Test

Figure 3.15. Climax: The Final Test.

1. *Display Figure 3.15, which shows Climax: The Final Test. Say:* At the Climax of the story, the hero faces her most difficult challenge and the stakes are at their highest, often life

and death. There may be a battle, showdown, duel, debate, contest, final court testimony, or argument where it seems that a meaningful relationship may end.

The Climax is the point of the highest emotional tension. It may or may not include much action. Whatever Transformations the main character has undergone have prepared him for this moment. It is the Final Test to see if the change in the hero is real or only temporary. This is the point where the reader's/viewer's heart is pounding as they wonder if the hero will attain her Prize or fail. Harry must face Voldemort in each of the *Harry Potter* books. After the glass slipper that would prove Cinderella's identity gets broken in the movie version, Cinderella has to prove that she is the girl from the ball and passes the test by producing the matching shoe from her pocket. Near the end of the story, there is often another twist or surprise.

2. *To help students identify examples, ask students to respond to prompts such as:* What did Dorothy have to steal from the witch in *The Wizard of Oz*? (her broomstick) Where does the Climax of *Charlotte's Web* take place? (the county fair)

3. *To help students generate additional examples, say:* Think of your favorite movie. When did the hero have to face his biggest challenge, compete in a contest, or pass a test? *Guide students in generating examples. Add age-appropriate examples familiar to your students. Remind students of the sample story if you read one to them.*

Final Reward

1. *Display Figure 3.16, which shows the Final Reward. Say:* Everyone gets their just reward. The hero usually returns with a Prize to share with the group such as love, money, or medicine. Peace, happiness, and balance return.

FINAL REWARD

Figure 3.16. Final Reward.

Sometimes the "group" is merely the main character and the reader. The reward may be the same Prize the hero has sought all through the story, or something different. Sometimes the real reward is knowledge, self-awareness, survival, or simply a good story.

There is often a celebration: a wedding, a parade, or a banquet. Wilbur receives a gold medal, and his owner gets twenty-five dollars. Cinderella marries the prince. Charlie gets the Chocolate Factory. This point in the story is where we find out how the hero thinks and feels about the consequences of his actions.

If the hero dies, there may be a funeral or other celebration of life. Something will remind us that life goes on. For instance, in *Charlotte's Web*, Wilbur the pig takes Charlotte's egg sac back to the farm and three of the babies stay with him to become his good friends.

Sometimes, if a character has died or failed due to foolish decisions, those left behind learn the critical lesson.

2. *To help students generate examples, ask them to respond to prompts such as:* What does Gryffindor House win at the end of the first *Harry Potter* book? (the house cup) *Guide students in generating additional examples. Add age-appropriate examples familiar to students. Remind students of the sample story if you read one.*

Review of the End

1. *Display Figure 3.17, which shows a review of the end section. Say:* Let's review the four elements we find at the end of the story. There is a turning point with a Chase or Escape along with some sort of a pursuit. The Death and Transformation scene may come before the Climax, or during. It shows the internal changes the hero has made. Finally, there is a Final Reward or consequence where the hero gets whatever he has earned through his Transformation. The resolution comes at the end as the loose ends wrap up, and a hero thinks about what has happened and considers how he feels about it.

Figure 3.17. Review of the end section: Chase and Escape; Death and Transformation; Climax: The Final Test; and Final Reward.

2. *You should now have three rows of pictures on the board if you have been displaying them during the lesson. Remind students that you won't always find all of these elements in a story, especially if it is very short. In addition, some might appear several times throughout a story. In* The Hunger Games, *there are many examples of Death. Entire movies have centered around Chase and Escape. You may not agree with your students (or with the analyses that follow) about what the Midpoint of a particular story is. The critical objective is to give students a schema or framework to use to think about stories, remember them, talk about them, and write about them.*

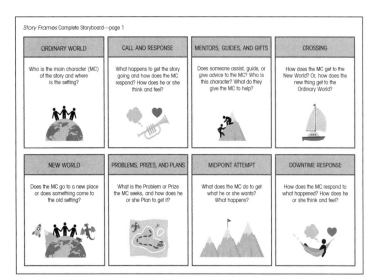

MEMORY FOR PICTURES

Figure 3.18 shows the Complete Storyboard. A full-size, downloadable and photocopiable version is provided with the downloadable resources for this chapter.

After using this analysis for a few stories, cut apart the pictures from the Complete Storyboard and ask students to scramble the 12 pictures to see how many they can put back in order. Be sure to review the information with students just before asking them to perform this activity. (This may happen on a different day.)

Laminate the images and add magnets to the back. A cookie sheet or magnetic white board may be used to arrange the pictures. Even students with severe academic challenges are surprisingly good at doing this if some hints and visual references are given ahead of time.

Review is a valuable memory strategy. If you want to show students how helpful review can be, have them attempt to recall the picture sequence without a review, then give them a review and see if performance improves. Collect baseline data using the forms in the downloadable resources.

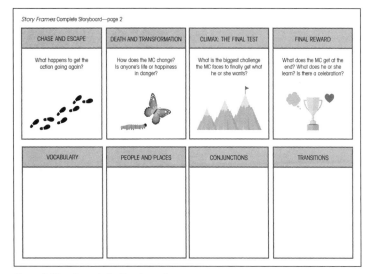

Figure 3.18. Complete Storyboard.

LESSON 3C: MEMORY FOR PICTURES

ACTIVITY

Objective:
Improve memory strategies

Time:
15 minutes

Grade Level:
Grades 1–8

Directions

1. Provide each student with the 12 icons cut out into squares and a Complete Storyboard to use as a guide.

2. Discuss REVIEWING as a strategy and instruct students to turn over the Complete Storyboard so it cannot be seen. Show students how they may test their knowledge by setting up the 12 images in three rows and then comparing it to the Complete Storyboard.

3. Discuss CHUNKING as a strategy and talk about memorizing one row of the *Story Frames* chart at a time.

4. Discuss using VISUAL CUES as a strategy and point out the fact that the two "worlds" are directly above and below each other with the boat connecting them. The mountain pictures are also directly above and below each other. The story ends with the trophy.

5. Instruct students to let you know when they are ready to put the icons in order from memory without the guide.

Whichever way you choose to start your presentation of *Story Frames*, the next step is to analyze several picture books using this structure. Picture books may be used for all ages because they are short and may be read in one session or class period. Some contain advanced vocabulary and cover topics that require higher order thinking. Activities based on both picture books and novels appear with the Literature Guides found in the downloadable resources. Chapters in Section 2 will discuss writing activities as well as activities for vocabulary development, grammar usage, executive function skills, and more.

THE SIMPLIFIED STORYBOARD

Figure 3.19 shows the Basic Storyboard. A full-size, downloadable and photocopiable version is provided with the downloadable resources for this chapter.

Some very simple stories for young children, such as the folktale "Little Red Hen," are characterized by repeating events and don't include all of the nuances of more complicated stories. Examples of other more basic picture books will be discussed in Chapter 4, Understanding Narrative Development. A simplified version of the storyboard, consisting of 8 elements rather than 12, may be used to discuss those types of stories as well as many longer stories. It may also be useful for young children, those with significant memory impairments, and second language learners.

The Frog Prince, Continued (1994) by Jon Scieszka with illustrations by Steve Johnson is a fun spoof of the old classic that students may retell with the Basic Storyboard as shown next. This story can also be retold using the Complete Storyboard; see the downloadable resources for a sample analysis and lesson.

1. **Ordinary World**—The Frog Prince and the princess live in a fancy castle where they are both happy for a long time, but after a while, they both become miserable.

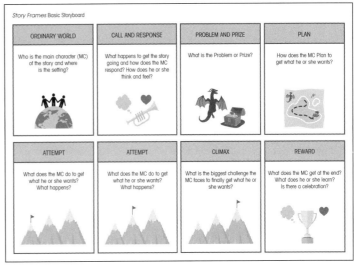

Figure 3.19. Basic Storyboard.

2. **Call and Response**—The princess tells the Frog Prince that they would both be happier if he were still a frog. This gives him an idea.

3. **Problem and Prize**—The Problem is that the Frog Prince still likes frog things. The Prize is to become a frog again.

4. **Plan**—He runs away to the forest looking for a witch who can turn him back into a frog.

5. **Attempt**—He finds Sleeping Beauty's witch, but she wants to cast a bad spell on him. Then he finds Snow White's witch, and she tries to give him a poisoned apple.

6. **Attempt**—He finds a pretty witch who seems much more helpful than the other two. She invites him to stay for lunch, but he realizes the house is made of gingerbread and that this is the witch from Hansel and Gretel's story.

7. **Climax**—He finds a fairy godmother who tries to change him into a frog but accidentally turns him into a carriage instead. He is worried he will stay that way forever. When the clock strikes midnight, he turns back into a prince.

8. **Reward**—He realizes how much he still loves the princess and runs back to the castle. They kiss, and both turn into frogs. They live happily ever after.

TIPS FOR ONLINE LEARNING AND TELETHERAPY

1. The Story Icon PowerPoint found in the downloadable resources may be used to discuss the 12 story elements by using the screenshare feature of Zoom.

2. Consider e-mailing the icon pages to students and then instructing them to print those pages, cut out the icons, scramble them, and put them back in order.

CONCLUSION: HOW TO INTRODUCE *STORY FRAMES*

When introducing *Story Frames*, remember that there are two lesson plan options found at the beginning of this chapter. Whether or not you choose to start with one of the stories available with the downloadable resources as an example text, try to help students make connections to other stories they have read in class. Always weave in the strategies of periodic review, Quick Draws, and the chunking of related information. Demonstrate how to look at the whole, then the parts, then the whole, going back and forth between the big ideas and the details. Finally, don't forget that the Basic Storyboard with only 8 elements may be more appropriate for simpler stories and younger students.

Using
Story Frames to
Build Literacy Skills

Section II focuses on using *Story Frames* strategies to build key literacy skills. Chapter 4 provides an in-depth look at the development of oral language, which is the foundation for written language. It discusses in detail how children develop oral narrative complexity. This chapter summarizes the narrative writing expectations outlined in the Common Core State Standards (CCSS), and the downloadable resources include a more detailed overview of the CCSS expectations across Grades 1–8. With these developmental expectations clearly in mind, Chapter 5 focuses on improving oral language and strategies for using oral retells to build the foundational skills of vocabulary understanding and use, sequencing, grammar usage and sentence construction, and story retelling. Chapter 6 explores how to make the transition from oral to written language, beginning with story retells and progressing to the creation of original stories. Chapter 7 discusses strategies for teaching expository writing and uses the *Story Frames* approach to analyzing narrative nonfiction as a means of helping students transition from creating and summarizing stories to creating and summarizing informational texts. Chapter 8 looks at how to improve reading and listening comprehension through visual strategies and questioning. Chapter 9, written by William Van Cleave, provides additional strategies for developing syntax and grammar. Chapter 10 tackles rhyme, alliteration, and phonological development, and how to express story knowledge through poetry. Chapter 11, written by Paula Moraine, focuses on executive function skills.

Understanding Narrative Development

4

This chapter will discuss how children develop a sense of narrative from earliest childhood through late elementary school and beyond. Young children's earliest oral attempts at narrative lack structure and unity; they feel disconnected and formless. Over time, however, their oral narratives and eventual written narratives become increasingly sophisticated and include recognizable grammar elements, as discussed in Section I.

Story elements are only one aspect of narrative, however. Eisenberg et al. (2008) examine narrative in terms of both *microstructure*—word usage and grammatical structures, and *macrostructure*—story elements and their organization. When we read, listen to, tell, or write a story, we are working with both microstructure and macrostructure. We are dealing with language at the word and sentence level in addition to thinking about story elements and structure. To understand narrative development, it is therefore necessary to understand language development. This chapter will begin with an overview of typical oral language development and how this lays the foundation for oral and written narratives. The chapter then describes in detail the progression of narrative development in children from preschool through late elementary school and beyond. Additional developmental and cultural considerations are discussed, along with connections to grade-level expectations for written narrative in Grades 1–8.

GENERAL ORAL LANGUAGE DEVELOPMENT

Story Frames is a resource specifically for Grades 1–8; however, our discussion of oral language development will begin at a much earlier age because many children with language delays exhibit the skill level of a much younger child. Understanding the developmental progression is essential for setting realistic goals. With that said, *Story Frames* has been used successfully with 4-year-olds in developmental preschool programs to work on sequencing and story retelling, with line drawings provided by the instructor for each element of the story.

Use of Phrases, Sentences, and Morphemes

In the article "Syntax Development in the School Age Years: Implications for Assessment and Intervention" Nelson (2013) discusses early oral language development and the transition from two-word phrases and sentences at age 2 to three-word utterances at age 3. She notes that even at this early stage, in these very short utterances, a variety of sentence structures are observable. She describes how young children typically follow Brown's (1973) pattern of acquisition of morphemes, which are used to expand both noun and verb

DOWNLOADABLE RESOURCES:

Keep this resource on hand for a quick summary of the Common Core State Standards for children's narrative development: Common Core State Standards expectations for narrative writing, Grades 1–8.

phrases; however, Nelson states that language development beyond the age of 4 is not nearly as linear or predictable as it is in the early preschool years. Sentences become longer and more complex, but they do so in a variety of different ways.

Brown (1973) lists the order in which most children acquire morphemes in spoken language, starting with -*ing* endings ("Mommy sleeping") at 19–28 months up to contractible auxiliary verbs ("Mommy is sleeping," "Mommy's sleeping") at 30–50 months. He judges these ages to be the point when a child would be expected to use a particular form correctly 90% of the time. Between the ages of 19 and 50 months, other grammatical morphemes observed include the following: *in, on, -s*, irregular past tense verbs, regular past tense -*ed*, and articles (*a, the*). See his work for a complete list of grammatical morphemes and expected age ranges.

Scott and Balthazar (2013) look at typical sentence development and how to use that continuum as a barometer for identifying children who may be at risk for delays. They observe that by kindergarten children should be using many complex sentences in their speech with very few verb tense errors. They report that until about age 10, the number of words in a sentence corresponds more or less to a child's age. For instance, a 2-year-old would be expected to use two-word utterances ("want cookie"), while a 3-year-old would use an average of three words per utterance ("I want cookie"). A 4-year-old would use an average of four words per utterance, and so forth, up to 10 words per sentence for a 10-year-old.

Language development undergoes a dramatic change between ages 3 and 5 and, not surprisingly, so does narrative development. According to Friend and Bates (2014), this includes improvement in executive attention and behavioral inhibition around age 4 as well as a significant increase in the use of verbs and conjunctions around ages 3–5. Children as young as 3 may use past tense in everyday speech, but they do not use it often when telling a story. By age 5, they show significant improvement in their ability to use verb tense markers, which help them describe the action and organize the events of a narrative.

Use of "Literate" Oral Language

Eisenberg et al. (2008) explore the elaboration of noun phrases and observe what they call a "literate language style" that appears during the school years in specific types of discourse such as narratives. This literate style includes more complex sentence structures and more specific word usage, and it helps to form a bridge between less formal spoken language and the type of language encountered in reading and writing. Although they point out the value of using narratives to identify students at risk for academic challenges, they also state that the microstructure (word usage and grammatical structures) of a student's oral story is a more accurate predictor of language impairment than the macrostructure (story elements and their organization). Because of this, they believe that sentence complexity overall, and noun phrase elaboration specifically, are excellent targets for intervention. This topic is discussed more in Chapter 6, which addresses written stories, and Chapter 9, which addresses grammar and syntax. A strength of *Story Frames* is the use of narratives to work on microstructure elements in addition to the macrostructure of the story plot.

In their study, Eisenberg et al. (2008) found that from ages 5 to 11, the use of two or more adjectives before a noun increased from 8% to 67% when the noun was the object of the sentence ("The boy popped the *big, green* balloon"). Use of describing words and phrases ("The girl drank the *chocolate* milk"; "The girl drank the milk *in the cup*") as noun expanders was about 30% greater overall for nouns in the object position of the sentence than for nouns in the subject position. They point out that the use of subject modifiers is not expected in conversation until age 12. The researchers deduced that it is most likely more manageable for young children to tack on details at the end of a sentence, after the main idea is fully developed, than it is to incorporate them with the subject at the beginning. For this reason, they suggest that instruction on noun phrase elaboration within stories focus on nouns in the object position of the sentence. They also found that the use of one picture prompt showing multiple characters or unusual events seemed to promote more noun phrase elaboration than did a sequence of simpler pictures. Based on their study, they outlined these noun phrase expectations for oral narratives:

- Age 5: Use of simple noun phrases with articles ("The boy kicked *the* ball")

- Age 8: Use of descriptive noun phrases ("The boy kicked the *blue* ball")

- Age 11: Use of prepositional phrases or clauses to modify a noun ("The girl hugged the cat *with white fur*")

ORAL AND WRITTEN NARRATIVES

By learning to talk about stories, students lay the groundwork for writing about stories. They use the framework of story grammar as a schema or structure to recall and understand the events of a story and create stories of their own (Roth, 2000, p. 16).

Oral language precedes written language, so it is essential to get students talking about stories long before expecting them to write about stories. Most children can create simple oral narratives by age 6, but students with language disorders often still have difficulty with both written and oral narratives into their teenage years (Montgomery & Kahn, 2005). Writing is a painstaking task for these students. As they grow older, the performance gap between them and their peers continues to grow wider (Roth, 2000).

Bailet (2004) reviewed the research on spelling instruction and intervention. She reports that children who struggle with reading typically struggle even more significantly with spelling, which affects overall written language abilities. In children with dyslexia, the gap between their own reading and writing (particularly spelling) abilities often continues to expand and the gains they do make in written language can be difficult to maintain. A study of 100 college freshman with dyslexia demonstrates that even struggling students who successfully complete high school continue to experience persisting difficulty with reading and spelling (Callens, Tops, Stevens, & Brysbaert, 2014).

Hedberg and Westby (1993) created a valuable resource on the assessment of oral narratives entitled *Analyzing Storytelling Skills: Theory to Practice*. They discuss levels of narrative development, the components of story grammar expected at each level, and the approximate age at which those levels occur. Westby revisited the stages of narrative development in her chapter on "Assessing and Remediating Text Comprehension Problems" in *Language and Reading Disabilities* (2012).

Hedberg and Westby (1993) build upon the work of Stein and Glenn (1979), who outlined the elements of story grammar still used today to determine the level of story structure a student incorporates into any given narrative. They also reference Applebee (1978), who described early forms of narrative development from preschoolers' first attempts to create stories to true narratives in the early elementary years. Applebee, in turn, drew upon the work of Vygotsky (1978) to describe the series of changes that occur in children's narratives as they relate to the child's evolving concept development.

Khan et al. (2016) completed a research study involving 3- to 6-year-olds and concurred with the stages of narrative (story schema) development outlined by Applebee (1978), specifically that goal-based narratives begin to appear around ages 4–5. In the Khan et al. study, 39% of 4-year-olds and 70% of 5-year-olds retold a story that included complete episodes using a wordless picture book.

Table 4.1, based on material from Westby (2012), shows children's levels of narrative development with approximate ages when the various story forms could be expected

Table 4.1. Narrative levels and comparison between authors

	Westby (2012)	Applebee (1978)	Stein and Glenn (1979) story grammar	Dean (2021) *Story Frames*
Preschool		Heaps (The child labels items, characters, actions, and places.)	None	None
	Descriptive sequence	Sequences (Centering is tied to describing one item, event, character, or place.)	None	None
	Action sequence (Narrative includes an event sequence but one event does not lead to the next.)	Primitive narratives (Centering is loosely tied to an event sequence.)	None	None
	Reactive sequence (Events are based on cause and effect but are reactionary and not yet purposeful.)	Unfocused chain (Chaining is added to centering with some causation, but the narrative has no goal or plan and nothing connecting the whole.)	Initiating event, direct consequence (limited), may include a setting and an ending.	The Call *may* include some type of reactionary Response. An Ordinary World (time or place) might be mentioned.
Early Elementary	Abbreviated episode (Goal may be stated or implied, but plans must be inferred by the reaction of the character to the problem.)	Focused chain (Chaining focuses on one central character participating in a sequence of connected actions or events.)	Initiating event, internal response, plan (inferred), consequence. *May* include a setting, reaction to consequence, and ending.	Call and Response, Prize (goal), Plan (inferred by listener). May include Ordinary World, Final Reward (consequence).
	Complete episode (Clearer evidence of goals; planning is stated or inferred by attempts.)	True narrative (Action and events move toward a conclusion, with one event leading to the next.)	Initiating event, internal response, implied plan, attempts, consequences. *May* include a setting.	Call and Response, Prize or Problem, Plan (implied by Attempts), Climax, Final Reward. *May* include Ordinary World.
Late Elementary	Complex episode (Obstacle arises to block attempt.)	Elaborated stories	All of the preceding items plus obstacles resulting in multiple attempts.	All of the preceding items plus Midpoint, Downtime Response, Chase and Escape.
	Multiple sequential episodes (A second episode follows the events of the first episode.)	Same		Repetitions of the Plan, Attempt/Consequence, Response cycle result in longer and longer stories.
Adolescent/ Adult	Embedded episode (A second episode is embedded within the events of the first episode.)	Same	Story grammar elements may be repeated and may disrupt the central action.	Flashbacks appear in the middle of a narrative and then the story returns to the central action.
	Interactive episode (Two or more interacting characters have their own plans and goals.)	Same	Story grammar elements may be repeated in different character's point of view.	Some or all of the *Story Frames* elements may be repeated in a secondary character's point of view.

Sources: Applebee (1978), Stein and Glenn (1979), and Westby (2012).

to appear. Also included are comparisons to Applebee (1978), Stein and Glenn (1979), and *Story Frames.*

It is important to remember that a child's verbal ability will surpass his or her written language, at least while spelling, syntax, and short-term memory are developing. Therefore, these levels may appear later in written narratives. Written narrative expectations from the Common Core State Standards (CCSS; National Governors Association, 2010) are listed in detail in this chapter's downloadable resources. Though not all states adhere to the CCSS, these standards show a nice progression of written language skills and it is interesting to note how they parallel narrative development.

THE PROGRESSION OF NARRATIVE DEVELOPMENT

The sections that follow describe in detail the progression of children's narrative development from preschool, through the early elementary school years, to the later elementary school years. As you read, be aware that young children's stories do not always fit neatly into one category (Applebee, 1978); however, there is consistency in when certain characteristics typically emerge.

Preschool: Connections and Causal Relationships

Preschool-age children's earliest narrative attempts begin with isolated descriptions, progressing to more connected descriptions and then simple action sequences. Narrative development at this early stage culminates in the creation of reactive sequences that include causal relationships between events.

Isolated Description   The child's effort to label items (people, things, actions) in a story represents a first attempt at creating a narrative. Hedberg and Westby (1993) refer to this type of early narrative as an *isolated description* that begins early in language development, around age 2. They observed that no story grammar elements are present at this level.

Applebee (1978) describes these early "stories" produced by very young children as *heaps.* The child "labels" items and actions with no connection between them, much the same way a child might stack or "heap" blocks of different colors and shapes. The labeled items may seem to come from a story, but nothing is organizing the people, things, or actions: "Goldilocks. Three bears. Go walk. Break the chair." When a child talks about a picture sequence from a book, the child appears to be labeling the items that he or she sees, rather than linking one page to another or one event to the next.

Applebee points out that adult writers, poets in particular, may choose to use this style, but it is a conscious decision used for a specific effect. In contrast, young children may have no other structure for organizing a "story" for quite a while. For children with language learning differences, this pattern may persist well into the school-age years. The information in these heap stories feels disjointed and unrelated.

Some popular children's books follow this structure. Examples include many of the Dorling Kindersley picture books for the very young as well as the *I Spy* series written by Jean Marcello with photographs by Walther Wick, which prompts the reader to search for a specific object among many others. These books are not intended to be "stories," but a child's early attempt at narratives may feel like these descriptions of individual items or characters. Slightly older children may use isolated descriptions that contain complete sentences, but the sentences are mostly unrelated to each other: "There is a cat. The ball is blue. The dog hid the bone. The cat chased the mouse."

Finally, just like the adult poet, or the author who uses a range of sentence types to add variation, children may choose at times to use earlier developing structures when they are capable of more sophisticated ones. Applebee says this is true of each stage of narrative development.

Descriptive Sequence   Next, the child goes beyond mere labeling to *describe* objects, settings, and characters. The narrative may include ongoing actions, but no sequence of one action followed by another action. The items described are interrelated, but there is no cause and effect or clear temporal connection. The sentences can appear in any order because one action does not lead to another and events do not occur in a sequence (Westby, 2012). There are still no story grammar elements present.

Applebee (1978) describes these stories as *sequences* that begin to have a center—in other words, a bond or connection of some type. His *sequences* stage appears to overlap with both the *descriptive sequence* and the *action sequence* phases of Hedberg and Westby (1993).

An example of a picture book that seems to follow a descriptive sequence is *Goodnight Moon* (1947), written by Margaret Wise Brown with illustrations by Clement Hurd. The narrator performs the ongoing action of saying "Goodnight" to a variety of objects that are connected by the fact that they are all in the child's room. This book contains engaging descriptions that go beyond the simple labeling of unrelated objects that would occur in the isolated description phase. With this simple text, the author and illustrator create a lovely mood and sense of setting, but there is no initiating event or action.

Action Sequence   At this level, according to Westby (2012), the child may sequence the action according to a timeline, but with no cause and effect relationship observed between actions or characters—that is, *this caused that to happen* or *this character influenced that one*. (Similarly, students can typically write stories sequencing two or more events in first grade, at ages 6–7, according to the CCSS written language expectations (see the Chapter 4 downloadable resource Common Core State Standards for Narrative Writing). Just as one action does not influence another action, one character does not influence another character. According to Hedberg and Westby (1993), children with language delays may persist with this type of storytelling into the school years. As these stories grow longer, they may be rambling and hard to follow because the connections are limited and the story has no real point or direction.

Applebee (1978) still describes these types of stories as sequences containing superficial links that may even seem to occur along a timeline, but not because one event leads to another. In these sequences, "centering" is based on a similarity. The story may center on one character performing a series of actions, or center on a series of characters performing related actions. A story of this nature can be quite long, but its heart or "core" is weak and, therefore, the possibility for story development is limited. Many 2-year-olds tell simple stories like this, but Applebee's study found 20% of the stories told by 3- and 4-year-olds still utilized this structure.

Applebee's (1978) next stage of narrative development, which correlates to the action sequence phase of Hedberg and Westby (1993) and Westby (2012), is the *primitive narrative*. It is slightly more involved than a simple sequence. In the primitive narrative stage, a more robust connection between details and events starts to appear. Applebee compares the cognitive process behind a primitive narrative to that used when gathering a set of items that go together based on utility, such as pieces of silverware or tools needed to perform a task. The child does not see these objects as belonging to a category, merely as items that work together. Applebee theorized that this is the way children at this stage of development understand stories—as a set of events and characters that go with Goldilocks or Cinderella; they do not delve any deeper into the story's meaning or importance. On the whole, he found that 20% of the stories told by 2- and 3-year-old children in his study implemented this structure, in comparison to 10% of the stories of 4-year-olds.

Many songs, rhymes, and books for young children (including board books) follow the structure of an action sequence and could conceivably continue forever by adding another verse or line. For example, in *Brown Bear, Brown Bear, What Do You See?*, written by Bill Martin Jr. and illustrated by Eric Carle (1967/1996), the narrative centers on the action of "seeing" carried out by a variety of different animals.

Reactive Sequence   Westby and Hedberg (1993) as well as Westby (2012) discuss how the addition of cause and effect raises a child's narrative to this next level. These stories have a chain of events with one event influencing the next one, but character behavior is reactionary rather than purposeful, with no clear goal and no planning. A formal "Once upon a time . . ." beginning, middle, end structure may appear. The child may add "and, so, then" to begin forming basic connections between actions (i.e., "and then . . . and then . . . and then . . ."). This growth in narrative proficiency parallels the Common Core writing expectations of second graders (ages 7–8) as they begin to develop one main event or provide a richer description of a short sequence of events.

Applebee (1978) likewise describes "chaining" as a process where each part of a narrative shares a clear connection to the next part. In what he calls an *unfocused chain*, the parts lack a thread connecting the whole. Each event or description relates directly to the next event or description, but the beginning likely has nothing to do with the end. The story still lacks focus or direction. A story like this can grow quite long, but length should not be confused with story complexity. If there is elaboration, it will feel like a tangent rather than a connection to the main action of the story.

According to Hedberg and Westby (1993), this is the first stage where the story grammar components of Stein and Glenn (1979) begin to appear. These components include an initiating event, a limited direct consequence, and possibly a setting and an ending. (Although the preschool child may mention a time or place, a setting is not expected until elementary school.) Traditional story grammar elements are limited at this level because of the lack of goal-directed behavior on the characters' part.

In regard to *Story Frames* elements, there will likely be a Call to adventure and an action Response or other consequence arising from the Call. The Ordinary World may be mentioned in terms of place or time, but it will likely not be described in detail.

Professional writers sometimes use this type of structure to create humor based on ridiculous results that arise from loose and often silly connections of causality between events. A good example is the picture book, *If You Give a Mouse a Cookie* (1985), written by Laura Numeroff and illustrated by Felicia Bond, in which the central character is a mouse. The narrative describes a series of loosely related actions that may arise from the simple act of giving a mouse a sweet, crunchy snack.

Early Elementary: Goals, Planning, and Internal Responses

In the early elementary school years, character goals begin to emerge in children's narratives, and causal relationships among events gradually become stronger. Narratives begin to include planning and goal-directed behavior on the characters' part, along with internal responses.

Abbreviated Episode   Hedberg and Westby (1993) and Westby (2012) observe that the first significant change from the oral narratives of early childhood to those observed in the early elementary grades is that goals appear that may be evident or implied. Plans still must be inferred by the listener of the story and may not exist in the child's mind. Often a character wants something and then suddenly has it, but how the goal was accomplished—in other words, a specific attempt on the character's part to achieve the goal—is missing. Actions are based on cause and effect but may not lead directly or logically from one to another to accomplish the goal. Internal responses based on emotions and thoughts appear. The child begins to be able to take the perspective of others. The child's growing understanding of emotions, what causes them, and what may result adds to the understanding of cause and effect. Similarly, in the Grade 3 (ages 8–9) writing expectations for the CCSS, the child develops a sense of cause and effect in his or her narrative writing, but it is not always based on logic.

Applebee (1978) describes a *focused chain* of events as having a connecting thread, but one that is superficial and concrete. Centering is still observed because there is often one central character performing a variety of actions. The actions have more focus and linkage than in previous stages of narrative development, but the story may feel like a series of adventures or events rather than one adventure that builds to a climax. Applebee reports that this is the typical narrative structure found in half of the stories produced by children at age 5.

Story grammar elements at this level include an initiating event, an internal response resulting in a goal, and a consequence. The story seems to leap from the character's desire for something to the possession of it. These narratives may include a setting, a reaction to a consequence, and an ending. Although a goal and the resulting consequence may be stated, the story is typically missing a clear plan and an attempt to reach that goal to connect the goal to the consequence.

In regard to *Story Frames*, a child might describe a Call to action, an inner Response to that Call, and description of a desired Prize or goal with a Final Reward or consequence at the end. How the outcome was achieved will likely be missing, which results in a story with only an implied Plan, with no clear description for executing it and no apparent attempt to carry it out. The story may include a description of an Ordinary World and an inner Response to the outcome after achieving the Final Reward.

A popular children's story that contains a goal but little attempt on the main character's part to achieve it is *Sylvester and the Magic Pebble* by William Steig (1969). Sylvester, the donkey, finds a magic pebble that makes wishes come true, but only if he is holding it. He wishes for rain, and it rains. He wishes for the sun, and it shines. One reason that this book may resonate with young children is because of this leap from wishing to having, which is often characteristic of the stories they create on their own.

When a lion frightens Sylvester, he wishes he could become a rock so the lion would not harm him. He turns into a rock, but when he wishes to be a donkey again, he cannot reach the pebble to make his wish come true. His internal response, feelings of hopelessness, worry, and fear are described. His only hope is that someone else will find his pebble and wish him back into being a donkey. There is goal-directed behavior on the part of his parents, who attempt to search for him, but they eventually give up while Sylvester grows hopeless. Eventually, Sylvester's parents happen to come by, have a picnic on the rock (Sylvester), and put the pebble on it, so he can finally wish himself back into being a donkey.

Complete Episode   The attempt to accomplish an aim combined with goal-directed behavior elevates the narrative from an abbreviated episode to a complete episode. Complete episodes typically emerge by age 8, according to Hedberg and Westby (1993). The main difference between this level and previous levels is these narratives have more visible evidence of planning, made apparent by the character's direct *attempts* to reach a goal. The previous levels typically lack these goal-oriented attempts. Children at this level grow in their awareness of emotions and ability to take the point of view of others and predict character behavior. Though Hedberg and Westby (1993) saw internal responses beginning to appear in the early elementary years, they did not expect complete episodes before age 8.

Applebee (1978) describes true narratives, similar to the complete episodes examined previously, as having more development and a stronger center, which allows for more elaboration than earlier narrative types. This is the final level in his description of the plot structure of children's stories. Themes and morals appear. Although the action does not always build toward a climax, the narrative definitely has the sense of moving toward a conclusion rather than rambling. Though he only observed about 20% of 5-year-olds to use true narratives, occasionally children as young as 3 or 4 told stories that resembled this form. Combining this observation with the observations of Hedberg and Westby (1993), one could expect true narratives to emerge in children's original oral narratives between the ages of 5 and 8. Similarly, the CCSS writing standards for Grade 4 (ages 9–10) expect a child of this age to write narratives with a conclusion that arises naturally from the sequence of events.

Khan et al. (2016) observed that between the ages of 3 and 5, there was a shift in the development of complete episodes in children's stories during story retellings. They hypothesized that this was due to the child's increasing ability to organize higher-order goals. They also found internal responses and reactions were not seen consistently before age 8. Stein and Glenn's (1979) story grammar elements at this level include an initiating event, internal response, implied plan, attempts, and a consequence.

Story Frames elements include a Call with an inner Response to that call and the description of a Prize or Problem to solve. Attempts to achieve the goal will most often, but not always, build to a Climax in a fairly linear fashion on a continuum with no obstacles appearing yet between one attempt and another. A Final Reward or consequence wraps up the story, with an internal response (how the main character feels about the events). The story may include a description of an Ordinary World. Although a child may be able to use the Complete Storyboard to retell a traditional story, he or she will need assistance to figure out the unfamiliar story elements, such as a Midpoint Attempt and Downtime Response. When creating an original story of their own, the Basic Storyboard would be more developmentally appropriate.

An example of storytelling at this level is Jon Scieszka's picture book *The Frog Prince, Continued* (1994) with illustrations by Steve Johnson. In this retelling, the legendary prince realizes he is quite unhappy living with the princess and runs away to find a witch who can turn him back into a frog. The goal is clear, but the plan is merely inferred by his *attempts* to reach his goal. Although his four attempts might classify this story as a complex episode (described following), the attempts are all pretty much the same—the prince asks a witch to turn him back into a frog. The last attempt occurs at the climax when the Frog Prince gives up on the witches and asks a fairy godmother to assist. She accidentally turns him into a carriage (consequence), which gives him time to reflect on the fact that his life with the princess was pretty good (reaction to consequence). In the end, he returns to the palace, kisses his wife, and they both turn into frogs.

Late Elementary: Obstacles and Elaborate Chains of Events

In late elementary school, children's narratives become more sophisticated, with obstacles between the character and his or her goal, which lead to a more complex series of events.

Complex Episode   Hedberg and Westby (1993) and Westby (2012) report that stories at this level begin to contain more elaboration and complexity, which usually arises from an obstacle getting in the way of achieving a goal. The obstacle results in a new attempt or multiple attempts to reach a goal, more than one plan, or several consequences. The additional attempts arise because of obstacles that make the first attempt unsuccessful.

The CCSS for writing at Grade 5 (ages 10–11) talks more in terms of pacing than obstacles, but the addition of obstacles naturally requires sophistication in pacing. Action rises, but then attempts are thwarted, which leads to downtime as characters explore internal responses and make new plans. Action rises again with new attempts. Applebee (1978) does not describe these higher levels of complexity in his analysis, and at this point all of the story grammar components of Stein and Glenn (1979) have appeared. However, there will be more repetition of these story components as multiple attempts to achieve a goal arise and obstacles appear.

Story Frames explores these obstacles by describing a Midpoint Attempt that is very different from the eventual Climax. At the Midpoint, the main character makes an attempt to achieve a goal that may be successful or not, followed by a period of Downtime as the hero responds to and reflects upon the Midpoint events. If the Midpoint Attempt resulted in failure, the Downtime provides an opportunity to make a new plan. If the hero was successful, the Downtime is an opportunity to celebrate; however, typically, a twist occurs with the Chase and Escape. This may be when the true obstacle appears. The Death and Transformation stage typically includes even more obstacles.

Other story analysis methods provide icons and descriptions for the earlier levels of story development, but with the addition of a Midpoint Attempt, Downtime Response, and Chase and Escape, *Story Frames* provides a bridge to the higher levels of analysis expected in the later elementary school years, middle school, and beyond. Children with learning disabilities often resist adding obstacles and complications to their stories, even in high school. Their writing objective is often to move from Point A to Point B as quickly as possible. They know that adding obstacles will slow down this process. They benefit from having this expectation built into the storyboard graphic organizer and from discussing examples of these types of complications in other stories.

A good example of how obstacles to an attempt can change the direction of a story and the course of a person's life is the picture book *Six Dots: A Story of Young Louis Braille* by Jen Bryant (2016). The book describes Louis's goal of wanting to be able to read and write even though he is blind. He plans to achieve this goal by becoming one of the best students at the Royal School for the Blind because only the best students are allowed in the library. When he finally arrives at the library, he is sorely disappointed. The words in the books are the size of his hand and, therefore, the books are massive but contain little information. He retreats to his bed without supper, wishing he was home. Soon an army captain sends a secret code to the school that inspires Louis to create a new reading and writing system for the blind, sending the action of the story and the trajectory of Louis's life off into an entirely new direction. Louis wants the army captain to help him, but the man has wars to fight and refuses the request, which creates another obstacle. Louis works on the code by himself and eventually creates the braille writing system.

Multiple Sequential Episodes   Multiple sequential episodes begin to appear in children's narratives around age 7 but can take quite a while to develop fully. A second episode follows the events of the first episode. At first, these multiple episodes are short, and it may feel like the narratives have regressed into a series of reactive sequences or abbreviated episodes without precise planning, goals, or attempts. A story may contain a variety of episode types (reactive sequence, abbreviated episode, complete episode, complex episode).

Hedberg and Westby (1993) observe that children with learning disabilities may skip the complex episode stage and go from a story with one reactive sequence to a narrative with chains of reactive sequences. In the writing of high school students with significant learning deficits, one may see many lengthy reactive sequences that lack planning, goal-oriented attempts, and clear consequences.

Hedberg and Westby (1993) also found that when children are about 9 or 10, their stories include much more detail and completeness. Their stories are more often chains of complete episodes containing clear plans, attempts, and consequences. As the child's storytelling ability increases, these episodes build with rising action, tension, and suspense. Characters' reactions to the events' consequences will be more prevalent. In *Story Frames* these episodes are observed with the repetition of the Plan, Attempt/Consequence, and Response cycle described in Chapter 2.

Many chapter books and novels for upper elementary and middle school students include multiple episodes. It is these episodes that cause these stories to be much longer than picture books. Multiple repetitions of the entire sequence of the 12 *Story Frames* elements may occur, but typically with an overarching beginning, middle, and end.

An example of a narrative with multiple episodes is *Fish in a Tree* by Lynda Mullaly Hunt (2015). This book follows the story of Ally Nickerson as she struggles to hide a learning disability, is diagnosed with dyslexia, and finally receives help from a caring teacher to overcome her challenges. That is the overarching plot, but other episodes within the story show her struggling to make new friends, dealing with peers who taunt her, being recognized for her exceptional artistic talent, and being voted class president.

Adolescent and Adult: Characters Influencing Each Other

In middle school and high school, student narratives become more sophisticated as stories are told from various vantage points, including multiple points of view, sometimes with disruptions in timelines.

Embedded Episodes   Around age 11, children start to create embedded episodes, and this skill continues to mature through adolescence. One chain of events is interrupted by another. A second episode is embedded within the events of the first episode. These may include flashing back or forward to embed one sequence of events into the ongoing and overarching action of the main storyline. Relatedly, within the Grade 6 (ages 11–12) CCSS writing standards, students are expected to use transitional words and phrases to signal shifts in setting and time. *Gingerbread for Liberty! How a German Baker Helped Win the American Revolution*, by Mara Rockliff (2015a) with pictures by Vincent X. Kirsch, includes embedded episodes. The initial description of the baker in his bake shop in Philadelphia is interrupted by a brief flashback that describes how he came to America when he was young so that he would never be hungry. The story then moves forward to the time when he reads about the Revolutionary War in the newspapers and goes off to support George Washington and his troops by baking gingerbread for them.

Interactive Episodes   According to Hedberg and Westby (1993), one of the last forms that starts to develop in the late elementary years and continues to expand during adolescence and adulthood is the interactive episode, which involves two or more characters with their own plans and goals influencing each other. This may start as dialogue between two characters as they react to one another. These stories may incorporate multiple points of view as the young adult learns to take more than one perspective at a time.

Embedding (discussed previously) may also be observed within the interactive episode, and the elements of story grammar may overlap. For instance, the gingerbread baker's solution (convincing the king's hired Hessian soldiers to join the war efforts of the Americans) becomes the king's problem. Relatedly, in the Grade 7 (ages 12–13) CCSS writing standards, students are expected to make clearer choices about point of view. In the Grade 8 (ages 13–14) standards, relationships between characters become more important. In the Newbery–award winning novel *The Whipping Boy* by Sid Fleischman (1986), the story is told from the perspective of the Whipping Boy, Jemmy, but his understanding of the point of view of Prince Brat develops as he takes on the role of the prince. In *Gingerbread for Liberty!*, we see the reaction of King George III as he wonders what happened to all of his hired soldiers.

ADDITIONAL DEVELOPMENTAL CONSIDERATIONS

Children combine the various components described to create a single episode or multiple-episode story. The complexity of episodes, as well as the number of story grammar elements included in an oral narrative, increases with age; however, it is essential to remember that these age levels are not always hard and fast. Khan et al. (2016) studied the age-related progressions in young children's story structure, and although they observed a definite sequence of progression, how early each stage appeared varied. Although one-third of 3-year-olds did not produce even one *episodic event*, about 25% were able to produce complete episodes.

The level of support a child receives will also impact the level of complexity of oral narratives. Applebee (1978), as well as Hedberg and Westby (1993), examined the original stories young children produced spontaneously. Story retells come with a context already provided. If the child receives picture support, his or her story might be produced at a higher level of complexity than specified in the age expectations described by these authors. Some educators use wordless picture books to elicit an oral narrative. Care must be taken when basing an assessment on a wordless picture book because the child may seem to understand cause and effect when all he or she is really doing is describing what is happening in the pictures where cause and effect is supported by the illustrations. Even so, Westby (2012) finds that wordless picture books are still quite useful in assessing many skills:

> To understand the stories, students must recognize what the characters are doing on each page. They must realize the relationships between activities on any two adjacent pages, as well as the relationships among all the actions in the book. They must understand temporal sequence and physical and psychological cause–effect relationships and plans and reactions of characters. (p. 178)

Applebee (1978) warns that many stories produced by young children will not fit neatly into one category or another. Categories overlap, and a child may use one form in one part of a story and shift to another form later on. He points out the need to more clearly describe the defining characteristics of one form of narrative versus another, which Hedberg and Westby (1993) did with their Binary Decision Tree for Determining Story Structure (p. 134). It identifies one or two attributes that elevate a story from one level to another. Using the decision tree, as well as their more detailed descriptions of each stage of development, Table 4.2 highlights the main differences between their levels. Westby (2012) further simplified the binary process to create a Story Grammar Decision Tree, which appears in Figure 4.1. It has been used by many educators to analyze student narratives and can be a helpful descriptor for setting goals and objectives in individualized education programs (IEPs). See Westby's 2012 chapter "Assessing and Remediating

Table 4.2. Defining characteristics of story levels

Story level	Defining characteristics
Isolated description	**Labeling** people, things, actions
Descriptive sequence	**Describing** people, things, actions
Action sequence	**Event sequence** but with no cause and effect
Reactive sequence	Event sequence based on **cause and effect that is reactionary** rather than goal-directed
Abbreviated episode	**Goal-**directed behavior is **implied.** A character wants something then suddenly has it. There may be attempts that are not clearly connected to the goal.
Complete episode	A clear **goal** is present. **Planning** is stated or inferred through a character's direct **attempts** to reach a goal.
Complex episode	An **obstacle** leads to additional attempts to achieve a goal.

Sources: Hedberg and Westby (1993) and Westby (2012).

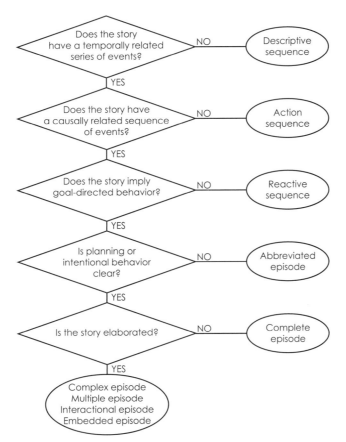

Figure 4.1. Story Grammar Decision Tree. (From Westby, C.E. [2012]. Assessing and remediating text comprehension problems. In **KAMHI, ALAN, & CATTS, HUGH [Eds.], LANGUAGE AND READING DISABILITIES, 3rd Ed.,** ©**2012.** Reprinted by permission of **Pearson Education, Inc.)**

Text Comprehension Problems" in *Language and Reading Disabilities* for examples of student stories at the various levels of development.

Story Frames can be used with children at different levels of narrative development. The Basic Storyboard with 8 elements was created for the young or early developing storyteller with the developmental stages discussed in this chapter in mind. The Complete Storyboard with all 12 elements can be used with older students. Blank Storyboards are provided in the downloadable resources, and Chapter 6 describes how to use them with students to create original narratives.

CULTURAL CONSIDERATIONS

Although narratives are an excellent way to assess discourse skills in a natural context, it is vital to be aware of how culture and other linguistic factors affect a child's narratives. Variations exist in information, organization, world knowledge, world experience, the purpose for sharing a narrative, and more. It is important to know how culture affects oral narratives before determining if a child has a cultural difference or an impairment of some kind. Be aware that their stories may not follow the story grammar model outlined by Stein and Glenn (1979) observed in mainstream American culture.

For this reason, Gutierrez-Clellen and Quinn (1993) suggest using a dynamic assessment by eliciting narratives to determine the narrative style and then teaching the rules expected for producing narratives for school and learning to "talk like a book." They recommend determining if the child can modify his or her narrative. Those who still have difficulty after the rules are taught may have a deficit in narrative production.

Westby (2001) discusses how the number of episodes, actions, or events varies across cultures. Stories may use three-part structures (favored by Western and Japanese cultures), four-part (some Native American cultures), five-part (other Native American cultures and some Chinese narratives), or even two-part structures (some Asian cultures). The relationship between story structure and plot events or character goals also varies. When retelling a story from another culture, people tend to modify it to match the story structure that fits their own culture. It is helpful to know a student's cultural background to judge if variations in narrative style represent a cultural difference rather than a delay or disorder.

With that in mind, Westby and Culatta (2016a) discuss the importance of teaching traditional story grammar structure to students from culturally diverse backgrounds because of the emphasis on this structure in mainstream Western education. Even if this is not the narrative structure of the home, it is still that of the school and essential for school success.

Gorman, Fiestas, Peña, and Clark (2011) point out that people in all cultures use storytelling to communicate, inform, relate experiences, entertain, and teach, as well as to share traditions and history. They designed a research study using wordless picture books to explore the effect of culture on the narratives of African American, Latino, and Caucasian, English-speaking first- and second-graders without history of language impairment. They found no difference in organization style across the three groups (although they did observe some differences in content). The majority of students from all backgrounds tended to create topic-centered stories. Researchers concluded that using wordless picture books depicting a clear sequence of events was a culturally less biased way to assess narrative structure than asking children to create personal narratives, which resulted in more variation in narrative structure and culturally relevant themes. Indeed, Bowles, Justice, Khan, Skibbe, and Foster (2020) suggest that narrative assessment has the potential to be less biased than other measures of language competence because narrative assessment is authentic, contextualized, and reflects a type of discourse naturally found in a young child's communicative interactions.

Abdalla, Mahfoudhi, and Alhudhainah (2020) recognized both the importance of narratives as an intervention tool and the lack of standardized tests in many languages to measure narrative and overall language competency. They set out to adapt a narrative assessment tool, the Edmonton Narrative Norms Instrument (ENNI), to study the use of story grammar elements in children ages 4–7 speaking Kuwaiti Arabic. They found these children were better at using the core story grammar elements of initiating event, attempt, and outcome, but less consistent with using what they called the "complementary" story grammar elements of internal plan, internal response, and reactions. The researchers surmised that with some adaptation of the story grammar subunits, standardized tests like the ENNI could be used as a "cross linguistic" measure.

For a more in-depth discussion of cultural factors, see Chapter 16, "The Influence of Culture on Storytelling," written by Carol Westby.

GRADE-LEVEL EXPECTATIONS FOR WRITTEN NARRATIVES

Many students find it difficult to structure their writing to meet the expectations of the various genres. Graphic organizers are a useful tool in this endeavor, and *Story Frames* incorporates storyboards for a variety of writing purposes. A full discussion of storyboards and how they may be used to facilitate the writing process appears in Chapter 6. Written language lags behind oral language, so the expectations for each grade level are somewhat different.

Scott and Balthazar (2013) observe that around age 10 (fourth grade), a student's written language starts to sound very different (much more formal) from his or her spoken language. By age 12, the length of written sentences catches up to the length of spoken utterances and may even surpass it. From that point through high school, written language shows increasingly more complex sentence structure and variety.

In the Common Core Curriculum, under Writing Standards for Literature, College and Career Readiness, Anchor Standard 3 (CCSS.ELA-Literacy.CCRA.W.3) focuses on creating narratives to develop both real experiences and imagined ones. This includes the ability to choose details and sequence events. Not all states use CCSS standards and many will have their own guidelines, but the continuum is still useful to note. Some fundamental expectations exist across each grade level for this anchor standard, but the sophistication increases with each passing year. These fundamentals include the following:

A. *Establishing an introduction*—from describing a basic situation and characters in the early grades to setting up a problem and exploring multiple points of view later.

B. *Incorporating narrative techniques*—from using basic details, descriptions, and simple reflections to fully developing events, experiences, and characters while creating multiple plotlines with character dialogue and pacing.

C. *Sequencing events*—from using temporal and transitional words and describing events that build on each other to incorporating phrases and clauses and creating a coherent whole while signaling shifts in time and setting.

D. *Using concrete words, phrases, and sensory details*. Starting at grade 4, the vocabulary, syntax, and imagery increases, resulting in more vivid verbal descriptions in the upper grades.

E. *Providing a conclusion*. At first, this will be simply a sense of closure, but ultimately, it is a reflection on the events and a resolution of the entire story.

The writing activities presented in *Story Frames* are appropriate for all grade levels, but the expectation for the quantity and quality of the writing produced will vary depending on age and ability. Because educators often find themselves working with students of various ability levels, it may be helpful to know how these CCSS expectations develop from grade to grade. The Chapter 4 downloadable resource Common Core State Standards for Narrative Writing lists these expectations for each grade.

ASSESSMENT

To determine if a narrative intervention strategy is effective, it is important to collect baseline data and monitor the progress of a student's ability to tell a story orally. See Westby's (2012) Story Grammar Decision Tree in Figure 4.1 for a simple yet effective tool to describe the level of story grammar complexity that a student uses to either retell a story or produce an original story. The Narrative Assessment Protocol 2 (NAP-2) as outlined in Bowles et al. (2020) was designed for children in prekindergarten through second grade. The test, along with training modules, is available for free at www.narrativeassessment.com. It is intended to be used by both speech-language pathologists (SLPs) and early childhood educators. It includes wordless books with a well-defined story grammar that provide the context for measuring skills at the microstructure and macrostructure level.

Progress monitoring for written work may be as simple as collecting writing samples in student portfolios throughout the year. Using the total number of words (TNW) written in connection to a prompt and monitoring the increase across the school year is a straightforward method used by Wood, Schatschneider, and Waznek (2020) to measure the Matthew Effect in second-graders' writing. (This is the principle that "the rich get richer and the poor get poorer"—students with strong literacy skills tend to keep improving while those with weaker skills fall further behind.) Counting the TNW in a student's writing sample and comparing it to a later sample using the same (or a similar) prompt can easily be implemented by teachers and SLPs; however, Westby and Clauser (1999, p. 266) caution that, "Short is not necessarily poor and long is not necessarily good. A short paper may be well structured. A long paper may ramble and not come to the point." With that in mind, TNW may be a better measure of the writing of young children. For older children, looking at syntactic complexity as measured by the number of subordinating conjunctions used may be a better gauge.

Subordinating conjunctions result in complex sentences and link ideas through the use of words such as *after, although, though, as, because, before, if, meanwhile, since, when/whenever, while, where/wherever, until, unless.* Coordinating conjunctions *(for, and, nor, but, or, yet, so)* result in compound sentences and are not always a good gauge of student progress because they can result in run-on sentences. When overused, they may reflect difficulty with punctuation and understanding sentence boundaries.

Several informal data collection tools are provided throughout *Story Frames.* For those who would like to use more formal measurements, such as SLPs who want to measure growth in narrative development as well as other key skills, there are several commercially produced tests that are useful for this purpose.

Formal measurements include standardized tests that have been normed on various age groups. They are typically given once every 3 years (or less) for students with an IEP and must be administered by someone with special training in evaluation and measurement, such as a diagnostician, SLP, or school psychologist. This usually occurs after strategies suggested by a student assistance team (SAT) have been unsuccessful. These tests typically cannot be given more than once a year unless alternate forms of the test exist (i.e., Form A and Form B), and signed parent consent is required. See your school district policies and procedures for how to refer a student for a formal evaluation. For students in special education, results of this type of testing may already exist in their student file. Some helpful tests include the following:

1. Test of Integrated Language and Literacy Skills™ (TILLS™) by Nickola Wolf Nelson, Elena Plante, Nancy Helm-Estabrooks, and Gillian Hotz (2015): Ages 6–18. This test measures oral and written language skills, including 15 subtests for areas such as vocabulary awareness, story retelling, listening comprehension, reading comprehension, delayed story retelling, social communication, and reading fluency. The writing cluster provides discourse, sentence, and word scores, including an analysis of the number of sentences used in a written retell compared to the number of content units included, which reflects, in part, the use of subordinating conjunctions to combine ideas.

2. The Test of Narrative Language–2 (TNL-2) by Ronald A. Gillam and Nils A. Pearson (2017): Ages: 5–15. This test measures a student's ability to answer questions about stories, retell stories, and create his or her own stories. It measures a student's ability to understand and tell narratives without the examiner needing to transcribe a language sample.

3. Peabody Picture Vocabulary Test, Fifth Edition (PPVT-5) by Douglas M. Dunn (2018): Ages 2.5–90. This test measures English hearing vocabulary. A student is asked to identify which illustration from a field of four pictures depicts the meaning of a word presented orally by the examiner.

4. The Clinical Evaluation of Language Fundamentals–5 (CELF-5) by Elisabeth H. Wiig, Eleanor Semel, and Wayne A. Secord (2013): Ages 5–21. This is a battery of tests designed

to assess general language ability. It measures receptive and expressive language as well as reading and written language. Subtests assess a variety of skills, including the ability to produce a sentence from a given word (formulated sentences), the ability to recall paragraph length material read aloud (understanding spoken paragraphs), the ability to assemble a sentence when a list of words are provided (sentence assembly), the ability to provide word definitions, and understanding of semantic relationships, which impacts a student's ability to understand sentences including temporal, spatial, and sequential information. A pragmatics profile looks at the effectiveness of social interactions.

TIPS FOR ONLINE LEARNING AND TELETHERAPY

1. Informal measurements of story grammar may be conducted online in a variety of ways, such as telling a student a story and asking him or her to retell it (with or without modeling) or by giving the student a prompt such as *Tell me what you do to get ready for school* and asking him or her to create a personal narrative. Another option is to show the student a single picture or series of pictures via PowerPoint and ask him or her to construct a story verbally. The testing condition should be noted in the evaluation report because each situation represents a very different level of scaffolding. The level of story grammar used by the student may then be determined using Westby's Story Grammar Decision Tree.

2. Several standardized tests may also be administered online to assess narrative ability and other key skills. Digital stimulus books are available for the CELF-5 and the PPVT-5. Practitioners who own a TILLS Examiner's Kit can access supplemental Tele-TILLS materials for working with students virtually.

CONCLUSION: HOW CHILDREN DEVELOP A SENSE OF NARRATIVE

Children develop a sense of narrative that grows as their cognitive processes and their understanding of interpersonal relationships mature. They begin with basic descriptions of actions and characters that are unrelated to one another and progress to the point where they understand how the actions of one character affect the reactions of another until eventually they are able to create stories taking the perspective of multiple characters who may have opposing viewpoints. The introduction of planning and goal-directed behavior increases as well. Written language expectations follow a similar pattern but lag behind oral language. In addition, cultural variations influence the types of narratives children create.

With the natural progression of oral language development in mind, Chapter 5 explores strategies for developing the vocabulary, sequencing, and grammar skills essential for both oral and written language. Specific strategies for oral story retells are included along with rubrics for evaluating the quality of story retells.

With the CCSS writing standards in mind, Chapter 6 then delves into written language and specific strategies for using *Story Frames* to improve composition at the sentence and paragraph level, with the eventual goal of creating story summaries and original stories. Chapter 7 explores similarities and differences between narratives and expository essays and discusses strategies for using narratives as a springboard for developing expository writing.

Oral Retells

Vocabulary, Sequencing, and Grammar

5

Children's sense of narrative begins developing in early childhood, as oral language emerges, and becomes more complex during the elementary school years as both their oral and written language skills grow. The American Speech-Language-Hearing Association (ASHA) 2001 position statement recognizes the reciprocal relationship between spoken and written language:

> Children with spoken language problems frequently have difficulty learning to read and write, and children with reading and writing problems frequently have difficulty with spoken language; and instruction in spoken language can result in growth in written language, and instruction in written language can result in growth in spoken language (www.asha.org).

Getting students to talk about stories builds a bridge between their ideas and their written products. Even when ideas flow freely, capturing them in writing can be tedious. Students often forget what they intended to say as they struggle with spelling and sentence formation.

Two foundational skills important for both writing and oral storytelling are vocabulary and sequencing. Children need to be able to use words as the building blocks of sentences and paragraphs, and they need to know how to present ideas that unfold in a logical order or sequence. Additionally, they need to form sentences that follow grammar conventions, gradually learning to use increasingly complex sentence structures in speech and eventually in writing.

The vocabulary and sequencing strategies discussed in this chapter may be used in conjunction with the storyboarding and Quick Draw (pictography) strategies found in Chapter 1. Once students have created their storyboards, they may use these for oral retells as well as written summaries. These retells also provide an opportunity to reinforce grammar understanding and give students practice building increasingly complex sentences orally.

Numerous tools are outlined in this chapter, but not all of them will apply to every student, classroom, or group. It is important to consider a child's strengths, needs, and developmental level when determining which activities are a good match for instructional goals.

DOWNLOADABLE RESOURCES

Keep these resources on hand for teaching the Chapter 5 lessons and activities.

- Lesson 5A, Vocabulary Foldables: Vocabulary foldable (sample and template); Vocabulary/Odd One Out data collection sheet
- Lesson 5B, The Story Game: The Story Game gameboard; game cards for Odd One Out (sample and template), Words in Sentences, and Word Definitions; Vocabulary/Odd One Out data collection sheet
- Lesson 5C, Story Sequencing: Complete Storyboard or Basic Storyboard
- Lesson 5D, Who Is Doing What? N/A
- Other: Semantic Web Builder, Story Element Score Sheet, Grammaticality Judgment game cards (sample and template), Grammaticality Judgment data collection sheet

VOCABULARY: WHAT THE EVIDENCE SAYS

A child's vocabulary is one of the biggest predictors of future reading and school success, and students who enter school with a limited vocabulary often never catch up to their peers.

Biemiller (2015) discusses how young students (K–2) learn new words and their meanings primarily through listening activities, such as hearing stories read aloud. He laments the fact that many teachable opportunities are missed when there is no explicit vocabulary instruction accompanying these read-alouds. For young children, he suggests sharing the same story multiple times, making the first exposure to the narrative a simple read-through with no explicit instruction, and then providing direct teaching of word meanings after the story is finished. He recommends additional word review after subsequent readings of the same story. He found that for many children in Grades 3–4, a simple increase in daily reading led to an increase in vocabulary knowledge, but some children made no progress in word knowledge with this approach and required more direct instruction.

Biemiller also suggests that in Grades 3–8, students should develop greater independence with finding and learning word meanings on their own, though some direct instruction will still be needed, especially in regard to affixes, compound words, and words with multiple meanings. In addition, he states that explicit instruction is still essential for learning key words that may be critical for understanding a specific passage or text.

The sections that follow discuss several recommended strategies and approaches for teaching vocabulary: picture noting, use of categories and semantic webs, use of small-group instruction for struggling learners, and approaches to teaching content-rich vocabulary for both nonfiction and fiction texts. Each can be used in conjunction with *Story Frames*.

Picture Noting

The ARK Institute of Learning presented an article in the 2015 summer issue of *Perspectives on Language and Literacy* entitled "Applying Imagery to Vocabulary Instruction" that outlined a strategy called *picture noting*. Similar to the pictography and *Stickwriting* discussed in Chapter 1, picture noting involves creating quick and simple drawings to represent new vocabulary. Abstract terms are a bit more challenging to represent, but with some ingenuity, images may be found or created to symbolize these words. A good resource can be found at www.thenounproject.com. For a nominal yearly fee, unlimited images may be downloaded to represent almost any concept. See the examples in Figure 5.1 of images used to represent abstract words and complex ideas. The teacher may want to provide students with pictures for abstract vocabulary or even for more concrete terms when time is limited, but students benefit from creating their own simple drawings and choosing images that make sense to them. These drawings may be added to the vocabulary foldables discussed later in the chapter.

Categories and Semantic Webs

Blachowicz and Fisher (2019) discuss the importance of extending word knowledge by teaching students to categorize words and focus on word relationships. They stress the benefit of playing with words to increase student engagement. To explore antonyms, these authors suggest creating a continuum between words with opposite meanings, such as *light* and *dark*.

light – whitish – pale – dim – shadowy – dark

Readers may be familiar with the use of semantic webs or maps to teach vocabulary. A semantic web shows the target vocabulary word in the center circle, connected to outer

Vocabulary words	Images
Revolution	
Liberty	
Persuade	
Surrender	

Figure 5.1. Vocabulary words with images. (© Carolee Dean.)

circles that show related words such as synonyms and antonyms or multiple meanings. Blachowicz and Fisher also describe a tool they call a *synonym web*, which they define as a type of semantic web that focuses on synonyms. These webs are especially helpful for understanding multiple meaning words. They suggest choosing a target word and then having students brainstorm synonyms, put the words into categories based on meaning, and finally create a web to show the words delineated in their categories and their relationship to the target word. Figure 5.2 shows an example of a semantic web for *light*. In addition to synonyms, a few idioms involving the word *light* as well as the antonym *dark* are included. See the Semantic Web Builder in the downloadable resources.

Classroom Versus Small-Group Instruction

Coyne, Capozzoli-Oldham, Cuticelli, and Ware (2015) found that even rigorous classroom vocabulary instruction did not provide enough support for many low-performing students. They needed intervention in a smaller group, numerous exposures to words and their usage, words presented in context, definitions they could understand, and the opportunity to answer questions about words. Weekly and monthly progress monitoring, using tests developed by teachers or found in study units, was crucial for determining if vocabulary instruction was effective.

The study by Gillam, Olszewski, Fargo, and Gillam (2014), discussed in Chapter 1, embedded vocabulary instruction into the study of narratives in an intervention led by a speech-language pathologist (SLP) in a general education classroom. The SLP highlighted target words, and these were used within sentences and paragraphs. Target words were reviewed often. Students considered at risk made progress in vocabulary development,

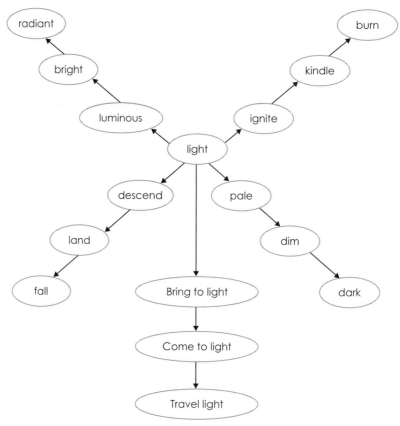

Figure 5.2. Semantic web for the word *light*.

but not nearly as much progress as they made in narrative comprehension, and they still lagged behind their peers in word knowledge. The authors reached a conclusion similar to Coyne, Capozzoli-Oldham, Cuticelli, and Ware (2015): Regular classroom instruction may be insufficient for struggling learners who need more explicit instruction of vocabulary, perhaps in a small-group setting.

Informational Text and Content Vocabulary

Wright and Neuman (2015) point out that with the adoption of the Common Core State Standards (CCSS; National Governors Association, 2010) the emphasis on understanding informational text, even in Grades K–2, has led to increasing challenges for students in regard to vocabulary acquisition. They outline several reasons why this type of vocabulary is more difficult to learn. The words found in informational texts are often directly related to challenging subjects such as science, history, math, or technology. They can represent entire concepts that are novel and unfamiliar. The key words tend to be repeated more often throughout a reading; therefore, if their meaning is unknown or misinterpreted, comprehension of the entire reading passage becomes very difficult. Even if a child has been exposed to the word, he may not understand its particular use within a specialized context.

These authors suggest what they call "content-rich vocabulary instruction" that takes place within the context of what is being taught in the classroom. This instruction includes repeated exposures to words and their meanings, analyzing of word parts, and utilizing words in a variety of contexts. Wright and Neuman also recommend reading a book that includes the target words several times, as well as reading a variety of books on the same subject. These strategies are in stark contrast to the practice of teaching vocabulary lists filled with words with no connection to each other and no relevance to the child's school day.

Shanahan (2015) discusses the reciprocal relationship between reading and vocabulary development. Students who struggle with decoding read less and are exposed to fewer new words; therefore, even when their decoding deficits are remediated, they may not have sufficient vocabulary for grade-level comprehension. He suggests pre-teaching target words before they appear in a text and reading aloud to students who struggle with decoding to expose them to higher level vocabulary. He points out that many schools sacrifice time previously dedicated to teaching science and social studies to focus more effort on reading instruction, which results in less exposure to the content-rich vocabulary found in these important subjects.

Content-Rich Vocabulary in Narrative Nonfiction Picture Books

Many high-quality commercial books may be used to analyze narrative structure while exploring important historical events and scientific concepts, and exposing students to content-rich vocabulary. For example, many stories discussed in the downloadable resources are narrative nonfiction stories chosen because of their connections to history/ social studies and science. Although these picture books were written primarily for elementary school students, most contain advanced vocabulary.

Consider the vocabulary found in Mara Rockliff's *Gingerbread for Liberty! How a German Baker Helped Win the American Revolution* (2015a). It is a fun and engaging, yet true account, of how Christopher Ludwick, a German baker, cooked for Washington's troops and convinced Hessian soldiers to leave the British side to fight for America. It's recommended for Grades 1–4, ages 6–9, but the terms used could be used for older students, especially struggling learners. The book contains many content-rich vocabulary terms like *revolution, independence, liberty, Redcoats, General Washington*, and *British*; other important terms and concepts such as *persuade, hired armies*, and *surrendered*; as well as multiple-meaning words like *shouldered* and *squash*. The Author's Note includes additional names and terms such as *Continental Army, Hessian*, and *Declaration of Independence*.

A similarly vocabulary-rich text for the same age range is *Mesmerized: How Benjamin Franklin Solved a Mystery That Baffled All of France* (2015b), also written by Mara Rockliff and illustrated by Iacopo Bruno. It outlines how Benjamin Franklin went to France to ask for financial support for the war and, while he was there, helped to expose Dr. Franz Mesmer as a medical fraud. This lively, colorful narrative explores both history and science. Consider this content-rich vocabulary: *King Louis the Sixteenth, Queen Marie Antoinette, Parisians, the scientific method, hypothesized*, and *placebo effect*, as well as multiple meaning words like *force, blind*, and *fumed*. The Author's Note includes additional terms such as *Antoine Lavoisier, Montgolfier gas, animal magnetism*, and *Dr. Joseph-Ignace Guillotin*.

In addition to these books written for younger children, consider the many picture books written for older students, such as *Bad News for Outlaws: The Remarkable Life of Bass Reeves, Deputy Marshal* (2009) by Vaunda Micheaux Nelson and illustrated by R. Gregory Christie. This book tells the story of one of the first Black deputy U.S. marshals. At 52 pages, it contains dense paragraphs of text, is intended for Grades 3 and up (actual reading level is fifth grade), and is appropriate for middle school as well as upper elementary students. The back matter includes a timeline of Bass Reeves's life, website links to historical information, books for further reading, additional information about Judge Isaac C. Parker as well as the Indian Territory, a detailed bibliography of the author's research, and definitions of Western terms like *desperado, lynching, posse, warrant, sorrel, tumbleweed wagon*, and *squatters*. Additional vocabulary terms found in the text include

Winchester, cattle rustlers, swindlers, dedication, marksmanship, sharpshooter, captives, silhouette, unflappable, pardoned, unsung, homesteader, and *legendary.*

For additional book examples as well as plot summaries, see the downloadable resources available online at the Brookes Publishing Download Hub (see this book's "About the Downloads" page).

USING *STORY FRAMES* TO SUPPORT VOCABULARY DEVELOPMENT

Story Frames supports the vocabulary strategies, ideas, and observations outlined previously, first of all by focusing story analysis on the use of several content-rich books that support the social studies and science curriculum. Additionally, by targeting terms that will be used in story retells and written summaries, *Story Frames* helps ensure that students see these words frequently and in meaningful contexts. Students require multiple exposures to target vocabulary to understand new words as well as opportunities to use these terms in their speech and in their writing. Students who struggle with word acquisition require multiple reviews of new words as well as explicit vocabulary instruction. These needs are easily met within *Story Frames.*

Introducing Vocabulary With Foldables

Vocabulary terms may be presented prior to introducing the story or after the first reading. Vocabulary foldables provide an engaging, multisensory way to introduce vocabulary. Figure 5.3 shows an example of a vocabulary foldable for *Six Dots: A Story of Young Louis*

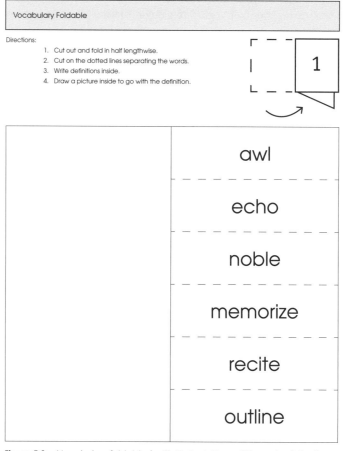

Figure 5.3. Vocabulary foldable for *Six Dots: A Story of Young Louis Braille.*

Braille (Bryant, 2016). A version suitable for copying, as well as blank vocabulary foldables to use with other books, are found in the downloadable resources.

LESSON 5A: VOCABULARY FOLDABLES

ACTIVITY

Objective:
Improve vocabulary understanding and use

Time:
45 minutes

Grade Level:
Second and up

Directions

First, provide students with a printed list of key words and synonyms or short definitions and then instruct them to do the following:

1. Cut out the blank vocabulary foldable.
2. Write the vocabulary terms on top.
3. Write the definitions inside on the right.
4. Draw a picture to go with each definition on the inside left. (See the section on picture noting earlier in this chapter.)

When the foldables are completed, students may work in pairs to test each other on the words or use the foldable to test their own knowledge.

After extensive review of the terms, students may also cut apart their foldables and glue each word and definition onto separate pieces of construction paper to create game cards. These cards may then be turned upside down and used to play a memory matching game with a peer.

Extending Understanding With Game Cards

To explore categories, students may work individually or in teams to create game cards in sets of four, listing three words that go together and one word that does not belong. To create the cards, students can use terms from the narrative and then brainstorm related words. They may then play a game called Odd One Out with a small group or a peer, in which the peer must name the item that does not belong and then name the category for the items that do go together. Figure 5.4 gives examples of Odd One Out game cards for *Six Dots*. More game cards for Odd One Out may be found in the downloadable resources, along with a gameboard.

ODD ONE OUT Which one does not belong? A. awl B. paper C. hammer D. screwdriver LET'S TALK: How are the others the same?	**ODD ONE OUT** Which one does not belong? A. listen B. memorize C. blanket D. recite LET'S TALK: How are the others the same?
ODD ONE OUT Which one does not belong? A. dominoes B. dice C. cards D. hammer LET'S TALK: How are the others the same?	**ODD ONE OUT** Which one does not belong? A. village B. headmaster C. army captain D. noble lady LET'S TALK: How are the others the same?

Figure 5.4. Sample game cards for Odd One Out, using vocabulary from *Six Dots: A Story of Young Louis Braille* (Bryant, 2016).

To further extend learning and test for understanding, additional game cards may be constructed using words in sentences, and still others may provide choices for definitions. In Words in Sentences, students decide which sentence uses the word correctly. In Word Definitions, students choose the definition that best goes with the word. Figure 5.5 shows examples for both types of cards. Additional game cards for *Six Dots* may be found in the appendix and online resources.

All three types of cards can be used to play The Story Game, as described in the lesson plan that follows. The downloadable gameboard for this game may be used with a variety of activities.

WORDS IN SENTENCES Which sentence best uses the word AWL? A. They played a game of awl. B. He used the awl to poke holes in leather. LET'S TALK: Use AWL in a sentence.	**WORDS IN SENTENCES** Which sentence best uses the word MEMORIZE? A. They will memorize the alphabet. B. They did a memorize of times tables. LET'S TALK: Use MEMORIZE in a sentence.
WORD DEFINITIONS What does AWL mean? A. a pointed tool for poking holes B. bad luck C. to hurt your eye D. a secret way to write	**WORD DEFINITIONS** What does MEMORIZE mean? A. to be good at math B. sing C. write D. remember

Figure 5.5. Game cards for Words in Sentences and Word Definitions.

ACTIVITY

LESSON 5B: THE STORY GAME

Objective:
Improve vocabulary comprehension

Grade Level:
Third and up

Time:
Will vary

Directions

For small groups of two to five, The Story Game may be used with Odd One Out, Words in Sentences, and Word Definitions. To play the game, follow these steps:

1. Give each student a set of A, B, C, D answer cards and instruct each to choose a card that corresponds to the correct answer.

2. Read the stimulus card that goes with the specific target.

3. Have students hold their chosen answer card where it can't be seen until you say, "Show me your answer."

4. Tell students the correct answer.

5. Have all students roll the dice and move their game pieces across the gameboard while you record the data. See Figure 5.6 for examples of how to collect data.

Requiring all students to choose an answer at once makes much better use of limited instructional time. Most importantly, students do not become distracted while waiting for peers to take their turns. The instructor or therapist also has more opportunities for data collection.

Vocabulary/Odd One Out Data Collection Sheet					

Directions: Give 1 point for every correct response, 0 for every incorrect response, .5 for partial.

Name:					
Date:					
VOCABULARY					
Choosing sentences					
Choosing definitions					
Using target words in a sentence					
Using target words during story retell					
ODD ONE OUT					
Different					
Same					
Word memory					

Figure 5.6. Data collection sheet for vocabulary activities.

Data Collection and Progress Monitoring

Figure 5.6 shows a data collection sheet that includes two categories, Vocabulary and Odd One Out, with space for recording data from the games described previously, in addition to other areas of vocabulary use that may be assessed but are not included in the game. The data sheet may be used to monitor five students at a time or to track an individual student's performance over time. (Not every instructor will want to use all of the following tools. Student needs change across settings and across grade levels.)

Under the category of Vocabulary, the data sheet includes rows for monitoring the student's abilities in the following areas:

- Choosing sentences (use the Words in Sentences cards)

- Choosing definitions (use the Words in Definitions cards)

- Verbally creating a sentence using target word(s)

- Using target word(s) during a story retell

Note that verbally creating a sentence will be much easier for students than using target words during a story retell.

Under the category of Odd One Out, the instructor may monitor a student's ability to determine which word does not belong (Different) and to describe how the other words go together (Same). A separate task that may be of interest to SLPs is the auditory perceptual skill of repeating back a list of words of increasing length and complexity. The word lists in Odd One Out may be used for this purpose by reading the list to the student and asking him or her to repeat it back from memory.

For larger groups or classes, teachers who have access to clickers may give them to students for data-collection purposes. Clickers are a type of classroom response system similar to remote control devices that allow students to click an answer choice based on a question the teacher has posted from a computer by way of an interactive smart-board or via an overhead projector. Each student submits an answer that is transmitted to the teacher's computer into software that records the data and makes it available for immediate or long-term use. Clickers are very engaging and allow a teacher to share the answer quickly, providing immediate corrective feedback even as student responses retain anonymity. Instructors also avoid the problem of students changing their answers and invalidating the data. Monitoring performance in this manner allows an instructor to follow a student's progress without continually needing to administer tests to do so. If the teacher does want to administer pre- or posttest measures, the game cards found in the appendix may be printed out as a unit and passed out to students who then circle their answers.

SEQUENCING AND COHESION: WHAT THE EVIDENCE SAYS

As mentioned in Chapter 4, the Common Core State Writing Standards for Literature place importance on the ability to chronologically sequence events at every grade level. As a student's ability to use transitional words, phrases, and clauses grows, the connections between the events become clearer. In the early grades, this sequence is fairly linear, but later, in sixth grade and beyond, the writer also uses these tools to signify shifts between settings and time frames.

Students in Grades 6 and beyond are expected to write arguments to support claims in the subject areas of history/social studies, science, and technical subjects. They must use words, phrases, and clauses to create cohesion between ideas (CCSS.ELA-Literacy. WHST.6-8.1.C).

The foundation for this cohesion in expository writing starts much earlier in children's oral and written narratives. Moats, Foorman, and Taylor (2006) analyzed the use of cohesive ties, along with other measures of written language, in the personal narratives of average third and fourth graders in struggling schools with high poverty. The researchers looked at two types of cohesion—lexical ties and transitional ties. Lexical ties involve the use of synonyms across sentences (e.g., *scared, afraid, frightened*). Transitional ties connect ideas through the use of conjunctions *(and then, and so, but, because)*, as well as words and phrases indicating temporal/spatial relationships and the sequencing of events *(once, first, after that, the next day)*. Students who struggled with foundational writing skills like handwriting, spelling, punctuation, and basic sentence structure had fewer cognitive resources left to use for planning and organization. As a result, they produced few cohesive ties. Even when reading skills were comparatively good, composition lagged behind and the quality (or lack thereof) of specific instruction in writing had significant effects on student performance.

Retelling a narrative, whether orally or in the form of a written summary, requires significant skill. Not only must students be able to temporally sequence events, but they must also use working memory to hold in mind the overall plot, while focusing on one element or event at a time and providing transitions that create a smooth bridge between events. Cohesion is needed to keep characters and their actions straight to convey a clear idea of who is doing what by avoiding ambiguous pronoun referents *(Bass Reeves, lawman, marshal, he, him… Louis Braille, child, student, creator, he, him)*.

Marzola (2018) suggests fostering reading comprehension in young children and those struggling with decoding by providing rich listening comprehension opportunities as students process stories read aloud to them:

> They can learn about predictable story structure and use graphic organizers, such as story maps, to aid their recall and retelling of stories. They can be engaged in drawing inferences, making predictions, analyzing characters, and following sequences of events. They can be exposed to rich vocabulary and background knowledge within meaningful contexts. (p. 611)

In this way, students improve their oral language abilities at the same time that they build the foundational skills needed for reading comprehension. Oakhill and Cain (2012) as cited in Oakhill and Cain (2016) conducted a study that revealed that a child's ability at age 7 to be able to take the events of a story written out in random sentences and place them in order into a coherent whole is a predictor of reading comprehension ability at age 11.

USING *STORY FRAMES* TO SUPPORT SEQUENCING

Story Frames easily lends itself to supporting sequencing, given its focus on a beginning, middle, and end that each contain distinct elements, and because of its emphasis on representing these elements visually. The sections that follow explain how to help students build sequencing skills during oral retells, gradually decreasing the amount of visual support provided.

Using Storyboards for Sequencing and Oral Retells

Storyboards using the *Story Frames* elements can be used to give students practice at sequencing events in a story and then orally retelling the story, as described in the following lesson plan.

LESSON 5C: STORY SEQUENCING

Directions

1. Pick a story from the ones provided in the downloads or choose another narrative appropriate for your students. It should be something short in the beginning. Read the story aloud.

2. Have students use the pictography strategies discussed in Chapter 1 and fill out a storyboard with images.

3. Cut apart the storyboard graphic organizer into 12 squares.

4. Ask students to reassemble the storyboard in its correct sequence. Start out working with 4 squares at a time. If they can easily do this, then attempt 8, then all 12.

5. Have students glue the pictures onto construction paper or into a file folder after making sure the sequence is correct.

6. For older students, leave space between the 12 story elements for the addition of transitional words and phrases.

7. When students become proficient at sequencing the story icons themselves, cut out the stick drawings (discarding the icons from each frame) to determine if the students can truly sequence the events of the story without using the icons as a visual support.

8. Once the storyboard is complete, have students orally retell the story, using each frame for a guide for what to include for that story element. Some students will need to physically point to each square so they stay on track and don't leave out important information.

9. If the storyboard will be used for creating a written summary or if you want students to use target vocabulary in their retell, add a list of keywords including vocabulary, character names, and places from the story. This list can be prepared ahead of time by the instructor or brainstormed with the class and then written on lined paper and glued onto the construction paper or file folder for easy reference.

A sample summary, *Story Frames* analysis, and lesson extension activity for *Six Dots* are provided as follows. Key events for each frame are italicized, with additional details in Roman type. Use this as a model for developing story analyses and lesson activities for books of your own choosing, and be sure to check out the additional story analyses available with the downloadable resources.

Objective:
Improve sequencing and story retell skills

Grade Level:
First and up

Time:
45 minutes initially; time varies with additional activities

Six Dots: A Story of Young Louis Braille

Author: Jen Bryant   Length: 40 pages
Illustrator: Boris Kulikov   Lexile 590L
Preschool to Grade 4

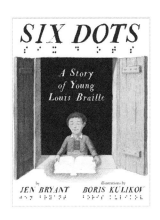

Louis Braille wants to read, but there are no books in his little village for children who are blind. He goes to the Royal School for the Blind and is excited when presented with a book with raised letters, but the words are the size of his hand and the books are huge. He then makes it his mission to create a reading and writing system for people who are visually impaired. (Note: Words in italics represent the core of the story element; additional information is not italicized.)

1. **Ordinary World:** *Louis is a curious child growing up in Coupvray, France.* He enjoys watching his father work with leather in his shop. He wants to use his father's tools, but his father tells him he is too small.

2. **Call and Response:** *Louis has an accident with his father's awl and becomes blind,* but he still wants to read like other children.

3. **Mentors, Guides, and Gifts:** *The Marquise sends a letter to the Royal School for the Blind asking them to accept Louis.* His family does not want him to go because he is only 10, but he tells them how important it is for him to learn how to read.

4. **Crossing:** *Louis goes to Paris.*

5. **New World:** *Louis lives at the Royal School for the Blind.* It is crowded and the food is cold, but he stays because he knows there are books there created for people who cannot see.

6. **Problems, Prizes, and Plans:** *The Prize is going to the library to read the books. The Problem is that only the best students are allowed in the library. Louis's Plan is to be one of the best students.*

7. **Midpoint Attempt:** *Louis is finally allowed to read one of the books.* He is excited until he finds out that the raised letters are so big that it takes half a page for one sentence. He knows he can't learn much from these books.

8. **Downtime Response:** *Louis is so disappointed that he goes to bed without any dinner and dreams of going home.*

9. **Chase and Escape:** *His friend wakes him and tells Louis to follow him outside. An army captain has sent the boys coded messages with dots.* Louis thinks the system is too complicated for the boys. Most of them quickly give up, so he asks the headmaster if the captain will help him create a better system.

10. **Death and Transformation:** *The captain refuses to help. Louis must work long hours on his own, but he finally transforms the army code into something the students can use.*

11. **Climax:** The Final Test: *Louis tests his system with the headmaster of his school and it works. He is able to transcribe an entire chapter of a book quickly and easily.*

12. **Final Reward:** *Louis comes up with an alphabet using a pattern of six dots. It is used around the world to this day.*

Extension: Connect the Dots   Have students look around the school and their community for examples of braille signage for room numbers, bathrooms, and elevators. Have them practice writing their names or secret messages in braille. Invite an adult with a visual impairment from the community to come to class and talk to students about his or her experiences. Find other suggestions about promoting "blind awareness" at www.nfb .org, the website for the National Federation of the Blind.

A file folder is useful for keeping all of the students' work together if they will be writing sentences and paragraphs and creating vocabulary foldables. If drawing is poor or labored, copy the instructor's version of the drawings for this activity. In the example in Figure 5.7, because the images were going to be used over several weeks, they were printed from www.thenounproject.com rather than using stick drawings. If stick drawings are vague, they can usually still be effective if used immediately; however, if time lapses it may be difficult for students to remember what their drawings represent.

See the following section for more information about story retells. For older students, this step may be skipped and the same storyboard may be used for writing sentences, paragraphs, and summaries. However, for some older students, the oral retell will still be an important part of the process and may provide an essential bridge to writing.

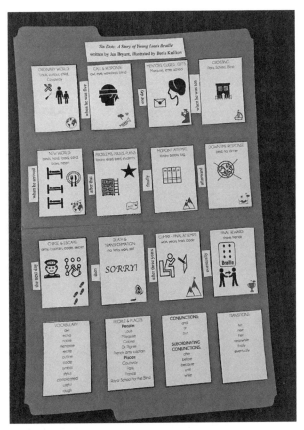

Figure 5.7. Twelve story elements with transition words.

Decreasing Visual Supports for Oral Retells

Initially, students may use their storyboards, which include their stick drawings and the icons, to verbally retell the story, including target vocabulary and key words. When a student is proficient with this step, he or she next retells the story by merely looking at the story element icons as reminders. When proficient with using only story icons, he or she retells a story without any visual supports. The story element icons may be used as prompts if the student gets stuck.

If other students are present during the story retells, keep them engaged by having them listen for target vocabulary. Younger students may raise a blank index card or a piece of paper with the target word on it when they hear it used in another student's retell. Older students may be provided with a list of vocabulary words and transition words. Instruct them to make a hash mark each time they hear a specific term used. This helps keep them engaged while drawing attention to key vocabulary and increasing the number of exposures to new words.

Students can break up into pairs to retell the story and focus on either listening for vocabulary or listening for story elements. The peer who is listening can point to each square and alert his partner if he skips information. Older students may use the Story Element Score Sheet in Figure 5.8 to rate a peer's story retell.

Data Collection and Progress Monitoring

Educators may monitor progress by determining the level of support and prompting needed for a student to complete story retells, the number of story elements included in the retell,

Story Element Score Sheet

Story element	Icon	Response includes	Score
BEGINNING			
Ordinary World		Main character and setting – Two	2
		One	1
		None or wrong	0
Call and Response		A call to adventure and feelings – Two	2
		One	1
		None or wrong	0
Mentors, Guides, and Gifts		Helper and gift – Two	2
		One	1
		None or wrong	0
Crossing		Where going and how they travel – Two	2
		One	1
		None or wrong	0
MIDDLE			
New World		New setting and new characters – Two	2
		One	1
		None or wrong	0
Problems, Prizes, and Plans		Problem and/or Prize and Plan – Two	2
		One	1
		None or wrong	0
Midpoint Attempt		Attempt and consequence – Two	2
		One	1
		None or wrong	0
Downtime Response		Action and feelings – Two	2
		One	1
		None or wrong	0
END			
Chase and Escape		New direction and action – Two	2
		One	1
		None or wrong	0
Death and Transformation		Danger and change – Two	2
		One	1
		None or wrong	0
Climax: The Final Test		Attempt and consequence – Two	2
		One	1
		None or wrong	0
Final Reward		Reward and resolution – Two	2
		One	1
		None or wrong	0
TOTAL		24 points possible	

Figure 5.8. Story Element Score Sheet.

the use of cohesive ties (including transition words and pronouns—e.g., *he, she, it, they*), key vocabulary, and grammar. Figure 5.8 shows the Story Element Score Sheet, which is useful for analyzing story retells. It may be used by students and instructors alike and a printable version may be found in the downloadable resources. When students reach the editing phase of their writing, they may use the Story Element Score Sheet to evaluate the content of their own work.

GRAMMAR: WHAT THE EVIDENCE SAYS

Colozzo, Gillam, Wood, Schnell, and Johnston (2011) note that when students with a specific language impairment (SLI) are focusing on oral storytelling as an objective, often more grammar errors will be observed in their speech. In addition, the authors found that students who continued to have good grammar during storytelling often did not use as many story elements as peers, did not elaborate, and were not as expressive. Proficiency in one seemed to be sacrificed for proficiency in another. They concluded that the students in the SLI group of their study "appeared to have limitations that made it difficult for them to tell stories that were both strong in content and grammatically accurate" (p. 1615). They predicted that students who started out with fairly good grammar might actually make more errors as their storytelling improved in story content and sentence complexity. These errors might actually be a sign of progress, demonstrating how students are balancing a variety of skills as they struggle with the multitasking required for storytelling.

Hochman and MacDermott-Duffy (2018) discuss the importance of explicit instruction in writing. Due to a lack of this instruction in many classrooms, even students with above average reading and speaking skills have difficulty with the writing process, especially in regard to revision, organization, and modifying a message for a specific audience. For students with learning disabilities who also struggle with basic sentence structure, grammar, word retrieval, spelling, and vocabulary, writing assignments can feel insurmountable. The authors suggest starting with oral language activities with young children as a foundation for writing. They also highlight the importance of writing about content areas at every grade level:

> Writing and thinking are inextricably linked. In order to enhance their knowledge of content, students should write about it. When students write about what they are learning, they gain more knowledge than if they are taught writing as a separate activity and assigned topics unrelated to the content of their classes. (p. 647)

One strategy these authors discuss is combining sentences through the use of conjunctions. Another is teaching students to use questions (who, what, where, when, why, how) to take a kernel sentence and expand it. Both activities result in sentences of greater complexity. The questioning strategy is used in the lesson plan found later in this chapter to expand sentences orally using illustrations from a picture book as a prompt.

USING *STORY FRAMES* TO SUPPORT GRAMMAR AND SENTENCE STRUCTURE

Activities within *Story Frames* can be used with oral retells to help students practice and strengthen grammar in oral language. The following activities reinforce grammatical concepts—not only correctness but also the ability to form increasingly complex and elaborated sentences orally. These skills provide students with a stronger foundation for writing.

Reinforcing Grammar Concepts and Correctness

Story Frames are effective for helping students use grammar correctly when they tell or retell stories orally. To reinforce grammar concepts, game cards for Grammaticality Judgment may be used to play The Story Game following the procedures previously discussed. This activity focuses on areas that often cause difficulty for young children, struggling students, and second language learners. These areas include recognizing the correct use of helping verbs, regular and irregular past tense verbs, and subject–verb agreement. Figure 5.9 shows examples for each of these areas based on *Six Dots*. These game cards are also provided in the downloadable resources, along with the data collection sheet shown in Figure 5.10.

Using Wh-Questions to Build Complex Oral Sentences

Returning to the idea that oral language precedes and supports written language, an entire session or class period or more could be dedicated to building complex oral sentences using the rich and colorful illustrations found in narrative nonfiction picture books. Marzola (2018) suggests picture description activities as a way to foster both oral language and reading skills. This is easy and fun to do using Wh-questions. Wh-questions often

GRAMMATICALITY	GRAMMATICALITY
(helping verb)	(regular past tense)
Which sentence sounds correct?	Which sentence sounds correct?
A. Louis born in France.	A. His father work with leather.
B. Louis was born in France.	B. His father worked with leather.
LET'S TALK: Fix this sentence:	LET'S TALK: Fix this sentence:
Louis born in France.	His father work with leather.
GRAMMATICALITY	GRAMMATICALITY
(subject–verb)	(irregular past tense)
Which sentence sounds correct?	Which sentence sounds correct?
A. He watches his father.	A. A noble lady write a letter.
B. He watch his father.	B. A noble lady wrote a letter.
LET'S TALK: Fix this sentence:	LET'S TALK: Fix this sentence:
He watch his father.	A noble lady write a letter.

Figure 5.9. Game cards for Grammaticality Judgment.

Grammaticality Judgment Data Collection Sheet					
Directions: Give 1 point for every correct response, 0 for every incorrect response, .5 for partial.					
Name:					
Date:					
GRAMMAR UNDERSTANDING					
Helping verbs					
Regular past tense					
Subject–verb agreement					
Irregular past tense					
GRAMMAR USAGE: SENTENCE REPAIR					
Helping verbs					
Regular past tense					
Subject–verb agreement					
Irregular past tense					
Sentence repair					
GRAMMAR USAGE DURING STORY RETELL					

Figure 5.10.   Data collection sheet for grammar activities.

work better for sentence expansion than traditional activities focused on parts of speech. The latter often include terms and concepts that are difficult for many students to understand. Students with learning disabilities may have difficulty with terms like *adjective*, *adverb*, and *conjunction* even in high school. Eberhardt (2019) laments the ineffectiveness of traditional grammar instruction (identifying and coding nouns and verbs) and recommends that grammar be taught in regard to a word's function within a sentence. After all, the same word may function as a verb or a noun depending on its syntactical role. *(He will ride the horse. It was a long ride.)* She suggests using question strips to build sentences so that the sentence parts can be easily manipulated. The use of questions to build complex oral sentences is outlined in the following lesson plan.

ACTIVITY

LESSON 5D: WHO IS DOING WHAT?

Objectives:
Improve the ability to answer Wh-questions; improve understanding and use of complex sentence structure

Grade Level:
Kindergarten and up

Time:
15 minutes

Directions

1. Display a book illustration via an e-book on a smartboard or using a document camera with the hard copy version so that all students can clearly see the nuances of the picture. Then ask the following questions:

    a. Who or what is the subject of the picture?

    b. What is he/she/it doing?

    c. How is he/she/it doing it?

    d. Where are they?

    e. When is it happening?

    f. Why are they doing it?

    g. Which one? (to add describing words)

2. After asking these questions, demonstrate how to put all of the answers together into one complex sentence. Use a visual example written on the board or constructed with sentence strips.

As an example of how to build sentences this way, consider the illustration on the fifth page of *Six Dots*. Louis is standing on a stool in his father's workshop. He is covering his eyes. A sharp tool called an awl is falling to the ground. His father is looking out the window.

    This illustration provides an excellent opportunity to talk about inferencing, as the book does not say explicitly that Louis poked himself in the eye, nor that he dropped the tool that is falling to the ground in front of him. Some students assume that he is shading his eyes because of the sunlight coming through the window. They completely miss one of the crucial plot points of the story, that this is how Louis became blind. Having discussions about the illustrations with students may reveal interesting gaps in their thinking.

    The questions outlined previously could be answered as follows:

1. Who or what is the subject of the picture? (noun = subject) Louis Braille

2. What did he do? (verb or verb phrase = predicate) poked

3. What did he poke? (object) his eye

4. How did he do it? (adverb, prepositional phrase) accidentally, with a tool

5. Where was he? (prepositional phrase) on a stool, in the workshop

6. When did he poke his eye? (adverbial clause with a subordinating conjunction) while his father was looking out the window

7. Why did he poke his eye? (adverbial clause with a subordinating conjunction) because he wanted to prove he was big

8. Which tool was it? (adjective) a sharp tool

After using Wh-questions to fully explore the illustration, demonstrate how to put it all together with a visual example written on the board or constructed with sentence strips. See the examples that follow.

    This sentence represents the structure of a simple kernel sentence:

        Louis Braille poked his eye.

Inform students that if they stopped here, this would still be a complete sentence. It includes a subject and a predicate, and that is all that is required. We can expand the sentence, however, and make it longer by asking Wh-questions about what is happening—questions like *where?*

        Louis Braille poked his eye in the workshop.

This is still a simple sentence. We have not added any conjunctions or clauses, only a prepositional phrase. We could stop here or keep going by asking additional questions about *when, how,* and *which tool?*

        Louis Braille accidentally poked his eye with a sharp tool in the workshop while his father was looking out the window.

That is still one sentence, but now it has become complex. We are still working with expanding the one idea of how Louis poked his eye. However, we have added an adverb telling how *(accidentally)*, another prepositional phrase telling which tool *(with a sharp tool)*, and a dependent clause telling when *(while his father was looking out the window)*. Now the sentence has become complex, with a dependent clause added to the original independent clause.

Next, after having a discussion about cause and effect and the reasons for Louis's behavior, the instructor could add another dependent clause telling *why:*

> Because he wanted to prove he was big, Louis Braille accidentally poked his eye with a sharp tool in the workshop while his father was looking out the window.

Struggling students have a lot of difficulty determining the content of a sentence, where it begins, and where it ends because sentences can be very short or quite elaborate. They might contain several nouns and verbs within multiple clauses; therefore, getting to the heart of the main subject and predicate isn't always easy. This difficulty causes challenges not just in student writing but also in reading and listening comprehension. See William Van Cleave's Chapter 9, "Function Trumps Form: Sentence-Level Instruction," as well as his book, *Writing Matters: Developing Sentence Skills in Students of All Ages* (2014), for additional suggestions on expanding written sentences.

A sentence of the length and complexity described previously is not a reasonable *writing* goal for all students, but answering most of these questions verbally, using the illustration as a guide, is not nearly as difficult. Even early elementary students can do this. These conversations expose kids to how rich and expansive a sentence can become. The activity will also help them to parse the sentence structures they hear and read later. This correlation will be discussed in greater detail in Chapter 8, "Toward a Deeper Understanding: Questioning and Comprehension Skills."

For additional practice, students can form their own sentences out of sentence strips using the same words, phrases, and clauses practiced orally as a group. When students are ready, fill in a chart like the one in Figure 5.11 with the class. Then make a copy for each

Questions	Answers
Who is the subject of the story?	Louis Braille
What did he do?	poked
What did he poke?	his eye
How?	accidentally, with a tool
Which one?	sharp
Where?	in the workshop
When?	while his father was looking out the window
Why?	because he wanted to prove he was big

Figure 5.11. Wh-questions and answers for sentence-building with *Six Dots: A Story of Young Louis Braille* (Bryant, 2016).

student. Instruct them to cut apart the answers to the questions and use the parts to build a sentence.

As mentioned earlier, Eberhardt (2019) recommends asking a series of Wh-questions and then creating sentence strips from the answers. She starts with two basic questions to establish the subject and predicate. Her first two questions are: *Who (what) did it?* and *What did they (he/she/it) do?* To expand the predicate (verb phrase) she asks the following questions: *Where? When? How?* To expand the subject she asks the questions: *How many? Which one? What kind?*

Greene and Enfield (1997) have created an extensive curriculum for Project Read called *Framing Your Thoughts: Sentence Structure.* It is explicit, systematic, multisensory, and incorporates graphic representations of the parts of a sentence and how to expand those parts. Their detailed manual uses Wh-questions to expand both the subject and predicate and is helpful for building both oral and written sentences of increasing complexity and richness. Written language will be explored in depth in the following chapter.

TIPS FOR ONLINE LEARNING AND TELETHERAPY

The narrative activities described in this chapter have been used successfully in teletherapy with a few simple modifications. Many of the online resources can easily be projected over the computer. Examples may be shown to students using the screen share feature of many online platforms such as Zoom. In addition, keep the following tips in mind:

1. E-mail all hands-on materials to the teletherapy monitor at the school prior to the session or the parent if the student is seen at home.

2. If you want to read the story and show the illustrations via document camera or via an e-book like Kindle using the Zoom screen share feature, be aware that some educators avoid sharing books online because of possible copyright infringements. See the *School Library Journal*'s article "Tackling Copyright Concerns When Taking Storytime Online" (Russell, 2019) for advice on this topic. If students have an account with www.bookshare.org or Learning Ally, it may be more appropriate for them to access books that way. Also, there are many free story resources available via YouTube and other sources that are intended to be shared online.

3. When playing The Story Frame Game, give all students their own color for ABCD choices. Have them all answer the multiple-choice questions at the same time by either holding up their letter or sliding their selection to the teletherapy monitor, who then reports their responses to the therapist. Manila folders may be placed between the students so they don't see peers' answers. Use virtual dice found on YouTube, which won't roll off the table and onto the carpet.

CONCLUSION: BUILDING LITERACY SKILLS THROUGH ORAL RETELLS

Oral language precedes written language, but there is a reciprocal relationship between the two in that growth in either contributes to growth in the other. This chapter provides strategies for instruction in foundational skills needed for both oral and written language.

These skills include vocabulary understanding and use, grammar usage, sentence expanding, story sequencing, and the use of cohesion to form smooth connections and transitions between ideas. With these underlying skills firmly in mind, Chapters 6 and 7 explore written language, while Chapter 8 examines reading and listening comprehension. Oral and written language, along with reading and listening comprehension, are all best fostered within a meaningful and engaging context. Narratives provide the perfect framework for honing the development of all of these areas.

From Speaking to Writing
Sentences, Paragraphs, and Stories

6

Writing is a challenge for all students, but even more so for those with learning challenges. Writing represents the culmination of the many skills already discussed—vocabulary understanding and use, grammar proficiency, perspective taking, understanding of text structures, spelling, syntax, organization, planning, and many more. In addition, a child's written work is a clear demonstration of his or her ability level or lack of ability. Many struggling learners have found ways to hide their reading challenges, but their writing challenges become glaringly apparent with the most basic writing assignments. In my experience, many teens with written language deficits refuse to produce any writing at all. They tear up their papers, distract the class with behavior antics, state that they have no ideas for their writing, or shut down and refuse to work.

Archer and Hughes (2010), Fisher and Frey (2008), and others discuss a three-step method for introducing new materials and methods to students that can be helpful for providing writing support. It's called the "I do, we do, you do" approach. Based on the gradual release of responsibility, it is beneficial for building the many skills students need for the complex challenges that come with structuring written work. This approach will be woven in throughout this chapter and the chapters that follow.

Chapter 4 outlined Common Core State Standards (CCSS) expectations for written narratives, and Chapter 5 wrapped up exploration of oral language story retell skills by discussing how to use Wh-questions to generate oral responses and then use those responses to create sentence strips. Wh-questions not only provide a valuable bridge from oral to written language, but also continue to serve as a guide for expanding sentences and clarifying meaning.

Working on sentence length and complexity is a valuable objective, and many workbooks are available to help develop this skill; however, these activities often contain little context. Sentences are unrelated, with no connection to a bigger picture. By using keywords from stories to create sentences that correspond to story elements on the storyboard, students have the chance to work on sentence structure in a meaningful context and continue their content area vocabulary development. Older students may use the same sentences to construct paragraphs and summaries.

Frishkoff, Collins-Thompson, Hodges, and Crossley (2016) discuss the importance of a child's seeing target words in a variety of contexts so students are exposed to shades of meaning. Dobbs and Kearns (2016) highlight how using

DOWNLOADABLE RESOURCES

Keep these resources on hand for teaching the Chapter 6 lessons and activities.

- Lesson 6A, Using Story Elements to Create Sentences: Plot Pages for Summary Writing; Three-Paragraph Summary Pages; Editor's Toolbox; Editor's Tools

- Lesson 6B, The Ties That Bind: Students' Completed Plot Pages; Three-Paragraph Summary Pages; Editor's Toolbox; Editor's Tools

- Lesson 6C, Bookends: Students' Completed Three-Paragraph Summary Pages; Editor's Toolbox; Editor's Tools

- Lesson 6D, Cash for Our Cause

(continued)

(continued)

- Lesson 6E, Book Talk: N/A

- Lesson 6F, Build Your Toolbox: Editor's Toolbox; Editor's Tools; Tool Inventory List

- Lesson 6G, Original Story Brainstorm: Basic or Complete Storyboard; Plot Pages for Summary Writing; Editor's Toolbox; Editor's Tools

- Lesson 6H, Twisted Tales: Basic or Complete Storyboard; Plot Pages for Summary Writing; Editor's Toolbox; Editor's Tools

- Lesson 6I, Story Ad Lib: Story Ad Lib Template

- Lesson 6J, Dicey Stories: PowerPoint Slide Deck for Dicey Story Choices; Editor's Toolbox; Editor's Tools

- Other: Online Instructional Tools PowerPoint Slide Deck; Plot Summary Basic worksheet (if using the Basic Storyboard)

academic vocabulary in written assignments demonstrates a deeper understanding of words. Haynes, Smith, and Laud (2019) discuss the benefits of using contextualized (topic-centered) versus decontextualized vocabulary during sentence, paragraph, and essay writing practice. When each sentence is about a different topic, as is frequently the case in many classrooms' sentence drills, a heavy cognitive load is created when students must shift between subjects. When vocabulary comes from the classroom's course content or from a story, writing practice allows students to go more deeply into a subject and helps reinforce understanding of the content and concepts rather than bouncing back and forth between unrelated ideas. Exploring new words in context also gives the student opportunity to practice vocabulary usage, which helps to solidify semantic concepts as well as grammar concepts as the student contemplates which form of the word best fits the sentence.

This chapter focuses on teaching students to write sentences that correspond to each story element and then use those sentences as the building blocks for more intensive writing activities. The discussion then shifts to working with the resulting rough drafts to build revision and proofreading skills, and how to approach editing, as well as the use of an Editor's Toolbox with students. Several student work samples are included, as well as a case study with multiple writing samples showing the skill progression of Elizabeth, a fourth-grade student with dyslexia who worked with *Story Frames* through a combination of direct therapy and remote online instruction.

FROM STORY RETELLS TO SENTENCE WRITING

Use of *Story Frames* to teach writing skills begins with using keywords to construct sentences. After sufficient practice creating sentences orally using Wh-questions, students use the keywords and vocabulary found in the *Story Frames* Storyboard (terms either provided by the teacher or brainstormed by the class) to create sentences to go with each story element for a specific story. The icons on the Storyboard correspond to the icons on the three Plot Pages in Figure 6.1 so that the student can easily see where the information is supposed to go and how it relates to the whole.

This approach helps with organization, too. Students with organizational and executive function challenges often require explicit guidance on how to make sense of a writing project. Many have difficulty tracking all of the different pages and worksheets involved in a complicated writing assignment. Providing them with a graphic organizer with icons that correspond to critical elements across the pages needed for an assignment can help them to more quickly locate their materials and know what to do with the information once they find it.

Getting Started With Sentences: Plot Pages

The following lesson illustrates how to get students started on Plot Pages, following the "I do, we do, you do" progression. This writing occurs after the story has been read, the storyboard Quick Draws completed, and keyword lists provided. First, in the "I do" phase, an instructor would model precisely how to create a sentence using keywords for the first story frame, the Ordinary World. Then, for the "We do" phase, the class can work as a group to construct a sentence for the next story frame, Call and Response. By this time, students will be halfway through Plot Page 1 and might then be expected to work on their own to complete sentences for the third and fourth story frames. Be aware that some students may still require ongoing modeling and support.

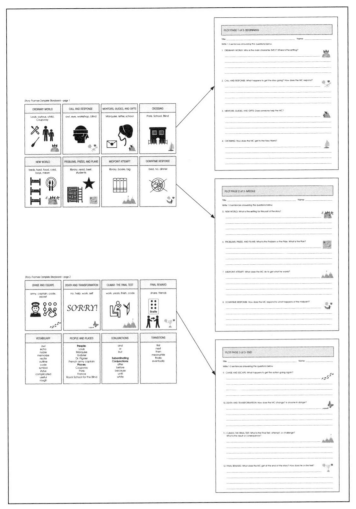

Figure 6.1. From Storyboard to Plot Pages: Writing sentences.

LESSON 6A: USING STORY ELEMENTS TO CREATE SENTENCES

ACTIVITY

Directions

1. Instruct students to locate their stick figure drawing and keywords that go with the Ordinary World on their storyboard.

2. Tell them to locate Plot Page 1. Model how to use the keywords from the storyboard to create one to three sentences everyone will write down for item 1. Point out that the item 1 icon matches the icon for the Ordinary World on their storyboard. Teacher modeling represents the "I do" phase.

3. Next, have students locate their stick figure drawing and keywords that go with the Call and Response on their storyboard. Work as a group to create one to three sentences. Have everyone write the class response for item 2 on Plot Page 1. Point out that the item 2 icon matches their storyboard icon for the Call and Response. When students work as a group, it represents the "We do" phase.

4. Tell students to locate their stick figure drawing and keywords that go with Mentors, Guides, and Gifts on their storyboard. Instruct them to work independently to use keywords to create one to three sentences and write this response for item 3 on Plot Page 1. Point out that the icon for item 3 matches the icon for Mentors, Guides, and Gifts on

Objectives:
Improve written organization and syntax skills; encourage use of key vocabulary

Grade Level:
Third and up

Time:
30 minutes for steps 1–4; 30 minutes each for steps 5, 6, 7, and 8. Note: Not every story needs to incorporate all 8 steps.

their storyboard. Walk around the room to make sure students can complete this step independently. They are now working at the "You do" phase. If they are not successful, return to the modeling of the "I do" phase or the group collaboration of the "We do" phase for anyone who needs that level of support.

5. Follow the same procedure outlined in step 4 for each additional story element.

6. Use the Plot Pages along with transition words to write a story summary on the Summary Page or a blank piece of paper. Model writing the first paragraph (I do), then work as a group to write the second paragraph together (We do). Finally, instruct students to write the third paragraph by themselves (You do). On subsequent story summaries, when students are proficient with this task, have them work more independently on the entire summary.

7. Use the Editor's Toolbox that follows to make edits.

8. Rewrite the story with the editorial changes (optional).

Building Sentence Complexity

To build more elaborate written descriptions, students may use the same Wh-strategies described in Chapter 5 for building sentences orally to expand their written sentences. Another way to build sentence complexity is to focus on using phrases, clauses, and conjunctions. When students are proficient at creating basic sentences using the steps outlined previously, challenge them to create more elaborate sentences.

The following suggestions for *Six Dots: A Story of Young Louis Braille* (Bryant, 2016) are based on William Van Cleave's Chapter 9, "Function Trumps Form: Sentence-Level Instruction." Children will show a wide range of ability levels regarding the skills described, and some kindergarteners will need much support to produce any writing at all. In the early grades, story retelling may be focused primarily on oral retells without any writing. For a more detailed description of activities and exercises for skill development, refer to Van Cleave's book, *Writing Matters: Developing Sentence Skills in Students of All Ages* (2014). What follows are examples of using his framework to expand the basic idea of the New World frame—that is, what happens in the middle of a story when either the main character travels to a new setting or something comes to the Ordinary World to change it.

In *Six Dots*, Louis enters the New World when he leaves his little village of Coupvray at the age of 10 to attend the Royal School for the Blind in Paris. The school was previously a prison and is still a very cold, damp place. His bed is hard, and he has to share a room with several other boys. The meals are usually cold, and there is never much to eat. The older boys tease the younger boys and steal from them. Louis misses home, but he endures these hardships because the best students get to go to the library where there are books for the blind.

The keywords for this story element are *beds, hard, food, cold, boys,* and *mean.* The teacher may come up with a list of keywords ahead of time, or the class can brainstorm words they predict they will need for summarizing each section of the story. Students can construct simple sentences, using the keywords, to capture the gist of this part of the story. They can also be encouraged to use more advanced sentence structures (compound, complex).

1. Simple sentences: The new school felt cold and damp. The beds felt hard. The food tasted cold. The older boys acted mean. Louis missed home. Louis stayed anyway.

2. Compound sentence with coordinating conjunction (Grade 1-2): The new school felt cold and damp, but Louis stayed anyway. The beds felt hard, and the food tasted cold.

3. Complex sentence with adverb clause (Grades 3–5): The new school was rough because the beds were hard. Louis stayed because he wanted to read. (Inverted) Because he wanted to read, Louis stayed at the school.

4. Complex sentence with adjective clause (Grade 6): Louis, who wanted to read books, stayed at the cold, damp school.

For a very young or struggling writer, it helps to provide keywords related to each story element that the student then uses to construct simple sentences. Older students may be able to create a list of keywords on their own. Many older students will still be inclined to use a basic sentence structure. For them, it is helpful to use the syntax concepts in Chapter 9 to encourage them to produce more sophisticated sentences.

FROM SENTENCES TO PARAGRAPH AND SUMMARY WRITING

Story Frames then uses the work students have done with sentences to teach them how to write paragraphs and, ultimately, multi-paragraph story summaries. After completing sentences that correspond to each of the 12 story elements (8 if using the Basic Storyboard), the student uses each Plot Page to write a paragraph. The beginning section of the storyboard corresponds to sentences from Plot Page 1, which become the first paragraph. The middle section corresponds to sentences from Plot Page 2, which become the second paragraph, and the end section corresponds to sentences from Plot Page 3, which become the third paragraph.

Using *Story Frames* in this way helps make the concept of a paragraph more concrete and clearer for students. Many students have difficulty with sentence structure and paragraph structure. In my experience, if a teacher asks students to define a paragraph, most will say it is five to nine sentences, depending on what expectations they have been taught. They have no concept that a paragraph, like a sentence, is a unit of information. To graphically represent the idea of a paragraph, show students the Complete Storyboard once again and remind them that the first row, the beginning, represents one paragraph. The second row, the middle, will become another paragraph, and the third row, the end, will become the third paragraph. Then hold up their sentence worksheets and point out that the sentences they have constructed will be the building blocks of their paragraphs. If they have written one to three sentences for each story element, each section (or paragraph) should contain four to twelve sentences.

There are several advantages to using *Story Frames* to teach paragraph structure.

1. Keywords are provided, which help with word choice and spelling, which frees up cognitive space for higher level tasks like creating more complex sentences, building cohesion, and taking the reader's perspective to ensure that sufficient information has been supplied.

2. Students don't have to rely on overly simplistic guidelines based on the number of sentences that should be included.

3. Paragraphs are based on content, which is graphically represented in visual form through stick drawings specific to each storyboard section.

4. Students who struggle with executive function deficits and organization can use the icons to determine what information needs to go in what location.

Story Frames and the chronological structure of narratives work like training wheels to help students grow toward higher levels of independence with their writing. If students use the sentences they have already written, they will have a reasonably logical summary that can then be smoothed out with transitions. Students often resist rewriting a

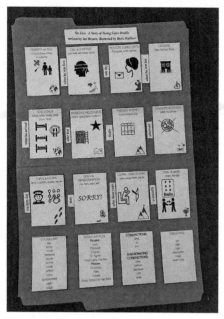

Figure 6.2. Twelve story elements with transition words.

rough draft and don't see a clear reason for doing so. It feels like busywork, and often it is, especially when they don't make any changes from one version to the next. With the *Story Frames* approach, moving sentences into paragraphs with transition words and phrases gives meaning and purpose to the "rewrite."

Connecting Ideas With Transitions

The student must do more than copy these sentences to create a paragraph. He must form smooth transitions between the sentences to show how the paragraph progresses. Refer students to the list of transition words printed at the bottom of the storyboard (see Figure 6.2). If the student has already created this graphic organizer with the transition words glued in between each story element, review it again to make sure he uses these cohesive ties between the sentences. If the student has not completed this activity, now might be a good time to do it.

The Plot Pages containing the sentences correspond directly to the graphic organizer for the paragraphs on the summary page in Figure 6.3. The

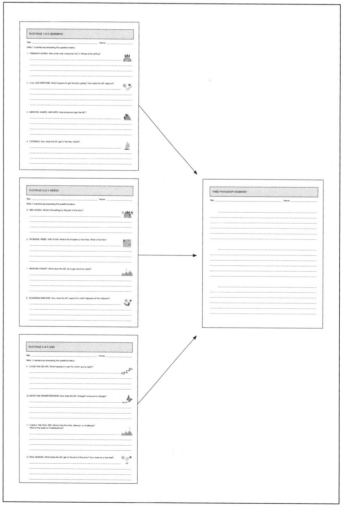

Figure 6.3. From sentences to paragraphs: Summarizing the beginning, middle, and end.

student will have more room for writing if he uses regular lined paper or types into a computer or word processing program, but it is still helpful to refer to Figure 6.1 to explain how the sentences will relate to the paragraphs.

LESSON 6B: THE TIES THAT BIND

ACTIVITY

Directions

1. Using the sentences on the Plot Pages, instruct students to write transition words or phrases at the end of each page to show a shift between paragraphs. Tell them a list of transition words may be found on their storyboard. Use a different color of pencil or pen so additions are easy to see. This may also be done for each sentence in the margin for older students.

2. Circle pronouns referring to people (*him, her, she, he, they*). Tell students to proofread the sentence to make sure it is clear who the pronoun is referring to. If this is not clear, instruct students to cross out the pronoun and write the name of the character above it.

3. Insert these additions when writing the story summary on the summary page.

Objectives:
Improve written organization and syntax skills; encourage use of transition words and cohesive ties

Grade Level:
Third and up

Time:
45 minutes

Creating an Introduction and Conclusion

To turn these paragraphs into a summary, the student then creates an introduction and a conclusion. They may add these components to the first and last paragraphs, or the introduction and conclusion may become additional paragraphs for older students. If they are standalone paragraphs, the summary becomes a five-paragraph writing assignment. For some students, merely constructing one paragraph based on one section of the story is enough of a challenge.

A review of student writing samples in CCSS Appendix C (found at http://www.corestandards.org/assets/Appendix_C.pdf), as well as specific standards for Writing Text Types and Purposes across Grades 1–8, reveals these expectations:

1. First grade: Students are expected to write an introduction that includes the title of a book, their opinion about the book, reasons for their opinion, and provide a sense of closure.

2. Second grade: In addition to the first-grade expectations, the introduction and conclusion are written as statements. One sentence for each would be a reasonable aim.

3. Third grade: Ideas are grouped into paragraphs. Introductions and conclusions may still comprise only single sentences, but might also appear in sections that resemble short paragraphs.

4. Fourth and fifth grade: An introductory paragraph clearly states the topic. Conclusions typically appear in their own paragraphs, but these may be short or may still only be statements of one or two sentences.

5. Middle school: Writing expectations continue to grow. Introductory and concluding paragraphs should be longer, but as sentences become more complex, sometimes the actual number of sentences is still low. There is a stronger sense that the conclusion arises from the argument or opinion presented in the preceding paragraphs.

To further explore the concept of introductions and conclusions, see the lesson plans that follow for the oral language activities called Bookends and Cash for Our Cause.

ACTIVITY

LESSON 6C: BOOKENDS

Objectives:
Improve summary writing skills; improve ability to write introductions and conclusions

Grade Level:
Third and up

Time:
30 minutes (not including time to read the book)

Directions

1. Create a visual of bookends by either using an image from the Internet or lining up a row of books and using two objects to hold the books in place. Explain that the purpose of bookends is to keep information together. Let students know that the bookends used for an introduction and a conclusion will be similar, but not exactly the same.

2. Many of the stories outlined in this book's downloadable resources are about a person who made a significant achievement or accomplishment of some kind. Read one of these stories. Let students know the story will be used to discuss how to create "bookends" for the information about the person included in the book.

3. To write an introduction, work with students to come up with the name of the main character (MC), their job or position, and what they accomplished (e.g., *Louis Braille, a blind student, created the braille writing system. Katherine Johnson, a mathematician, helped save Apollo 13.*) Ask these questions and write student responses on the board:

    a. Who is the main character of the story?

    b. What was their job or position?

    c. What did they do that was so important?

4. To create a conclusion, work with students to restate the name of the MC and what they accomplished. Write responses on the board. Then add a sentence or phrase about why the accomplishment was so amazing, surprising, or important. Mention any awards the MC might have won (e.g., *Louis Braille changed the life of blind people everywhere when he created the braille alphabet. It's hard to believe he accomplished this feat when he was only 15 years old.*)

Many students, even in high school, struggle with writing multi-paragraph essays. They believe that a conclusion is nothing more than a restating of the introduction. This notion results in conclusions that don't serve their real purpose, which is to sum up the essence of what has been said and reinforce a theme or emphasize a point. Students sense the meaninglessness of conclusions that do nothing more than repeat what has already been said and are left feeling that the current writing assignment is yet another example of busywork.

Conclusions are important for everyday communication. They help us "seal the deal" when we make requests or try to persuade someone to action. They help us summarize our feelings on important topics. They bring clarification to conversations. What follows is a fun way to work on introductions and conclusions that focuses on verbal persuasion. Because it doesn't involve any writing, it is suitable for students of all ages and ability levels.

ACTIVITY

LESSON 6D: CASH FOR OUR CAUSE

Objectives:
Improve social communication; improve the ability to make requests, take perspective, and structure verbal interactions

Grade Level:
First and up

Time:
45 minutes

Directions

1. Share a few appropriate *Go Fund Me* campaign ideas with students and discuss the various reasons why someone might want to request money from others.

2. As a class, brainstorm different topics for a child-centric fundraising campaign, such as requesting capital for starting a business like opening a lemonade stand, funds to buy something important for the school, contributions for someone who needs an operation, donations to go on a band trip or participate in some other school-related activity the student couldn't afford otherwise, donations for other needy students, money for purely selfish reasons (like going on a vacation or buying video games).

3. Tell each student to come up with a reason for requesting money, decide on an amount needed, and design a short verbal pitch using the following format:

    a. Create an introduction stating why he or she wants the money and what he or she plans to do with it.

    b. Give three specific reasons why others should donate to his or her campaign.

    c. Provide a conclusion that restates what he or she wants but gives a little more incentive for encouraging others to donate. For instance, will the contributors get something in return? Will they help someone in need? How many people will benefit?

4. Each student shares his or her pitch with a small group of three or four students and peers provide suggestions for how to make the pitch better.

5. Each student revises his or her pitch and shares it with the class.

6. The class votes on the best pitches and the students who created the top three receive $20 of play money.

Book Talk, a similar activity, can be used to create short oral summaries for books. The lesson plan that follows provides a fun way to model how a short book summary might sound. Like the Cash for Our Cause activity, it helps young children to begin to understand the elements of a persuasive speech, an understanding which lays the foundation for later persuasive writing. Book Talk also contains the added benefit of encouraging peers to read books.

   Librarians often conduct what they call "Book Talks" by sharing short pitches for a variety of books to encourage student interest in new titles. Before beginning the activity that follows (which should be conducted over two class sessions), educators should model their own Book Talk by discussing several books they want to encourage students to read.

LESSON 6E: BOOK TALK

ACTIVITY

Directions

1. Plan a library visit and let students choose any book they like OR provide a selection of books.

2. Give students time to read the books or assign them as homework.

3. Type up a list of titles selected by students and authors with a scale of 1–5 printed next to each title so students can vote on how many stars they choose to give each book based on how interesting it sounds.

4. Students show the book they have selected to the class as they give a verbal summary of the book using the following guidelines:

    a. Tell the title, author, genre (picture book, biography, mystery).

    b. Give three reasons why they think their peers will like the book.

    c. Provide an exciting conclusion that makes peers want to read the book.

    d. Remind peers of the author and title so they can look for the book by name and tell them why they should give it a 5-star rating.

5. While students pitch their books, their peers rate them.

6. When all of the students have given their pitch, students circle their top three choices for books they may want to read.

7. The teacher tallies the top five books based on students' selections and shares the list of favorites with the class.

Objectives:
Improve the ability to create verbal summaries; improve the ability to persuade

Grade Level:
Second and up

Time:
Two 45-minute sessions

Practical reasons for repeating the author and title are built into the activity. To highlight the value of repetition, share with students a few appropriate infomercials and have them tally how many times a specific phrase, product name, or phone number is repeated. Discuss why these commercials repeat this information so often—so consumers remember the product name and want to buy it.

FROM FIRST TO FINAL DRAFTS: EDITING

The Editor's Toolbox in Figure 6.4 and Editor's Tools in Figure 6.5 may be incorporated at any point in the writing process. Full-size versions are available online, along with blank tools and a Tool Inventory List (including additional editing tools; see Figure 6.6). See the lesson plan that follows, entitled Build Your Toolbox. The instructor can modify which tools go into which student's toolbox so each student is working at his or her challenge level. Many students have no idea what to do when a teacher tells them to check their work. Giving them one specific task to complete at a time, along with a visual "tool," helps make this abstract concept more concrete and achievable.

For struggling learners and younger students, be selective about which tools to use and pick ones that are developmentally appropriate. A first grader might only check for capitals and final punctuation and stop at that, while second graders could also be required to check their spelling using the word lists provided on the storyboard. More advanced students might be expected to use a dictionary. Older elementary school students could add adjectives or phrases for descriptions and check for run-on sentences by circling every time the word AND is used. I tell students they can only use AND one time in a sentence to connect two independent clauses (clauses that could be individual sentences). If they have used too many ANDs, they must cross one out, end that clause with a period, and start the next clause (sentence) with a capital letter.

Many writers slip back and forth between past and present verb tense. Even professional authors have to check for consistency in verb tense. Summaries can be written in either past or present, but a student needs to choose one and stick with it. A valuable grammar exercise is to ask students to circle all of the verbs in their writing assignment and then change the verbs that don't fit the selected tense. Be aware that many students with learning challenges have difficulty understanding this concept. When asked to change the word *ran* to present tense, they might replace it with *walked* or *jogged*.

Middle school students are growing in their ability to understand the nuances of word choice and consequently should be demonstrating a greater use of synonyms to both replace overused and vague terms and to avoid repetition of words. This is a way to create cohesion while avoiding redundancy. For example, when writing about an important historical figure, students could create a list of alternative terms such as *George Washington, general, president, commander, hero, he, him.* For cohesion, they need to make sure that pronouns match the intended antecedents and that transition words are used to indicate shifts in time, place, and ideas. Students can be required to add a specified number of subordinating conjunctions *(because, before, after, while, although, when)* to written assignments to vary sentence length and complexity. Finally, students can read over their entire paper pretending to be a reader unfamiliar with the topic to check for clarity.

EDITOR'S TOOLBOX

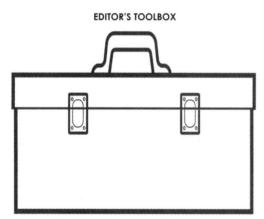

Figure 6.4. Editor's Toolbox. (© Carolee Dean.)

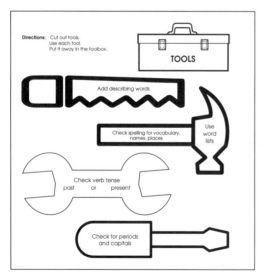

Figure 6.5. Editor's Tools. (© Carolee Dean.)

TOOL INVENTORY LIST

Directions: Teachers, circle the number beside the tools you want each student to use. Students, cut out the tools and glue them onto objects for your toolbox.

1	Check for capital letters and final punctuation.	8	Make sure pronouns clearly go with the person they are referring to.
2	Check spelling. Use the word lists to help.	9	Add transition words. See the list on your storyboard.
3	Add describing words or phrases.	10	Make complex sentences by adding words like *because, after, while, although,* and *when.*
4	Check verb tense: PAST or PRESENT.	11	Check for clarity. If someone else was reading your work, would it make sense?
5	Do a run-on sentence check by looking for overuse of AND.	12	
6	Find synonyms to replace overused and vague words.	13	
7	When talking about your main character, use other terms besides his or her name.	14	

Figure 6.6. Tool inventory list.

LESSON 6F: BUILD YOUR TOOLBOX

ACTIVITY

Directions

1. For each student, circle the numbers corresponding to the tools you want them to use on the Tool Inventory List.

2. Print out a copy of the empty tools.

3. Instruct students to cut out the tool descriptions you have circled and glue them onto the tools. Laminate the tools.

4. Print out the toolbox and laminate it.

5. The tools may be attached to the toolbox with Velcro.

6. Instruct students to go through their work using one tool at a time. When they finish with a tool, instruct them to put it away in the toolbox.

Objectives:
Improve editing, revision, and proofreading skills

Grade Level:
First and up

Time:
45 minutes

Many professional writers choose to turn off spelling and grammar check aids while drafting a story. They focus on content when building their first draft and then make multiple sweeps through a story or novel. The first time through, they might check for spelling and grammar. On subsequent edits, they may focus on the accuracy of the time-line or on making sentences more descriptive. Some authors who know they tend to over-use a particular word may search their document for that word to see where they can substitute another.

With this understanding of how professional authors work, encourage students to create first drafts of stories, summaries, and essays without spending too much time and effort worrying about grammar and spelling. They can always go back through their work to make spelling and grammar corrections, check punctuation, and to make sure the verb tense is consistent. For students whose spelling is so poor that they later have no idea what they have written, encourage them to use speech-to-print accessibility tools that will type out what they speak. Having students dictate to an instructor is often a useful accommodation.

FROM SUMMARIES TO ORIGINAL STUDENT STORIES

At this point in *Story Frames*, many commercially produced stories will have been shared with students and their plots discussed in detail. Students have examined the elements of stories and how they fit together, but they haven't learned how to create or put together these elements themselves. They've examined written *products*, but their work on the writing *process* has thus far focused on summary.

This process may seem straightforward. However, students may find it hard to generate story ideas, and students who have struggled with writing before may be so intimidated by the prospect of writing their own story that they are afraid to try. The lesson plans that follow include various approaches the instructor can use to not only provide support but to also make writing more fun and less stressful for students, such as:

- Introducing story writing using the "I do, we do, you do" progression

- Working with original fairy tales and spoofs to help students create their own "twisted tales"

- Using "random acts of writing"—such as Story Ad Libs or a roll of the dice—to generate ideas and build some levity into the process

The "I Do, We Do, You Do" Approach

Instructors can use the "I do, we do, you do" progression described previously to get students started on creating original stories. For the "I do" stage, the instructor can model how to use a blank storyboard to brainstorm an original story. For the "We do" stage, the class repeats this process. Finally, for the "You do" stage, each student is expected to use a blank storyboard to create her own story brainstorm, as well as to create keywords and vocabulary to go with each part of her story. She would then use this brainstorm to write sentences for each story element on the Plot Pages. Finally, she would use the Plot Pages to construct a complete story with added details and transitions. These steps are detailed in the lesson plan that follows. Expect it to take three sessions.

ACTIVITY	LESSON 6G: ORIGINAL STORY BRAINSTORM
Objectives: Improve story writing; increase sentence complexity; increase the use of new vocabulary terms; improve event sequencing **Time:** Three 45-minute sessions	**Directions** 1. Project the blank storyboard or create one on a whiteboard and then model quick drawing and writing keywords to go with an original story. 2. Use the blank storyboard and encourage the class or group to come up with ideas for each story element. 3. Give each student a blank storyboard and instruct each student to use Quick Draws and keywords to create an original story brainstorm. 4. Instruct students to use the storyboard to create sentences corresponding to each story element on the Plot Pages.

5. Have students use the Plot Pages along with transition words to write an original story.

6. Have students use the Editor's Toolbox to make edits.

7. Have students rewrite the story with the editorial changes.

Twisted Tales   Even after reading and analyzing multiple stories using *Story Frames*, students may find it difficult to make the leap to generating story ideas. It often helps to have another story to use as a guide. The following 3-day lesson plan uses traditional fairy tales to create original spoofs.

LESSON 6H: TWISTED TALES

Directions

1. Read a few traditional fairy tales to the class.

2. Read two or more of the fairy tale spoofs from the downloadable materials for this book.

3. As a class or small group, compare and contrast the spoof with the original story.

4. Use the Basic Storyboard or Complete Storyboard to brainstorm a spoof as a group.

5. Instruct students to use the Basic Storyboard or Complete Storyboard to brainstorm their own story spoof.

6. Use the Plot Pages to create sentences to go with each part of the story.

7. Write paragraphs for the beginning, middle, and end of the story, adding transition words.

8. Use the Editor's Toolbox to edit the story.

<table>
<tr><td>**ACTIVITY**</td></tr>
<tr><td>**Objectives:**
Improve story writing; increase sentence complexity; increase the use of new vocabulary terms; improve event sequencing</td></tr>
<tr><td>**Grade Level:**
Third and up</td></tr>
<tr><td>**Time:**
Three 45-minute sessions</td></tr>
</table>

Random Acts of Writing

Even with the level of support provided in the previous lesson plans, many struggling learners will still crumple their papers, put their heads on their desks, and state boldly, "I don't know what to write about." The writing process is still too intimidating, and they have already experienced so much failure with writing that they are afraid to attempt any writing task, even with a high level of support. For these students, and even for students without these challenges, it helps to take the seriousness out of the writing process and invite in some fun by providing experiences with Random Acts of Writing: Story Ad Libs and Dicey Stories.

Story Ad Libs   For the following activity, a fill-in-the-blank story template was created that resembles the commercial Mad Libs game, in which players work with a brief story that has one or more words missing from each sentence. In traditional Mad Libs, the blanks are labeled by part of speech—noun, adjective, and so on. One player views the incomplete story, prompts other players to supply the missing parts of speech, and writes their responses in the blanks. This player then reads the completed story aloud. *Story Frames* builds on this concept by having players supply story details. Some parts of the story will need to be added more intentionally, but the Story Ad Lib element gets students started. Figure 6.7 shows page 1 of the Story Ad Lib. The complete three-page Story Ad Lib template may be found in the downloadable resources.

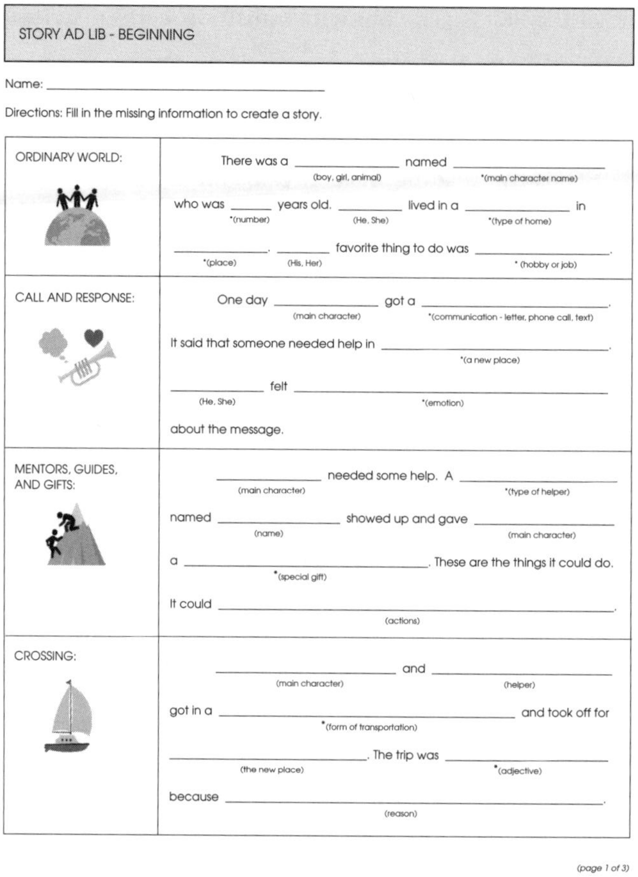

STORY AD LIB - BEGINNING

Name: ____________________

Directions: Fill in the missing information to create a story.

ORDINARY WORLD:	There was a ________ (boy, girl, animal) named ________ *(main character name) who was ____ *(number) years old. ________ (He, She) lived in a ________ *(type of home) in ________ *(place). ________ (His, Her) favorite thing to do was ________ * (hobby or job).
CALL AND RESPONSE:	One day ________ (main character) got a ________ *(communication - letter, phone call, text). It said that someone needed help in ________ *(a new place). ________ (He, She) felt ________ *(emotion) about the message.
MENTORS, GUIDES, AND GIFTS:	________ (main character) needed some help. A ________ *(type of helper) named ________ (name) showed up and gave ________ (main character) a ________ *(special gift). These are the things it could do. It could ________ (actions).
CROSSING:	________ (main character) and ________ (helper) got in a ________ *(form of transportation) and took off for ________ (the new place). The trip was ________ *(adjective) because ________ (reason).

(page 1 of 3)

Figure 6.7. Page 1 of Story Ad Lib.

ACTIVITY

Objectives:
Improve story writing

Grade Level:
First and up

Time:
40 minutes (20 minutes for Steps 1–3; 20 minutes for Step 4)

LESSON 61: STORY AD LIB

Directions

1. Complete the section for the Ordinary World by asking students to give verbal responses for each blank (character, type of home, location) without showing them the Story Ad Lib.
2. Complete the story elements for each section of the Story Ad Lib.
3. Read the Story Ad Lib to students. Fill in any missing information to complete the story.
4. If age-appropriate, give each student a blank Story Ad Lib and instruct them to create a story either with a partner or alone. Working with a partner results in a sillier story that includes the element of surprise because only the partner can see the prompts. Once all the mystery items are filled in, the students can work together or alone to complete the other missing information that is NOT designated by an asterisk.

The Story Ad Libs approach can help students create focused and structured stories. The following story, "Rainbow Magic Land," was created by Gigi, a second-grade student with dyslexia seen three times a week to work on decoding and spelling. She had high verbal skills but significant challenges in reading and writing. Nevertheless, she reported she often wrote stories at home on her own. When she told stories verbally, she tended to go off on tangents that were interesting and creative, but sometimes hard to follow. The Story Ad Lib exercise helped her stay focused on each story element. Because of her age and significant challenges with spelling, she dictated her responses for the Story Ad Lib.

Rainbow Magic Land

Beginning

There once was a girl named Rainbow. She was 19 years old. She lived in a castle in a cloud in Rainbow Magic Land. Her favorite things to do were dance, sing, travel, meet new people, solve problems, do gymnastics and create rainbows.

One day Rainbow got a royal letter. The Royal invitation looked like rainbows, rubies, and glitter. The thing was shaped like a heart shaped valentine sticker to go with it. It told her that a prince wanted to dance with her at a ball. She felt happy and scared and afraid and respected. She did want to go, but she needed to ask the queen if she could go.

Rainbow needed some help to get to the ball because the carriage couldn't get over the rainbow. A unicorn named Magic Sparklehorn showed up and gave Rainbow a rainbow magical dress. These are the things it could do. It could do her hair, match her mood with style and color, put on her makeup and provide necklaces and rainbow sparkles and crowns.

Rainbow and Sparkle got in a rainbow princess carriage and took off for the other palace on the other side of the world. It was a short trip because the rainbow was so magical it would take them only two seconds to get there.

Middle

When Rainbow and Sparkle arrived in Glitterland Magic land, the first thing they noticed was the prince. He was wearing a suit full of glitter. Next, they saw a servant carrying two crowns. She was ecstatic about getting that crown. She will do anything to get the rainbow crown. The people were pretty. They thought Glitterland was a magical place.

The prize was a rainbow crown. The problem was that the prince's mom didn't want him to get married. The plan was to be super nice to the queen. They felt excited about the plan.

Rainbow was giving the queen candy. She was making smores and putting on a magic show. Sparkle is flying with the queen and giving her a makeover. She wants her son to marry her. She gets to wear the crown during the ball, and she gets to dance with the prince.

Afterward, they went to the wedding store to think about what happened. She felt happy. She wanted a new gown for the wedding, but her luggage with the dress would not fit on the carriage.

End

Suddenly, she has to throw out her dress to the whole kingdom and one person will get to keep it.

It seemed like all hope was lost when she threw it out. Then something changed. The prince of Glitter caught the dress.

The biggest test happened when they had to walk all the way back to Glittertown with her luggage. Glittertown and Rainbow Magic Land needed a new name. The prince and princess came up with Rainbow Glitter Magic Land.

In the end, Rainbow got the rainbow crown. She learned that the prince was a life-saving person. She felt needed.

It is clear to see how Gigi's voice and personality shine through in this story despite the highly formulaic nature of the Ad Lib. At one point between the middle and end sections, the tangential quality of her storytelling started to take the action off in a different direction about the dress that was unrelated to the main action. Because of the highly structured nature of the Ad Lib, she returned to the main action of the story. At this point, the narrative started to feel like an unfocused chain where one action leads to another but does not necessarily fit in the sequence of beginning to end. Even so, her clever ideas and creativity are ever present throughout the story.

If more time had been spent on editing and refining, some shorter elements would have become complete paragraphs, and she could have worked on transitions between ideas, but a complete and polished story is not always the goal of instruction. When using *Story Frames*, sometimes the objective is to simply retell a story, sometimes to work on sentence or paragraph structure, and sometimes to focus on microstructure elements such as vocabulary and grammar.

Dicey Stories   For the Dicey Stories lesson plan, a chart of six options is created for each story element corresponding to the numbers 1–6 on the die. This list may be completed ahead of time by the instructor or created with the class providing suggestions. Students may pick one of the choices provided or roll the dice and choose items randomly. Students then use these random selections to brainstorm a story and create sentences for each story element. Even the most reluctant writers enjoy random and playful activities, especially if the story is written as a group, and they can use their silly ideas to play off of each other.

After creating an Ordinary World in this manner, the student may be ready to launch out on their own and complete the rest of the story brainstorm without using the dice and the choices provided. He may return to the dice options as desired and should be allowed to do this if he prefers. If a student says he does not "know" what to write, remind him this type of story process is about choosing rather than "knowing." Often choosing randomly helps this process along.

ACTIVITY

Objectives:
Improve story writing; increase sentence complexity; increase the use of new vocabulary terms; improve event sequencing

Grade Level:
First and up

Time:
45 minutes

LESSON 6J: DICEY STORIES

Directions

1. Create a chart with six options for each story element, either before the session or with the class. Alternately, use the options from the PowerPoint slide deck for Dicey Story Choices found in the online resources. Some story elements may require multiple charts. For instance, Figure 6.8 shows six different options each for setting, character, and action.

2. Roll the dice and use the selections to create one to three sentences to go with each story element.

3. For a group story, use the PowerPoint slides for the Dicey Story Builder to write one to three sentences as a group. Have students dictate their responses, and then type them onto PowerPoint slides, projecting them for the class to see.

4. Repeat the prior procedure for each story element.

5. Use the Editor's Toolbox to edit the story.

6. Select free images from the Internet to go with each slide. This is an excellent time to teach students about honoring copyrights and where to go to find free images. One good source is www.pixabay.com.

7. (Optional) Print the slides and bind them together so each student has a copy of the book.

For older students, after the experience of writing a story as a group, you may wish to upload the PowerPoint slides and instruct them to create their own stories alone or in pairs. These stories may be cut and pasted from the PowerPoint slides into a Word document.

This approach can be used with students across a wide range of ages, with or without disabilities. The following story excerpt is from "Quest for the Snow Sphere," a story completed during a group writing project spanning several weeks, led by myself and an occupational therapist (OT) with a group of 10 students ages 18–22. These young adults were

Directions: Roll the dice to choose 1) a main character, 2) what the main character is doing at the start of the story, and 3) a setting. Put these three things together to create an opening sentence.

MAIN CHARACTER

1	Teenager	4	Athlete
2	Prince or princess	5	Grandparent
3	Scientist	6	Animal

WHAT ARE THEY DOING?

1	Watching TV	4	Riding a bike
2	Cleaning	5	Sleeping
3	Cooking	6	Doing homework

SETTING

1	Trailer	4	Restaurant
2	House	5	Work
3	School	6	School

Figure 6.8. Sample Dicey Stories options.

involved in a community-based instruction program for students with significant cognitive challenges that focused on job training as well as communication skills and leisure activities. All students had low IQs, some were on the autism spectrum, and one had a traumatic brain injury. One young man did not communicate through speech but used a communication device with icons that he chose by activating a switch with his knee because he lacked fine motor control of his hands.

For the Dicey Stories activity, the students verbally created lists of choices that the OT typed into the computer. The young man described previously had dice rolling as a feature on his device, so his job was to make the final selections for the group. Once the selections were made, the students took turns dictating sentences that incorporated their selections. When they finished their story, the group went through the editing process, correcting punctuation and grammar with the therapists' assistance. Afterward, the group chose images from the Internet to go with the group story. Students who were able to do so took part in binding the books with equipment purchased for the community-based program. The teachers leading the program were in the process of setting up a workstation for various print-related activities, and the bookbinding experience provided valuable skill development.

Quest for the Snow Sphere

CBI Program
Students,
Ages 18–22:
Class Story

Crystal was a fifteen-year old girl who lived on a farm with her mom and dad in Texas. She was bored out of her mind because she hated taking care of cows and plowing the field. They lived in a triple-wide trailer and every time the wind blew it blew right through the house and knocked everything down. She had a special power. When her parents called her to do chores, she could make herself invisible.

One day it started to snow and it got very cold. The snow didn't stop until everything was covered in 8 feet of snow. The Ice Witch sent the snow storm because she didn't want the people to cross the bridge into her territory and find her Ice Cave. She had been sleeping underground in the cave for twenty-five years, but then she was awoken by the sound of tractors and she didn't want anybody to find her Magical Mystical Snowball Sphere. The Governor of Texas appeared on the family's home computer screen and asked Crystal to sneak into the ice cave and steal the Magical Mystical Snowball Sphere because he heard that she had the power to make herself invisible.

She said to the governor, "I can't!"

"Why not? We need you," replied the governor.

"Because I'm afraid that I'm going to be stuck in the storm and I can't get out of my house because of the snow."

"Don't worry. I'll send Glenda the Good Witch to help you. She will bring you red hot ruby slippers. What do you think of that?"

"How will the shoes help me?" asked Crystal.

The Governor said, "They're magic and they will melt anything your feet touch. But be careful, they'll burn everything in your path like a hot tamale."

"Do I get to keep the shoes when I'm done?"

"Only if the Magical Mystical Snowball Sphere is brought safely to me, and don't drop it and break it into pieces or the whole planet will be destroyed by storms. Earthquakes, tsunamis, hurricanes, F5 tornadoes, blizzards, firestorms, floods, and dust storms will all be unleashed from the sphere at once."

"Oh my! Isn't there somebody taller or stronger or hunkier or how about a weight lifting dude?"

This excerpt represents the Ordinary World and the Call and Response. The story, which goes on through all of the story elements, was inspired by *The Wizard of Oz* and contains some elements of a spoof. The teen voice becomes clear as the dialogue progresses. Each student took home a book at the end of the year.

I ran into one of the young ladies at a pizza restaurant 2 years after she graduated, and she told me that she still had the story we created as a group. "Do you remember that book we wrote?" she asked me.

I assured her that I did.

"I read it every day," was her reply.

It was a silly story, but still a memorable one. For this young lady, it became a keepsake and a treasure. The students worked on many social skills during the process, including turn-taking, perspective-taking, and working collaboratively.

TIPS FOR ONLINE LEARNING AND TELETHERAPY

The writing activities described in this chapter have been used successfully in teletherapy with a few simple modifications. Many of the downloadable resources, especially the PowerPoint slides, can easily be projected over the computer. Examples may be shown to students using the screen share feature of many online conferencing/communication programs. Zoom is a useful platform because it provides a whiteboard, allows for screen sharing, has tools for making notations on a variety of documents, and is encrypted for privacy. A Health Insurance Portability and Accountability

Act (HIPAA)–compliant form of Zoom is also available, but many other online platforms for class instruction or teletherapy could also be explored. Tips that teachers or teletherapists can try include the following:

1. Prior to the session, email all hands-on materials (Storyboards, Plot Pages) to the teletherapy monitor at the school or to the parent if the student is seen at home. Instruct them to print these and have them ready for student use.

2. Create files for students in DropBox, Google Docs, or Google Classroom and have them type directly onto the forms. Text boxes may need to be created.

3. Using the Whiteboard feature of Zoom, click on the image of a pen and model Quick Draws and picture noting directly on the whiteboard. If the annotate feature is being used, you may need to take screenshots to save student work. Another option is to open a blank PowerPoint presentation and use the Draw feature to save student Quick Draws.

4. When adding stick figures to a storyboard, display a blank storyboard using the screen share feature and then use the Annotate feature (also a pen) to model Quick Draws on the storyboard.

5. Share Word documents easily via the screen share feature of Zoom, then turn over control of the keyboard to the student via the remote control option and have the student type directly into the document. If you have concerns about computer security issues, you may prefer to have the student work in Google Docs. Also, at this writing, if the student is using a Chromebook, it may not interface with Zoom for remote control access.

6. Display the Editor's Toolbox via PowerPoint slides. See an example in the online resources in the PowerPoint for Online Instruction Tools.

7. When reviewing a student's writing, it is important to know what level of support she received and how many drafts she completed. Work samples should always be shared with parents and other professionals with this vital information included.

The section that follows describes in detail how *Story Frames* was used in teletherapy with an individual student.

TELETHERAPY CASE STUDY: ELIZABETH

Elizabeth was a fourth-grade student diagnosed with dyslexia who had significant spelling and reading challenges. Even so, she showed a keen interest in writing stories on her own and shared many of these stories during our sessions. She was seen four times a week after school by me in my capacity as an SLP and Certified Academic Language Practitioner specializing in dyslexia. The sessions were mostly conducted via teletherapy with occasional meetings in person. The last 5 minutes of most sessions were dedicated to narratives, listening to and analyzing stories, and sharing original stories Elizabeth had created. This proved to be an important motivation because much of the dyslexia work was tedious and challenging. It helped Elizabeth to understand what all of her hard work was for. It is beneficial to keep the big picture in mind and show students the purpose of this work—which in her case related directly to her love of writing.

Baseline: Original Story 1

Before *Story Frames* and narrative structure were introduced, Elizabeth shared the following story, "Flying with my Friends," that she had recently created on her own. The story has been typed exactly as she wrote it in her original version. It has not been edited for spelling or punctuation, and she received no adult support for writing or organizing her ideas. Words in parentheses were added later for clarity. At first glance, this writing sample may appear less sophisticated than the previous examples in this chapter, but it is actually much more advanced because the student received no outside direction, assistance, or structure. In addition, this writing was self-motivated rather than assigned.

Elizabeth's Original Story 1

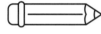

*Grade 4 (baseline before **Story Frames**)*

Flying with my Friends

One day Lusy and Emmaly wher (were) walking into the Forest and thay saw a pack of weird dragons And they thot that if thay got close anuthe (enough) to tuch (touch) one thay cold (could) Ride one and So thay walked close and closeer and thay looked ferce (for) the dragon thay want.

The nexed moning (next morning).,Emmaly do you want to see the dragons, Losy sed,,Sher (sure) Emma sed, Then thay sprinted of (off) and Thay went bake (back) to war (where) thay wher (were) then thay did not see them atall so then thay got Rilly wored (really worried) so thay looked all day For them and then Thay whent (went) back home and wen thay wher (were) at the hous thay saw ther dragon and got so happy

Then we finally get on them and thay wake up thay weht Krasy (went crazy) and then thay came down and they are nice to us so thay let as Rid them and we Ride and Ride and Ride. In till the sun gose done(goes down) the (then) we go home.

Losy was gone for so loge (long) That Emally was Feling (feeling) bad and so Emmaly and RoRo went to go Find them and thay Fond them Losy, cold (called) Emmaly, Losy anserd (answered) with wat do you want She replide (replied). I want you to cum bake home. She yeld Plesa. Cum home! Losy ses that She wil com home but she will have to go at Sepret (separate) times then (than) Emmaly. So. Emmaly left Losy was paking (packing) up and then Losy left.

The nexed (next) day thay are all so happy. Thay Just fond out That The dragons wher at ther houes to look For them to so Losy and COLO left to go on a Ride because she was mad at Emmaly. So Emmaly and Losy had a fight then Emmaly sed I am not your Frend eny more! And Losy goot Sad. And the dragons wher canfused (confused).

Then Thay Thot (thought) that if thay went on a Ride That wold coll them done (that would calm them down) so thay went on a Ride ner the montons (mountains). And thay did.

In this initial story, cause and effect is clear at times, but not always. Characters have emotional responses, but the reasons for them are not always clear. The story includes problems (the dragons are gone; a friend is gone for a long time.) It also includes attempts to solve problems (they look for the dragons; Emily calls out for Lucy), which implies planning or at least goal-directed behavior. One event led to another for the most part, but there was no clear thread connecting the beginning to the end. Much of the story felt like a reactive sequence (Hedberg & Westby, 1993) or an unfocused chain (Applebee, 1978).

Incorporating *Story Frames*: Story 2, First Draft

Shortly thereafter, I introduced the story elements for *Story Frames* and read aloud *Six Dots*, which we discussed in terms of the 12 elements. Elizabeth then used a storyboard to retell the story. The following week, Elizabeth shared the story that follows, "Lost far far Awa (Away)!" that she had created completely on her own at home, of her own initiative, incorporating nearly all of the *Story Frames* elements. Spelling is still a challenge, but the complexity of the storytelling has grown exponentially, and now the sequence of cause and effect events builds to a climax.

Grade 4 (after introduction to **Story Frames**)

Elizabeth's Original Story 2

Lost far far Awa (Away)!

Ther was a boy named Rory and Rory was living with his mom and Dad and then one day we had in erth crak (earth quake) his mom wus criying and then his Fother, sed stay thayr the Fier Fiters (fire fighters) will come and get you, so thay left Rory and thay noked (knocked) over a cando (candle) and it started a Fier and Rory was Skard . . .

And so the Fierfighers came and got the Fier away. So the Rory got skard (scared) and he Got adopted By one ove the Fier Fiters so he adopted hem so thae thay had a good time.

But then The Rory Relised (realized) that was not his Rell (real) his dad so he had a Fight with his dad and he went to his tree hows.

And so the dad fellt bad so he coled (called) The pilese (police) and the pilese sed thay cold triy to Find his mom and dad and Thay did . . .

So when the Rory Fond out he was so happy! He cold hardly belef (believe) it and the step dad was sad. And so the step dad that (said) that if he throw a party he wold gane Roreys trust so he set a partty.

And Finaly He saw them he was so exited (excited) but When he saw them Thay wher vary mean to Him and 3 weacks pased (weeks passed) and he thot that Thay did not like him eny more so he got rilly said (really sad) and He was so lost. So he Whent to his bed rome (room) and sat and thot (thought).

And he Finaly know (knew) That he did not belog (belong) with his rell parance (real parents). So He told them that he did not want to Be with Them he wanted to Be with is Step dad So he left and his Reall parents wher (were) so happy That he was leaving. And Rory whent back to his step dad and lived a vary log (long) life.

Notice how the new story contains a clear initiating event that creates a situation that builds from one event to another to a climax. The problems are clear. Although it is the adult that solves the initial problem and goes to the police to find the missing parents, the planning is more transparent. It is the child at the end, though, who makes the decision to tell his parents that he wants to live with the stepdad (adoptive father). The obstacles that arise lead to new actions and reactions, and thus the narrative has many of the elements of a Complex Episode. This story has a greater sense of resolution than the first story and the emotional content is much deeper. Reasons for emotional responses are also clearer, though not completely explained.

This story might even be described as an interactive episode, the latest stage in Hedberg and Westby's levels of narrative development, with one character influencing the other. Figure 6.9 shows a page from Elizabeth's original story and artwork. Considering that this story is a first draft created with no adult direction or support, her progress is clearly evident. She quickly internalized the story elements and raised the level of her writing in the process.

Figure 6.9. Elizabeth's original story and artwork.

Editing: Story 2, Final Draft

Next, I typed Elizabeth's story into a Pages document, and using the Zoom screen share feature, she was able to edit her work with support. Using the tools from the Editor's Toolbox displayed via PowerPoint slides, she first corrected spelling errors using the spell check feature of Pages, working on one paragraph at a time. She was given extra assistance for words that spell check did not accurately detect, but some spelling errors persisted, as is typical of her age.

Next, she worked on punctuation and capitalization, with the cue to look for the overuse of the word "and." She was instructed to choose which "and" to delete to more clearly end one sentence and begin another. By the end of the editing process, conducted in short segments over several days, she was using this strategy independently. I also gave her a mini-lesson on the use of quotation marks. Finally, for the third step in the editing process, Elizabeth added descriptions.

Each of these steps required her to reread the paragraph she had written, thus working on reading in conjunction with writing. She showed enthusiasm for this process as she watched her story improve and expand. Her edited story follows. Though her work still has some errors, it has been elevated to a much higher level through the editing process.

Lost Far Far Away!

By Elizabeth

There was a boy named Rory and Rory was four. Rory was vary sweet. Rory was living with his mom and dad in a brick house. Then one day he had a loud earth quake! His mom was crying and then his Father, said, "Stay here the fire fighters will come and get you."

So they left Rory and they nocked over a candle stick. It started a big fire and Rory was scared . . .

The firefighters came and got the fire away. So then Rory got scared because he was not with his mom and dad. When three weeks passed he got adopted by one of the fire-fighters. They went to the zoo. They also went to the museum. Last but not least they went to the bowling alley. It was the first day he go him and he wanted it to be special. They had a really good time.

When it was his fifteenth birthday his friends started questioning him about why do you and your dad look nothing alike. Rory realized that was not his real his dad so he had a fight with his dad and he went to his tree hows because they started talking really mean to each other.

Then the dad felt bad so he called the police. The police sed they cold try to find his mom and dad and they did! So when the Rory Fond out he was so happy! He cold hardly believe it and the adopted dad was sad. So the adopted dad thot that if he throw a party he wold gain Rory's trust so he set a party.

Finally he saw them he was so exited but when he saw them they were vary mean to him. Three weeks passed and he thot that they did not like him any more so he got really said and he was so lost. So he went to his bed room and sat and thot.

He finally know that he did not belong with his reel parents. So he told them that he did not want to be with them. He wanted to be with his adopted dad.So he left and his real parents were so happy that he was leaving. Rory went back to his adopted dad and lived a vary long life.

The End

It should be noted that there are more sophisticated spell check programs available that lead to even greater independence for students, such as *Co:Writer Universal* by Don Johnson Incorporated. This resource offers word prediction, a topic dictionary, and a text-to-speech feature that will read what a student has written aloud for support during the writing process. This same feature may be used at the completion of writing to review one's work. The spell check feature is more keenly tuned to picking up the type of errors that struggling writers make. These errors are often misinterpreted by traditional spell check methods.

Storyboarding and Summarizing: *Emmanuel's Dream*

Finally, I read aloud the picture book *Emmanuel's Dream: The True Story of Emmanuel Ofosu Yeboah* (Thompson, 2015) to Elizabeth. It is the true story of Emmanuel Ofosu Yeboah, a young man with one leg who rode a bicycle nearly 400 miles around Ghana to raise awareness about people with disabilities. Elizabeth quick-drew pictures to go with the story using the method for picture noting outlined by Ukrainetz (1998). She then worked with me to determine which pictures should go with each story element, and then reproduced these on a storyboard previously emailed to her family. Using the storyboard and keywords, she next created sentences for each part of the story and wrote these on the Plot Pages. Figure 6.10 shows her progression from Quick Draw to Storyboard to Plot Pages. Note that she has shifted from print to cursive, which is a key feature of the dyslexia remediation program used in therapy. It should also be noted that she chose "Elizabeth" as a pseudonym and was experimenting with the spelling of the name on the Quick Draw page. The sequence of the Quick Draw items shows some challenges with spatial perception that was remedied in subsequent sessions with other stories.

Although her original stories were quite colorful, Elizabeth's teacher reported that she had difficulty summarizing nonfiction articles for class. As a result, we started reading short biographies from *Goodnight Stories for Rebel Girls–2* by Elena Favilli and Francesca

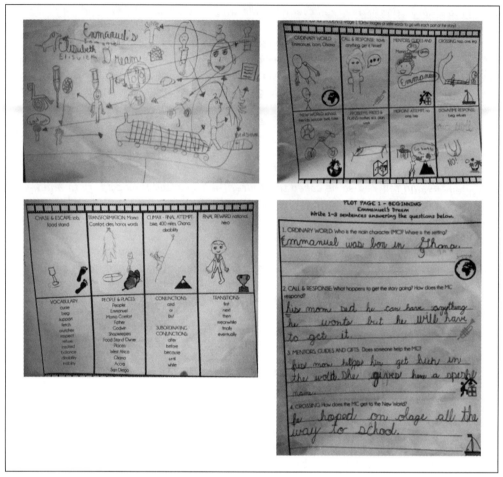

Figure 6.10.   Elizabeth's storyboard for *Emmanuel's Dream: The True Story of Emmanuel Ofosu Yeboah* (Thompson, 2015).

Cavallo (2017). Each story is only about two pages long and features a woman who has made a positive contribution to science, history, art, or social justice. A similar text that I have used with boys is *Stories for Boys Who Dare to Be Different: True Tales of Amazing Boys Who Changed the World Without Killing Dragons* by Ben Brooks (2018). What I really appreciate about this book is that although it includes famous figures like Louis Braille and Confucius, it also celebrates lesser-known heroes, like Favio Chávez, a music teacher who helped impoverished children in Paraguay create instruments out of trash, and a boy who grew out his hair to donate it to people with cancer.

After reading an excerpt from *Goodnight Stories for Rebel Girls*, Elizabeth was instructed to provide what we called the Big 5:

- One introductory sentence stating who the story was about and why that person was important

- Three supporting sentences including relevant details

- One concluding sentence mentioning a recognition/award or another interesting observation about the person

This activity is similar to the previous Book Talk lesson plan. Sometimes these summaries were written, but most of the time they were oral. Because of the oral nature and because the stories were so short, we were able to complete several in short order (one a day at the end of our sessions). The frequency and repetitive nature of the activity helped to solidify the concept of basic paragraph structure with an introduction, supporting details, and conclusion.

We used the same Big 5 strategy to write thank you letters, a practical and authentic literacy activity. Elizabeth stated who she was thanking and why, three specific reasons she was grateful, and a concluding statement such as, "I hope to see you soon." The carryover of the strategy helped to solidify the concept of the Big 5 and highlight its practical value. Prior to this, Elizabeth's thank-you notes were vague and repetitive—*Thank you so very, very much* was a common and repeated statement.

Stories like *Six Dots* and *Emmanuel's Dream* are powerful not only because they contain detailed illustrations and beautifully written narratives, but because they show the struggles of real children with disabilities and how they overcame them. These true-life heroes remind us that obstacles may stand in the way of our dreams, but they don't prevent us from reaching them—they merely help us shape our vision.

CELEBRATING STUDENT WRITING

A great way to celebrate student writing is to compile a book of student stories at the end of the year. Students are more invested in the editing and rewriting process when they know their stories will be celebrated and read by others. One year when there was a moratorium on field trips because of the cost of buses, we were able to take a group of middle schoolers on an excursion by walking to a nearby elementary school. The older students read the stories they had created for the younger ones. We stopped at a park on the way back, and parents bought pizza for a group picnic. Many sessions were spent rehearsing the stories and practicing to read them aloud, which had a practical purpose because these teens were preparing to read to younger children. It was a prime opportunity to practice reading fluency. Knowing their stories needed to be appropriate for a younger audience also helped to curb some of the violent themes that often appear in the narratives of adolescents.

Although most libraries offer summer reading incentives, students do not always take advantage of them. Providing a book to take home for the summer gives students additional reading opportunities and something to cherish.

Stories written by students seen via teletherapy can be emailed to parents for printing. Elizabeth enjoyed illustrating her stories. One of the stories she typed during therapy was sent home with space left on each page for her illustrations, which she worked on after the writing of the story was completed.

CONCLUSION: HELPING ALL STUDENTS BECOME WRITERS

This chapter illustrated how to use *Story Frames* and keyword lists to create sentences that can then be used for writing paragraphs and summaries. Engaging activities for creating original stories were also explored. Specific editing strategies were discussed. Many activities for inspiring reluctant writers were provided. Even with the supports outlined in this chapter, some students may still feel intimidated by the prospect of writing something as long and complicated as a story. Chapter 10 focuses on poetry and explores many simple poetry formats useful for writing about a story. These activities may be a more appropriate starting place for younger students and students with significant academic challenges, as well as those who have experienced extensive writing failure. They are much shorter projects, but they still require a student to demonstrate a thorough understanding of a story.

The work of the young authors shared in this chapter and the chapters that follow remind us how essential it is to fan the flames of creativity with all students, but especially with those who struggle with literacy.

From Story Writing to Expository Writing

Bridging the Gap With Narrative Nonfiction

7

Other types of genre writing beyond the narrative are expected of even very young children. The Common Core State Standards (CCSS) require children as young as kindergarten and first grade to demonstrate an understanding of persuasion by stating an opinion and to develop exposition by sharing information specific to a topic.

How these abilities typically develop is summed up in Table 7.1, Genre Development in Writing, which was presented at the 2016 International Dyslexia Association Conference in Orlando, Florida by Gary Troia. Troia covered the expectations at various grade levels for writing in the genres of narrative, persuasive, and expository text.

The narrative nonfiction picture books outlined in the downloadable resources for this book follow narrative text structure but also include many informational text features such as glossaries, bibliographies, timelines, and well-researched facts. Because of these shared features, these types of narratives may provide a bridge to reading informational text and eventually to writing expository essays.

WHAT THE EVIDENCE SAYS

Some authors feel that the delineations between narrative and expository writing are not as clear as previously believed. An expository essay may have many similarities to a narrative, but it also contains differences with distinctions that are important for a student to understand. Petersen and Petersen (2016) discuss these similarities in an article in *Perspectives of the ASHA Special Interest Groups* entitled "Re-Conceptualizing Expository Language as Narration." In contrast to others who view the two skills as independent, these authors believe they exist on a continuum. They point out apparent differences. Narrative writing focuses on describing a sequence of events on a timeline, while expository writing is objective, contains more content area vocabulary, and includes longer and more complex sentences. The authors also highlight similarities, including links between causes and effects and the need to decide which details to include and which to leave out. In their article, Petersen and Petersen show examples of how descriptions in specific narratives could also be used in expository writing. They state:

> It is important to recognize just how much information is embedded in model narratives, and just how similar the language complexity is between a model narrative intervention story and a parallel expository passage. It is generally the same language, just organized differently. (p. 114)

They were referring to specific types of stories used in a narrative intervention, so it is important not to overgeneralize their statement to all narratives, but they also point out that the intention of a narrative and a piece of expository writing can be similar. Both

DOWNLOADABLE RESOURCES:

Keep these resources on hand for teaching the Chapter 7 lessons and activities.

- Lesson 7A, Noun Phrase Titles: N/A
- Lesson 7B, What's My Text Type? What's My Text Type chart
- Lesson 7C, Expository Writing—Problem and Solution: Expository Essay Brainstorm; Transition Word list
- Lesson 7D, Compare and Contrast Essay Comparing Narrative Nonfiction to Informational Text: Key Features worksheet; Transition Word list
- Lesson 7E, Letter to the Author: N/A

Table 7.1. Genre development in writing

Grades	Narrative	Persuasive	Expository
K–1	Proto-narratives (heaps of actions or chains of cause and effect sequences)	Simple statements of opinion on a subject, perhaps with reasons	Simple expressions of topic-related information
2–3	True narratives with simple episodic structure	Opinions with reasons (mostly experiential)	Mostly list-oriented facts and minimal details based on experience and some source materials
4–6	Elaborated episode structure (goals and plans, coordinated setting, plot, and character traits) with somewhat more literate language style	Opinions with reasons (experiential, emotional, and minimal factual/logical) though often no markers of negotiation (counter-arguments)	Facts and details organized around major themes/qualities (marked in text) based more on source materials
7–12	Sequential, interactive, and nested episodes with multiple characters, competing goals, and figurative language	True persuasion with factual/logical appeals that are related and focused with supporting data and counterarguments	Relationships between themes/qualities are elaborated and information is based on vetted sources with citations

From Troia, G. A. (2016, October). Learning progressions for writing genres and instructional supports for students with LD/dyslexia. In G. A. Troia (Chair), *Development, assessment, and instruction of writing skills in children with and without learning disabilities.* Symposium conducted at the meeting of the International Dyslexia Association, Orlando, Florida; reprinted by permission.

can have the aim of informing, explaining, persuading, or even arguing a point. Lesley Roessing further explores the connection between narrative and expository text in Chapter 13, where she discusses memoir writing as a bridge between narrative and expository texts.

One emphasis of the CCSS is the sequential, detail-oriented writing needed for argumentative and informative essays, but even these standards hint at the connection between narrative and expository writing. In addition to writing standards linked specifically to narratives, the CCSS also outline writing standards for history/social studies, science, and technical subjects. In Grades 6–12, students are required to not only write informative and explanatory texts on these subjects but also "narrate" them as they might do for a commentary or a story.

It is still important to emphasize the differences between narration and exposition. Uppermost is the need to decide which details to include in a piece of exposition versus a story. It is vital that students understand how these details differ between genres.

Using Similar Strategies Across Genres

Pictography is a strategy discussed at length in Chapter 1, which was first described by Ukrainetz (1998) as a narrative representation tool focused on teaching students to use stick drawings as a quick and easy way to recall the action of a story. In 2019, Ukrainetz further developed the concept of pictography to use with students in a strategy she called "Sketch and Speak" as a note-taking aid for understanding and remembering expository text. In her study, students in Grades 4–6 with language-related learning disabilities were seen one-on-one or in small groups of two. They first listened to information read aloud from an expository text and then discussed with a speech-language pathologist (SLP) the most important ideas and where that information should be recorded on a note-taking sheet with categories of information already specified. The SLP read the selection aloud a second time, stopping frequently to prompt the student to consolidate the information in the paragraphs into "quick and easy" sketches. After each sketch, the student reconstructed the main idea of that section into a fully formed oral sentence. At the end of the session, the student created a detailed oral report of the information based on all of the sketches.

During the second session, the students started where they left off with a complete oral summary of their sketches (without referring back to the expository text). Then they went back, sketch by sketch, first creating a sentence orally, then reducing their oral sentence into a more traditional bullet style written note, and then finally using the bulleted note to once again restate the full sentence orally. When finished with their bulleted notes, students went back through their notes to give a full summary one more time. Independent note taking and oral summaries improved over just six 30-minute sessions. A strength of the study was the amount of time spent on oral rehearsal as well as the focus on the executive function strategies of preview and review, and working with the whole, then the parts, then the whole when constructing oral reports. Although the study did not emphasize prior training in pictography, it is easy to see how using a strategy familiar to the student in his or her work with narratives would help to provide a foundation for using a similar strategy for expository text.

Using Strategy Instruction and Genre Study to Improve Expository Writing

Shen and Troia (2018) reviewed two evidence-based approaches (Hayes, 1996) that have shown success in improving the expository writing of students with learning disabilities. The first was Hayes' Strategy Instruction, which focuses on cognition and motivation by providing specific strategies and teaching students self-regulation through building executive function skills in areas like goal setting and self-monitoring. The second was Russell's Genre Study, which stresses context and views "genre" as a structure that changes based on context. During Genre Study, students take part in multiple literacy activities to more deeply explore a genre. They learn characteristics specific to a genre and which elements to watch for to determine genre type. Both approaches lead students step-by-step through the process of planning, drafting, revising, editing, and hopefully publishing their work by sharing it in an authentic way. Both also include teacher modeling, scaffolding, collaboration, and independent practice similar to the "I do, we do, you do" strategies (Archer & Hughes, 2010).

Shen and Troia discuss the numerous challenges students with learning differences face when writing expository text due to factors including limited vocabulary, struggles with both generating and organizing ideas, and weaknesses in foundational skills like spelling, grammar, and sentence structures. They often view themselves as less capable writers. Because time allocated for writing instruction is often limited and students with learning disabilities need even more practice and strategic instruction than their peers, the authors recommend connecting writing to the curriculum to reinforce curricular concepts. Teachers should provide enough support to make writing a positive experience and, whenever possible, provide choices for topic selection so that students can tap into their personal interests and background knowledge. The authors also stress the importance of writing for a real audience as opposed to an imaginary one. Worse, of course, would be completing writing assignments unrelated to any meaningful context for no audience at all. See the Letter to the Author lesson plan at the end of this chapter for an example of a highly engaging authentic writing activity conducted with a group of high school students with significant learning disabilities.

Understanding the Importance of Text Structure Knowledge

Hennessy (2021) in her book, *The Reading Comprehension Blueprint: Helping Students Make Meaning from Text*, dedicates an entire chapter to text structures because of the powerful role that understanding the structural features of text plays in comprehension. Many skilled readers seem to acquire this skill naturally, which helps them to remember details, organize patterns, and process information, as well as to make predictions about what is coming next. Understanding the macrostructure of narrative and how it differs from persuasive or expository text (and its various subtypes) makes it easier to search a text for key information and understand how the parts relate to the whole.

Hennessy outlines the five main types of expository/informational text (description, chronological sequence, compare and contrast, problem and solution, cause and effect) first discussed by Meyer (1985; as cited in Hennessy, 2021). Based on these types, Hennessy created a Graphic Summary of Foundational Components of Instruction for Teaching Informational Text, found in Figure 7.1, which includes characteristics of the text type,

Type of text	Characteristics of text	Signal words for reading, discussion, and writing	Key questions	Visual representations
Description	Person, place, thing, or idea being described and how it is described	For example, such as, characteristics (look, sound, feel like)	Who or what is being described? What is included in this description?	
Chronological sequence	The order of events/steps in a process	Before, during, after, as soon as, first, second, next, then, initially, afterward, finally	What is happening? In what order? Does the order matter? Can it be changed?	First → Then → Next
Compare and contrast	How two or more things are alike (compare) or different (contrast)	Same, as well as, similar, in common, different, although, however, on the other hand, in comparison, either/or	What is being compared? In what ways are they alike? How are they different?	
Problem and solution	What is wrong (problem) and how to fix it (solution)	Because, resolved, result, so that, consequently	What is the problem? Why is it a problem? What is being done? Does it work?	Problem → Who or what; Solution → Possible solutions → Final solution
Cause and effect	How or why an event happened (cause) and what resulted from event (effect)	Because, since, as a result of, was caused by, led to, therefore, when/then, if/then	What happened? Why did it happen? What caused it to happen? What is affected?	Cause Effect

Figure 7.1. Graphic summary of foundational components of instruction for teaching informational text. (Reprinted from Hennessy, N. L. [2021]. *The reading comprehension blueprint: Helping students make meaning from text* [p. 144]. Baltimore, MD: Paul H. Brookes Publishing Co.)

signal words, key questions to ask, and a visual representation to help students readily identify the type. She also mentions argumentation (pro/con essays), which is not listed on her chart but is a structure often explored in school.

It can be difficult for students to tell the difference between these various types of informational text and comprehend the information they contain for several reasons (Hennessy 2021). These include having little or no background knowledge of the content, encountering text that is dense and filled with unfamiliar terms, struggling with complex sentence structures, coping with abstract ideas, and finding more than one type in a reading passage. Hennessy highlights the importance of teaching students the characteristics of various text types and providing opportunities to identify those characteristics as a way to improve text comprehension: "Knowing whether an author is describing, comparing, linking causes and effects or problems and solutions, or sequencing steps or events is critical to the construction of meaning" (p. 134). Understanding the structure also helps students determine the author's purpose.

Hennessy suggests teaching text structures one at a time, starting with description and chronological sequence, then compare and contrast, because it happens to be the structure taught most often, and finally delving into problem and solution, and cause and effect, which are often confused but can be tackled with even young children (second grade) if taught carefully and explicitly. She recommends initially using model texts that incorporate only one text structure. After gaining proficiency with each structure individually, students are then ready to tackle texts that contain multiple structures.

It is interesting to note how the various expository text structures parallel the progression of narrative development found in children's oral narratives outlined in Chapter 4. See the comparisons found in Table 7.2, which highlights the similarities between the stages of narrative development (Hedberg & Westby, 1993; Westby, 2012) and the various expository text structures. These are further explained as follows.

1. Description: In the preschool years, a child's earliest attempts at producing a narrative involve *isolated descriptions* and *descriptive sequences*.

2. Chronological sequence: In the later preschool years, children produce loosely connected *action sequences* in their narratives. Events may occur on a timeline, but with no cause and effect.

3. Compare and contrast: Although not directly tied to the narrative sequence outlined by Hedberg and Westby (1993) and Westby (2012), the notion of *compare and contrast*

Table 7.2. Similarities in the development of expository text and oral narratives

Expository text	Oral narratives
Description	Isolated descriptions Descriptive sequences
Chronological sequence	Action sequences: Events may occur on a timeline but with no cause and effect.
Compare and contrast	Not tied to narrative sequence but present in the concept of hero/villain, Ordinary World/New World, and so forth.
Cause and effect	Reactive sequence: Cause and effect is reactionary. Abbreviated episode: Stronger sense of goal-directed behavior.
Problem and solution	Complete episode: Planning as a result of problem solving and solution-oriented behavior Complex episode: Obstacles arise to block characters' attempt to find solutions and create more problems.
Argumentative	Interactive episode: Stories are told from multiple points of view and take more than one perspective.

Sources: Hedberg and Westby (1993) and Westby (2012).

emerges with the idea of heroes and villains, the Ordinary World and the New World, plans that succeed or fail, good and bad consequences, and the reactions to those events, people, and consequences.

4. Cause and effect: In the later preschool years, the *reactive sequence* is based on cause and effect but is reactionary and not yet purposeful. The principle of "effect" emerges as the child begins to include limited direct consequences in a story, such as a character reacting to an initiating event. In the early elementary years, the *abbreviated episode* includes a stronger sense of goal-directed behavior, but it may still only be implied. There may be a reaction to a consequence and a clearer conclusion, which shows an even greater understanding of the relationship between cause and effect.

5. Problem and solution: With the development of the *complete episode*, planning becomes more purposeful and is often the result of problem solving and generating solutions. Events move toward a conclusion as problems and solutions become more defined and characters strive to either solve a problem or achieve a prize or goal. In the late elementary years, within the *complex episode*, obstacles arise to block a character's attempt to reach a goal and find a solution, while problems become even more prominent in storytelling.

6. Argument: In the *interactive episode* stage of narrative development, which begins in the late elementary years and develops more fully in adolescence, a student acquires the ability to tell stories from multiple points of view and take more than one perspective. It is this ability to take more than one perspective that allows a student to see both sides of an issue and prepares the adolescent to undertake a pro/con argument.

One way to bridge the gap between stories and expository text is to explore the research that authors conduct to write their books. Even fiction authors typically carry out extensive research. This is often reflected in author notes and bibliographies.

For my young adult novel, *Take Me There* (Dean, 2010), the story of a 17-year-old boy who goes looking for his father who is in prison in Texas, I researched both sides of capital punishment, including interviewing a man who had served 11 years on death row and was ultimately exonerated when it was revealed that someone else had confessed to the murder for which he had been convicted. I also visited the Texas Prison Museum in Huntsville and interviewed Jim Willett, the curator and former warden who personally oversaw the executions of dozens of inmates. I read his book, *Warden: Texas Prison Life and Death from the Inside Out* (Willett & Rozelle, 2005), and he shared with me numerous photos and stories about life at The Wall. I wrote a debate scene that I ultimately omitted from the book but have shared with students. When works of fiction cover controversial topics, one connection between narrative and expository text is to have students create a scene where two characters debate a topic. We often see these types of scenes played out in movies and TV shows.

In 2012, I organized a panel for the YALSA (Young Adult Library Services Association) Young Adult Services Symposium entitled: *A Matter of Facts and Fiction: Giving Teens a Research Edge through YA Author Panels.* I, along with four other young adult (YA) authors, shared a pilot program where we went to high schools to talk to teenagers about research strategies for writing both fiction and nonfiction. The purpose was to get teens excited about research and inspire teachers to link YA fiction with curriculum goals and objectives in expository writing. Vaunda Micheaux Nelson, a former librarian, winner of the Coretta Scott King Author Award, and one of the speakers on the panel, is also a picture book author whose *Bad News for Outlaws: The Remarkable Life of Bass Reeves, Deputy U.S. Marshal* (2009) appears in *Story Frames*.

Supporting the Subskills Needed for Expository Writing

Genre study and text structure help students understand the macrostructure of text, but to craft a piece of expository writing they also need a host of skills in the microstructure, the basic building blocks of words and sentences. These range from the physical act of writing or typing to the cognitive skills required for planning and completing a draft. Hebert, Kearns, Hayes, Basiz, and Cooper (2018) suggest that for struggling students, providing ideas and topics for expository writing along with target vocabulary with correct spellings already included helps to lighten the "cognitive load" (p. 858) so students can focus their energies on the executive function skill of organizing the information to fit the text structure specified (whether it be description, compare and contrast, sequence, cause and effect, or problem and solution). The focus of working memory then shifts from remembering spelling patterns and generating ideas to goal setting and planning. Lesson plans in this chapter incorporate key word lists to support student writing.

Literate language, necessary for both narrative and expository writing, is commonly thought of as the language of literacy, though it starts well before the school years. According to Benson (2009), literate language contains more sophisticated vocabulary, abstract concepts, and complex sentence structures compared to the more common/concrete vocabulary and simple sentence structure of oral language. Oral language and literate language are interrelated, though, and may be better defined in terms of formal versus informal. There is crossover. Formal language may appear in young children's oral discourse, including their social–symbolic play, and informal language may be appropriate for writing for specific subjects and certain genres. These situations depend more on the context than the avenue of delivery (writing versus speech).

Benson lists several linguistic forms common to literate language including mental verbs (*think, decide, know, wish*) and linguistic verbs (*say, yell, ask*). Coordinating conjunctions found in literate language include *but, so, yet,* on Benson's list, but excluded *and* (as well as *and then*), which are common in oral language but tend to be overused in children's written language. The use of subordinating conjunctions (*because, before, after, while*), adverbs (*quickly, slowly, soon*), and elaborated noun phrases are also hallmarks of literate language, according to Benson.

To determine how often a child is using these structures, Benson describes how researchers analyze oral narrative discourse samples by tallying the number of literate language features used and dividing that number by the number of communication units (C-units). That analysis may be beyond the scope of what many teachers or SLPs want to undertake for progress monitoring, but analyzing a piece of writing or a story retell by tallying the total number of words, and also calculating the number of conjunctions and elaborated noun phrases utilized, could streamline the process. Benson reports that growth in language development as well as prediction of language impairment is correlated with the use of conjunctions plus mental/linguistic verbs in preschool oral language samples, while the use of conjunctions plus elaborated noun phrases was more highly correlated with the oral language proficiency of 7- to 10-year-olds.

Elaborated noun phrases include the use of modifiers coming before the noun (the big, bad wolf) and qualifiers coming after the noun *(The Boy in the Striped Pajamas* [Boyne, 2006]; *The Girl Who Drank the Moon* [Barnhill, 2016]; *My Friend Flicka* [O'Hara, 1941]). Expanded noun phrases make excellent book titles, as evidenced by the previous examples. Furthermore, a student's ability to understand a story well enough to encapsulate it in a new title is a good measure of comprehension. Questions including this type of device are frequently found on high stakes tests. See the Noun Phrase Titles lesson plan that follows for a deeper exploration of this concept.

ACTIVITY	**LESSON 7A: NOUN PHRASE TITLES**

Objective:
Improve use of relative clauses and prepositional phrases for noun phrase expansion

Grade Level:
First and up

Time: 30 minutes

Directions

1. Share with the class book titles that incorporate relative clauses, such as *The Girl Who Drank the Moon* by Kelly Barnhill, and prepositional phrases, such as *The Boy in the Striped Pajamas* by John Boyne, and appositives, such as *Let 'er Buck! George Fletcher, The People's Champion* by Vaunda Micheaux Nelson (2019).

2. Discuss as a class how to invent a new title for a picture book, chapter book, or novel by using a relative clause or prepositional phrase. Write the new title options on the board and vote on a class favorite. Examples:

    *   *Six Dots: A Story of Young Louis Braille* (Bryant, 2016): The Boy Who Invented an Alphabet; The Boy Who Created a Code; The Boy in the Library
    *   *Counting on Katherine: How Katherine Johnson Saved Apollo 13* (Becker, 2018): The Woman Who Saved the Astronauts; The Woman Who Was a Computer; The Woman at the Chalkboard

3. For older students, keep a list of the new titles. At the end of the semester or unit of study, see if they can remember the stories well enough to match the new titles with the old. A matching game could be created out of the old and new titles written on pieces of construction paper.

Nippold, Ward-Lonergan, and Fanning (2005) studied persuasive writing in typically developing children, adolescents, and adults. They found that a child's ability, on average, to use subordinate clauses (nominal/noun and adverbial clauses) was similar between the age groups studied (ages 11, 17, and 24), though the use of relative clauses did increase from childhood to adulthood. A relative clause is a subordinate clause that starts with a relative pronoun *(who, that, which, whose, where, when)* and acts like an adjective to describe or add information about a person, place, or thing (e.g., Bass Reeves was a lawman *who arrested his own son for murder*). Other differences across the age groups included overall essay length and an increase in literate vocabulary, including abstract nouns and terms like *typically, however, therefore, finally*, and *consequently*, as well as advanced verbs like *acknowledge, assert, reflect, argue*, and *disagree*.

Nippold et al. suggest strategies for improving the use of literate language in struggling writers by encouraging them to combine simple sentences into more complex ones by using subordinate clauses like those described previously. Although typically developing children at age 11 use many of these forms, struggling writers often do not and require specific instruction to incorporate them. Another suggestion was giving students cue cards containing key words and phrases to prompt them to use target terms in their essays that might include abstract vocabulary, sophisticated verbs, and adverbial conjunctions (*consequently, typically, finally, furthermore, however*). The latter also results in more complex sentence structures.

To develop flexible thinking and the ability to see two sides of an issue, the authors recommend engaging students in group discussions exploring varying points of view before requiring them to write on a topic. Like previous authors, they suggest that writing should be connected to the curriculum and should focus on topics that students value.

With these subskills in mind, along with the practical suggestions made by these and other authors throughout this chapter, the next section looks at ways that narratives can be used as a springboard for expository writing.

USING *STORY FRAMES* TO SUPPORT EXPOSITORY WRITING

Story Frames and its emphasis on text structure can help students bridge the gap between narrative and expository text, especially when it comes to writing. The activities described in Chapter 6 incorporate nonfiction details and sequences of events into writing a narrative summary. This section will look at how to use some of these same tools to explore writing an informative essay.

Methods for Teaching Text Types

Looking back at Hennessy's (2021) delineation of text structure types and using a narrative nonfiction picture book as a model text, a teacher can encourage students to match text types to examples after they have a clear understanding of the various text types. They can then create their own text types based on Hennessy's graphic summary of foundational components (Figure 7.1) and target a narrative nonfiction picture book, as I did with *Six Dots*.

LESSON 7B: WHAT'S MY TEXT TYPE?

ACTIVITY

Directions

1. Give each student a copy of Figure 7.2, What's My Text Type?, with paragraph examples based on *Six Dots: A Story of Young Louis Braille*. These paragraphs were created by using the information found in the picture book to produce paragraphs matching the various text types.

2. As a class, discuss the various text types as outlined in Hennessy's Graphic Summary of Foundational Components.

3. Decide which paragraph matches which type of text.

4. For older students: Read another narrative nonfiction picture book to the class and model how to use the information found in the narrative to create a variety of paragraphs based on text types.

5. Print Hennessy's Graphic Summary of Foundational Components and highlight which text type paragraph each student or group will be responsible for creating—description, chronological sequence, compare and contrast, problem and solution, or cause and effect.

6. Instruct students to create a paragraph that represents their specific type of text. Students may work individually or in groups.

7. Read the examples aloud and ask the class to identify what type of paragraph each example represents based upon Hennessy's Graphic Summary of Foundational Components.

Objectives:
Improve text structure knowledge; encourage critical thinking

Grade Level:
Fourth and up

Time:
30 minutes for Steps 1–3 (plus time to read the story); time varies for additional steps

Developing an Expository Essay Based on Problem and Solution

Using *Six Dots* as an example, a student could start with the idea that will serve as the introduction—that if a person works hard, he can overcome challenges related to a disability. Then the students could discuss Louis Braille's problem (becoming blind) and his goals at the beginning of the story. (He wants to read but there are no books for the blind in his village.) Then students can explore his attempt to find a solution in the middle of the book. (He goes to the Royal School for the Blind because they have books for the visually impaired, but the books are huge and don't contain much information. Then an army captain brings a secret code made of dots, but he won't help Louis adapt it.) Finally, students can discuss Louis's ultimate success (Louis works for 3 years all on his own to perfect the code and create the braille alphabet).

Some details will be the same as those found in the story summary, but some will be different because of the more intense focus on problem and solution. The emphasis of expository writing is on supporting a thesis or claim. The purpose of a narrative is to relate

WHAT'S MY TEXT TYPE?

Directions: Read each example paragraph and ask students to identify what text type matches each example.

PART ONE	
Example Paragraphs	**Text Types**
1. Louis's father told him not to touch the tools in the workshop because he was too little. Louis didn't listen. As a result, he poked himself in the eye with an awl, which caused his eye to get infected. He scratched his eye because it itched, and that led to his other eye getting infected. As a result, he became blind at the age of 5.	a. Description b. Compare and contrast c. Cause and effect
2. Louis was similar to a lot of boys in the village. He went to school, played games, and wanted to learn to read. One big difference, though, was that he was blind and there were no books for children with visual impairments in his village.	
3. When Louis went to live at the school for the blind he was disappointed to discover that the building was cold and wet and there wasn't much to eat. He slept in a room filled with a lot of other boys and some of the older ones were mean. It may have been called the Royal School for the Blind, but there was nothing fancy about it.	
PART TWO	
1. The problem with the army captain's code was that it was too complicated for the students and they quickly grew tired of it. Also, the dots represented sounds rather than letters. Louis asked the army captain to help him improve the code, but with no luck. Consequently, Louis worked on the code alone, by himself, for 3 years until he created what we now know as the braille alphabet.	a. Compare and contrast b. Chronological sequence c. Problem and solution
2. First, Louis perfected his code. Then he asked the headmaster to read him a chapter of a book while Louis transcribed it with his new alphabet. Finally, when the headmaster was done reading, Louis turned over his paper and read back the entire chapter using his new writing system.	
3. The braille alphabet is similar to the standard English alphabet because each series of dots represents a specific letter. On the other hand, the braille alphabet is made up of raised dots that must be read through, while the standard English alphabet is made up of symbols that are read by sight.	

Figure 7.2.   What's My Text Type? (Example paragraphs based on *Six Dots: A Story of Young Louis Braille*; Bryant, 2016.)

Introduction:		
Describe the main character's problem. What was his goal at the beginning of the story?	What were some of his attempts to find a solution in the middle of the story? Was he successful or not?	Describe the main character's success at the end of the story. How did he solve his problem?

Conclusion:

Figure 7.3. Expository Essay Brainstorm for problem and solution.

a sequence of events. See Figure 7.3 for a sample Expository Essay Brainstorm, used in the lesson plan that follows.

LESSON 7C: EXPOSITORY WRITING—PROBLEM AND SOLUTION

Directions

1. Read *Six Dots: A Story of Young Louis Braille* to the class.

2. Work as a group to fill out the Expository Essay Brainstorm based on the following:

    a. Discuss Louis Braille's problem and his goals at the beginning of the story.

    b. Explore his attempt to find a solution in the middle of the book.

    c. Discuss Louis's ultimate success and how he achieves it.

3. Brainstorm key vocabulary from the book.

4. Provide a transition word list (see Figure 7.4, from Hennessy's [2021] Graphic Summary) specific to problem and solution essays *(because, resolved, result, so that, consequently).*

5. As a class, brainstorm an introduction with a thesis statement and a conclusion.

6. Demonstrate how to write the introduction and first body paragraph (I do).

7. Have the class provide input for the middle (second) body paragraph (We do).

8. Have students work independently to draft the third body paragraph (You do).

ACTIVITY

Objectives:
Improve expository writing skills; encourage use of academic vocabulary; improve the ability to identify problems and solutions

Grade Level:
Fourth and up

Time:
Two 30-minute sessions

Compare and Contrast	same	different
	as well as	although
	similar	however
	in common	on the other hand
	in comparison	either or
Problem and Solution	because	
	resolved	
	result	
	so that	
	consequently	

Figure 7.4. Transition words list. (Adapted from Hennessy, N. L. [2021]. *The reading comprehension blueprint: Helping students make meaning from text* [p. 144]. Baltimore, MD: Paul H. Brookes Publishing Co.)

9. Invite the class to come back together to check their third paragraph for accurate details and brainstorm a conclusion (We do).

10. When students have gained proficiency with the process, have them use the graphic organizer to brainstorm a new book and write a complete essay on their own or with support.

Older students might also be required to find nonfiction texts and resources to include in their essays to further support their claims. Alternately, these resources could be compared and contrasted with the picture book for a discussion on the two types of texts, as outlined in the lesson plan that follows for writing a compare and contrast essay.

Comparing and Contrasting Narrative and Expository Text Features

Another strategy Hennessy (2021) shares is searching a text for key features such as titles, headings, diagrams, glossaries, and indexes, as well as chapter and section headings. An entire essay could be written comparing the key features, similarities, and differences, between a work of narrative nonfiction and a piece of informational text addressing the same subject, person, or point in time. The Key Features Worksheet in Figure 7.5 may serve as a discussion starter or the brainstorm for an essay as described in the following lesson plan.

ACTIVITY

LESSON 7D: COMPARE AND CONTRAST ESSAY COMPARING NARRATIVE NONFICTION TO INFORMATIONAL TEXT

Objectives:
Improve essay writing skills; encourage critical thinking

Grade Level:
Third and up

Time: Varies depending on books read and length of essay

Directions

1. Read a narrative nonfiction picture book to the class, such as *Sadako* by Eleanor Coerr (1993), a story about a young girl who dies of radiation poisoning after the dropping of the atomic bomb.

2. Explore a nonfiction title on the same subject, such as Dorling Kindersley's (2015) *World War II: Visual Encyclopedia*. Demonstrate for students how to search a resource book for specific information when appropriate rather than reading the entire book.

KEY FEATURES WORKSHEET

Directions: Describe the features used in each type of text. If a book does not include that feature, write NONE.

	Picture Book	Informational Text
Title		
Subtitle		
Author		
Index or list of chapters		
Word definitions: At the end in a glossary or somewhere else?		
Pronunciation guide: At the end of the book or within the text?		
Chapters or section headings		
Bolded text		
Sidebars: How often? Every page?		
Back matter added at the end of the book (appendix, glossary, index, etc.)		
Photos or illustrations		
Graphs, charts, maps, or other visuals		
Timeline		
Acknowledgments		
Bibliography or references: How many? Are they books, articles, or websites?		

Figure 7.5. Key Features Worksheet: Narrative nonfiction picture book versus informational text.

3. Complete the Key Features Worksheet found in Figure 7.5. For young children (second and third graders or struggling learners), creating a list of features and discussing similarities and differences may be enough of a challenge. For older students, make the list collaboratively the first time (I do). On subsequent essays, have students work together in teams to create lists (We do), and then individually (You do).

4. Brainstorm key vocabulary with the class for each book and create a list for students to use in their writing. On later essays they may generate these lists with peers or individually, or they may add to the collaborative list.

5. Provide a transition word list (see Figure 7.4, from Hennessy's [2021] Graphic Summary) specific to compare and contrast essays (*same, as well as, similar, in common, different, although, however, on the other hand, in comparison, either or*).

6. Use the Key Features Worksheet to write a two-paragraph essay comparing and contrasting the two books, using the block method with the first block or paragraph focused on how the two books are the same and the second block or paragraph focused on how they are different.
   a. Paragraph 1: How the two books are the same. Class collaborates with teacher writing the paragraph (I do).
   b. Paragraph 2: How the two books are different. Students work in pairs (we do), or individually (you do), to write the second paragraph.

7. For older students, create a four-paragraph essay by adding an introductory paragraph at the beginning and a concluding paragraph at the end. Use "I do, you do, we do" strategies as needed.
   a. Introduction, including thesis statement
   b. Body paragraph 1: How the two books are the same
   c. Body paragraph 2: How the two books are different
   d. Conclusion

8. To create a five-paragraph essay, use the point-by-point method. Choose three features to highlight and then compare and contrast both books and how they apply that specific feature in each paragraph. Use "I do, you do, we do" strategies as needed.
   a. Introduction, including thesis statement
   b. Body paragraph 1: key feature 1—compare and contrast both books
   c. Body paragraph 2: key feature 2—compare and contrast both books
   d. Body paragraph 3: key feature 3—compare and contrast both books
   e. Conclusion

9. Using a model example or student example, demonstrate how to revise a paragraph by getting rid of unneeded or redundant information and adding details (I do). Revise an additional paragraph with the class (We do). Have peers work in teams to help revise each other's paragraphs (We do). Instruct students to work independently on a paragraph to revise.

10. Edit work using the Editor's Toolbox. In addition, instruct students to refer to the transition word list to make sure they have included appropriate transition words.

11. Cite references. Demonstrate how to do this, then have students work in pairs, and finally individually. When appropriate, demonstrate how to use resources like www.easybib.com.

For a high school level analysis, after exploring several pairings of narrative nonfiction picture books and informational texts, the class could discuss patterns of similarities and differences, and each student could write an essay about the overall topic of similarities and differences between narrative nonfiction and informational text.

Creating Opportunities for Authentic Writing

Earlier I mentioned the importance of creating authentic writing for an authentic audience. I would like to share a letter writing experience that proved to be very effective with high school students. The subject matter was fiction, but the person students were writing to was very real.

The Grades 9–10 special education English teacher and I collaborated on a project where we had students read Cynthia Leitich Smith's graphic novel, *Tantalize: Kieren's Story* (2011). It's a retelling of her vampire novel, *Tantalize* (Smith, 2007), but from another character's point of view. Students also read a simplified version of Bram Stoker's (1897) *Dracula*. They tracked the plot and characters of both books, wrote compare and contrast essays, and created their own hybrid characters and stories. (The main character was a hybrid werewolf.) In addition, I brought in a variety of vampire novels, including the original Bram Stoker (1897) version, so that students who finished the first two books would have related material to read in class.

It was an afterthought to ask them to write letters to Cynthia, the author of *Tantalize*, 3 months after we'd finished her book, but the results were astounding. Both the classroom teacher and I were amazed by how much writing students produced in two 40-minute sessions. Even our most reluctant writers, those who never finished the story project, completed three-paragraph letters. Afterward, the teacher and I brainstormed about what made the letter project so successful because we definitely wanted to do it again. Following is the list we came up with.

1. *Make sure students have read the book.* This may seem obvious, but as an author I have often conducted school visits with students who have never read my books. Many authors make the reading of their novels a requirement for attendance. There is a very good reason for this—it's so much more meaningful to connect with someone whose material you are familiar with and have enjoyed. It's what makes a two-way conversation possible.

2. *Get excited about the books you are asking your students to read.* If you can't get excited about a story, it will be very difficult for students to get excited. The classroom teacher and I talked about *Tantalize* with great enthusiasm before we asked students to read it. We discussed Cynthia as an author and shared her other books with the class to encourage students to explore other titles in the series. For a nonfiction connection, we read Cynthia's excerpt from *Dear Teen Me: Authors Write Letters to Their Teen Selves* (Anderson & Kenneally, 2012). I told the class how thrilled I was that I would be seeing Cynthia at an upcoming book festival and how delighted I knew she would be at receiving their letters. I knew her personally and had talked to her ahead of time, so I knew this was the case.

3. *Make letter writing a meaningful literacy experience.* As educators, we realize that writing an essay is a beneficial activity. We have specific goals and benchmarks in mind when creating such assignments. But our students don't necessarily view this type of writing as intrinsically valuable. The letters were important to them because they represented true communication with another person who they knew would be reading what they wrote for a purpose deeper than checking their punctuation and assigning them a grade.

4. *Brainstorm content with the class.* Writing letters may address just as many benchmarks and standards as writing essays if the activity is structured with specific goals in mind. I told the students what material I wanted in each paragraph as follows:

   • Paragraph one: This was the introduction where they told a little bit about themselves and mentioned which book of Cynthia's they had read.

   • Paragraph two: Students were instructed to describe their favorite character or scene from the graphic novel.

   • Paragraph three: This was the wrap up and conclusion and students were instructed to end with a question.

   During our brainstorm, I asked for examples from the class and wrote them on the board. I then typed the examples so that students who struggled with spelling and sentence/paragraph structure would have a template to follow. Though we did not require it, a fourth paragraph could involve asking students to share a meaningful quote from the book and why it was important.

5. *Make rewriting a natural part of the process.* Wong (2000) points out that even students without learning disabilities need to be taught that planning and revising are part of the writing process. To stress the importance of revising, I brought fancy stationery from home and told the students they needed to write a sloppy copy first so their final draft would be perfect. No one complained about the editing process, and one girl even stated she had completed an additional draft on her own at home.

As I expected, Cynthia was delighted to receive the student letters and promptly wrote back, addressing all of their questions. I had contacted her ahead of time, which I highly recommend. Make sure the author is on board before asking your students to undertake such an endeavor. It's also important to make sure you have current contact information.

If conducting this activity, I recommend that the teacher read through the student letters and write a cover letter including the questions, many of which will be repeated. This will help the author give a quicker response.

You don't have to personally know authors to have your students write letters to them. Many YA authors may be contacted through online websites or blogs and they love connecting with young readers. Local chapters of the Society of Children's Book Writers and Illustrators may also have contact information. To bring in a nonfiction or even a multimedia component, find articles written by or about the author, or find online interviews. *Dear Teen Me* (Anderson & Kenneally, 2012), mentioned previously, includes letters written by dozens of young adult authors to their teen selves. The lesson plan here consolidates the process we followed.

ACTIVITY	**LESSON 7E: LETTER TO THE AUTHOR**

Objectives:
Improve revision and organization skills

Grade Level:
Fourth and up

Time:
Varies

Directions

1. Read a book. Contact the author ahead of time to make sure he or she is willing to correspond with students. If the author is not available, find someone else connected to the book directly or to the subject matter who is willing to return a letter to students. If the class is reading *Six Dots*, perhaps that person could be a local teacher of students with visual impairments.

2. Instruct students to write a three-paragraph letter based on the following structure (or another structure if you prefer different content):

   a. Paragraph one: Introduction. Students tell a little bit about themselves and mention the title of the book they have read.

b. Paragraph two: Middle. Students describe their favorite character or scene.

c. Paragraph three: End. Wrap up the letter and end with a question.

3. Revise the content of the letters. Have students exchange letters to proofread.

4. Edit for punctuation and grammar.

5. Rewrite the letters on stationery.

6. The teacher reads through the letters and writes a cover letter to the author listing the questions and consolidating repeated questions or information.

7. Send the letters to the author.

8. When the author responds, read the response to the class.

TIPS FOR ONLINE LEARNING AND TELETHERAPY

1. Email the worksheets and brainstorms to the school or home. They may then be printed for the student to write on.

2. Create a Google file for student work and have the student access worksheets and brainstorms directly from his or her computer.

3. Download the What's My Text Type? chart and share it onscreen for the students who can use the annotation feature of Zoom to draw a line between the paragraph example and the matching text type.

4. Share YouTube videos of author interviews.

5. Demonstrate how to conduct online research.

CONCLUSION: MOVING FROM NARRATIVE TO EXPOSITORY WRITING

The focus of this chapter was using nonfiction narratives as a bridge between story writing and expository writing. These types of books share many of the same features of expository writing, and lesson plans were provided to highlight these features. Additional lesson plans explored comparing a picture book with informational text and writing a problem and solution essay based on the central problem of a character in a book facing a real-life challenge. The chapter ended with an authentic literacy activity that included writing a letter to an author. To further explore how narratives may be used as a bridge to expository writing, see Chapter 13, in which Lesley Roessing explores using student memoir writing as a bridge from narrative to informational text, and check out her book, *Bridging the Gap: Reading Critically and Writing Meaningfully to Get to the Core* (2014).

Toward a Deeper Understanding

Questioning and Comprehension Skills

8

Many skills that support good reading and listening comprehension also support oral and written language abilities. Strategies explored in previous chapters targeted vocabulary development, sequencing, summary writing, understanding grammatical forms, creating visual images, and understanding text structures. In addition to proficiency in these areas, students must have the skills needed for deeper understanding of a text. They must have adequate background knowledge to be able to compare what they are reading or hearing to their personal experiences. They must be able to make inferences and understand complex sentence structures.

This chapter will focus primarily on building on these underlying skills to be able to answer questions about a text as well as to generate questions of one's own. It will wrap up with a discussion of Bloom's Revised Taxonomy (Anderson & Krathwohl, 2001) and how it relates to questioning, as well as the other skill areas previously discussed.

ASKING AND ANSWERING QUESTIONS: WHAT THE EVIDENCE SAYS

Having students answer questions about a text and generate their own questions is a strategy with several applications for improving comprehension. It can be used to help students visualize what is happening in a text and improve their sentence-level comprehension, including comprehension of complex syntactic structures.

Improving Comprehension Through Mental Imagery

Bell (1991, 2007) uses a series of questions to improve comprehension through mental imagery. In *Visualizing and Verbalizing: For Language Comprehension and Thinking*, she teaches students a variety of what she calls "structure words" to describe first a picture, then a word, then sentences, then multiple sentences and paragraphs. Students learn to verbalize what they are picturing in a way that others can clearly understand and to create visual images from what they hear others describe. They use these same strategies to create mental images of what they read. When students have a solid foundation in creating sentences and paragraphs verbally, they then move to sentence construction using the imaging and describing strategies they have honed as a bridge to writing. Bell's structure words include Wh-questions like *what, where*, and *when*. Her program is invaluable for students who need more intense practice with creating visual images.

The ability to form mental images is key to being able to remember what is read and answer questions about it. In discussing some of the executive function skills necessary for reading, Hudson, Scheff, Tarsha, and Cutting (2016) describe the importance of being

DOWNLOADABLE RESOURCES:

Keep these resources on hand for teaching the Chapter 8 lessons and activities.

- Lesson 8A, Describing Book Illustrations: Eight question types: Wh- icons

- Lesson 8B, Concept Script for Wh-questions: Eight question types: Wh- icons

- Other: Wh-questions PowerPoint Slide Deck, with sample questions for *Six Dots: A Story of Young Louis Braille* (Bryant, 2016)

able to use working memory to organize and update concepts while relating them to what is being read, especially regarding expository texts. Narratives require the ability to maintain the overall structure and meaning of a story while considering its parts. Hudson et al. report that students with a specific reading comprehension deficit, as a group, showed less gray matter volume in the brain regions responsible for creating mental images as measured by magnetic resonance imaging (MRI) brain scans. Difficulty with forming mental images can have a negative impact on both reading and listening comprehension. It is difficult to recall a narrative's many component parts if visual imagery is weak.

Oakhill and Cain (2016) suggest teaching students to use mental imagery by telling them to visualize the events of a narrative as if the story was a movie playing in their mind's eye. Additional strategies they suggest for improving comprehension include training students to ask themselves Wh-questions (who, what, where, when, why) about a text to be able to make inferences about missing information. Also important is the ability to monitor one's own comprehension to be aware of when a text does not make sense. They recommend asking open-ended teacher-generated questions like, "How do you know?" to develop higher-order thinking skills such as inferencing. Even picture books for young children often leave out critical information that must be inferred from the illustrations and deduced from the rest of the text.

Improving Comprehension at the Sentence Level

Scott and Balthazar (2013) discuss the importance of asking students questions at the sentence level, directly after exposure to complex syntactic structures, because this is often where comprehension breakdowns occur. They also recommend asking students to paraphrase a complex sentence. This works better for longer sentences than shorter ones since students are not as apt to merely repeat the words. The authors discuss many factors that can make the subject-verb-object (S-V-O) relationship that is key to understanding a sentence more challenging. A sentence's length and complexity can be impacted by the number and placement of noun modifiers, the number of clauses, embedded information, use of subordination, passive versus active structure, and any change in the standard S-V-O word order. Often students assume that the person, place, or thing in the sentence with the closest proximity to the verb is the subject.

Asking questions can also help with understanding complex sentences. Cain (2016) discusses how oral language understanding in the preschool years provides the foundation for reading comprehension in elementary school and beyond. In addition, students with weak phonological skills in preschool often struggle with decoding later on. Difficulty with decoding can result in limited exposure to the vocabulary and syntax found in books, which can also impact overall comprehension over time. Both groups, those with poor comprehension of oral language and those with deficits in phonological awareness, often struggle with reading comprehension in their later elementary years, even if their early challenges are only marginal. For this reason, she recommends that listening skills be fostered well before children are expected to read by exposing them to stories that contain robust vocabulary within sentence structures of increasing complexity. This is also useful for students who have limited experiences with print due to deficits in decoding.

Nelson (2013) discusses the importance of using grammar knowledge to break down complex sentences both for comprehension and for building more complex sentence structures for writing. Simple sentences develop before compound sentences (two independent ideas joined with a conjunction). Compound sentences develop before complex sentences (an independent clause and a dependent clause joined by a subordinating conjunction such as *because*). After these distinctions, Nelson says the developmental progress is unclear.

Therefore, she concludes that beyond simple and compound sentence structures it does not matter in what order concepts are presented for teaching students to create complex sentences. This flexibility allows an instructor to focus on forms that correspond to content rather than selecting one specific type of sentence and creating drills around that type. Nelson also points out that answering questions about what is read and writing a summary are important ways to improve comprehension.

In outlining specific strategies for improving reading comprehension, Marzola (2018) discusses using Wh-questions to facilitate comprehension at the sentence level. She specifically points out the value of describing illustrations:

> Students can be encouraged to "read" picture books to hone their comprehension skills. Describing the characters and actions in pictures begins the process of comprehension. It also sets the tone for helping students to focus on what factors come into play in comprehending text. (pp. 610–611)

She laments that the standard in education has been to "test" knowledge using questions, but not to "teach" any actual strategies for answering those questions. Proficient readers seem to develop such skills naturally. Not all students do, however:

> Good readers ask themselves questions before, during, and after reading. Yet, many students do not self-question spontaneously. They need to have good models of questioning during all three periods of the reading process to have an effect on their comprehension. (p. 623)

Marzola concluded that self-questioning during the reading process was the single greatest strategy for effectively improving reading comprehension. Also, understanding the structure of stories improved a student's ability to answer these Wh-questions.

In summary, to be able to answer questions, students require many skills, including the ability to make visual images and to understand text structures. When students can self-question, they can use this tool to make sense of complex sentences, monitor a text for missing information, compare what is happening in a text to their background knowledge, make inferences, and monitor their comprehension.

USING WH-QUESTIONS TO SUPPORT COMPREHENSION

Story Frames utilizes Wh-questions (who, what action, what thing, where, when, how, which one, why) to improve reading and listening comprehension, and as discussed in the previous chapter, to structure writing. But not all questions are created equal, and students with learning challenges respond differently to different question types.

Spencer et al. (2019) studied various types of reading comprehension questions and their level of difficulty based on complexity of text. They also evaluated adolescents with a wide range of reading abilities to determine their strengths and weaknesses on a variety of measures. They determined that word reading ability (based on a test of real words and non-words), vocabulary as measured by word knowledge, and inferencing ability impacted accuracy with answering multiple-choice questions, more so than working memory or cognitive flexibility, although working memory had a greater impact on questions that involved free recall (providing the last word in a sentence). The researchers controlled for background knowledge and IQ, so those were not a factor.

The complexity of the text that was read was measured by cohesion, decoding, vocabulary, and syntax. The level of cohesion challenge impacted a student's ability to answer multiple-choice questions more than the other factors. Cohesion, vocabulary, and syntax impacted free recall questions, and all four impacted oral reading fluency. The question types found to be most difficult were questions requiring inferencing (making predictions and drawing conclusions beyond the information provided in the text) and critical analysis (determining author purpose, text type, patterns of text, and organization). The easiest were literal questions.

None of these results is surprising, but in my personal experience I have found that many elementary school students with receptive language challenges have difficulty with literal questions as well, even when the text is read aloud to them and decoding is not an issue. Many seem to have challenges with understanding what is being asked of them in a Wh-question. They do not appear to have a clear understanding of the meaning of the different types of Wh-questions. Another possibility is that if they don't know an answer, they reach for an answer they do know regardless of the type of question being asked. The underlying problem may be challenging to detect, especially on multiple-choice tests, but the foundational weakness is exposed when students are required to give a verbal or written answer rather than just choosing one option among many. When you ask a question like, "When did Louis Braille become blind?" and a student answers with, "In his father's workshop," or "Because he was playing with the tools," it is clear he has the ability to recall the literal details from the story, but not the correct details for the question being asked. He is answering *where* and *why* questions when he was asked a *when* question.

A student may have a detailed understanding of the story events, be able to retell the events in sequence, and still have difficulty answering questions about the story. Training a student to understand question types to discern what information needs to be included in an answer provides valuable preparation for standards-based assessments. It also provides practical, real-world skills for interacting with others. Many social interchanges, in and out of school, involve asking and answering questions, and many misunderstandings arise when young people and adults alike misinterpret questions.

For these reasons, *Story Frames* uses icons to make these abstract questions more concrete. Figure 8.1 shows eight question types and their icons. A reproducible version of these icons is located in the downloadable resources. These are the same questions asked to help students build complex sentences, as discussed in Chapter 6. Their

"WHO" questions ask about a person or character.	"WHAT" questions sometimes ask about things.	"WHAT" questions sometimes ask about actions.	"WHERE" questions ask about places or locations.
"WHICH" questions ask us to describe people, places, or things.	"WHEN" questions ask about a period of time.	"HOW" questions ask us to describe actions.	"WHY" questions ask us to give reasons.

Figure 8.1. Types of questions. (© Carolee Dean.)

application will be discussed in greater detail in the activities that follow: picture reading and Social Stories.

Picture Reading

The picture reading strategy discussed by Marzola (2018) is easily adaptable to the picture books discussed in the downloadable resources. These books contain illustrations filled with details and nuances that make them entertaining as well as educational. They are rich with images that help students develop oral language complexity, which in turn leads to the understanding of complex sentences that are necessary for reading comprehension as well as for written expression.

The story that follows is from the Greek myth of Prometheus. It may be read aloud to students or used as an outline and retold by the teacher and adjusted for grade level. The illustration depicts the Midpoint Attempt of the story.

Prometheus and the Gift of Fire, **adapted from the Greek myth**

Illustration: Prometheus and the Gift of Fire. (Created by Christopher Jochens; used by permission.)

1. **Ordinary World.** A terrible war raged between the Titans, led by Cronus, and the Olympians, led by Zeus. The Titan, Prometheus, refused to take sides, so when the other Titans lost, he was not banished with them to live in Tartarus in the underworld. After the war ended, the world was a very quiet, empty place.

2. **Call and Response.** Zeus asked Prometheus for help to fill the earth with living creatures. Prometheus didn't really like Zeus, but he was excited about creating other living beings.

3. **Mentors, Guides, and Gifts.** Prometheus's brother, Epimetheus, helped Prometheus by giving special gifts to all of the newly formed creatures—wings, speed, night vision, sharp teeth, and so on. Unfortunately, he didn't leave anything for Prometheus's greatest creation, man. This was very upsetting to Prometheus.

4. **Crossing.** Prometheus went up to Mount Olympus looking for something special to bring back to the people living on the earth.

5. **New World.** Covered in clouds, the top of Mount Olympus could not be seen by the mortals below. A beautiful place with lush, green forests, it was home to the gods' ruler, Zeus. The gods had their own palace where they ate ambrosia, a magical food that gave them immortality.

6. **Problems, Prizes, and Plans.** Prometheus wanted to steal fire from Hephaestus, the god of fire, so that he would have a gift to give mankind. He knew if he was caught, he would be punished, so he planned to hide a flame inside of a leaf.

7. **Midpoint Attempt.** Prometheus found the forge where Hephaestus kept his fire burning. He stole one tiny flame and hurried back to earth with it.

8. **Downtime Response.** When Prometheus shared the fire with humans, it soon spread. Now the men of the earth were able to have light and heat and to cook their food, and they were happy.

9. **Chase and Escape.** Zeus was very angry when he looked down and realized Prometheus had brought fire to man. He asked Hephaestus to create Pandora, the first woman, and send her to earth to marry Epimetheus. For a while, Prometheus thought he had escaped the wrath of Zeus, but Zeus was actually busy planning a very nasty trick.

10. **Death and Transformation.** As a wedding present, the gods gave Pandora and Epimetheus a special box but said they must never open it. Curious, Pandora peeked

Table 8.1.   Wh-questions and answers for *Prometheus and the Gift of Fire*

Questions	Answers
Who is the subject of the picture?	Prometheus
What is he doing?	Sneaking
How?	Alone
Where?	Into a cave; up on Mount Olympus
Which one?	Hephaestus's cave
When?	One night
Why?	Because he wanted to steal fire from the gods

inside—and death, hate, disease, war, and every imaginable bad thing came out. She tried to shut it, but it was too late. Fortunately, the last thing to escape was a tiny winged creature, Hope. Wherever it went, Hope helped transform the people below, making them strong so their difficulties wouldn't destroy them.

11. **Climax: The Final Test.** When Zeus found Prometheus, he chained him to a very high mountain and sent an eagle to peck at him and torment him all day long. (For older students, you might add that the eagle ate his liver each day, and each night it grew back so the eagle could eat it again the next day. There was no way for the immortal Prometheus to escape this fate, for he could not die.)

12. **Final Reward.** Although Prometheus spent many years living in pain and watching horrible things happening down below to the people on earth, he never gave up hope. Eventually, a mighty warrior named Heracles (Hercules) came to free him.

The prompts in Table 8.1 outline how the Wh-questions icons may be used to help students describe the illustration of Prometheus stealing fire. The same questions with minor modifications may be asked to help students describe any illustration from any picture book (see the following lesson plan). Review the strategies in Chapter 6 for specific ideas on how to use similar prompts for writing.

ACTIVITY	**LESSON 8A: DESCRIBING BOOK ILLUSTRATIONS**

Objective:
Improve the understanding of Wh-questions; improve descriptive language

Grade Level:
First and up

Time:
30 minutes

Directions

1. Give each student a copy of the Wh-question icons.

2. Project a book illustration on a smartboard or screen via a document camera or Kindle book.

3. Model how to use each Wh-question icon to describe what is going on in the story.

4. Model how to verbally use all of the responses together to build a complex sentence.

5. Turn to another illustration. Ask students to volunteer to verbally answer one of the Wh-question prompts to help describe the illustration. Go around the room until all questions have been asked.

6. Ask another volunteer to see how many responses he or she can include in one complex sentence.

7. When finished with one illustration, move on to another. Not all Wh-questions will have an apparent answer for every illustration.

Using Concept Scripts to Teach Wh-Questions

Narrative-Based Language Intervention (NBLI) is a term used by Swanson, Fey, Mills, and Hood (2005) to describe a language intervention approach that uses the context of a story to address narrative abilities as well as other key skills, such as syntax and grammar. Dodd (2012) discusses the value of using narratives in an NBLI approach in working with students with complex language challenges, including autism, because stories exemplify a natural context while providing ample opportunity to work on a variety of functional skills. She was concerned, though, that many commercially produced stories, though well written, are too cognitively and linguistically advanced for students with complex challenges. Dodd suggests adapting commercially available stories or creating stories while modifying the complexity of story text, syntax, and semantics. She recommends that the text be clear and avoid the need for inferencing. Sentence structure should be short and simple unless the student can handle longer more complex structures. The number of new words should be limited and defined within the text. Dodd also recommends using visual images and photographs when creating stories.

Carol Gray (2000) outlines a method for creating Social Stories in a variety of books, as well as on her website on the subject. Her method includes using repetitive and straightforward language, personal examples, and concrete visual images (when not distracting or confusing) to explicitly teach children on the autism spectrum about topics and situations that most children learn through experience (Gray & Garand, 1993). Other goals of Social Stories include teaching routines and academic concepts within a social context.

Students on the autism spectrum often have difficulty with abstract concepts such as Wh-questions. They are not the only ones. Many students benefit from the use of what I call Concept Scripts to make these abstract concepts more understandable.

I was working with a middle school student on the autism spectrum with significant intellectual impairment who had difficulty with Wh-questions that affected his interpersonal relationships, his ability to have conversations with peers and teachers, and his ability to answer questions in class. I had previously used the strategies of Carol Gray to create a Social Story of sorts about pronoun use (another area that caused interpersonal as well as academic difficulty when he referred to boys as "her" and girls as "him"). That story was so successful that I applied a similar approach to teaching him Wh-questions.

Carol Gray outlines 10 defining characteristics for a story to be called a true Social Story. Though inspired by her work, the lesson plan that follows does not adhere to those criteria and is not specifically for students on the autism spectrum. Nor does it follow the story grammar conventions of a true narrative, so I've used the term Concept Script to identify a "story" created to teach a specific linguistic skill that may or may not strongly impact social as well as academic progress. The lesson should incorporate strategies outlined by Gray (2000) and Dodd (2012), such as, using 1) simplistic, child-centered text; 2) syntax at the child's level of development; 3) familiar terms or terms that are clearly defined; 4) personal examples relevant to the child; and 5) visual images or icons to represent abstract ideas.

LESSON 8B: CONCEPT SCRIPT FOR WH-QUESTIONS

ACTIVITY

Directions

1. Use the Wh-question icons and their descriptions to elicit conversations with a student or a class about personal examples that relate to each question type. See the examples that follow. (Note: If tackling another challenging concept or idea, include students in the search for icons or visual representations of the idea. The website www.thenounproject.org is a good place to search.)

2. Use the student responses along with the icons to create pages for either a personal Concept Script or a class-elicited Concept Script.

Objective:
Improve the understanding of Wh-questions

Grade Level:
First and up

Time:
30 minutes

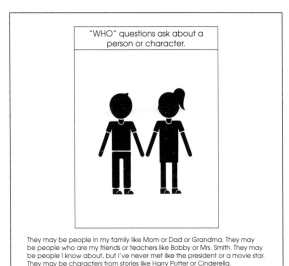

"WHO" questions ask about a person or character.

They may be people in my family like Mom or Dad or Grandma. They may be people who are my friends or teachers like Bobby or Mrs. Smith. They may be people I know about, but I've never met like the president or a movie star. They may be characters from stories like Harry Potter or Cinderella.

Figure 8.2. Concept Script sample page.

3. Print the pages and staple into a book.

4. Read the Concept Script with the student whenever needed to reinforce Wh-questions.

Following are examples of questions and responses for a Concept Script about Wh-questions. Figure 8.2 shows what a page from a Concept Script of this nature might look like. When generating a script with more than one student, the term "we" may replace "I."

1. *WHO questions ask about a person or a character.* They may be people in my family like <u>Mom or Dad or Grandma</u>. They may be people who are my friends or teachers like <u>Bobby or Mrs. Smith</u>. They may be people I know about but have never met, like the <u>president or a movie star</u>. They may be characters from stories like <u>Harry Potter or Cinderella.</u>

2. *WHAT questions sometimes ask about things.* They might be small things like a <u>penny, a bug, or a pencil</u>. They may be big things like <u>a house, a rocket, or a train.</u>

3. *WHAT questions sometimes ask about actions.* They may be actions that happen when I am moving around like <u>running or jumping</u>. They may be actions that happen when I am sitting still or even sleeping like <u>thinking, feeling, or dreaming.</u> These are often called verbs. Some small verbs like *is, am,* and *are* refer to a state of being, like <u>I am happy.</u>

4. *WHERE questions ask about places or locations.* They may be very large places like <u>at my school</u> or <u>on the moon</u>. They may be very small places like <u>in my backpack or on my finger.</u>

5. *WHICH questions ask us to describe people, places, or things.* They help us know which person or thing someone is talking about like <u>my *oldest* brother, my *new* school, or my *green* socks.</u>

6. *WHEN questions ask about a period of time.* They may be about times in the past like <u>yesterday, in the time of the dinosaurs, or when George Washington was president</u>. They may be about times in the future like <u>when I graduate or my next birthday</u>. They may even be about things happening right now.

7. *HOW questions ask us to describe actions.* These describe how I walk or talk or perform other actions and include words like <u>slowly, quickly, alone, and backward.</u>

8. *WHY questions ask us to give reasons.* These questions might be about explaining our actions like <u>because I was tired</u> or <u>so that I would get a good grade</u>. These questions might be about explaining other people's actions, such as characters in books, like <u>because he wanted to win a trophy</u> or <u>because she wanted to be helpful.</u>

9. *Other questions.* Sometimes these question words may ask different things than are described here. Then I have to think about what the person who is asking the question really wants to know. Here are some examples: What time is it? What were you thinking? How did you know that?

Questions serve a wide variety of purposes, including determining how well a student can remember details. One valuable way to use questioning with students is to use mixed

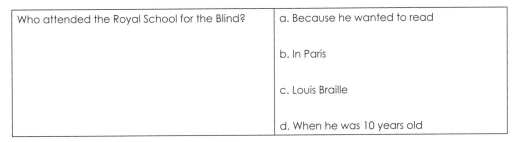

Who attended the Royal School for the Blind?	a. Because he wanted to read
	b. In Paris
	c. Louis Braille
	d. When he was 10 years old

Figure 8.3.   Mixed question.

questions. These questions include answer choices that are all true, but only one choice answers the specific question and relates directly to the type of question being asked. This is an excellent way to determine if a student understands question types. Figure 8.3 shows an example of these mixed questions, mixed because the answers fit with a variety of question types besides the one being asked. Examples of specific Wh-questions for *Six Dots* are located in a PowerPoint file in the downloadable resources that may be used both with face-to-face classes and via teletherapy and online instruction. The final questions in the PowerPoint file are mixed questions.

HIGHER-ORDER THINKING

Standardized tests and the preparation for them have become such a strong focus in education that this method of data collection via multiple-choice options often becomes the norm for assessing a student's level of understanding for a variety of skills, including reading and listening comprehension. However, the ability to make judgments and decisions based on multiple-choice options is not a practical skill in work or life. Students need to be able to do more than memorize information for the short term. They need to develop the ability to understand concepts on a deeper level so they may apply that knowledge to analyze, evaluate, and create. As important as these skills may be, however, they are not always easy to define or measure.

One way educators have tried to do so is through Bloom's Taxonomy of Educational Objectives. From 1949 to 1956, Bloom and a group of university specialists across the country worked to create a measurement tool to be used as a classification system for curriculum objectives, activities, and test items (Krathwohl, 2002). They came up with six main categories in the cognitive domain, ordered from simple to complex and concrete to abstract: knowledge, comprehension, application, analysis, synthesis, and evaluation. Figure 8.4 shows the categories with examples. A framework that builds on Bloom's original taxonomy can be used with *Story Frames* to address these higher-order comprehension skills and is described as follows.

Bloom's Taxonomy, Revised

Anderson and Krathwohl (2001) attempted to further quantify these higher-order skills when they revised Bloom's Taxonomy of Educational Objectives to create a continuum for educators to use to determine the level of cognitive complexity a child can demonstrate. They took Bloom's one-dimensional continuum and created a two-dimensional framework. The two dimensions are the *cognitive dimension* and the *knowledge dimension*. Figure 8.5 shows the increasingly complex categories within each dimension and how they can intersect, as described on the next page.

Table 1
Structure of the Original Taxonomy

1.0 *Knowledge*
    1.10 Knowledge of specifics
        1.11 Knowledge of terminology
        1.12 Knowledge of specific facts
    1.20 Knowledge of ways and means of dealing with specifics
        1.21 Knowledge of conventions
        1.22 Knowledge of trends and sequences
        1.23 Knowledge of classifications and categories
        1.24 Knowledge of criteria
        1.25 Knowledge of methodology
    1.30 Knowledge of universals and abstractions in a field
        1.31 Knowledge of principles and generalizations
        1.32 Knowledge of theories and structures

2.0 *Comprehension*
    2.1 Translation
    2.2 Interpretation
    2.3 Extrapolation

3.0 *Application*

4.0 *Analysis*
    4.1 Analysis of elements
    4.2 Analysis of relationships
    4.3 Analysis of organizational principles

5.0 *Synthesis*
    5.1 Production of a unique communication
    5.2 Production of a plan, or proposed set of operations
    5.3 Derivation of a set of abstract relations

6.0 *Evaluation*
    6.1 Evaluation in terms of internal evidence
    6.2 Judgments in terms of external criteria

Figure 8.4. Bloom's Taxonomy of Educational Objectives. (From Krathwohl, D. R. [2002]. A revision of Bloom's taxonomy: An overview. *Theory Into Practice, 41*[4], 213. Reprinted by permission of the publisher [Taylor & Francis Ltd., http://www.tandfonline.com].)

The Cognitive Process Dimension

The Knowledge Dimension	1. Remember	2. Understand	3. Apply	4. Analyze	5. Evaluate	6. Create
A. Factual Knowledge						
B. Conceptual Knowledge						
C. Procedural Knowledge						
D. Metacognitive Knowledge						

Figure 8.5. Bloom's Revised Taxonomy (Anderson & Krathwohl, 2001). Cognitive complexity increases moving from left to right on the chart; knowledge complexity increases moving top to bottom. Thus, the intersection of 1–A (remember factual knowledge) is simpler than that of either 3–A (apply factual knowledge) or 1–C (remember procedural knowledge). (From Krathwohl, D. R. [2002]. A revision of Bloom's taxonomy: An overview. *Theory Into Practice, 41*[4], 216. Reprinted by permission of The College of Education and Human Ecology, The Ohio State University, https://ehe.osu.edu/.)

The Cognitive Dimension   This dimension contains six major categories that increase in the degree of complex thought needed to carry them out: remember, understand, apply, analyze, evaluate, and create. Each involves a more challenging level of higher-order thinking. The idea is that to *remember* details and facts requires less cognitive ability than to *understand* (demonstrated by a student's ability to give examples, classify information, compare, contrast, explain, infer, and summarize). To *understand* requires less cognitive ability than to *apply* understanding, and so forth.

In addition, under each of the six major categories the authors further break down each cognitive process into actions that show a student's actual ability to perform that process. For instance, under *remember* they list *recognizing* and *recalling* as ways to demonstrate how much and how well a student may remember.

The Knowledge Dimension   This dimension moves from concrete understanding to more abstract comprehension. It includes four levels of abstractness: factual, conceptual, procedural, and metacognitive. Each of the six cognitive categories intersects with the levels of abstractness on a grid, with the six cognitive dimensions heading the columns across the top and the four knowledge dimensions heading the rows going down. Therefore, the lowest skill requirement would involve the intersection of remember + factual (remembering facts), while the highest challenge, in terms of both cognitive ability and knowledge, would be create + metacognitive (using self-knowledge or strategic knowledge to plan out and create something original based on or inspired by the subject matter).

With the revised taxonomy in mind, it is plain to see that most of the Wh-questions described in this chapter fall into the remember + factual category, with a few questions requiring the inferring that appears in the understand category. This is a good starting place and easy to measure, but very low on the scale. Using *Story Frames*, instructors can move beyond Wh-questions and give students tasks that call on higher-level thinking.

Using *Story Frames* Across the Taxonomy

What follows is a hierarchy of Bloom's Revised Taxonomy, along with examples of *Story Frames* activities, so an instructor may see how cognitively loaded the different tasks will be. If a child is struggling with a higher-level task, this may indicate that a task lower on Bloom's Revised Taxonomy would be more appropriate. On the other hand, if a student is bored or does not seem challenged, a higher-level task may be indicated. Many of these activities have been described in previous chapters. By using the taxonomy as a guide, an instructor may better understand a child's level of cognitive conceptualization and set learning objectives accordingly.

Remember: Recall Details   Within this most basic cognitive dimension, instructors can use the following *Story Frames* activities, listed in order of least to greatest knowledge demand.

1. Factual: Answer questions about a story that require a student to recall specific details.

2. Conceptual: List the story elements that appear at the beginning, middle, and end of the story.

3. Procedural: Draw stick figures to go with each story element.

4. Metacognitive: Retell the events of the story by describing what is happening in each story element using the storyboard as a guide. Relate an event in the story to a personal experience or background knowledge.

Understand: Make Meaning   Within this slightly more demanding cognitive dimension, instructors can use the following activities, again listed in order of least to greatest knowledge demand.

1. Factual: Match words to definitions. Create a short summary of the main events or central idea of the story.

2. Conceptual: Tell which word does not fit in a list of four words and explain why the others go together. Give an example of another word that fits in that category. Compare two books by the same author or on the same topic and discuss similarities.

3. Procedural: Follow the procedure to create a vocabulary foldable. Follow the rules to play the Odd One Out game.

4. Metacognitive: Use background experience and context clues to make inferences about information not clearly stated in the text and to answer questions that require inferencing.

Apply: Use Information to Perform a Task or Procedure   Within this still more demanding cognitive dimension, instructors can use the following *Story Frames* activities at increasingly difficult knowledge levels.

1. Factual: Retell the events of the story using cohesive ties.

2. Conceptual: Use the Plot Pages to incorporate keywords to build sentences for each part of the story.

3. Procedural: Complete a Venn diagram comparing and contrasting two books by the same author or two books on a similar subject.

4. Metacognitive: Describe a picture in the book using Wh-questions to expand ideas.

Analyze: Break Into Parts and Compare the Parts to the Whole   Within this somewhat higher-level cognitive dimension, instructors can use these activities.

1. Factual: Describe the Ordinary World. Then describe the New World. Make a list of attributes and characteristics of each.

2. Conceptual: Describe how the main character (MC) grows and changes as the story progresses from beginning to end.

3. Procedural: Sequence the events of the story by scrambling the storyboard elements and then putting them back in order. Complete a Venn diagram comparing different elements of the story, such as the Ordinary World versus the New World. Compare and contrast characteristics of the hero at the beginning of the story and at the end. Complete the brainstorm for an expository essay, determining which ideas and facts from the narrative sequence would be appropriate to use and what additional facts or information are needed.

4. Metacognitive: Discuss how the setting and the action affect growth and change in the MC. Describe the transformation of the MC. Write a compare and contrast essay describing how the MC grows and changes. Determine a theme for an essay based on one's personal beliefs, values, and experiences.

Evaluate: Make Judgments Based on Specific Criteria or Standard   Within this even higher-level cognitive dimension, instructors can use these activities.

1. Factual: Listen for the use of keywords in a peer's story retell and tally how many times a word has been used.

2. Conceptual: Use the Story Element Score Sheet to determine if an author has used all of the story elements or determine how many story elements a peer has included in a retell.

3. Procedural: Follow directions for editing a story using the Editor's Toolbox.

4. Metacognitive: Use the Story Element Score Sheet to judge the quality of one's own story or essay writing.

Create: Use Knowledge and Skills to Reorganize Into Something New At this most demanding cognitive dimension, instructors can use the following activities, progressing from least to greatest knowledge demand.

1. Factual: Brainstorm ideas for an essay or an original story using the books read in class as a springboard. Decide on a topic. Make a list of keywords, characters, and places.

2. Conceptual: Plan out the events of the story using the *Story Frames* storyboard or outline an expository essay using the Expository Essay Exercise in Chapter 7.

3. Procedural: Use the Plot Pages graphic organizer to create sentences and then use those sentences to create paragraphs to form an original story or essay.

4. Metacognitive: Create a hook to engage a reader for either an essay or a story. Go back through a story or essay to determine if information is missing. Research a topic to add details to both original narratives and essays. Check for cohesion and smooth transitions between ideas.

The taxonomy is helpful for coming up with ways to stretch a student's comprehension of the stories he hears and the stories he reads. Oral language and written language are not just valuable skills in their own right, they also help students to express how much they understand about what they read and what they hear.

Deficits in word recognition and decoding are defining characteristics of dyslexia, whereas difficulty with listening comprehension may be a symptom of a comprehension-based reading deficit. Many students struggle with both. Students with word recognition challenges alone will often show markedly better performance in comprehension tasks when texts are read aloud to them. Providing this support while their decoding skills improve will allow these students to be exposed to higher-level vocabulary and text structures than what they would be able to read on their own. Students with comprehension deficits, on the other hand, may not benefit from the accommodation of having a text read aloud if their reading comprehension (independent reading) and listening comprehension skills are at a similar level. They may benefit more from explicit instruction in the critical skills outlined early in this chapter, which include the development of vocabulary awareness, sentence comprehension, understanding complex grammatical structures, making inferences, and, of course, forming mental images.

TIPS FOR ONLINE LEARNING AND TELETHERAPY

Building on the suggestions for online learning presented in earlier chapters, the following tips are specific to this chapter.

1. The lesson plan for Describing Book Illustrations may be modified by e-mailing the Wh-question icons to the school or home where students can print and cut out the images.

2. The teacher or therapist introduces the question icons by pulling up the file provided in the downloadable resources and using the screen share feature of Zoom or another platform to discuss each image.

(continued)

(continued)

3. The student holds up one icon at a time to describe a picture projected by the educator on the screen. The educator helps the student verbally build a complex sentence. This may just be an oral exercise, or a Word document in which either the teacher or student types the sentence.

4. I created a PowerPoint file called Silly Pictures that I filled (one image per slide) with royalty-free images from sites like www.pixabay.com. I often use it at the beginning of the year or right before breaks when I want to do a fun, low-key activity but still work on learning objectives. Students use their Wh-question icons to describe each picture. I duplicate the PowerPoint file for each therapy group so that I can type their responses directly onto the slide next to the image.

5. The PowerPoint file with Wh-questions for *Six Dots* may easily be shown to students online.

6. The lesson plan for Concept Scripts may be modified by projecting the pages on the screen and filling in the information with student input. The pages can be used as a Word document or each page may be turned into a slide on a PowerPoint file.

CONCLUSION: BUILDING
READING AND LISTENING COMPREHENSION

One of the best ways for students to improve reading and listening comprehension is through questioning—being able to answer questions and to generate questions about a text. Specific strategies were outlined that emphasized the importance of visual imagery and understanding text structures. The chapter then moved beyond basic questions to outline activities for developing higher level thinking skills through the use of Bloom's Revised Taxonomy, looking at both the cognitive dimension and the knowledge dimension outlined by Anderson and Krathwohl (2001), moving from concrete understanding to more abstract comprehension.

Function Trumps Form
Sentence-Level Instruction

WILLIAM VAN CLEAVE

9

Teachers have a complex history with the term *grammar* and the kinds of instruction it might entail. Some have childhood memories of memorizing (or failing to memorize) long lists of words (e.g., an alphabetical list of prepositions), learning parts of speech songs (e.g., *School House Rock!*'s "Conjunction Junction"; Warburton, Dorough, & ABC, 1973), and labeling parts of speech in extensive sentence activities—of a drill-and-kill philosophy that many students loathed and not a few found challenging. Unfortunately, this restrictive, limited kind of grammar instruction remains prevalent in many schools despite an overwhelming body of research that denies its usefulness (Hudson, 2016; Jones, Myhill, & Bailey, 2013). Perhaps just as many schools have eliminated grammar instruction entirely (Carter, 1996; Kolln & Hancock, 2005; Locke, 2009; Rothery, 1996—all as cited in Hudson, 2016), wishing to avoid practices that students typically detest and that research does not support. Another prevalent approach teaches grammatical concepts incidentally as problems in student writing occur. Unfortunately, such hit-or-miss instruction leaves students with an "understanding of grammar [that] is unlikely to be more than an unstructured list of unrelated items" (Hudson, p. 293).

Interestingly, Myhill and her colleagues conducted studies where students learned "specific grammatical patterns" and applied that understanding "directly to writing tasks" (as cited in Hudson, 2016, p. 296). Her studies revealed that grammar instruction that focuses on application improves writing (Hudson, p. 296). An understanding of text structure, only possible with initial direct, explicit instruction in what is to be recognized, has also been shown to positively impact comprehension (Scott, 2009).

Just last week, a well-intentioned teacher came up to me during an all-day workshop at her school and showed me a packet she had diligently downloaded and printed from Teachers Pay Teachers. On each page, students were expected to label a different part of speech in prewritten sentences. Thinking that because she was in a syntax workshop she had found an ally, she proclaimed that it was essential that students be able to label parts of speech in sentences and that these sheets would prove students' knowledge, provide her with easy-to-grade reinforcement, and build an effective and essential foundation. Her intentions were good, but misguided. Her student goal was identifying parts of speech successfully. Unfortunately, without moving several steps past an initial labeling activity, students are unable to apply their understanding to the development of reading comprehension and writing skills. Helping students develop this deeper understanding requires a shift in how educators think and talk about sentence-level writing.

A SHIFT IN TERMINOLOGY: FROM GRAMMAR TO SYNTAX

Using the term *syntax* instead of *grammar* in working with students and teachers stimulates a curiosity about a new field, rather than a sense that we are moving into familiar—and tedious—territory. Syntax also reflects a more accurate understanding of the kind of work we want to do with our students. Grammar means different things to different people. Syntax, on the other hand, has one distinct meaning: It is the arrangement of words to create sentences, in essence, word order.

It is somewhat amusing to hear primary teachers claim, "I can't believe John's paper! He wrote nine sentences with eight *and*s and one period!" The goal, of course, is to teach students not to write these lengthy run-on sentences and to instead write effective and varied sentences. But children first write as they speak. Anyone who has listened to a 5-year-old child relate a story will recognize such a paper as a reflection of the way the child speaks. Elementary students write as simplistically as they speak—perhaps more so. Their thoughts in writing are choppy, and their sentences lack complexity and variety. This is normal and expected in young children, but as they mature, they need to be able to expand their "sentence repertoire."

Over time, in a typically developing student, written syntax diverges from spoken syntax. The former becomes more sophisticated and complex; many features crop up frequently in written syntax, but not often in spoken syntax. Listening to a speaker requires auditorily processing and retaining the thoughts and ideas conveyed. Listeners can only hold onto so much syntactic complexity and richness before they lose both retention and comprehension. The syntax of an essay, a textbook, or even a novel or short story can be much more sophisticated and complex. The reader can examine the language at her own pace and return to particular words or passages to reflect. Crafting written sentences is somewhat parallel to reading them. The skilled writer can think about how to combine ideas effectively to convey an idea. She can determine when a sentence has too many ideas, or not enough. She also can choose and then revise the words she uses to convey her ideas.

A number of factors impact struggling students attempting to write sentences. A few of them are worth mentioning here:

- Both elementary students and those with writing deficits often struggle mightily with transcription skills, which include the motor component (handwriting and word processing), spelling, and mechanics. When a student who has difficulty with transcription attempts to write her thoughts, "bottlenecks" in her transcribing impede both the quantity and quality of her text (Alves, Branco, Castro, & Olive, 2012, as cited in Connelly & Dockrell, 2016). For additional information on transcription difficulties, see Berninger and Wolf (2009) and Graham (2009–2010).

- Struggling students, as a secondary consequence of their learning differences, typically have reduced reading experience. They do not read at their grade level as often as their grade-appropriate peers, if at all. As a result, they neither have access to the varied, grade-appropriate syntax that would improve their comprehension of sophisticated ideas, nor do they possess the ability to generate similarly varied and sophisticated sentences in their own writing.

As is the case with all aspects of literacy, students who struggle need direct, explicit instruction in syntax. Effective instruction will help them improve their sentence-level reading comprehension and the variety and effectiveness of their sentence-level writing as well.

A SHIFT IN HOW WE THINK ABOUT PARTS-OF-SPEECH INSTRUCTION

When it comes to parts of speech, function trumps form. Instead of asking what a word *is,* instructors should teach students to ask what it *does.* Ask students or teachers what part of speech the word *man* is, and they are likely to state confidently that it is a noun. They would be right most of the time, but consider the command, "Man the lifeboats!" Here it is used as a verb. I lived in South Carolina for over a decade, and while I was there I learned that *tree*, a word I had always considered to be solely a noun, can be used as a verb, hence, "The dog treed the cat." You can be a *smooth* operator (adjective) but also *smooth* the bedspread after you make the bed (verb). A *table* (noun) sits in some kitchens, but at a meeting at work, you might *table* a discussion until later (verb). Thousands of words serve more than one function, depending on how they are used in a particular sentence. Following are some discussion points that will illuminate both traps to avoid and practices to embrace.

Adjectives: Teach Function, Not Location

Though a student might learn that adjectives appear before the nouns they describe, this is a trick based on locating an adjective, rather than understanding how it functions. Consider this sentence:

> The *funny* man wore a *plaid* suit to the party.

The location of *funny* and *plaid* (in front of the nouns they describe) is irrelevant. Each of these adjectives describes (or modifies) the noun it accompanies. *Funny* describes the demeanor or personality of the man; *plaid* describes the pattern of the suit. Considering the function of these words helps students understand how they relate to other words in the sentence. Adjectives are not just describing words, they specifically describe *nouns* and *pronouns*. When a student encounters an adjective, he or she must find what it describes. Doing so verifies that it is an adjective, but more interestingly builds comprehension as the student considers a word's relationship to other words in the sentence. Consider another example:

> The woman was both *kind* and *intelligent*.

Though *kind* and *intelligent* are adjectives, they are not located in front of the noun they describe. These predicate adjectives (adjectives located after a linking verb) are not anywhere close to the noun they describe, but clearly this is a *kind* woman and an *intelligent* woman. Again, an understanding of the way *kind* and *intelligent* relate to *woman* builds a comprehension link and reinforces the notion that function trumps form. The term *adjective* merely allows students to communicate about the word.

Adverbs: Teach Function, Not Suffix *-ly*

Teachers sometimes instruct students that adverbs typically end in *-ly*. Again, this is a trick designed to help students locate adverbs in existing sentences, a skill that improves neither reading nor writing skills. It turns syntax work into a seek-and-find whose goal is to locate words ending in suffix *-ly* and mark them as adverbs. Moreover, it is inaccurate and misleading. Some adverbs do in fact end in suffix *-ly*. Here's a sample sentence:

> The dog barked *loudly* and *anxiously* as the postal carrier walked *quickly* up to the porch and *promptly* delivered the mail.

Each of the four italicized words is an adverb, not because it ends in suffix *-ly* but because it describes a verb. *Loudly* and *anxiously* describe how the dog barked; *quickly* describes how the postal carrier walked; and *promptly* describes when he delivered the mail. Consideration of how words are related to other words in a sentence is more thought-provoking and useful than labeling; it raises interesting questions and challenges students to explore and deepen their understanding. Again, the term *adverb* merely facilitates the conversation.

Not all words ending in suffix *-ly* are adverbs. Consider the following:

> The *elderly* woman's *untimely* passing interrupted my *weekly* routine.

Elderly, untimely, and *weekly* are adjectives, again despite the fact that they end in suffix -*ly*. *Elderly* describes the woman, *untimely* describes her passing, and *weekly* describes the author's routine. Similarly, students in a class might enjoy discussing the Cowardly Lion from *The Wizard of Oz*. While *cowardly* ends in suffix -*ly*, it clearly describes the lion, making it an adjective.

Also, students who are taught that adverbs end in suffix -*ly* might find the italicized words in this sentence confusing:

> We need to leave *soon*, so if you do not get your belongings together *now*, you will be grounded *forever*.

All three of the italicized words are adverbs, and not one includes suffix -*ly*. Many of the adverbs older students will use, in fact, answer the question "when," and some of these "when" adverbs lack the -*ly* suffix (e.g., *soon, never, often, sometimes, now, always*).

Prepositions and Conjunctions: Teach Function, Not Word Lists

One of the most troubling practices in sentence-level instruction today concerns memorizing long lists of prepositions and conjunctions, typically in alphabetical order. This rote memory activity is particularly challenging for struggling writers; it has as its only goal the labeling of a particular part of speech in a prewritten sentence. And worse, it provides misinformation to students.

One of the words typically memorized on an alphabetical list of prepositions is *after*. Consider these two sentences:

> *After* our bike ride in the park, we stopped for fresh lemonade.

> *After* the girls finished their homework, they went to the movies.

In the first sentence, *after* functions as a preposition because it begins a phrase, while in the second, it functions as a conjunction because it begins a clause. Memorizing that *after* is a preposition serves only one purpose—to label it as a preposition in a prewritten sentence. Because the research does not support excessive labeling, and because *after* often serves another function, such a practice is both a waste of time and misleading as well. Again, rather than focus on what the word *is*, students should instead focus on what it *does*. The preposition *after* in the first sentence begins the phrase "after our bike ride" and explains that stopping for lemonade occurred after an event, a bike ride in this case. In the second sentence, *after* begins a dependent clause and helps sequence two activities, the girls finishing their homework and the girls going to the movies. The difference is subtle but important. Later in this chapter, significant time will be devoted to clauses, and this focus may help to clarify the differences here.

A Rewarding Way to Use Parts of Speech

The parts-of-speech portion of syntax instruction can be both useful and satisfying. Use the terminology (e.g., noun, adverb, conjunction) as a means of discussing the functions of words in both reading and writing—as a means to the end, rather than the end product itself, or, as Cameron puts it, "that grammatical terminology is simply the tool that facilitates the investigation and analysis" (1997, as cited in Myhill & Watson, 2014). Remember that function trumps form.

Consider this sentence:

> The *boy* played on the *playground* at the *school* in our *town*.

Boy, playground, school, and *town* are nouns. Though some would define *noun* as "person, place, thing, or idea" (with *idea* being introduced only to older students who are capable of abstract thinking), they miss the most important part of the definition in their haste to simplify it for labeling. A noun *names* a person, place, thing, or idea—it's a namer, and the words *noun* and *nominate* interestingly share a common root in Latin. The four nouns in the previous example sentence *name*. This is essential because it shows what a noun *does* rather than what it *is*.

Here is another interesting sentence example:

> *Soon*, Marcus and Anna must get ready to leave for the movies.

Soon tells when Marcus and Anna must get ready. Words that describe verbs are called *adverbs*. Using the term *adverb* facilitates our discussion of the word *soon* and allows us to consider it in a familiar context with other words that share the same function. Discovering that the adverb *soon* tells when Marcus and Anna must get ready is also useful for comprehension, particularly because *soon* is not adjacent to the verb it describes.

Here's an example that a student of most any age might write, but the discussion a teacher could have with her students about the words' function would require a student ready to handle the information:

> Eli loves to ski.

Every sentence in English requires a verb. A student's first reaction would be to circle "ski" as the action of the sentence. Actually, "to ski" is an infinitive, and it serves as a noun. But never mind all of that. What will prove fruitful, even to younger students, is a discussion of what is actually happening in this sentence. Is Eli skiing? Not at all. In fact, Eli could love to ski and be in a hospital bed with a broken leg up in a sling, correct? The action in this sentence is love. "I love to ski" is similar to "I love chocolate." This kind of rich discussion is syntax at its best. It considers function and also works comprehension skills deeply. It focuses attention where it should be—on how words work with other words to convey meaning. The labels are merely the vocabulary to facilitate the discussion.

Summary: Teach Function and Relationships to Improve Reading and Writing

Memorizing alphabetical lists of prepositions or conjunctions and learning identifying tricks (e.g., adverbs end in *-ly*) raises a number of concerns:

- Rote memory, or the memorization of meaningless, disconnected facts, is often extremely challenging for struggling students. Such activities are both tedious and frustrating, especially because they do not help students improve reading comprehension and syntax skills.

- The purpose of such activities is to help students locate and label words, something the research has shown to be ineffective in building better readers and writers.

- Even if a teacher determined that labeling was an important goal in her class, a student who encountered a word and wanted to "test" whether it was a preposition or not would have to recite the memorized list in order to recall whether the word is on the list. Consider the preposition *with*, which appears near the end of the alphabetical list, and it becomes clear how time-consuming the process could be.

- Many words, including some that appear on the preposition and conjunction lists and some that end in suffix *-ly*, serve more than one function, depending on the sentence in which they appear. A student could observe a word such as *after* in a sentence, recall that it is on the preposition list, label it as a preposition, and still misidentify it if the word in that particular sentence served a different purpose.

- Finally, and most importantly, this kind of labeling diminishes the role that parts of speech can play in genuine reading comprehension. Knowing that *smooth* is an adjective in "smooth operator" and a verb in "smooth the bedspread" is useful, not because the student knows the terms *adjective* and *verb*, but because those terms allow for a discussion of purpose—the way words relate to other words and the way they convey meaning. It involves comprehension.

GOOD PARTS OF SPEECH INSTRUCTION: A MODEL

Figure 9.1 shows a version of the activity sheet I developed for the MTSS Writing Committee work conducted for the Pennsylvania Training and Technical Assistance Network (PaTTAN). This example is based on *Six Dots: A Story of Young Louis Braille* (Bryant, 2016), one model story used in *Story Frames*. Teachers who choose to adopt this I.E.C.C. format for syntax instruction would first introduce a concept to students. Then, the students would **I**dentify examples of that concept in context; **E**xpand by generating examples to add

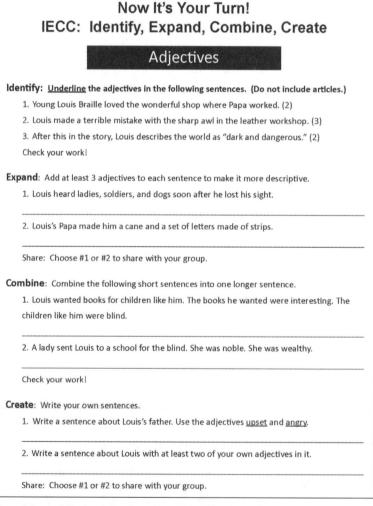

Figure 9.1. Activity sheet developed for MTSS Writing Committee work for the Pennsylvania Training and Technical Assistance Network (PaTTAN), based on *Six Dots: A Story of Young Louis Braille* (Bryant, 2016).

to prewritten sentences; **C**ombine simplistic sentences into more sophisticated ones with a focus on the concept under study; and finally, **C**reate sentences that include examples of the concept. Ideally, such work would involve texts students are studying in their academic coursework.

The I.E.C.C. format makes it clear that labeling is merely a launching point for the deep syntax activities that truly build better readers and writers. The *expand* and *combine* steps ask students to apply their newfound knowledge immediately to build better sentences that use the studied element. A number of studies (Andrews et al., 2004; Graham & Perin, 2007; Hillocks, 2003; Hillocks & Mavrognes, 1986—all as cited in Hudson, 2016, p. 296) point particularly to the latter as a best practice in writing instruction. Bruce Saddler's work (2007, 2012) has focused particular attention on this area as well. Finally, each sentence-level activity should involve sentence *creation,* which allows students the chance to apply their knowledge in context. Using this I.E.C.C. template for teaching parts of speech has been transformative in my work with teachers, as it has forced the conversation that prioritizes function over form and pushes teachers to create activities that improve student readers and writers.

To summarize:

I – Identify

E – Expand

C – Combine

C – Create

These activities and others can be found in *Writing Matters: Developing Sentence Skills in Students of All Ages* (Van Cleave, 2014) and *Sentence Sense, Books A* and *B* (Van Cleave, 2015 and 2017, respectively), the workbooks based on *Writing Matters*. Because the research on syntax instruction argues convincingly in favor of creating activities based on the texts and topics students are studying, it also makes sense for teachers to generate activities based on the content of their courses.

THE SECOND LAYER OF SYNTAX INSTRUCTION: SENTENCE COMPONENTS

Too often, sentence-level instruction remains in the realm of parts-of-speech instruction and never ventures into understanding of sentence *components.* An exploration of these components allows for an understanding of the way *groups* of words interact and also gives students the building blocks both to write and to read/understand a variety of different kinds of sentences. Some of the fundamentals, including subject/predicate and simple and compound sentences, are first-grade concepts. Most of the rest of the content here begins to be taught in the third grade.

Unfortunately, teachers in English language arts sometimes resist the transition from teaching parts of speech to teaching sentence components because of one or more of the following:

1. They do not themselves have a good grasp of sentence parts and higher-level syntax knowledge.

2. They incorrectly believe that students without the ability to regurgitate parts of speech and their definitions are incapable of grasping sentence components and construction.

3. They think their students are not mature enough or old enough for this kind of content.

Too often, students only learn about sentence components, including clause structure, in middle school, if at all. Teachers often express concern that their students "still don't know what an adjective is" and sometimes use this as a reason to spend months on parts of speech, even in the upper elementary and middle school grades. Doing so means that students often do not learn about and explore clauses until winter or even spring each year, and as a result, their understanding of and ability to apply clause knowledge never solidifies. Because the fundamental building block of all sentences is the clause, an understanding of how they work and how to manipulate them can be a game changer in terms of writing and reading comprehension. Research indicates that an understanding of syntactic components positively impacts reading comprehension (Brimo, Apel, & Fountain, 2017; Scott, 2009).

Third-grade language standards, such as the Common Core State Standards (CCSS) and various states' standards, suggest that students should be able to generate simple, compound, and complex sentences. It is therefore useful for instructors beginning in third grade to introduce students to clause structure. Mainstream third graders are indeed ready for this kind of work. Compromises and adjustments have to be made for students functioning below grade level, however, not because they lack the ability but because their reading/writing skills may mandate different immediate priorities.

Foundational Sentence Building Blocks

Sentences, regardless of complexity, are made up of foundational building blocks. Students need to have a thorough understanding of these building blocks both to expand the variety of their own sentences and to understand the more sophisticated sentences they read.

In *Writing Matters* (Van Cleave, 2014), each concept includes a definition and useful strategies for instruction. Table 9.1 outlines these terms and their definitions.

Subject and Predicate   As early as first grade (or even kindergarten), students can and should be introduced to two core sentence components: the subject and its predicate. Students can begin with definitions that work exclusively for action verbs (the ones listed in Table 9.1). Except in the case of an imperative sentence (command), every English sentence contains at least one subject and its predicate. Consider the following:

> S   P
> Marcia ate breakfast.

Marcia is the simple subject, or the *doer*, because she is doing the eating. *Ate* is the simple predicate, or the *do*, because it is what Marcia is doing. At first students should be asked to explain the relationship between *doer* and *do* using simplistic sentences like this; that is, sentences with little or no elaboration or detail. Doing so allows students to develop comfort with the vocabulary of subject–predicate and the relationship each has with the other.

Table 9.1.   Terms and *Writing Matters* definitions

Term	*Writing Matters* definition
Simple subject	Noun or pronoun doing the action—"the doer"
Simple predicate	Action of the subject/main verb—"the do"
Compound subject	Two or more nouns/pronouns that share the action
Compound predicate	Two or more actions that share a subject
Complete subject	Simple subject and the words used to describe it
Complete predicate	Simple predicate and the words used to describe it

From Van Cleave, W. [2014]. *Writing matters: Developing sentence skills in students of all ages* [2nd ed.] Greenville, SC: W.V.C.ED.; reprinted by permission.

It cements students' understanding of these important building blocks. Here is a slightly more sophisticated sentence:

S   P
In the nearby park, the boy played catch with his older brother.

In this sentence, the fact that there are several nouns *(park, boy, catch, brother)* makes identifying the subject more difficult. If a student were to choose *park* as the subject (because this is the first noun in the sentence), the instructor might say, "What is the park doing?" There is no answer to this question. The student can then be asked, "What is the action?" *Played* is a straightforward action to find, and the instructor can then elicit the subject from the student with the question, "Who is playing?" Students need a lot of practice with the core concepts of subject and predicate. Rather than tasking students with long, tedious worksheets with dozens of sentences to label, instead have students practice locating subjects and predicates over time, in shorter sessions. As students grow more comfortable with the basics, add nuances, such as compound subjects and predicates, linking and helping verbs serving the role of predicate, and, eventually, predicates followed by pesky infinitives.

Students at *all* grade levels should spend some time with subject–predicate relationships. They are required of all sentences, and they are the key components of clauses; understanding clauses helps students with sentence variety and comprehension. Interestingly, a number of approaches to teaching comprehension suggest that students should locate subject–predicate pairs in complex text. Once they have found the subjects and predicates in a sentence, the descriptive phrases and other structures will, in essence, fall away. If students are unable to find the subject–predicate relationships within sentences, they are unlikely to understand the sentences they read, whether they know the terms *subject* and *predicate* or not.

Recently, in a high school workshop for teachers, a 27-year veteran biology teacher came up at break to tell me he had applied this subject–predicate experiment with the genetics section of his AP Biology textbook. The students, who had always grappled mightily with this reading, spent some time highlighting subjects and predicates, and they had a better grasp of the processes the text described. Ideally, subject–predicate location is an automatic, comfortable process, so the comprehension payoff does not take an extra, specific identifying step. When work with locating subject and predicate begins early and continues with increasingly complex text as students grow older, the payoffs can be significant and more automatic.

Clause Structure   Subjects and predicates are the only required components of clauses. Table 9.2 again presents information taken from *Writing Matters*. Mainstream third graders can handle this content comfortably.

Establish a firm knowledge of clause structure, as clauses are relatively concrete and have specific, recognizable ingredients. While you are establishing the basics, *phrase* can

Table 9.2.   Subject–predicate terms and *Writing Matters* definitions

Term	*Writing Matters* definition
Subject	Who or what is doing the action—the "doer"
Predicate	Action/main verb—the "do"
Clause	Group of words with subject and its predicate
Independent clause	Clause that can stand by itself
Dependent clause	Clause that cannot stand by itself
Phrase	Group of words without subject and predicate

From Van Cleave, W. [2014]. *Writing matters: Developing sentence skills in students of all ages* [2nd ed.] Greenville, SC: W.V.C.ED.; reprinted by permission.

really be "the other stuff"—until students are sophisticated enough to handle that material. Teachers who teach phrases before or at the same time they teach clauses often confuse their students and with little value.

Clauses are the building blocks that create sentences. Understanding clauses will help students develop their syntactic repertoire, as both readers and writers. More specifically, a deep understanding of clauses assists students with the following:

- ❑ Sentence generation
- ❑ Sentence variety
- ❑ Sentence expansion
- ❑ Sentence combining
- ❑ Comprehension at the syntax level
- ❑ Avoiding and eliminating run-ons and fragments
- ❑ Tackling sentence-level errors on standardized tests

Teachers and their students should know what a clause is. Syntactic errors are almost always linked to students' understanding (or misunderstanding) of the clause. If something confuses a student (or instructor new to teaching this content), returning to what a clause is will often clear up their confusion.

Students should spend time completing clause/phrase sorts, understanding that if a group of words contains a subject and its predicate, it is a clause. Three of the six groups of words below are clauses; the other three are phrases. See if you can discern a clause from a phrase.

_____ 1. at the river's edge
_____ 2. the shark entered the bay
_____ 3. Wilbur looked up into the web
_____ 4. under the old stone bridge
_____ 5. when the children sat at the picnic table
_____ 6. in the pot on the stove in our kitchen

Numbers 2, 3, and 5 are clauses. Each has its own subject–predicate relationship (i.e., shark–entered; Wilbur–looked; children–sat, respectively). The other three are phrases. In fact, number 6 has *three* consecutive prepositional phrases!

Students should do a lot of clause/phrase sorting. Return to this kind of activity frequently, again with short practice sessions. Identifying clauses allows students the opportunity to review subjects and their predicates, and also to practice with the units of language they need to build different kinds of sentences. When a student misidentifies a group of words, the teacher should use careful questioning to elicit the correct understanding and a deeper understanding of the concept addressed. The discussion might go something like this:

Jake: "The shark entered the bay" is a phrase.

Instructor: What makes you think so?

Jake: It's not a clause.

Instructor: What does a clause have in it?

Jake: A subject and verb.

Instructor: Do you see a predicate or verb?

Jake: Oh wait. "Entered" is a verb.

Instructor: Good. What entered?

Jake: The shark. I guess this is a clause after all.

Instructor: You bet.

Independent and Dependent Clauses   Luckily, there are only two kinds of clauses, independent and dependent. Again, students should sort these, this time discerning whether clauses are independent (can stand by themselves as sentences) or dependent (*cannot* stand by themselves as sentences). With the six examples that follow, three are independent clauses and three are dependent clauses. If any of them give you pause, it may help to read them aloud. Native English speakers, comfortable with English syntax, can typically hear the difference. Sometimes, students for whom English is a second language struggle with this, not because the concept is difficult but because they lack familiarity with English syntax. Because these are all clauses, each contains a subject and its predicate.

____ 1. if the battery in your watch dies
____ 2. I bought a new phone last week
____ 3. after we ate supper this evening
____ 4. although I am particularly hungry this morning
____ 5. the boys cleaned their room on Sunday morning
____ 6. at dusk the couple took a walk in the nearby park

Numbers 2, 5, and 6 are independent; numbers 1, 3, and 4 are dependent. You may notice that some of the clauses contain phrases. Sentences are made of clauses, and those clauses may contain phrases. Just as they do with clause/phrase work, students should return to independent/dependent clause sorting again and again, focusing particular attention on the necessary skill of locating subject and predicate/main verb.

Occasionally, a student may incorrectly identify a dependent clause as an independent one. (Rarely does a student identify an independent clause as a dependent one.) Often, their confusion stems from difficulty recognizing the ways in which dialogue can differ from standard, declarative sentences. Consider the following:

Example 1

> Angelica: Why have you been frowning all morning?

> Frederick: Because I have a headache.

Example 2

> Dori: Can we go to the movies tonight?

> Mom: Only if you finish your homework.

These kinds of dialogues are parts of everyday conversations and also typical of narrative writing. In each case, though, the responder is speaking with a dependent clause, not a complete sentence. Dialogue does *not* reflect standard expository writing and should not be used as a model for sentence writing instruction. When a student incorrectly identifies a dependent clause as independent, discuss with him the difference between speaking and writing and the difference between a complete thought and one that is *dependent* on a prior statement, which is the case in the previous dialogues. If Frederick were to answer in a complete sentence, he would say, "I have been frowning all morning because I have a headache" and Mom would say, "You can go to the movies tonight only if you finish your homework."

Using the Building Blocks to Construct Sentences

Students should use their knowledge of subject/predicate and independent/dependent clause to build different kinds of sentences. As they grow more comfortable with the structures they have learned, they will write more sophisticated sentences, not just in isolation but also in their paragraphs, essays, and stories. As their sentence repertoire develops and becomes more automatic, their sentence-level comprehension will also improve.

The examples used in this chapter are either general and relatable to most any reader, or particular to the text *Six Dots*. Remember that the research argues that syntax-based activities should be connected to content writing. In other words, an I.E.C.C. parts-of-speech sheet or a sentence-building activity would best be created about material the students are studying, whether fiction or nonfiction. These authentic writing activities help students comprehend the text they are studying more deeply and also encourage deeper thinking about that material. An additional benefit is that the generated sentences will be more substantive when they are about "something" rather than whatever happens to cross the student writer's mind. These authentic writing activities also fit naturally with the *Story Frames* approach.

Once clauses are established as the building blocks of all sentences, students can then think about different kinds of sentences (simple, compound, complex, and compound–complex) as merely clauses combined in different ways. Rather than a restrictive or limiting practice, using this conceptual framework frees students to develop sentences with increasing variety and sophistication as they learn new possibilities for sentence creation based on new ways to combine clauses. Further, knowing how clauses can (and cannot) be combined allows students to hone their ability to determine what is and is not a sentence and how to punctuate sentences, based on the clause components they contain. The fact that punctuation is not arbitrary, but instead follows a system of specific rules, is often a comfort to students who have been plagued with punctuation issues in their writing. Again, the information that follows showing sentence types with grade-appropriate explanations is borrowed from *Writing Matters*:

Sentence types with grade-appropriate explanations		
Term	**Explanation for Grades 3 and up**	**Explanation for Grades K–2**
Simple sentence	One independent clause (I)	Complete thought with subject and its main verb/predicate
Compound sentence	Two independent clauses joined by comma + coordinating conjunction (I, fanboys, I)	Two complete thoughts joined by comma + and/but/or
Complex sentence (with adverb clause)	One independent clause and one (or more) dependent clause (D, I, or ID)	N/A

Simple Sentences Some simple sentences (one independent clause) are simplistic:

Jake slept.	Nancy ate a pear.
The sun set at 8:00 p.m.	Marcus laughed.
We can drive home.	The horse galloped in the meadow.
Trish and Tamika raced.	The light flickered and went out.

Others are far from simplistic, but they are still simple sentences because they comprise a single independent clause. Simplistic simple sentences can be made quite interesting and creative through a bevy of elements useful in expansion. Believe it or not, these two sentences are also simple sentences grammatically:

At just after midnight, *Andrew Telleman*, husband to Margo Telleman and father to five children, *awoke* at the sound of burglars in the downstairs hall of his house.

Without consideration for others on the team, *Marco left* the cooler open and *ruined* the recently packed lunches.

In the first sentence, *Andrew Telleman* is the subject, while *awoke* is the predicate or main verb. In the second sentence, *Marco* is the subject and *left* and *ruined* make up the compound predicate. (A simple sentence can have a compound subject or compound predicate as long as it consists of just one independent clause.)

Compound Sentences   A progression of skills for teaching compound sentences might look like these examples.

Progression of compound sentences	
Stage 1: Grades K–2	Two complete thoughts joined by comma + and/but/or
Stage 2: Grades 3–4	Two independent clauses joined by comma + and/but/or/yet/so
Stage 3: Grades 5+	Two independent clauses joined by comma + coordinating conjunction
Stage 4: Grades 8+	Advanced compound sentences: two independent clauses joined by semi-colon

Typically developing children, even before they enter school, frequently speak in compound sentences. First graders can learn about compound sentences, though they would use the concept of *complete sentence* instead of *independent clause* to describe the components on either side of the comma/conjunction structure. The conjunction serves as glue to hold the independent clauses together but does not alter the meaning of the parts. The chart that follows provides examples of sentences at this level, which are referred to as stage 1 examples with *and, but,* and *or.*

Stage 1 examples with *and, but,* and *or*		
First independent clause	**Comma + and/but/or**	**Second independent clause**
Our new puppy Ginger loves to take walks	, and	Marvin is responsible for giving her lots of exercise.
The team can go out for pizza after the game	, or	we can get on the road home immediately.
The bowl crashed to the floor	, but	no one claimed responsibility.

It may make sense to limit the use of *so* as a coordinating conjunction; students often overuse it in their writing anyway, so focusing on it in instruction does nothing to improve a student's sentence repertoire. *Yet,* on the other hand, functions much like *but,* although it provides some variety. The following chart shows stage 2 examples with *so* and *yet.*

Stage 2 examples with *so* and *yet*		
First independent clause	**Comma + so/yet**	**Second independent clause**
We were hungry	, so	we walked to the corner bakery for cookies.
Ginger was exhausted after her long walk	, so	she took a nice nap on the couch.
The student struggled with math and science	, yet	his work in English and social studies was remarkable.
Scientists classify the duckbill platypus as a mammal	, yet	they lay eggs unlike other mammals.

Instructing students to use *for* and *nor* as conjunctions should wait until students can grasp their meaning and use them effectively. Direct instruction can assist students in understanding how they function in text but also in how to use them in writing. A few examples are shown here.

Stage 3 examples with *for* and *nor*		
First independent clause	**Comma + for/nor**	**Second independent clause**
Elijah began to scream at the top of his lungs	, for	his mother refused to give him a second cookie.
Yoda tries to teach Luke patience in *The Empire Strikes Back*	, for	he fears Luke will rashly rush into danger.
William does not like mushrooms	, nor	does he like lima beans.
We could not go to the pool	, nor	could we play golf because of the lightning.

When a student is ready to cover all seven of these coordinating conjunctions (stage 3), the mnemonic *fanboys*, f(or), a(nd), n(or), b(ut), o(r), y(et), s(o), can be useful to help students remember them. Only these seven words can serve the function of coordinating conjunction. Because the prefix *co-* means "with or together," it should come as no surprise that these conjunctions keep the clauses they join on equal footing. When I ask students to write a compound sentence, they will often respond, "So, that's I, fanboys I [independent clause + comma + coordinating conjunction + independent clause], right?" This is a great way for them to think about the structure of what they intend to write.

Complex Sentences With Adverbial Clauses   If a student writes exclusively in simple and compound sentences, his writing will sound repetitious, tedious, and often jarring. Students who expand their sentence repertoire through incorporating complex sentences into their writing significantly improve the flow and sophistication of their writing.

Remember that complex sentences comprise one independent clause and one (or more) dependent clauses. In the complex sentences that are most accessible to young students, the dependent clauses begin with subordinating conjunctions and are therefore adverbial. The following chart shows some examples where the dependent clause, which begins with its subordinating conjunction, starts the sentence.

Examples where the dependent clause starts the sentence		
Dependent clause beginning with subordinating conjunction	**Comma**	**Independent clause**
When your alarm rings	,	you need to get out of bed.
If we get any more snow	,	school will be canceled for sure.
Whenever she got a migraine	,	Cindy preferred to sit in a dark room.

Each of these complex sentences begins with a subordinating conjunction, which functions as the first word of the dependent clause. In other words, their structure is D, I. Subordinating conjunctions *always* introduce dependent clauses; it is their only function. When a subordinating conjunction begins a complex sentence, a comma is required to separate the dependent clause from the independent clause that follows it. Look carefully at the three sentences. The portions that follow the commas could stand by themselves as sentences, meaning they are independent clauses.

When they are ready, students can be taught that sometimes complex sentences begin with an independent clause that is then followed by a dependent clause. This style of complex sentence takes no comma. The following chart shows examples of sentences that begin with an independent clause.

Examples where the independent clause starts the sentence	
Independent clause	**Dependent clause**
The dog tugged anxiously at his collar	*because* he wanted to chase a squirrel.
His boots were caked with mud	*whenever* he hiked the south field.
Nan must finish her homework	*before* she can watch television.

In these sentences, the part before the italicized word is an independent clause, meaning it could stand by itself as its own sentence. The italicized words are subordinating conjunctions, which serve to introduce the dependent clauses. These sentences, then, are ID (independent clause + dependent clause). Again, no comma is required.

The subordinating conjunctions that begin dependent clauses are some of the most powerful words in English. Not only do they allow for the creation of complex sentences, they also significantly impact meaning. While students should not be required to memorize lists of conjunctions, providing them a list as reference for sentence building makes a lot of sense. The following chart shows a relatively complete list of subordinating conjunctions taken from Binder Insert A (see www.wvced.com). Students should begin with just a few conjunctions, adding to their list as they grow more comfortable with the language and structure.

Subordinating conjunctions		
Time	**Cause**	**Manner**
after	as	as
as	because	as if
as soon as	since	as though
before		
just as	**Comparison**	**Purpose**
now that	as	in order that
once	just as	so that
since	than	
until		**Condition**
when	**Concession**	as long as
whenever	although	even if
while	even though	if
	though	unless
Place	whereas	whether
where	while	
wherever		

The power of these words cannot be underestimated. Consider the sentences that follow.

Eliza ran through the house screaming *after* her brother was studying.
Eliza ran through the house screaming *while* her brother was studying.
Eliza ran through the house screaming *just as* her brother was studying.
Eliza ran through the house screaming *because* her brother was studying.

They are identical except for the subordinating conjunction. Spend a few minutes considering how that single word change affects the meaning of the entire sentence.

While the D, I, and ID complex sentences here can be further complexified with the addition of other dependent clauses, they still remain complex because a complex sentence is one independent and one (or more) dependent clause. See the chart that follows for examples of sentences with more than one dependent clause. A sentence must contain an independent clause, but the number and position of the dependent clauses can vary.

Sentences with more than one dependent clause			
Dependent clause	**Comma**	**Independent clause**	**Dependent clause**
Whenever the clock chimes	,	I jump out of my skin	because it startles me.
If you protect the cut with a bandage	,	it will stay clean and dry	although the sticky tape may irritate your skin.

Complex Sentences With Adverbial Clauses: Sample Lessons   Arguably, many subordinating conjunctions fall into the category of academic vocabulary. As such, they are useful not just for writing, but also reading comprehension. Mainstream third-grade students are ready to learn about clauses, subordinating conjunctions, and complex sentences for the first time. Early on, these young students often benefit from specific, isolated complex sentence lessons where the instructor introduces only one or two of these subordinating conjunctions. Sometimes *when* is a good subordinating conjunction with which to begin. The discussion can be rich and include a number of different elements.

After a quick review of the concepts of subject, predicate/main verb, clause, and independent/dependent clause, the instructor might first introduce a straightforward complex sentence, comprising a dependent clause, comma, and then independent clause. Because the subordinating conjunction begins the dependent clause, in this structure it also begins the sentence. Here is an example:

When Louis scratched his damaged eye, the infection spread to his other eye.

Discussion of this sentence and the structure it represents might include the following:

- Distinguishing *when* as a subordinating conjunction from situations where it is used as an interrogative. For example: "I ate breakfast *when* the sun came up" versus "*When* are we leaving?"

- Examining the function of *when* in the sentence as the word that makes the first clause function with the second clause, both for structure (subordinating conjunction required to make the clauses join) and for meaning. For example: What question does *when* answer? (It's a time word.) What is its purpose as a time word here? (To say that the scratching of his eye coincided with the infection spreading to his other eye.) What can you infer from this? (The infection spread *because* Louis scratched his damaged eye.)

- Examining the difference between the complex sentence and two disconnected simple sentences. For example: "When Louis scratched his damaged eye, the infection spread to his other eye" versus "Louis scratched his damaged eye. The infection spread to his other eye."

These activities use clause structure to enhance comprehension. Next, it is important for the instructor to move to sentence generation with activities such as sentence expansion, sentence combining, and sentence generation.

Sentence Expansion   Help students locate places where adjectives, adverbs, and even prepositional phrases can be added if they are ready. Sentence expansions might include examples such as these:

> When Margaret lit the campfire, the children cheered.
> *becomes*
> When Margaret lit the campfire **in the small clearing**, the **happy** children cheered **loudly**.
> *or*
> When Margaret **finally** lit the **tiny** campfire, the **enthusiastic** children **around it** cheered.

Taking time to share and discuss student results, though time consuming, is essential.

Sentence Combining   Show students simple sentences and ask them to combine those sentences using the conjunction *when*.

> The computer malfunctioned. Nancy spilled coffee on it.
> The ant crawled onto the boy's paper plate. He flicked it into the woods.

Encourage a discussion of how *when* changes the meaning. Also, help students decide which clause should take the subordinating conjunction, thereby becoming dependent. "When Nancy spilled coffee on it, the computer malfunctioned" suggests that the coffee caused the malfunction. "When the computer malfunctioned, Nancy spilled coffee on it" suggests that Nancy was frustrated enough by the malfunction to spill coffee on the computer. These nuances in meaning are useful in terms of comprehension and engaging to students, who will find the possibilities both varied and amusing. This is the kind of syntax instruction that builds students' knowledge and also engages them in deep, meaningful sentence-level discussion.

Sentence Generation   Use tandem writing to begin the process, particularly with young or struggling students. Provide them with the dependent clause and allow them to generate the independent clause.

> When Louis first practiced with the French army captain's code,
> When Louis began experimenting with his new alphabet,

Again, contextualizing our syntax work with examples based on a studied text is worthwhile and supported by the research.

Similar activities can be done with ID complex sentences, where the dependent clause follows the independent clause. The fact that many complex sentences can be D, I, or ID, depending on author preference, is illuminating to student readers and writers. Look at these examples with the conjunction *if*:

> *If* Louis had not injured himself as a young child, braille never would have been invented.
> Braille never would have been invented *if* Louis had not injured himself as a young child.

Ask students if one structure is better than the other. The answer is no, of course, though preceding sentences in a paragraph may make one preferable. Many D, I sentences can be flipped to create ID sentences. This is about repertoire, about having a number of options at our fingertips as we write. When these different options are truly automatic, writers generate text that contains genuine sentence variety, one essential goal of expository writing.

Once students are comfortable with D, I, and ID sentences, complex sentences with more than one dependent clause can be introduced. Students will have already generated some of these, whether they recognized it or not.

Sometimes, using sentences from the novel students are reading is useful. If you decide to try this, though, choose carefully, as dialogue and some other writing do not employ the syntax necessary for good expository writing.

Complex Sentences With Adjectival/Relative Clauses   All complex sentences have one independent and one (or more) dependent clause, but the dependent clause in this style of complex sentence is adjectival/relative. It is adjectival because it describes the noun or pronoun it follows; it is relative because it relates back to the noun immediately preceding it. The first word of the dependent clauses in these sentences is most often *who, which,* or *that,* so this text will focus exclusively on them. Consider these examples:

> Braille, *which is a system of raised dots developed by Louis Braille,* allows blind people to read.
> Dr. Pignier, *who was Louis's headmaster at the school in Paris,* had an open mind about Louis's plans.

The italicized portion in each of the examples is the dependent clause. In this particular structure, it separates the independent clause's subject from its predicate. Cheryl Scott's (2009) research has illuminated an important fact in our understanding of syntax: The further the subject of the independent clause is from its predicate, the harder the sentence is to understand. Furthermore, this kind of sentence, the complex sentence with adjective clause, appears more often in expository text—in textbooks, articles, and essays. Because students read more fiction than nonfiction, they lack experience and practice with this kind of syntax. The sophisticated structure coupled with challenging new content often leaves students confused and even overwhelmed. In essence, the student must retain the main subject as she reads the long, interrupting dependent clause, and then connect it with the main predicate—all while holding onto the meaning of the aside.

The CCSS recommend introduction of this relative or adjective clause construction in sixth grade. Though that may make sense for student *writers,* it may prove useful to show students this construction as early as fourth grade for *reading.* These upper elementary students need not write examples unless they are ready to do so. Nevertheless, exercises where they are asked to identify the subjects, predicates, and clauses; read the independent clause and its dependent clause separately; and discuss the role the dependent (adjective or relative) clause plays with the independent clause may prove useful for comprehension. In the Louis Braille sentence shown previously, the relative or adjective dependent clause is long enough that the reader may lose the main clause's meaning while he is untangling and comprehending the dependent clause. Picking up the strand of the independent clause again requires strong enough decoding skills to read fluently, as well as the working memory to hold onto one thought while the other is being processed.

Complex Sentence With Adjectival Clause: A Model Lesson Sequence   While complex sentences with relative/adjective clauses can be challenging, they are also powerful. Begin instruction with a good example:

> Louis Braille, *who learned about a special raised-dot code developed by a French army captain,* simplified the original code to create something more accessible for people who are blind.

Explain that this kind of sentence is still complex because it comprises one independent and one (or more) dependent clause. The italicized section is the dependent clause, though it does not begin with a subordinating conjunction. Instead, it takes a relative pronoun, *who*, which also serves as the clause's subject. This dependent clause is called a relative or adjective clause. The relative clause in the example *relates back* to Louis Braille. Furthermore, it *describes* Louis Braille, a noun, and is therefore an adjective clause because adjectives do, in fact, describe nouns.

Then, try the following sequence:

1. First, show students some examples of these complex sentences containing relative or adjective clauses.

    The water cycle, which lacks true beginning and end points, includes evaporation, condensation, precipitation, and collection stages.

    Our family vacation, which included car troubles, poor weather, and insects in our hotel rooms, allowed us to strengthen our connection through adversity.

2. Then, ask students to generate examples. Typically, the most useful relative pronouns to use are *who, which*, and *that*.

    *   If students struggle to generate good examples, have them generate simple sentences and then insert relative or adjective clauses as a second, separate step. Here is an example:

        Gregor Mendel is commonly credited with discovering the modern science of genetics.
        , who was born in 1822 and died in 1884,

    *   They may need to jot down content in note form first. Often, when students attempt to create sentences in a content they are not familiar with, either the content or the syntax or both suffer.

3. Only later, when students have grown comfortable with the process of generating new sentences with adjective clauses, and also deciphering those written by others, should they be taught about punctuation of those sentences. In brief, non-essential relative clauses require commas to set the information apart and allow for its removal from consideration. A more detailed explanation of the punctuation rules for this kind of sentence can be found in *Writing Matters* or another syntax resource of your choosing.

A Word on Punctuation

In most instances, punctuation follows a set of explicit, black-and-white rules that can provide comfort and security to a student who has learned them. Start with the axiom, "When in doubt, leave it out." The modern English writing system uses a streamlined approach to punctuation, limiting it to specific syntactic constructions. Rather than memorize rule after rule in an intense lesson series, which typically includes dozens of incorrectly punctuated sentences for students to proofread, teach punctuation as it occurs in the syntax you introduce. For example:

Compound sentences are joined by a *comma* and coordinating conjunction: I, fanboys, I

In a complex sentence, if the dependent clause is first, it takes a comma: D, I

It does not take a comma if the dependent clause is last: ID

This kind of teaching contextualizes punctuation with the sentences that include it, pushing students to apply their understanding of a particular structure to genuine sentence practice. Though certainly students I have taught make punctuation errors, those who have a solid knowledge of clause structure and the punctuation that works with it can typically correct their own errors.

CONCLUSION: THE IMPORTANCE OF SENTENCE-LEVEL INSTRUCTION

This chapter has explored some of the content important for student writers as they develop their sentence repertoire. The kinds of teaching that make good sense are clearly outlined in the model lessons sections and can be applied to more sophisticated concepts, such as the semicolon, the appositive, and the participial phrase, which are not covered in this chapter. There is no doubt that syntax matters, and direct, explicit instruction of the foundations of sentence structure coupled with engaging, interactive sentence-building activities will provide students with the tools they need to develop their writing and reading comprehension skills.

Poetry

Exploring the Power of Language and Story Through Verse

10

As discussed previously, oral language (speaking and listening) plays a vital role in the development of both reading and writing. It is the foundation on which written language is built (Heggie & Wade-Woolley, 2017, Shanahan, 2006). Poetry, which started as an oral tradition and is still best appreciated when read aloud, can create a powerful bridge between spoken and written language. It helps develop phonological awareness—that is, "sensitivity to the sound structure in spoken language" (Singer, 2018, p. 835), an important part of the foundation for other literacy skills. In fact, Singer states that rhyming is the first phonological awareness skill to develop, followed by syllable counting, detecting the position of a sound within a word, and so forth. Rhyme provides an engaging context for playing with sounds and word parts and gives children the opportunity to develop phonological awareness skills through a naturalistic experience.

Chapter 10 begins with an exploration of rhyme and alliteration, two poetic devices children encounter early in school. Not all poetry rhymes, however. Several forms based on syllabification and parts of speech are explored later, with practical suggestions and lesson plans for using them with students to improve their understanding of stories and concepts. Many commercially available story units incorporate poetry as a way for students to demonstrate their understanding of a story. Poetry options are especially helpful for struggling learners who may not be at the stage where writing a summary is a practical goal. Through the activities outlined in Chapter 10, they have the opportunity to grow as writers and demonstrate their improvement while still working at the word, phrase, and sentence level. This foundation and the sense of accomplishment it brings then functions as a bridge to longer sentences and summaries.

After exploring phonology and sound-related activities through rhyme and alliteration, and syllabification through the use of haiku, this chapter expands on haiku and delves into the cinquain and diamante forms to examine language concepts that go far beyond sounds and syllables, such as grammar, parts of speech, character development, and simplified summaries.

DOWNLOADABLE RESOURCES

Keep these resources on hand for teaching the Chapter 10 lessons and activities.

- Lesson 10A, Rhyme Sort: Spider Named Glider rhyme sort activity
- Lesson 10B, Acrostic Riddle
- Lesson 10C, Alliteration Station: N/A
- Lesson 10D, Prepositional Phrases: 5 syllables
- Lesson 10E, Adjectives Out of Order: 7 syllables
- Lesson 10F, Verb Phrase: 5 syllables: Haiku Builder
- Lesson 10G, Haiku Stories: Work completed in lessons 10D–10F
- Lesson 10H, Story Hai-Clues: N/A
- Lesson 10I, Character Cinquains: Character Cinquains activity
- Lesson 10J, Character Diamonds: Character Diamonds activity
- Other: Odd One Out activity for rhyme

RHYME AND ALLITERATION: HARNESSING THE POWER OF SOUND

Rhyme occurs when the ending syllables of words are similar. This is not always the case, though, as evidenced by *slant* or *near rhyme* where words share similar vowel sounds or final consonants but not both or not in the same order *(fast, pants; dock, slick)*. True rhymes *(cat, bat, hat)* that are short and simple in structure also form the basis of word families *(-ad, -am, -ell, -ock, -uck, -ick, -ice)*. It is no surprise that nursery rhymes feature many of these word families. Worksheets abound that explore them, but songs and poems do so in a fun and natural context and also include rhythm, which worksheets cannot.

Applebee (1978) describes the rhythm found in poetry and spoken language as a "physiological phenomenon" (p. 31) linked to the rhythms of the body. He observes how young children are captivated by poetry that is read aloud even if it has adult subjects. When children cannot understand the words, it is the rhythm of the language that resonates with them.

Alliteration occurs when a series of words or words in close proximity have similar beginning sounds *(silly, sir, soon; dismal, den; slice, sleep, sly; Miss Mary Mack)*. They are repeated multiple times in tongue twisters *(Peter Piper Picked a Peck of Pickled Peppers)* and are found in prose as well as poetry. Older students can search the novels in verse discussed in this book's downloadable resources for examples of alliteration.

Many children are exposed to rhyme and alliteration in preschools and in homes where parents or older siblings share rhyming books (as well as songs and fingerplays), but many children lack these early literacy experiences or have difficulty grasping the concepts and, therefore, don't benefit fully from the sound awareness exposure these activities naturally provide. Continuing to bring attention to rhyme and alliteration during the school years helps children develop phonological awareness skills. The activities that follow are not meant to replace robust phonics instruction but are provided to give a context for drawing attention to sounds, syllables, and parts of speech and reinforcing these concepts when studying narratives.

What the Evidence Says

Hudson, Scheff, Tarsha, and Cutting (2016) describe how difficulty with phonological awareness can be observed by children's lack of awareness of rhyme, alliteration, and syllable segmentation. Bryant, MacLean, Bradley, and Crossland (1990) conducted a longitudinal study that monitored 65 children from ages 4 years, 7 months to 6 years, 7 months. They examined phonological awareness and the development of reading and spelling skills and found that sensitivity to rhyme led to improved phoneme awareness. Better phoneme awareness, in turn, led to positive outcomes in reading.

Culatta, Kovarsky, Theodore, Franklin, and Timler (2003) conducted a pilot study for Head Start classrooms to develop and measure the effectiveness of language and literacy instruction for struggling preschoolers who were already showing delays in language development. One strategy they explored included rhyming and letter naming. They described rhyming as a metalinguistic skill that develops before children are consciously aware of syllables or phonemes: "Rhyming, a metalinguistic capacity that emerges before explicit awareness of the syllable or phonemic structure of words, has a strong and specific relationship to more advanced phonological awareness abilities" (Culatta et al., 2003). They found that early rhyme recognition, as well as rhyme generation, was related to later reading ability. In other words, awareness of rhyme in children as young as 3 and 4 could predict later reading success.

Playing with the sounds of language draws attention to sounds before a child is exposed to the alphabet or phonics. These researchers wanted to motivate young children to experiment with linguistic targets in meaningful and engaging experiences with game-like activities such as:

1. Odd One Out. Six words/pictures were shown to the child, who had to find the one that did not fit the rhyme scheme.

2. Rhyme sort. Children were shown a picture of a dog named Mickey along with several other dogs with various names (some rhyming with Mickey and others that didn't). They were instructed to place the dogs with names that rhymed in the same doghouse with Mickey.

3. Rhyme generation. Students were instructed to come up with words that rhymed with a target word.

4. Share rhyming books. The researchers suggested reading *Sheep in a Jeep* by Nancy Shaw (1988) or similar books out loud to students.

Working With Stories in Verse

Many stories for young children are told in rhyme, and several famous poems that students frequently memorize in high school represent rhyming stories. These include "Casey at the Bat" by Ernest Lawrence Thayer, "The Raven" by Edgar Allen Poe, and "Paul Revere's Ride" by Henry Wadsworth Longfellow.

In addition, many epic poems do not rhyme but are based on specific types of meters, such as *The Song of Hiawatha* by Henry Wadsworth Longfellow in trochaic tetrameter and the *Iliad* and the *Odyssey*, attributed to Homer, in dactylic hexameter.

The guides available in the downloadable resources examine books for students in Grades 3–8 and include several novels in verse. Most poems contained in these books do not rhyme but include other poetic devices such as alliteration, repetition, simile, and metaphor.

As an example, *The Spider and the Fly* (Howitt & DiTerlizzi, 2002), a picture book with beautiful black and white illustrations by Tony DiTerlizzi, is a retelling of the famous cautionary poem by Mary Howitt. The eerie artwork, reminiscent of an old Alfred Hitchcock thriller, is appropriate for older students as well as very young ones. An analysis of the story's narrative structure is available with the downloads for this book, but the poetry is discussed following. The rhyme scheme provides many opportunities for phonological awareness activities. Figure 10.1 shows an adaptation of the Rhyme Sort activity previously described by Culatta et al. (2013). Students place spiders with names that rhyme with Glider in the web and spiders with names that do not rhyme outside the web. Reproducible copies are provided with the downloadable resources.

An example of Odd One Out follows. Students must decide which word does not fit with the rhyme scheme of the other words in that row and cross it out. Then they use the same lists to generate an additional word that does rhyme. The space at the end is left blank for students to fill in a rhyming word.

Odd One Out

Directions: 1. Cross out the word that does not belong in each row.

   2. Add a word in the empty space that rhymes with the others.

fly	spy	wing	sly	
there	shelf	stair	hair	
slice	spice	web	nice	

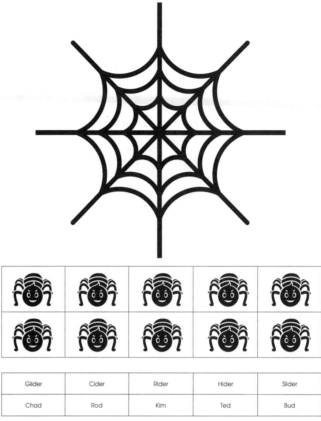

| Glider | Cider | Rider | Hider | Slider |
| Chad | Rod | Kim | Ted | Bud |

Figure 10.1. A Spider Named Glider game.

| **ACTIVITY** | **LESSON 10A: RHYME SORT** |

Objectives:
Improve phonological awareness skills and auditory discrimination

Grade Level:
Kindergarten and up

Time:
30 minutes

Directions

1. Give each student a copy of the spider web shown in Figure 10.1. If desired, they may glue yarn onto the web to turn it into an art activity.

2. Give each student a copy of the spiders and names. Instruct them to cut out the names and glue them onto the spiders.

3. Instruct students to place Glider in the center of the web. Tell students that this web belongs to Glider, and he only allows other spiders to join him if their name rhymes with his. Instruct students to place spiders with rhyming names in the web with Glider.

4. Encourage students to create more spiders with additional names they invent and write in the blanks, forming word families.

The Spider and the Fly also provides ample opportunity to work on /s/ blends in both initial and final position for students with articulation challenges. Many students on the speech-language pathologist (SLP) caseload may struggle with speech–sound production in addition to literacy challenges. Students with articulation difficulties often have weaknesses in sound–symbol associations that later manifest as reading deficits. They may also have listening comprehension difficulties and other learning challenges. In addition, when it comes to reading aloud, many struggling learners leave out some of the sounds in blends. When spelling words with /s/ blends, many students do

Table 10.1. Initial /s/ blends from *The Spider and the Fly* (Howitt & DiTerlizzi, 2002)

Initial /s/ blends		Medial and final /s/ blends	
spy	spider	rest	crested
store	story	fast	prettiest
stair	snugly	last	
step	slowly	ask	
sleep	sweet		
sly	slice		

not hear the /s/ sound, which is unvoiced, so bringing attention to these cluster sounds is beneficial.

Table 10.1 shows a list of /s/ blends taken from the story. A list like this could be made for any picture book to highlight the sounds within the words found in the text. This is helpful for students who struggle with phonological awareness as well as for students who struggle with articulation. They could even go on a treasure hunt through a book to help find words containing blends. Looking at the initial /s/ blends, they could group words that go together and then add other words with the same initial sounds to create a tongue twister based on the story—for example, "The spider spied a special fly and spun a sparkling web." Tongue twisters are engaging for articulation practice as well as for drawing attention to initial word sounds.

Using Poetry as a Learning Tool

In addition to providing fun and playful opportunities to segment and blend words, poetry is a practical learning tool for several other reasons: It serves as a powerful memory aid, a natural motivator, and a fun way to provide repetitive practice.

Powerful Memory Aid Many teachers have used rhymes as well as songs to teach difficult concepts to students of all ages. A song may be repeated many times, as needed, to reinforce a concept, rule, or idea. It may be sung when students need a quick reminder of a spelling or grammar rule. Many of us still remember the *Schoolhouse Rock!* grammar songs from our youth (Warburton, Dorough, & ABC, 1973).

Following is a song I created to help my high school students remember to indent paragraphs, but I've also used it with elementary and middle school kids. The tune sounds like a military march and the students echo what I sing. Often, volunteers will get up and march around the room with me. There are also hand gestures. Tunes like this are helpful when teachers sense they are starting to sound like a broken record by repeating the same rule or concept over and over again. If they sing a short song instead, it lightens the mood.

> Make a dent two fingers wide . . .
> Don't let that first sentence hide . . .
> If you do all will be lost . . .
> And your grade will be the cost . . .
> Do not . . . line up . . . that first sentence . . .
> Do not . . . line up . . . that first word . . .
> Make a dent, dent, dent . . .
> Make a dent, dent, dent . . .
> Make a dent!

Most of us have also had the experience in college of using an acronym to memorize a challenging list of information for a final exam. An acronym is an abbreviation formed from the first letters of each word in a phrase and pronounced as a word. Sometimes these letters will form an existing word, as in SOAP note (**s**ubjective, **o**bjective, **a**ssessment, **p**lan). Some teachers use the term CLOVER to help students remember the six syllable types (**c**losed, fina**l** stab**le** syllable (or consonant-**l**-e), **o**pen, **v**owel team, silent **e**, **r**-controlled). Sometimes the acronym will merely represent the initials of a group of words, such as individualized educational program (IEP). As parents, many of us have relied on the BRAT diet to deal with children's stomach upsets: bananas, rice, applesauce, toast. Medical school students and other graduate-level students rely heavily on these acronyms for the many lists they must memorize. The acronym SCALP is used to remember the layers of the scalp (skin, connective tissue, aponeurotic layer, loose connective tissue, pericranium). Just try to dredge up that list without the acronym.

Acronyms tied to a recognizable word or sentence are especially memorable and happen to be the same structure found in acrostic poems, where the letters of a word run down the page with each letter representing a word or phrase across the page.

Another type of acronym is a group of letters that form a non-word (something that sounds like a real word but isn't), such as PEMDAS, which represents the order of operations in mathematics (parenthesis, exponents, multiplication, division/addition, subtraction). Because PEMDAS can also be tricky to remember, the mnemonic "Please Excuse My Dear Aunt Sally" is sometimes added. For a fun activity exploring acrostic poetry, see the lesson plan for the Acrostic Riddle. Note that the poem example that follows rhymes, though most acrostics do not.

ACTIVITY

LESSON 10B: ACROSTIC RIDDLE

Objectives:
Improve sound segmentation skills; improve auditory discrimination; improve deductive reasoning and problem solving

Grade Level:
Second and up

Time:
45 minutes

Directions

1. Read the SKITTLES poem that follows to students.

2. Instruct them to write down the first letter they hear in each line. Indicate the start of a new line by holding up a finger. Younger students may need the first word of each line written on the board. They may then segment the first word to identify the initial sound.

3. Ask students to solve the riddle by putting the first letter from each line together to form a word.

4. Instruct them to try writing their own acrostic poems based on their name or a character in a story. They may use single words or phrases.

5. Randomly read these acrostic poems to the class and have them guess which student or character the poem is about.

    SKITTLES

    S – Strawberry, cherry, orange, and
    K – Kiwi lime
    I – I love the cheerful colors
    T – Tropical is sublime
    T – Tangy and so chewy
    L – Lemon is a treat
    E – Everyone loves this candy
    S – So very good to eat

Natural Motivator   Young children naturally love rhyme, as evidenced by the numerous songs, rhymes, and finger plays used in early childhood education. This extends into the teen years with rap music. The fast-paced rhymes, rhythms, and beats in rap naturally draw attention to the words and motivate children of all ages. Many teachers use rap to teach concepts for students, young and old. When a concept is put into a rap, it's easier to remember, not to mention fun to perform, which leads to the next reason to use poems and songs in the classroom: They lend themselves to repetition.

Repetitive Practice   Students need many repetitions of a concept to remember it consistently, and children with learning disabilities need even more exposures than their peers to grasp a meaning or idea firmly. Drills and worksheets soon become exhausting and tedious, but students can participate in songs, rhymes, and raps without growing tired of them. They often crave repetition of these activities. Rhyme provides a natural context for repeatedly practicing language and even articulation targets in a fun, engaging context.

LESSON 10C: ALLITERATION STATION

ACTIVITY

Directions

Objectives:
Improve sound segmentation skills; improve auditory discrimination

Grade Level:
Kindergarten and up

Time:
45 minutes

1. Define *alliteration* and *tongue twister*. Explain: "*Alliteration* is the repetition of consonants at the beginning of words, two or more, like 'watch and wait.' A *tongue twister* is a sequence of words that is difficult to pronounce quickly, either because of alliteration or variation."

2. Share a few tongue twisters with the class such as, "She sells seashells down by the seashore" and "Peter Piper picked a peck of pickled peppers."

3. Pick a target sound. You may want to require it to be on a specific subject, theme, or story if working with older students.

4. Instruct students to write down as many words as they can think of that start with that sound.

5. Model how to write a tongue twister using words that start with the target sound (I do).

6. Complete another tongue twister as a class or group (We do).

7. Instruct students to create their own tongue twisters individually or in pairs (You do).

Suggestions: For older students, search a variety of poems and books for examples of alliteration. Two from children's literature discussed in this book are listed here:

- "All they wanted was a wave of Dr. Mesmer's wand" (p. 17, *Mesmerized: How Ben Franklin Solved a Mystery that Baffled All of France* [Rockliff, 2015b]).

- "Nellie feasted on fiery curry and lounged in the cool ocean breeze" (p. 12, *A Race Around the World: The True Story of Nellie Bly and Elizabeth Bisland* [Rose, 2019].)

Rhyme, alliteration, and other devices common to Western poetry are not the only elements of poetry that can be useful for instruction. Concise, carefully structured poetic forms can also be used to:

- Teach and reinforce grammatical concepts

- Summarize key moments or details from a story

- Generate discussion about stories

- Explore characterization, including how characters change over the course of a story.

What's more, these forms give students the opportunity to grow as writers without the pressure of drafting lengthy paragraphs or essays. The next sections explore the instructional use of several short forms commonly introduced in elementary school: haiku, cinquain, and diamante.

HAIKU: CAPTURING THE ESSENTIALS

Haiku is a Japanese form of poetry frequently explored in the early elementary years and beyond. It comprises 17 syllables (or onji) divided into 3 lines of 5-7-5 syllables. It tends to focus on allusions and comparisons. Nature or the seasons are often the subjects of these poems.

> snow gently falling (5)
> a candle in the window (7)
> riding home at night (5)

Haiku is an excellent intervention tool for students with language-based learning disabilities. It is also a powerful educational tool for general education students. There are several reasons for this:

1. It provides a meaningful and playful context for working on syllabification and other skills.

2. It is versatile in that a variety of different objectives may be addressed either in isolation or simultaneously.

3. The form is short but packed with meaning.

Haiku Grammar Builders

Although you may choose to concentrate on word choice and not worry about parts of speech or even grammar, haiku allows you to turn the spotlight around to make grammar the focus of your lesson. Haiku provides abundant opportunities to work on parts of speech in an engaging, natural context. Forget about worksheets of unrelated sentences with no connection to each other. Choose a part of speech to explore and then brainstorm as a group or individually, keeping in mind the principle of "I do, we do, you do." Keep each student's brainstorms in a special folder because they will be used later to create original haiku. You may use plain notebook paper with a heading at the top for each category.

Grammar concepts you can easily address through haiku include prepositional phrases, adjectives, and verb phrases, which can be used to build a haiku line by line.

Line 1: Prepositional Phrase   Prepositional phrases serve a variety of purposes, including telling us where an action is happening. This is important not only for sentence structure but also for giving and following spatial directions. (Put your book . . . *in the box, on the table, under your chair.*) Young children benefit from acting out spatial directions that are relevant to their personal setting (throw the ball . . . *under the swing . . . over the sandbox*). Children on the autism spectrum and others who are very concrete thinkers may need to act out these spatial relationships with an object such as a ball, toy car, or bean bag before they can understand prepositions found in stories shared in class.

A prepositional phrase could be used to build the first line of a haiku, as in the following lesson.

LESSON 10D: PREPOSITIONAL PHRASES: 5 SYLLABLES

ACTIVITY

Directions

1. Tell students to put this heading at the top of a blank piece of paper:

Prepositional Phrases: 5 syllables

2. Help them brainstorm a list of prepositional phrases associated with a book or topic. One of these will be the first line of the student's haiku.

3. Write down examples and put them in a manila folder marked Haiku Folder. These examples are from stories outlined in this book's downloadable resources.

   • In a cold, damp school (*Six Dots* [Bryant, 2016])

   • On the battlefield (*Gingerbread for Liberty* [Rockliff, 2015a])

   • In the wild, wild west (*Bad News for Outlaws* [Nelson, 2009])

   • All around Ghana (*Emmanuel's Dream* [Thompson, 2015])

Objectives:
Improve understanding and use of prepositional phrases

Grade Level:
Second and up

Time:
15 minutes

Line 2: Adjectives Out of Order   It is also fun to explore a subject using "adjectives out of order," a strategy discussed by Noden (1999) in *Image Grammar*. The most noteworthy example of this technique is the title of the Newbery Award–winning novel, *Sarah, Plain and Tall*. Consider how much less effective the traditional word order would have been—*Plain and Tall Sarah*. Simply changing word order can have a substantial impact on how literary or "poetic" a phrase sounds. Adjectives Out of Order has students describe a subject or main character in a 7-syllable phrase using this approach.

LESSON 10E: ADJECTIVES OUT OF ORDER: 7 SYLLABLES

ACTIVITY

Directions

1. Tell students to put this heading at the top of a blank piece of paper:

Adjectives Out of Order: 7 syllables

2. Help students brainstorm a list of examples associated with a book or topic. Examples should follow this structure: [Subject], [adjective], and [adjective]. One of these will be the second line of their haiku.

3. Write down examples and put them in the Haiku Folder. These examples are from stories outlined in the downloads for this book:

   • Louis Braille, blind and alone (*Six Dots*)

   • The baker, jolly and fat (*Gingerbread for Liberty*)

   • The marshal, honest and brave (*Bad News for Outlaws*)

   • Emmanuel, proud and strong (*Emmanuel's Dream*)

Objectives:
Improve use of adjectives

Grade Level:
Second and up

Time:
15 minutes

Notice how phrases from this Adjectives Out of Order activity describe *the subject* of a story, but do we know yet what the subject is doing? We do not. We need a verb phrase/ predicate to tell us that in the final line of the haiku.

Line 3: Verb Phrase   Guide students to explore predicates by creating 5-syllable verb phrases. Start with a verb. Write it on the board and then help students to expand the verb into a phrase by asking questions such as "how, what, where, when, how, or why?" Examples include: *worked* (how did he work?) *without stopping; cried* (when did he cry?) *in the morning; wailed* (what did he wail?) *a mournful song; rode* (where did he ride?) *into the night; wept* (why did he weep?) *because it hurt; slept* (where did he sleep?) *under the stairs.*

ACTIVITY	**LESSON 10F: VERB PHRASE: 5 SYLLABLES**

Objectives:
Improve understanding and use of verb phrases and predicates

Grade Level:
Third and up

Time:
15 minutes

Directions

1. Have students put this heading on a blank piece of paper: *Verb Phrases – 5 syllables*.

2. Help students brainstorm a list of examples associated with a book or topic, following the structure shown previously. One of these will be the last line of their haiku.

3. Write down examples and put them in the Haiku Folder. These examples are from stories outlined in the downloadable resources:

   • Created a code (*Six Dots*)

   • Made bread for the troops (*Gingerbread for Liberty*)

   • Tracked down the outlaws (*Bad News for Outlaws*)

   • Pedaled with one leg (*Emmanuel's Dream*)

After brainstorming these parts of speech either individually or as a group, put them all together to create an original haiku. See the example in the Haiku Builder in Figure 10.2.

Haiku for Story Review

The activities described in the previous section build students' understanding of grammatical concepts. Because students construct each line based on story content, these

Line 1	5-syllable prepositional phrase	In a cold, damp school
Line 2	7-syllable subject with adjectives out of order	Louis Braille, blind and alone
Line 3	5-syllable verb phrase/predicate	Created a code

Figure 10.2.   Haiku Builder with examples from *Six Dots: A Story of Young Louis Braille* (Bryant, 2016).

activities also reinforce their understanding of the story and provide a creative format for writing about the story. The activities that follow, Haiku Stories and Story Hai-Clues, can be used to review stories and provide practice writing.

Haiku Stories   In the Haiku Stories activity, students will use the lines they created during the grammar-building activities to construct a haiku about a story they have read.

LESSON 10G: HAIKU STORIES

Directions

1. Instruct students to locate their three haiku planners for Prepositional Phrases, Adjectives Out of Order, and Verb Phrases.

2. Tell them to choose one line from each planner to complete a haiku about a book they have read.

3. Instruct students to use Figure 10.3, the Blank Haiku Builder, to write a haiku about a story they have read. Here are some examples:

> *Six Dots*
> In a cold, damp school
> Louis Braille, blind and alone,
> Created a code
>
> *Gingerbread for Liberty*
> On the battlefield
> The baker, jolly and fat,
> Made bread for the troops
>
> *Bad News for Outlaws*
> In the wild, wild west
> The marshal, honest and brave,
> Tracked down the outlaws
>
> *Emmanuel's Dream*
> All around Ghana
> Emmanuel, proud and strong,
> Pedaled with one leg

ACTIVITY

Objectives:
Improve planning and organizational skills

Grade Level:
Second and up

Time:
15 minutes

Line 1	5-syllable prepositional phrase	
Line 2	7-syllable subject with adjectives out of order	
Line 3	5-syllable verb phrase/predicate	

Figure 10.3. Blank Haiku Builder.

It is possible to fit a large variety of goals into the haiku format—just specify for your students the requirement for each line. Syllables are essential building blocks for words, but few content-related activities are available at the syllable level. Poetry provides a creative framework for developing skills for understanding syllables and using them to create a written product.

Story Hai-Clues   In this activity, students write a haiku about a story of their choosing and have other students guess the story title from clues in the haiku. This activity may be better suited to students who have prior experience working with haiku, as it provides less built-in scaffolding.

ACTIVITY	**LESSON 10H: STORY HAI-CLUES**

Objectives:
Improve deductive reasoning skills and syllabification skills

Grade Level:
Third and up

Time:
45 minutes

Directions

1. Ask students to think of a book they've read or a movie they've seen. Instruct them to write a haiku with each line describing a setting, action, character, or something else from the story: Line 1: 5 syllables, Line 2: 7 syllables, Line 3: 5 syllables.

2. After they have written their hai-clues, share the poems with the class and see who can use the clues in the poem to guess what story the student is describing. Here are some examples:

    > A lonely cupboard,
    > A ride on a magic train,
    > A school for wizards

    > Mopping dirty floors
    > Riding in a pumpkin coach
    > Dancing with a prince

    > A farm in Kansas
    > A storm and a crazy trip
    > Meeting the Munchkins

Haiku can be used effectively to help students capture the essence of a story or topic in a few well-chosen details, while at the same time strengthening their understanding of grammar and syllabification. The forms discussed in the next section help students capture the essence of a character in a few lines—including how a character grows and changes.

CINQUAINS AND DIAMONDS: SKETCHING A CHARACTER

There are many other types of poetry, but it is not within the scope of this book to discuss them all. This section explores two forms of poetry and how these forms may be used to address different objectives related to characterization and language use. Refer to the downloadable resources for activity sheets to accompany each lesson plan.

Character Cinquains

A cinquain is a five-line poem that may utilize any subject, but for this activity the focus will be on a person from a story. The first line of the poem starts with a character name. The second line describes the character. The third line identifies verbs describing the character, the fourth line uses a phrase telling something about the character, and the fifth line represents another word or perhaps a nickname for the character.

LESSON 10I: CHARACTER CINQUAINS

Directions

Instruct students to choose a person from history or a character from a story and write a cinquain describing this person following this structure:

Line 1: Noun
Line 2: Two adjectives describing the noun
Line 3: Three verbs that tell something about the noun
Line 4: A 4-line phrase telling something about the noun
Line 5: A synonym for the noun

Example:

George
honest, brave
fighting, leading, battling
crossing the Delaware River
General

Objectives:
Improve understanding of parts of speech; improve use of descriptive language; improve understanding of characterization

Grade Level:
First and up

Time:
30 minutes

Character Diamonds

A diamante poem is shaped like a diamond. This form is discussed in detail in *A New Poetry Form: The Diamante* by Iris Tiedt (1969). The first and last lines are each a one-word noun. Lines two and six consist of two adjectives. The third and fifth lines comprise three verbs each. The fourth (middle) line is a sentence connecting the two nouns. This form can be used to write about a character and how that character changes over the course of a story, as described in the following lesson.

LESSON 10J: CHARACTER DIAMONDS

Directions

1. Introduce the structure of the diamante poem that appears at the end of this lesson plan.

2. Explain that the students will write a diamante poem about a character and how that character changes over the course of the story.

3. Show and discuss the Avi example that follows this lesson plan (I do).

4. Work with students to generate an example using a story that has been read in class (We do).

5. Instruct students to work independently to create a diamante poem offering support and assistance as needed (You do).

Objectives:
Improve characterization; improve understanding of parts of speech; improve use of descriptive language

Grade Level:
Second and up

Time:
30 minutes

Diamante Structure

Line 1: One noun that tells what kind of person the character is at the beginning
Line 2: Two adjectives describing what he or she was like at the beginning of the story
Line 3: Three verbs describing the character's actions
Line 4: A sentence or phrase describing how the character changed
Line 5: Three verbs describing the character's new actions
Line 6: Two adjectives describing what he or she is like at the end of the story
Line 7: One noun that reveals what kind of person the character has become at the end of the story

For our purposes, the top half of the poem will signify what the main character is like at the beginning of the story. The second half of the poem will show what he or she is like at the end, and the sentence in the middle will describe how this transition takes place. We will also take a bit more latitude and use more than one sentence (line), or even a paragraph, if desired.

One of the things that make stories so compelling is the opportunity to watch characters grow and change. Great classics like "Cinderella" usually focus on this type of transformation. For this activity, we will explore a character using a diamante poem to demonstrate it.

The following example is from *Crispin: The Cross of Lead* by Avi (2002).

Peasant

Timid Afraid

Running, Hiding, Cowering

He discovers he is the son of the Lord Furnival.

Plotting Confronting Rescuing

Brave Courageous

Freeman

TIPS FOR ONLINE LEARNING AND TELETHERAPY

The following tips for working with students online are specific to this chapter.

1. For the Rhyme Sort lesson plan, copy and paste the spider web from the downloadable resources onto a Google slide. After adding the names to the various spiders, create screenshots of the spiders and copy them onto the slide with the spider web. The spiders can then be moved in and out of the spider web for demonstration purposes. Email the spider web and spiders to the home or school. The monitor working with the student(s) may assist them with constructing the spiders and the web.

2. For Odd One Out, choosing which word in a list does not rhyme with the others, the educator shares the word lists with students via screen share and uses the annotation feature of Zoom to allow students to cross out the word that does not rhyme with the others.

3. Project all poetry examples using the screen share feature of Zoom or another online platform.

4. For the Haiku Builder activity, student responses may be typed into a PowerPoint file or Word document and shared via screen share.

CONCLUSION: USING POETRY AS A TOOL FOR INSTRUCTION

The activities in this chapter demonstrate how poetry in its many different forms can extend the number and variety of learning objectives that may be addressed through narratives. Students benefit from summarizing stories in the methods described in previous chapters, but the poetry activities outlined here provide additional avenues for expressing understanding and examining topics in new and adventurous ways. These alternative methods of expression are especially effective for struggling learners so they have a variety of ways to express their knowledge and understanding. There are several novels in verse outlined in the downloadable resources that provide further opportunity to explore poetry.

This chapter is just a sampling of the poetic devices, forms, and applications that can be used in literacy instruction. There are many others that may be adapted to teach grammar, characterization, and story structure in new and exciting ways. Now that your creative juices are flowing, you will likely come up with some novel applications of your own.

The playful activities in this chapter help us to remember that stories are fun. The ways we talk about them and share them should be fun too!

Enhancing the Learning Experience
Coherence and Executive Functions

PAULA MORAINE

11

When do we hear students say that writing is fun? In contrast, students like to listen to stories. Beginning at a very young age, students are delighted when it is story time. Stories are engaging, entertaining, and even educational when students listen to them, watch them, and later read them. Receptive engagement in stories activates mental processes such as mental imagery and memory. Listening to a story can conjure up pictures and sensations, sometimes making us feel like we are being transported into a different dimension.

While receptive engagement in a story is pleasant, we will actively comprehend the story better when we can give it our best attention, draw on previous knowledge of the subject as we try to understand, and form purposeful mental images of the story. Our attention is most helpful in comprehending a story when it is engaged robustly, actively using mental imagery and linking the story to previous knowledge. Writing stories, though, is a completely different experience, and requires us to activate an entire set of skills related to our executive functions. Learning how to write a story requires a more complex engagement with our executive functions than what is needed for listening to a story. Writing can become fun for those students who integrate the receptive and expressive language skills using the processes we know to be executive functions.

EXECUTIVE FUNCTIONS

Executive function is no longer a vaguely understood term, yet there is still no single, explicit, universally accepted, absolute definition of executive function. A quick search on the Internet will yield an array of responses, defining executive functions with varying phrases such as processes, neurological skills, or cognitive functions. Some authors use the words *executive function* as an umbrella term; others call executive functions a set of cognitive processes. Even the number of executive functions varies from description to description. An uncomplicated definition describes executive functions as what we use to manage our resources in order to achieve a goal. While definitions are an important aspect of understanding executive functions, it can also be simply stated that executive function skills are the neurocognitive skills we require to engage in the goal-directed control of thought, action, and emotion (Zelazo, Blair, & Willoughby, 2016).

Executive Functions in Education

The purpose of every school is to teach, the goal of every student is to learn, and therefore, the fundamental purpose of any educational endeavor is to engage in a process of growth, development, and change. While engaged in this learning process, each student uses his or her gradually developing executive function skills to complete any learning-related task. But why is this process of growth, development, and change so difficult for so many students? Is it the same reason why so many struggle with robustly developing reliable executive functions? What could or would make developing executive functions, and specifically writing skills, a bit easier?

Education that is based on the insight that eventually every student needs to connect with his or her own internal set of skills, abilities, and approaches is a good starting place. The executive function skills of attention, memory, organization, planning, goal-directed behavior, initiative and inhibition, and flexibility slowly and individually develop in each individual (Moraine, 2012). The essential question throughout this gradually evolving process is: What makes the process of growth and development of executive functions a healthy process?

Salutogenesis

Salutogenesis is a term that means "origin of health," formed from the two parts of the word, *saluto*—meaning "health" and *genesis*—meaning "origin of." Originally, the term was used in the fields of both physical and mental health based on the contrast between salutogenesis and pathogenesis: "Pathogenesis improves health by decreasing disease and infirmity and salutogenesis enhances health by improving physical, mental, and social well-being" (Becker, Glascoff, & Felts, 2010, pp. 25–32). Salutogenesis, "the study of health origins and causes, starts by considering health and looks prospectively at how to create, enhance, and improve physical, mental and social well-being" (Antonovsky, 1979). In educational terms, we often approach a student with the "what's wrong" questions: "What is the disability? What can I do to decrease this disability?" In salutogenic terms, the question becomes: "What can I do to enhance and improve this student's experience of his or her own learning process?"

Antonovsky based his principles of salutogenesis on the overall model known as the *sense of coherence*, defined as:

> . . . a global orientation that expresses the extent to which one has a pervasive, enduring though dynamic feeling of confidence that one's internal and external environments are predictable and that there is a high probability that things will work out as well as can reasonably be expected. (Antonovosky, 1979, p. 123)

Antonovsky's perspective is that a sense of coherence can be understood in developmental terms, arising initially from experiences in childhood and adolescence, and maturing in the early adult years. The process of acquiring a sense of coherence follows a path that is slow, gradual, and uneven. A sense of coherence is not a single, ultimate goal, but rather a journey with twists, turns, and unexpected challenges. Antonovosky (1987) highlights the uneven trajectory when he states: "The adolescent, at the very best can only have gained a tentative strong sense of coherence, which may be useful for short-range prediction about coping with stressors and health status."

This principle of the evolution of a sense of coherence aligns with our understanding of the developmental nature of executive functions. When we consider this in an educational context, the notion is that executive functions exist on a continuum. Once we understand that, it also becomes understandable that the sense of coherence is a result of the developmental process during childhood and adolescence. This would indicate that the sense of coherence basically is seen as an outcome of individual life experiences, learning processes, and environmental influences (Jensen, Dür, & Buijs, 2017). When we acknowledge its gradual development, we can more easily align with the understanding that executive functions slowly develop over time, mature gradually, and are the product of manifold life experiences as well as educational processes and inputs.

Clarifying what constitutes the sense of coherence, Antonovosky specifically attributed it to three components: *comprehensibility, meaningfulness,* and *manageability.* In an educational context, these can be understood in the following way:

- *Comprehensibility:* Does the student understand the content being taught? Does the student understand/comprehend what is being asked of him or her? Does the student understand what is going on in general? Does the student have a sense of order or even predictability in his or her learning? Are the expectations clear?

- *Meaningfulness:* Does the student find the learning interesting and/or meaningful? Does the student care about the content being learned? Does the student find the experience of learning valuable or worth the effort? Is the learning relevant?

- *Manageability:* Does the student believe that he or she has the necessary skills, ability, and support to learn? Does the student experience the learning environment as one that is under control and manageable? Specifically, is the learning environment under the student's control? Does the student have the right tools for learning? (Moraine, 2012, p. 19)

The executive functions that control thought, emotion, and action are directly linked to the experiences of comprehensibility (thoughts), meaningfulness (emotions), and manageability (actions). Students need to engage actively in all three areas to be successful in any educational endeavor. The more user-friendly we can make the act of written expression, the more students will be able to write. As we teach students to tell their stories, we can make the writing process understandable, engaging, and accessible. While we are at it, let's make it a bit of fun, too.

The Executive Function Toolbox

Executive functions have been defined simply as the brain processes that control our attention and behavior (Barkley, 2012). In education, the student is engaging in a continuous process of attention and behavior, listening and doing, and receptive and expressive language. Specifically, during the writing process, the student is required to know what to write about, internally generate interest in the topic or content, and have sufficient skills to produce accurate sentences and paragraphs. This is a complex set of tasks that requires the student's active attention and controlled behavior. Writing requires a full set of executive function skills. There is far too much to share with students about executive functions, so instead of speaking about these functions in theoretical terms or overwhelming them with too many concepts, it is most beneficial to offer students insight into the basic and fundamental activities of executive function through the tools of attention, mental image, and review/preview.

Attention: Active and Passive   We all have attention and we all use attention in our own, individualized way. The common element, though, is that we all have *active attention* and *passive attention* (Moraine, 2012). With our active attention, we choose what to focus on or think about. We use our senses to purposefully see, hear, touch, move, etc. We then process those sensory inputs more or less consciously. We engage our passive attention at all times as well, often even more than our active attention. We notice colors, sounds, smells, movements, thoughts, ideas, feelings, sensations, etc., on a continuous loop. We rarely disengage from our passive attention, but we frequently disengage our active attention.

We are actively or passively engaged in our thoughts, feelings, and actions at all times, but this engagement is not evenly distributed. Our active attention can be engaged in intentional actions while our passive attention is simultaneously processing all manner of internal and external stimuli. Attention is controlled through the ever-changing alternations between active and passive attention. For example, reading is generally considered to be an activity of receptive language. From the perspective of attention, though, we are actively decoding the words, creating mental images of the words, connecting the content to previous knowledge, and actively synthesizing for meaning and relevance. Our passive attention is simultaneously flitting around any thoughts, images, or feelings that are randomly generated by the more controlled content laid down by our active attention to the reading.

The writing process is generally considered an activity of expressive language. First, we apply our active attention and create a mental image of what we will write. Initially, there is nothing passive about this process, but this is exactly the point where so many students struggle. Actively creating mental images is difficult, and many students find it easier to passively respond to content that is provided. The writing process, therefore, is frequently built up gradually for students, with educators providing them with a carefully constructed series of ideas and images to begin the process. Expressive language originates within the student, first as spoken language and later as written language. We are not always fully conscious of each word we speak; it is more or less automatic and based in our passive attention. Writing our words down requires a fully conscious process; it is more intentional and based in our active attention.

Being aware of our active and passive attention, and consequently gaining control of our attention, is best achieved using a variety of tools based in executive function. Two of the most essential and critical tools for engaging our executive functions are review/preview and mental image. A third is the use of synthesis and analysis.

Review and Preview   All of our executive functions take place in relation to time. We are, at every second, in the present. From our present moment, we are able to look back to the past and gather previous experiences that inform our understanding of the present moment, and then look ahead to determine what action we need/want to engage in for the future. These experiences of integrating past, present, and future form the basis of our executive function skill of engaging in goal-directed behavior. Figure 11.1 shows the continuum that proceeds from the present, to gathering previous experiences of the past, to forming goal-directed decisions for the future.

We engage our executive function skill in this way millions and millions of times per day. Students make many decisions in the writing process, and a decision can be something as simple as choosing what kind of paper to write on. The thought process can go something like this: *The last time I wrote an essay for school, I used lined paper and that helped me keep my writing even, so I will use lined paper again.* This brief review and preview took place in a nanosecond of time. It can also be a much more complex and conscious process, such as deciding what to write: *My teacher gave us the writing assignment at the end of class.*

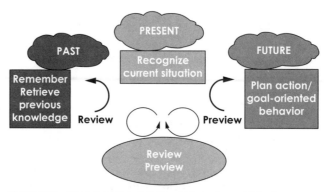

Figure 11.1. The continuum of review and preview, which allows us to integrate past, present, and future to engage in goal-directed behavior.

He gave us a paper with the assignment guidelines and if I re-read that paper, I will have a better idea of what to write and where to start. Because review and preview are part of every second of every day, examples are limitless. Intentional practice of review and preview is strongly advised. It is a good idea to review a whole day, a class period, a specific topic, or a page/paragraph of reading, The more students use their active attention to become aware of the unconscious review and preview process, the easier it is for them to practice review and preview purposefully and with their full, active attention.

Mental Images   In a modern world, inundated by constant visual onslaught, it might sound counterintuitive to state that modern students form too few mental images. More visual images have been consumed by the average 10-year-old than some older adults have consumed in a lifetime. Yet, it cannot be assumed that a child/student is able to form independent mental images. Underestimating this fact leads to ineffective teaching and learning. When we tell stories, it might be an enjoyable experience for students, but when we ask questions related to the content of the story, a student is likely to remember details from the story only if these details relate directly to his or her own previous experience or previous knowledge. The teacher may need to provide the student with background vocabulary and build mental images using the pictography approach discussed in Chapter 5, picture noting for learning new vocabulary.

The mental images have to exist for the student in order for these images to be accessed and used to comprehend the content of the story. Once any new content or vocabulary has been heard or presented, it can go through a process of review in order for it be safely deposited in the memory. Using mental pictures as a method of making a memory deposit allows the student to retrieve that information using visual strategies. These become images that can be accessed on command and used for comprehension. When the content is understood or comprehended, reimagined for meaning or relevance, and processed using active attention, then the content is readily available for use. After this procedure using comprehension, meaning, and application of skills, writing becomes a coherent experience and the content can be used in written expression.

Synthesis and Analysis   Another underappreciated tool in the executive function toolbox is synthesis and analysis, which essentially is working from the whole to the parts or from the parts to the whole. In my experience, students are often given assignments in small chunks, without a sufficient idea of what part this assignment plays in an overall learning goal. Gradually, enough parts are added to allow the students to synthesize these parts into a whole. The opposite often happens when students are asked to analyze text. A small portion of the text is chosen, then deeply and analytically dissected. Once it is dissected and the test completed, the text is not reconstructed or synthesized back into its whole. The models we present students are too often either/or models—assignments that are many small parts that are not related to a whole picture, or the drilling down from a whole picture into the small, component parts.

As educators, we might know for ourselves what the learning goal is because we know the curriculum and are aware of the intended learning outcomes. Students are not always aware of the intended learning goals and, therefore, do not have an overview or sense of orientation. The student is then described as having deficits in executive function because she cannot see the whole picture, or she is described as having deficits in executive function because she cannot analytically drill down to the parts.

One of the strengths of the *Story Frames* analysis is its reference to the whole, then the parts, then the sections (beginning, middle, end), then the whole. Table 11.1 offers a framework in which to see both the whole overview of *Story Frames* in all 12 steps, as well as *Story Frames* chunked in terms of the three essential elements of comprehensibility (thinking), meaningfulness (relevance), and manageability (tools and skills sets). (The link between

Table 11.1. *Story Frames* elements and the elements of a sense of coherence: Comprehensibility (thinking), meaningfulness (relevance), and manageability (tools and skills sets)

Story Frames	Verbs	Executive function
Ordinary World Call and Response Mentors, Guides, and Gifts Crossing	be, are, were	Comprehensibility Thinking—Understanding Accessing previous knowledge through the use of review
New World Problems, Prizes, and Plans Midpoint Attempt Downtime Response	felt, wondered, hoped	Meaningfulness Relevance—Feeling Understanding the present situation well enough to see what goals are needed
Chase and Escape Death and Transformation Climax: The Final Test Final Reward	challenged, changed, learned	Manageability Action—Deeds Seeing and assessing the future and setting goal-directed decisions and behavior

the two can be strengthened through the choice of verbs and descriptive language, as will be discussed in the following section.)

Students are so frequently described by what they cannot do that we consider it normal to speak from a deficit perspective. Their writing assignments are judged and graded, but too infrequently the edits are offered back to the student as supportive guidance for a new draft. We could turn instead to the insights of a salutogenic model and ask the questions: In what way can I support the student's writing process through understanding, emotional relevance, and needed skills? How can I employ the executive function skills of attention, mental image, and review and preview to support the writing process?

A SALUTOGENIC LESSON PLAN

Written expression instruction can easily be built on a salutogenic lesson plan that uses *Story Frames* to strengthen executive function. The lesson can start with a warm-up of previously learned skills. These practice skills can include grammar and sentence construction, as well as practice with the parts of speech, phrases, clauses, sentence types, voice, tense, etc.

Then, the goal will be to create a lesson that is:

- Comprehensible: Establish understanding/comprehensibility through asking the "What" questions, leading to idea generation, categorization, and creating mental images.

- Meaningful: Ask the "Why" questions by engaging with the content, explaining its importance, and generating access to the experience of the story.

- Manageable: Ask the "How" questions by identifying the style of the writing, the writing skills needed, and the techniques for writing, and then editing the writing once it has been put in draft form.

The lesson can start with a prompt that guides the student through practice of these previously learned skills, beginning with a sentence or sentence starter, a question, or keywords. Then, the educator guides the student in actively creating a mental image so the student can form a preview of the writing, ideas, and pictures that can be generated and order or categorize these pictures for use in the writing. Now, it is time to choose a style of writing, such as descriptive, narrative, discussion, etc. See the lesson plan framework in Figure 11.2.

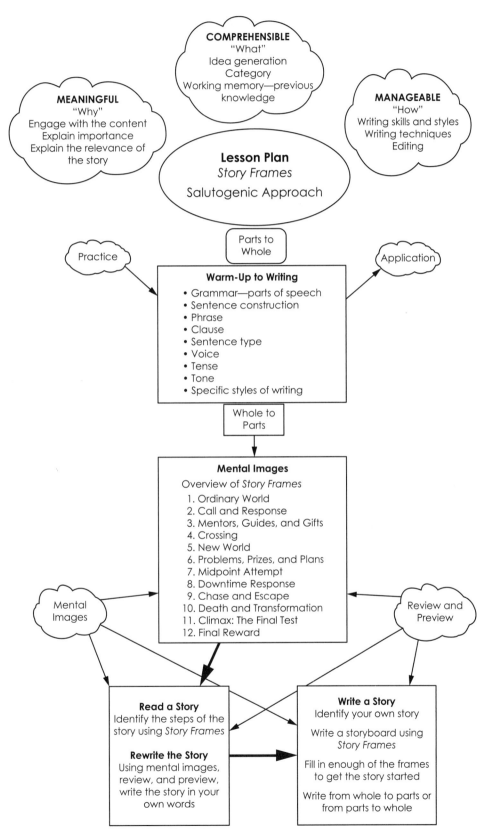

Figure 11.2. Lesson plan framework: *Story Frames* and the salutogenic approach.

Using *Story Frames* enhances the basic lesson plan. After the warm-up, the educator can teach the structure of *Story Frames* using a whole-to-the-parts approach. Each of the following steps requires both active and passive attention based on mental images:

1. Share the overview of the *Story Frames* using the 12 steps of a story *(preview)*

2. Read a story *(receptive language)*

3. Retell and/or rewrite the story using the story frames *(review)*

4. Brainstorm ideas with the students for their own story *(expressive language)*

One reason I encourage the students to rewrite the story they just heard in their own words is to allow them time to practice creating mental images based on receptive language skills, followed by putting those images into their own words using expressive language skills. When they are not yet concerned about having to create their own story, they can more easily access the previously learned mental images provided by the story and, in turn, easily learn how the *Story Frames* work. When it is time to write their own story, the work is more engaging and enjoyable for them because they already feel successful. They have just experienced having a whole storyline or plot in their mind, and they have just written it down.

Even if the story is a retell and not a fully original story, the sense of the story is now personalized. It can feel as if they actually created the story. This experience can easily transfer to their own writing when they are generating their own ideas for a story. An internal sense of story structure is created through this simple process of retelling and rewriting the story they just heard. Retelling and rewriting generates confidence in the student writer. They understand what the story is telling, they have made a relationship with the characters and storyline, and because they can "hear" the story in their mind, it is easier to formulate sentences and write the whole story.

When setting out to write an independent composition, it is not essential for the students to have the entire story in their minds before they begin writing. Some of the most impressive stories have been written by students who wrote some of the beginning, some of the middle, and some of the end of their story before they finished writing in the details (parts to the whole). These students established the framework for the whole story before filling in all the details. Once a student is using review and preview based on mental images, and switching between active and passive attention with ease, then the student can use a whole-to-the-parts approach, or a parts-to-the-whole approach, with equal success.

Table 11.1 gives some examples for linking the sections of the *Story Frames* to comprehensibility, meaningfulness, and manageability through the choice of verbs and descriptive language. Linking verb choices to the stages of past, present, and future in the telling of a story can be a quietly powerful means of communicating meaning.

STORY FRAMES AND EXECUTIVE FUNCTION: THE SECRET LANGUAGE OF STORIES SUMMER WORKSHOP

Each summer I offered a summer writing intensive workshop for students in middle and high school. Samantha joined one of these summer writing workshops at the end of her sixth-grade year. She had a strong interest in writing, but she struggled to organize her imaginations into words. Her school focused on the brief constructed response (BCR) style of writing, and Samantha tried hard to write within the guidelines dictated by this specific formula. Rather than enjoying the process of writing, she became anxious about being criticized for not being able to answer the exacting, analytical questions required by the BCR. She joined the small group of summer students for a writing workshop aimed at strengthening writing skills using *Story Frames*.

We began with a preview of how we would approach the stories, both those we heard and those we would eventually write. Speaking about each step of the *Story Frames,* we put up a picture to serve as an icon for the step, then added a few words to help us remember what part of the story was told by each step. Once we had a strong preview of the entire process established, we read *Gingerbread for Liberty! How a German Baker Helped Win the American Revolution* (Rockliff, 2015a). First, we read the story together, then we retold the story in the group, letting each student add their own favorite or important part of the story. I asked the students to describe what they each pictured, making sure they had access to the mental images connected to the vocabulary. For example, it is important not to assume every student can picture what genuine German gingerbread looks like! Mental images kept the story alive in their imaginations by reviewing the story for sequence and content, giving them ideas for writing their own review of the story.

Samantha chose to write the story in the voice of General Washington.

*Gingerbread for Liberty—*Reflective Rewriting

Samantha,
end of Grade 6

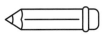

My soldiers and my country are suffering, the revolution is our only hope. I am no longer merely George Washington, I am now a General, in charge of hundreds of people.

It was just a normal day, my soldiers were threatening to quit because of starvation and out of nowhere there came an old and fat man. Before I could even ask him what he wanted he said, "I would like to join your army."

Naturally, I looked at his kind face, and his round tummy, and asked what he might have to offer the army.

"I am a baker," Christopher Ludwick said proudly, "And I love my America!"

I asked him what he could bake because my soldiers were hungry and need strength for our fight for independence from England.

He replied," Of course! In fact, I am one of the best bakers in Philadelphia!"

"Thank goodness!" I thought to myself, "I won't lose my soldiers to starvation"

I told him, "Well, one way you could be of service is to bake food for my starving soldiers."

"I would be glad to!" he replied in excitement. The new baker, Ludwick, set up his bakery faster than I could imagine, and in no time he was baking loaves of bread and gingerbread as fast as the soldiers could eat them. I was amazed at what this man could do.

Now that the soldiers are no longer starving, I need to return to the issues of the war. Soon after Ludwick joined us, I find myself standing at the side of the shore, staring at the biggest display of force and warships I had ever seen I start to realize the immense challenge I am facing if I want to win this war.

Ludwick, standing by my side, says to me, "I recognize where these soldiers are from! They are from Germany, my homeland! Perhaps I can persuade them to join our side, with your permission of course."

"How many more surprises is this man full of?" I wonder to myself.

"If you get caught you may get killed," I warn him.

"Then I will be killed serving our country. This is a risk that I must take for America," Ludwick bravely responds.

"Alright, you have my permission," I sigh.

Without any more words, Ludwick gets into a boat and begins to sail towards the soldiers and their many boats. Still standing on the shore an astonishing sight met my eyes, Ludwick boarded the ship of the mercenary soldiers and started to talk to them.

A few minutes later, when they were done talking, the warships started to sail toward shore without fighting!

Ordinary World	Call and Response	Mentors, Guides, and Gifts	Crossing
New World	Problems, Prizes, and Plans	Midpoint Attempt	Downtime Response
Chase and Escape	Death and Transformation	Climax: The Final Test	Final Reward

Figure 11.3. Storyboard.

Each student was given the option to write on paper, use speech to text, or type on the computer. Samantha chose to handwrite her drafts and type her final copies. She enjoyed handwriting and explained that she could think better when she wrote on paper. The graphic organizer and more structured response style of writing forced a specific type of thinking on her, and she explained that she could not use her imagination when she wrote in that way. Handwriting allowed her to feel freer with her images.

At this point in the process, we reviewed how each student connected the *Story Frames* in their own writing of the story and found that the *Story Frames* could be easily adapted to several styles of reflective rewriting without losing the integrity of the original storyline.

Now it was time to provide the students with the scaffolding for their own writing. Using a simplified storyboard shown in Figure 11.3, the students each started filling it in with their original ideas. Some wrote on the white boards, some wrote on paper, and a few chose to use computers at this point in the writing process. Samantha wrote on paper with lots of colored pens.

Each student filled out parts of this storyboard with their own story, but no two students filled it out in the same order or level of detail. They put down a few ideas in one section, then another, and went back and forth across the story, filling in sections as the ideas came to them. Sometimes the action in a frame toward the end gave them an idea for the beginning. Occasionally, they would fill out the middle of the story before they could "see" the beginning or ending details. Samantha was quick to see some of the beginning details, and quite a few of the middle details, but she did not see how it would end. I assured her she could move around in her story and write it as it came to her.

We were approaching the end of our time together, and Samantha had decided on her storyline, felt confident that she could write the pictures that had formed in her mind, and started writing. If she got stuck on a detail, she returned to her storyboard to remember where the characters had been and where she wanted them to go. The workshop came to an end before she could type up her conclusion, but this is the story she created using *Story Frames*.

**Samantha,
end of Grade 6**

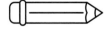

The Journey to Stone Lagoon
By Samantha

Lying on a tropical island beach was a beautiful baby, with her proud parents next to her. The baby had a striking and unique look due to her red and black striped hair. Such an unusual characteristic had brought both praise and ridicule to this young girl. It was a beautiful day. Her parents understood that their daughter was destined for a special life, they just didn't know exactly what that would be. They had decided at her birth to be supportive of what was to come and knew that they were her parents for a reason. The baby was named Fern.

The sun was shining, the breeze was blowing, the waves were quietly receding at low tide. This beach was part of their home, as an extension of the wonderful, strong tree house that Fern's father had built before Fern was born. That tree house was the only home Fern had ever known. The little family of three were planning to live on this wonderful island forever. They had access to all the food and water they needed and had no reason to fear anything. Little did this happy family know the great sorrow that was soon to come into their lives.

Coming to this very beach was the Mother Goddess of Lava and Fire. Her name was Blaze. Blaze was obsessed with taking over the world. Her plan was to reach every beautiful spot on the globe and turn it into a dreadful, ugly landscape. Blaze was the daughter of Eris, the Goddess of Chaos, and the daughter of Ares, the God of War, so she knew nothing about love or kindness. Her home was a volcano and was the only home she had ever known. It was in the volcano where she was born, where she was raised, and where she was trained in the arts of evil. Blaze had fire for hair and molten lava for clothes. Blaze gazed at the beautiful island, and it annoyed her so much. This happy family irritated her like a gnat that keeps buzzing in your face and never leaves you. She approached the beach with a fireball ready in her hand. Terrified at the specter of the blazing fireball, the mother grabbed her baby and sprinted into the woods where the baby would be safe. The father had started for the woods, but was struck by a fireball, nearly instantly ending his life on that lovely beach. Hiding the baby safely in the woods, the mother rushed to the beach to help her husband, only to find him charred to death. Grief stricken, she kneels beside her dead husband and weeps. Blaze strikes a fireball at the mother, swirls around, and cackling she leaves the beach in ruins.

Fern was quietly sleeping in the woods where her mother had hidden her. She was completely unaware of the recent death of her parents, and she had no idea that another potential threat was looming close to her. A wolf, named Spikes, was close, having picked up on the scent of a small human. Spikes had been wandering in the woods near his lair. He was a lone wolf, since from birth he carried a blessing and a curse in his coat. The hair on his back was in the form of spikes, strong, pointed, and full of protective power. He had to be careful to not let them discharge when he was around his friends, but the spikes, or fire fur, helped him in times of conflict. The scent he picked up was curious, so he pursued the scent until he found the baby. This baby was unusual, in that she had red and black striped hair. He decided that he liked the way her hair was, but there was still one problem. The baby did not have anyone to care for her. Just moments ago, her parents had been killed by the evil Goddess Blaze. "This must be their daughter," he thought, "after all, who leaves their daughter out in the wilderness by themselves?"

The wolf thought long and hard, then came to the conclusion that he would be the one to look after her. He would teach her the wolf ways and the human ways. So, without further hesitation, Spikes took Fern on his back and carried the sleeping baby to his tree house, rocketing with his feet on fire up to his tree house. Once he got in, he set Fern on his bed and pulled together a bed for her. Sure that she was safe, he climbed on his bed with her and slept peacefully.

This wolf and child odd couple got along very well. The wolf would hunt and bring back berries and a piece of meat to share. Fern was getting older and smarter, learning everything Spikes could teach her. They were great partners. One day, Fern was exploring the forest when the strangest thing happened. Fern found a dead tree. It was very unusual to find something dead because the forest was like paradise. Fern used her heightened sense of smell to find the person who did this to the tree. Her senses told her that the person she would need to find was located at the stone lagoon! It was then Fern realized that if this *creature were to come back, it would destroy the whole forest! Suddenly she formulated a plan in her head. The stone lagoon was a long way away, and her senses were not limited only to what was nearby. She knew that she and Spikes would go on a journey to find the person who committed this terrible deed! Fern sprinted to the tree house and started packing the supplies that they would need. As soon as they were packed and ready to go, they marched out of the house and started their journey.*

Samantha continued to write this story and completed the workshop. She wrote everything up to the conclusion, but she had a good idea of how to end it, so she was happy to keep writing after the workshop ended. It had become her writing, her idea, her story, and her style of storytelling.

Samantha and I continued to work together during the seventh grade, and at the end of her seventh-grade year Samantha described how the process of writing stories in the workshop changed her approach to writing in all her classes in school. She became more confident, more creative, and more structured in her writing after her exposure to writing with *Story Frames*.

CONCLUSION: *STORY FRAMES* AND THE SALUTOGENIC APPROACH

The *Story Frames* approach provides structure, image, and content to the writing process. *Story Frames* establishes an external support system for the writer in the same way that a map gives us guidance and orientation when we travel. Using *Story Frames* gives the students access to explicit step-by-step directions leading directly to the intended destination. Offering such an outline or guide for students to consider both prior to and while writing instills confidence and a sense of connectedness.

The inner structure for writing can be provided by the salutogenic approach to executive functions. Activating the student's capacity for mental images and directly teaching the student how to preview and review starts the necessary process of inner engagement. Active and passive attention working together with mental imagery and review and preview opens up access to the full range of executive skills we use for receptive and expressive language. It then becomes possible for the student to unite skills in the craft of writing together with personal insight and executive function. The writing process becomes:

- Comprehensible, because the student understands the basic principles of what is being asked, understanding and comprehending what is being asked of her in the writing process

- Meaningful, because the student feels as if she can relate to the content of the story she is writing, the story becomes a part of her own story, and is therefore relevant

- Manageable, because the writing is taught with consistent practice of the basic tools of writing, and the student becomes more skilled in the craft of writing

When the outer structure of *Story Frames* meets the inner structure of a salutogenic approach to executive functions, the student experiences security, confidence, and success.

Shaping Writers, Shaping Lives

The Power of Personal Narrative

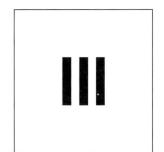

"If you would not be forgotten, as soon as you are dead and rotten, either write things worth reading, or do things worth the writing."

—Benjamin Franklin

Benjamin Franklin admonishes us to either write about things of importance or to do things worth writing about. Personal narratives encourage both. In teaching young people to narrate their own experiences, we give them another valuable schema—a structure for chronicling and reflecting upon the events of their lives. Chapter 12 provides an introduction for Section III, which includes storyboards for personal narratives inspired by the 8-element structure of the *Story Frames* Basic Storyboard with slight variations. In Chapter 13, Lesley Roessing, university lecturer, shares strategies for memoir writing and explains how memoir can be a bridge to expository writing. In Chapter 14, Amy Miller, director of the May Center for Learning, shares how students transform personal experiences into superhero stories in a project she runs called the Dyslexia Justice League. She discusses using superheroes and the Hero's Journey format to help students explore personal struggles and develop a growth mindset. In Chapter 15, Mary Jo O'Neill, parent advocate, discusses how getting parents to write down their family story provides a powerful tool for advocacy. Her chapter highlights a type of persuasive writing that has real-world implications for students receiving special education services. Finally, in Chapter 16, university lecturer, researcher, and leading authority on narrative development, Carol Westby, discusses the importance of considering multicultural perspectives in the writing of personal stories and the ways storytelling varies across countries and cultures. Her chapter also discusses strategies for empowering English as a Second Language (ESL) students, while celebrating diversity.

Introduction to Writing Personal Narratives

12

Personal narratives are central to human experience. They are found even among very young children and are a vital part of our daily lives. They help us make sense of our world, as well as to build social relationships. The importance of personal narratives continues into adulthood. Narratives have the power to convey feelings, ideas, beliefs, and information that might otherwise be forgotten if presented outside the realm of the story.

Grandparents tell stories to entertain. Teachers tell stories to motivate and educate. Parents tell stories to school officials to advocate for their children. Preachers tell stories to inspire. Marketers and politicians tell stories to persuade. Lawyers tell stories to convince jurors of a defendant's innocence or guilt. Newscasters tell stories to inform. People who have overcome addiction tell stories to share their experience, strength, and hope.

Psychologists dig deep into the human psyche by listening to the stories of their patients. College admissions advisors determine which candidates would be a good fit for their university by reviewing personal essays. Detectives solve crimes and uncover motives by listening to stories of witnesses, victims, and criminals. Some human resource directors ask potential employees to write a personal story as part of the interview process.

Literate adults should be able to write and speak persuasively and informatively. The ability to do so has both professional and personal implications. Proficiency with telling personal narratives supports these skills. Additionally, adults and children who lack the ability to relate personal events often struggle with social interactions. This chapter begins by discussing how personal narratives are linked to academic success—not only because of their connections to writing, speaking, and listening skills, but also because of their connections to less obvious characteristics that contribute to success, such as social-emotional skills, executive function skills, and a sense of ownership and agency about what one writes. Following this discussion are lessons you may use to begin teaching personal narrative writing to your students.

WHAT THE EVIDENCE SAYS

Although retelling fictional narratives orally while incorporating story elements, sequencing events, and providing details and adequate information is a good predictor of school success, the ability to construct personal narratives and tell them to others effectively may serve a similar role in predicting success with social communication, especially in regard to conversational skills, because conversations often focus on

DOWNLOADABLE RESOURCES

Keep these resources on hand for teaching the Chapter 12 lessons and activities.

- Lesson 12A, Personal Event Narrative Brainstorm (based on a Problem or Prize): Personal Event Narrative Brainstorm template (Problem or Prize)

- Lesson 12B, Personal Event Narrative Brainstorm (based on a Climactic Event): Personal Event Narrative Brainstorm template (Climactic Event)

- Lesson 12C, Family Questionnaire: Family Questionnaire form

understanding and telling stories (Westby & Culatta, 2016b). This section discusses what the evidence says about personal narratives in relation to the following:

- Academic standards in writing, speaking, and listening

- Other important skill areas, such as social-emotional learning and executive function

- Students' sense of ownership and agency regarding their writing

Academics: Anchor Writing Standards, Speaking, and Listening

Throughout Grades 3–8, the Common Core State Standards (CCSS) require students to write narratives for the goal of developing both personal and fictional experiences. Anchor Writing Standard 3 states that students will write about "real or imagined experiences." Though not all states utilize the CCSS, all state standards encourage research, inquiry, and the ability to narrate events.

A prime example of a personal narrative is the age-old prompt, "What did you do over summer vacation?" A question of this nature allows a student to immediately draw on readily accessible information to create a written sequence of events.

Anchor Writing Standard 8 says students will: "Gather relevant information from multiple print and digital sources, assess the credibility and accuracy of each source, and integrate the information while avoiding plagiarism." The ultimate goal of this standard is for a student to be able to gather information from a variety of sources and judge if it is relevant and accurate. In elementary school, this process begins with the ability to recall personal experiences, talk about them, and write about them. Describing events that are real and relate to personal experience lays the foundation for later writing about real events in the larger world.

This ability to describe real-life events in the elementary years forms the foundation for the simple research expected early in the Writing Standards as well as for the more complicated research that follows, as in Writing Anchor Standard 7. This standard relates to both short research inquiries as well as projects that require more intensive questioning and in-depth knowledge of a subject.

Research and the ability to gather information from a variety of sources becomes the focus in middle school for Writing Standard 8. However, the ability to describe personal experiences provides the foundation for the inquiry skills needed to explore other sources.

Not all educators see a clear delineation between narrative and expository text. As discussed in Chapter 7, Petersen and Petersen (2016) describe them as existing on a continuum. Lesley Roessing, university lecturer and former director of the Coastal Savannah Writing Project, explores using memoir as a bridge between writing narratives and writing informational text (expository and persuasive) in her book, *Bridging the Gap: Reading Critically and Writing Meaningfully to Get to the Core* (2014). Because memoir is, in essence, narrative nonfiction, it contains elements of both narrative and informational writing. Examining personal experiences is an effective way to bridge the gap between these two types of writing. See Chapter 13 for a full discussion of Roessing's strategies for using memoir writing to develop expository skills.

Speaking and Listening Anchor Standard 4 requires that students support their claims with evidence in a clear and well-organized manner so that listeners can easily understand both their reasoning and their intended purpose. The requirements to accomplish this evolve as a student progresses through the grades. Young children are expected to verbally describe familiar people, places, and things, as well as events in kindergarten and first grade, and to tell a story or recount a personal experience in the second, third, and fourth grades. In Grades 5–6, the ability to verbally tell a personal story shifts to reporting on a topic, expressing an opinion, and sequencing ideas with relevant facts and details that support the main idea of a text. In Grades 7–8, the emphasis is on presenting claims and making key points in a clear and well-organized manner while providing sufficient descriptions, facts, and details.

When verbally recounting personal events in this speaking and listening strand, the focus moves from simply describing events in kindergarten and first grade to having a clear structure and sequence for events with descriptive details in Grades 2–4, including a point or main idea in fourth grade, while stating definite opinions and making explicit claims in fifth grade and up.

The skills students develop through speaking and writing personal stories are a starting point for developing skill in other types of speaking and writing. Furthermore, the ability to relate what is read via research to what one encounters through personal experience is essential for the development of empathy and perspective-taking. It is also essential for the development of a theory of mind—that is, "awareness that other people have perceptions, feelings, and thoughts that are different from their own" (Dickinson & Morse, 2019). In typically developing children, this understanding usually emerges during the preschool years.

Social-Emotional and Executive Function Skills

Personal narrative is useful not only for encouraging literacy skills—writing, speaking, and listening—but also for developing strengths in other areas. These include abilities in the social-emotional domain as well as executive function.

Social-Emotional Learning   Narrative involves not only language and cognitive skills but also a social-emotional component. Retelling a personal experience comes naturally for some students, but not for all. Rollins (2014) studied the production of personal narratives of young adults with autism spectrum disorder (ASD) who were high functioning and compared those results to their production of storybook narratives. She found that students with ASD were able to produce more complete narratives based on storybooks compared to stories relating their personal experiences, with which they had significant difficulty. Specifically, students with ASD struggled with explaining how they felt about personal events and drawing conclusions based on those feelings. These personal reflections were a challenge, even if the student was able to talk about feelings and draw conclusions when retelling a fictional story about an imaginary character. Rollins discussed the value of using narrative discourse to evaluate pragmatic language skills because of its importance in social communication and because so many linguistic, social, and cognitive skills must be integrated at one time to be able to create an oral narrative.

Additional evidence also supports the importance of the social component of narrative and the role of theory of mind. Kim (2016) studied the listening comprehension of first-grade students in Korea as it relates to narrative texts. Kim found that while many factors contributed to listening comprehension in young children, theory of mind was the most significant predictor of success in her study, followed by working memory, grammatical knowledge, inferencing, vocabulary, comprehension monitoring, and attention. Theory of mind requires a student to take another person's perspective and understand both other people's thoughts and their emotions.

To follow how a story develops, a child must understand a character's or writer's point of view, including goals, beliefs, emotions, and reactions (Graesser, Singer, & Trabasso, 1994). When students share personal narratives with peers, it provides an excellent opportunity to practice perspective-taking. When personal stories include an insight into cultural experiences that may be unique, everyone benefits. Grace Lin, Newbery Honor Winner and author of *Where the Mountain Meets the Moon* (2009), explores this idea in her TEDx Talk, "The Windows and Mirrors of Your Child's Bookshelf" (2016). She describes the importance of children both seeing themselves reflected in the books they read and getting a glimpse into other cultures. When children share personal stories about their unique experiences, they're providing a glimpse through this window.

Executive Function   Friend and Bates (2014) studied the relationship between narrative and executive function in 4- to 5-year-olds and found that the skills required for both developed "asynchronously." One did not precede the other, but a strong interdependence existed—development in one supported development in the other. The ability to sequence and organize events is an important executive function skill. Many students struggle with relating personal events (whether verbally or in writing) in a way that makes sense to the listener. This difficulty is not just apparent in school and not only in young children. Many teens, especially those with language-based learning challenges, experience difficulty relating experiences to adults or even peers.

The social-emotional and executive function skills involved in telling a narrative have implications not just for students' lives at school but for other aspects of their lives as well. For instance, the need to provide an explanation to a law enforcement officer, a judge, a student resource officer, or an administrator can escalate into a potentially critical situation if a teenager does not have the ability to provide personal information, share emotions appropriately, take another's perspective, or draw conclusions.

Empowering Students: Ownership and Agency

Another reason to promote personal narratives is that topic choice is key to success in writing, especially for students struggling with literacy, and this means giving them the freedom to write about personal experiences. They often feel cut off from literacy experiences because they don't think they have anything to say and don't see that their voice is important. (Roth, 2000; Graves, 1985). Students have a natural tendency to make up stories about the worries, concerns, and experiences personal to them (Duchan, 2004), and they have a high interest in stories about their own lives (Montgomery & Kahn, 2005). Allowing students to choose their own topics helps them know that their ideas are worth writing about.

Danzak (2011) studied the relationship between language proficiency and identity in the writing produced by English language learners. The chosen format for the study was bilingual autobiographies because, as Danzak points out, when literacy experiences connect to students' personal lives, it gives them more background knowledge to draw upon and increases their investment and engagement in learning. In addition, autobiographical writing helps students incorporate cultural and social identity into meaningful writing activities utilizing a familiar context. Danzak states that topic choice is key, including the ability to decline writing about topics that are uncomfortable. Carol Westby explores the topic in greater detail in Chapter 16, "The Influence of Culture on Storytelling."

Teachers play a crucial role in helping close the gap in the trajectory of a young student's ability to write personal narratives. Wood, Schatschneider, and Wanzek (2020) conducted a research study entitled, "Matthew Effects in Writing Production During Second Grade" and found that although students with low socio-economic status progressed in their writing of personal narratives at a slower rate than more advantaged peers (as measured by growth in the total number of words written in response to the prompt, "One day when I got home from school . . ."), there was significant performance variance between classrooms. Though the researchers did not measure or quantify the specific differences between the teaching styles and classroom environments, they hypothesized that student writing was impacted by the quality of instruction, resources in the classroom, time spent on writing, and opportunities for peer support.

Freedom to choose a topic does not mean that everything a student writes will be an autobiography. Often, though, even fantasy stories of superheroes who fight injustice and battle inner demons may include more autobiographical information than we realize. Metaphors often hold more truth than confessions and are easier to process as the abstract becomes concrete. It is important to give students a degree of freedom over the topics they choose to write about.

Westby and Culatta (2016b) created a tutorial for speech-language pathologists (SLPs) working in the schools to give them strategies for helping students develop personal narratives. They outline two types of narratives: 1) personal event narratives and 2) life stories. Personal event narratives focus on one significant event (or short series of related events). Life stories, which are more appropriate for older students, look at their entire life or a span of time in their life. Westby and Culatta discuss four strategies useful for creating personal narratives, including reminiscing, reflecting, making coherent connections, and signaling plot structure.

Reminiscing with caregivers about experiences they have shared helps children develop autobiographical memories and can predict how well they will be able to build complex narratives later on. Westby and Culatta suggest ways to encourage reminiscing by asking questions about popular trade books. Using this strategy, a teacher, therapist, or parent could use books from the downloadable resources for *Story Frames* to ask questions to encourage reflection. The following books discussed in *Story Frames* provide examples of stories to stimulate reminiscing, along with related questions.

1. *Gingerbread for Liberty! How a German Baker Helped Win the American Revolution* by Mara Rockliff (2015a): Did you or someone you know ever use a practical skill (like cooking) to help someone else?

2. *Mesmerized: How Ben Franklin Solved a Mystery That Baffled All of France* by Mara Rockliff (2015b): Recall a time when someone tried to trick you or someone you know. What happened? Have you or someone you know ever used logic or the scientific process to solve a problem?

3. *When Washington Crossed the Delaware: A Wintertime Story for Young Patriots* by Lynne Cheney (2004): Think of a time you or someone you know attempted to do something that seemed impossible. How did it turn out?

4. *Six Dots: A Story of Young Louis Braille* by Jen Bryant (2016): Think of a time you or someone you know couldn't do something others could do easily. What happened? How did you feel?

5. *Sadako* by Eleanor Coerr (1993): Think of a time when someone was sick. What did people do to show their support?

6. *Thank You, Mr. Falker* by Patricia Polacco (1998): Have you ever felt bad because other people were better at something than you were? Have you ever discovered you had a special talent?

7. *A Race Around the World: The True Story of Nellie Bly and Elizabeth Bisland* by Caroline Starr Rose (2019): Think of a time when you were in a competition with someone who was a friend or maybe a stranger. What happened?

8. *Magic Ramen: The Story of Momofuko Ando* by Andrea Wang (2019): Have you or someone you know ever tried to invent a new food or recipe? How did it turn out?

TEACHING PERSONAL NARRATIVE WRITING

The following activities and lesson plans provide questions and storyboards for creating a variety of personal narratives. For drafting and editing suggestions, refer to Chapter 6. Templates for the following activities are located in the downloadable resources.

ACTIVITY

LESSON 12A: PERSONAL EVENT NARRATIVE BRAINSTORM (BASED ON A PROBLEM OR PRIZE)

Objective:
Improve ability to sequence events and relate personal information

Grade Level:
Third Grade and Up

Time:
45 minutes

Directions

1. Instruct students to think of a time when there was something they really wanted *or* a problem they needed to solve (or both)—in other words, a Problem or a Prize.

2. Tell them to answer the questions on the Personal Event Brainstorm that follows. A full-size, photocopiable version is located in the downloadable resources for this book.

3. After answering the brainstorm questions, have students complete the Personal Narrative Storyboard shown here and provided in the downloadable resources.

4. Instruct students to use their storyboard to write a personal story.

Personal Event Brainstorm

Directions: Think of a time when there was something you really wanted or a problem you needed to solve (or both). In other words, a Problem or a Prize. Answer the following questions:

1. Where were you and who was with you? (Setting)
2. How did it all start? (Call to Adventure)
3. What was the Problem or Prize?
4. Did you have a Plan? If so, what was it?
5. What did you do to carry out your Plan? (Attempt)
6. What happened and how did you Respond?
7. What was the final outcome? Did you learn anything? Was there a purpose or point to your story? (Reward)

Personal Narrative Storyboard (based on a Problem or Prize)

Directions: After answering the Personal Narrative Brainstorm questions, use your answers to help complete the Personal Narrative Storyboard shown here.

Ordinary World (Setting)	Call to Adventure	Problem or Prize and Plan
Attempt	Response	Reward

Westby and Culatta (2016b) point out that personal stories do not always fit into a story grammar format with an initiating event, a problem, or a plan. These stories may instead focus on a sequence of actions leading to a climax (or high point) followed by a resolution. The following brainstorm activity is based on a climactic event.

LESSON 12B: PERSONAL NARRATIVE
BRAINSTORM (BASED ON A CLIMACTIC EVENT)

Directions

1. Instruct students to think of a time when something dramatic happened in their lives and consider what led up to this event.

2. Tell them to answer the questions on the Climactic Event Brainstorm shown here and located in the downloadable resources.

3. After answering the brainstorm questions, have students complete the Climactic Event Storyboard shown here and provided in the downloadable resources.

4. Instruct students to use their storyboard to write a personal story.

ACTIVITY

Objective:
Improve ability to sequence events and relate personal information

Grade Level:
Third Grade and Up

Time:
45 minutes

Climactic Event Brainstorm

Directions: Think of a time when something dramatic happened in your life and what led up to this event. Answer the following questions and then use the storyboard to sketch or write about the series of events.

1. Describe the setting.
   a. Who was with you?
   b. Where were you?
   c. When did it happen?

2. What happened?
   a.
   b.
   c.

3. Describe the big event or climax.

4. Why was this experience significant?

Climactic Event Storyboard

Directions: After answering the Climactic Event Brainstorm questions, use your answers to help complete the Climactic Event Storyboard shown here.

Who, When, Where? (Setting)	Event or Action	Event or Action
Event or Action	Big Event	Significance

Family Questionnaire

One way to honor cultural differences is to encourage students to write about family traditions, which are often heavily impacted by cultural influences. The Family Questionnaire can also encourage reminiscing as well as intergenerational perspective-taking. The stories of our elders help us know where we have come from and inform where we are going.

The following activity encourages reminiscing between students and family members. It may function as a standalone project or it could lead to writing a narrative about a family member's experience, a shared experience, or a family tradition.

ACTIVITY

Objective:
Improve ability to conduct research and ask questions

Grade Level:
Third Grade and Up

Time:
30 minutes at school and 30 minutes at home

LESSON 12C: THE FAMILY QUESTIONNAIRE

Directions

1. Read students one of the stories discussed earlier in this chapter and ask the reminiscing questions to spur a class discussion.

2. Discuss what reminiscing means and how the Family Questionnaire will give students an opportunity to reminisce with older family members.

3. Send students home with the Family Questionnaire form shown here and provided in the downloadable resources. Instruct them to complete the assignment and return it to class.

4. Ask students to share their experiences with the questionnaire and discuss the responses of their family members.

Family Questionnaire Form

Directions: Ask someone in your family to pick one or more of the following questions and talk about it with you. On a separate piece of paper write down his or her response.

1. What was your favorite holiday or tradition when you were young? What was special about it? What was different or special about the way your family celebrated it?
2. What was the most memorable gift you ever received? What was it and who gave it to you?
3. Who did you admire most when you were growing up? Why?
4. What was something funny or surprising that happened to someone in your family? Describe what happened.
5. Did anyone ever have a serious accident? What happened?
6. Have you ever been really scared? What happened?
7. What is your favorite family recipe? Have you ever had a chance to make it with others? What was your job?

Interviewing family members is a way to gather information from a source that is still personal to the student. It provides an opportunity for a young child to conduct early research and practice interviewing techniques. The Family Questionnaire provides a simple format for upper elementary and middle school students to collect material for the purpose of writing about family traditions and experiences.

A Word of Caution

Sometimes when children find their voice and write their stories, emotions arise and situations are revealed that require intervention beyond the scope of the classroom teacher or SLP. It is important to know when to refer students for help from a social worker, psychologist, or counselor. In addition, sometimes outside agencies must be involved. It is essential to understand professional obligations regarding reporting abuse and neglect.

TIPS FOR ONLINE LEARNING AND TELETHERAPY

1. Any of the downloadable questionnaires or brainstorms may be shared with students over the Internet. Either have students add replies via Adobe Acrobat Reader's Comment tool or copy them onto a PowerPoint file and create text boxes where student writing will appear.

2. Creating separate files for each student in PowerPoint or Google slides helps to organize information. Individual online notebooks may be created for each student in Google Docs or Google Classroom to keep track of all of their student writing in one location.

3. For privacy, make sure that access is password-protected. As an extra precaution, students may use initials for their last name or create a pseudonym.

CONCLUSION: HONORING PERSONAL STORIES

This chapter discussed how a student's early writing about true life experiences builds a foundation for later research and expository writing. The connections between personal narratives and the development of social-emotional and executive function skills were also explored. The importance of topic choice for creating ownership and agency was also highlighted, especially in regard to second language learners and struggling writers. Finally, suggestions were provided for reminiscing with caregivers and a lesson plan outlined on how to interview family members. Additional lesson plans provided structure for brainstorming and writing personal narratives.

Whatever type of narratives you explore, consider honoring student writing by creating books of stories (both fictional and personal) that can be sent home over summer vacation. Students love reading the stories they and their peers have created. Although most cities provide free summer library programs and reading incentives, students from disadvantaged homes frequently do not participate in them.

Stories have the power to change lives. They help us connect and they help us reflect. The ability to tell personal narratives shapes not just who we have been but who we wish to become. The remaining chapters in this section provide a variety of approaches to writing personal stories.

Memoir
Writing Our Lives

LESLEY ROESSING

13

We write for many reasons—to entertain, to inform, to persuade, to enlighten, to show what we learned, to find out what we know. But the most important reason young writers can write is to discover who they are and to reflect on the people, places, items, and events that made them the persons they are and the adults they will become. In other words, memoir writing. As writers learn about themselves while "researching" and writing their memoirs, memoir writing becomes inquiry. And memoir writing becomes a journey of self-discovery.

WHAT IS MEMOIR WRITING?

Memoir writing is a form of personal narrative but is created from the memories of the writer. Tim O'Brien, author of *The Things They Carried* (1998), once said in a speech, "You don't need to tell a true story to tell the truth." Memoir is based on how writers remember events and what those events meant to them. Memoir differs from personal narrative in that memoir includes reflection on the importance of the persona, place, memento, or event, while a personal narrative is a story of events as they happen.

WHY TEACH MEMOIR WRITING?

Writers become better writers by writing. Memoir entices students, especially reluctant writers, to write. All children like to write about themselves. Through memoir writing, writers can learn strategies that will transfer to all writing.

Memoir writing leads to more meaningful writing. Teachers need to coach developing writers to discover and craft their personal stories to impart the joy and power of writing. Quality of writing improves when writers write about what they know, what they have experienced. Memoir writing, specifically, induces students to write more, write better, and write more willingly and meaningfully.

Affectively, memoir writing compels writers to reflect. The difference between memoir and autobiography or personal narrative, as mentioned previously, is that memoir includes reflection. Teachers can tell their writers that the "R" in memoir stands for reflection. In short, memoir = memories + reflection.

Reflection induces writers to think about the story behind the story and possibly the story that will come after the story. That deliberation causes the writer to ask critical questions: *What did this small moment mean to my life? How did this event, person, place, or object influence or change me? How did it contribute to the person I am today and the future person I will become?*

Academically, memoir provides a bridge between narrative and informative writing. Many times, writers see no connection between the two. They are frequently taught in entirely different manners, and writers tend to lose their voices as they make the change. Memoir, which is essentially narrative nonfiction, is that perfect connection between the two modes. As writers search for information from their past, they are employing experiential knowledge as the basis for their "research."

Through writing memoir, writers also discover and uncover their own passions and convictions, leading them to choose more effective topics for argument writing. In this way, memoir writing can inspire, or lead to, ideas and, again, a voice in opinion and argument writing.

Most importantly, memoir bridges the achievement gap. Research supports the fact that prior knowledge is a major determinant of academic achievement. Memoir is one area in which *all* students come to the table with the necessary background knowledge—their experiences. Memoir writing values these experiences and levels the playing field as all children—economically, culturally, and academically diverse—inherently have the essential "material" necessary to achieve memoir writing. Not all students have the prior knowledge, skill, or motivation to write to prompts on standardized tests, but once writers learn to write meaningfully on topics that matter, they can transfer those skills to other topics, even to "on-demand" writing tasks.

Finally, children and adolescents are natural storytellers. Ask a group of children to tell you about a person they know and the stories spill out; ask them what those people or events mean to them and, after a short reflection, they can tell you. Ask a group of teens why they missed an assignment or broke a rule, and the most incredible, implausible stories will emerge. Getting them to write those stories leads to more proficient writing and becoming storytellers, a skill that will help them in any future profession. And, in that way, memoir allows all children to see themselves and their lives reflected in a text and realize that their lives matter.

The process I've used to teach memoir writing to students includes:

- Reading, listening to, and analyzing mentor texts

- Brainstorming using techniques such as collecting memories on a memories chart, creating a map of one's childhood home or neighborhood, and free writing in response to diverse prompts

- Choosing a topic, such as a significant object, person, event, or crisis

- Choosing a format; possibilities include poetry and graphic formats as well as more conventional prose narratives

- Putting it all together: drafting, revising, editing, and presentation

The sections that follow discuss each part of this process in depth.

USING MENTOR TEXTS

Like any writing, memoir writing is taught most effectively by first reading mentor texts. Mentor texts are exemplars of good writing. Through deconstructing mentor texts, students are able to identify ideas and crafts they can adapt and make their own.

Listening to Mentor Texts

It is effective to begin with an aural text, such as Jerry Seinfeld's "Halloween" (2008). As the students listen to this memoir, they jot down the elements they notice, such as dialogue; narration; settings; specifics; description; sensory details; names and other proper nouns; humor; point of view; diverse subtopics, in this case, costumes, neighbors, and family quotes; onomatopoeia; similes; and an ending with a short reflection.

Reading Brief Mentor Texts

After the class creates an anchor chart of elements that render memoirs more effective, students read and deconstruct a short, written memoir. For example, looking at the first few lines of George Ella Lyon's poem, "Where I'm From" (1999), students are asked to note what they notice about *what* and *how* the memoirist writes. The remarks that follow are from an actual classroom conversation about this poem.

Charlie starts, "I notice smells, 'Clorox and carbon-tetrachloride.' I am not sure what carbon-tetrachloride is, but I am picturing a chemical smell." Students look it up and find out that carbon-tetrachloride was used in dry-cleaning establishments. A biography of Ms. Lyon reveals that her father worked as a dry cleaner, and students infer that either her father came home from work smelling of the chemical or she visited him at his business. Either way, that smell takes her back to her childhood. Another student chimes in, "Clothespins, Clorox, and carbon-tetrachloride are sort of like alliteration—almost the same beginning sound."

Students observe that people's names are included in the memoir, and a student says, "Imogene and Alafair sound a little old-fashioned, so they could be parents or grandparents," and others notice the family sayings, such as "Perk up." Students can then share maxims from their own families.

Reading Full-Length Mentor Texts

It is even more effective if students read full-length memoirs, independently or in book clubs, so they can observe how the memoirists write about different influences in their lives. Memoir as a literary genre is experiencing great popularity, and memoirs are available in diverse reading levels, genres, formats, and on a wide variety of topics. As writers read memoirs, they are reading like writers and noticing and noting *what* the memoirists include and *how* they write—what is effective and what may not be as successful.

For younger writers or for shorter readings, there are memoir picture books, such as those written and illustrated by Patricia Polacco. Ms. Polacco's books cover a variety of memoir topics: *Meteor* (1996) is about a town event; *Thank You, Mr. Falker* (1998) is about an influential person; and *Some Birthday* (1993) is about a personal event. *My Ol' Man* (1999) and *My Rotten Redheaded Older Brother* (1994) are about family and relationships. *Betty Doll* (2001) is about a memento special to her mother, while *Thunder Cake* (1997) shares a family ritual.

Reading Memoir Poetry and Graphic Memoirs

Besides prose memoirs in essay length and novel length, there are memoir poems: George Ella Lyon's "Where I'm From," discussed previously, has developed into a genre of its own; Dolly Parton's lyrics for "Coat of Many Colors" became a picture book (Parton, 1996); Billy Collins shares his narrator's past with the poem "The Lanyard" (2005), which may not be autobiographical for the poet but is written in the form of memoir and reveals how ordinary objects can spark memories and pursuits of meaning. Cynthia Rylant's free-verse poetry about her home in Beaver, West Virginia, is collected in *Waiting to Waltz: A Childhood* (2001) and offers examples of memoir poetry on diverse topics: objects ("Wax Lips"), places ("Henry's Market"), people ("Mr. Dill"), relationships ("Pet Rock"), events ("Spelling Bee"), and even crises ("Forgotten"). There are full-length verse memoirs, such as Sonya Sones' (2016) *Stop Pretending: What Happened When My Big Sister Went Crazy*, the account of her thirteenth year when her sister "went crazy."

Table 13.1. Reading Like a Writer chart

Excerpt From Mentor Text	What I Noticed	What I Can Use/ Add to My Memoir
"I'll wear anything I have to wear. I'll do anything I have to do . . ." (Sein-feld, 2008)	Parallel construction Dialogue	When begging my parents to let me study abroad in Scotland, I could write, "I will write to you every day. I will go to classes every day."

Graphic memoirs, such as *Persepolis: The Story of a Childhood* (Satrapi, 2004) or *El Deafo* (Bell, 2014), and Rania Telgemeier's books, have become popular with readers of all ages. And there are oral memoirs and video memoirs. Listening to memoirs, such as "The Garbage Man" (2015) on NPR's *Snap Judgment,* provides excellent mentor memoirs.

Student writers read a memoir and analyze *what* the author wrote and *how* the author wrote, deconstructing those texts to discover how authors develop their writings. After the teacher demonstrates how to take those deconstructed elements and reconstruct them into a memoir, the students are ready to brainstorm their own topics to prepare to draft. Table 13.1 shows an example of the Reading Like a Writer chart.

It may appear unusual to allot nearly as much time to reading memoirs as writing, but deconstructing and studying the structure, ideas, and crafts of professional mentor texts, as well as examples from previous students, teaches writers how to write their own works. Those who need to follow the mentor text more closely will do so, while others who may be more creative will be inspired to use them as springboards for their own original, inventive ideas.

BRAINSTORMING

Students report that one of the greatest roadblocks to writing is finding a topic, especially a topic about which they have something to say, about which they *want* to write. Brainstorming is one of the most important steps to writing. As Sholem Asch, American novelist, dramatist, and essayist, is credited with saying, "Writing comes more easily if you have something to say." Three helpful techniques for brainstorming are having students collect topics on a memories chart, creating a map of their childhood home or neighborhood, or free writing in response to verbal or nonverbal prompts.

Memories Chart

After noting that Lyon's "Where I'm From" was fashioned from a variety of childhood topics, such as people, places, events, activities, environment, religion, family sayings and stories, and foods, writers brainstorm topics from their own childhoods, collecting them on a memories chart to help elicit ideas for writing. Figure 13.1 shows a sample ideas chart that can easily be employed.

Using a projector, the teacher would model noting entries onto a chart, relating a 1-minute story about each entry, while students fill in their charts in any order, jotting thoughts and ideas in whatever boxes they find appropriate, in whatever order their memories surface. Some students will glance up at the model chart and listen as they become stuck; others will stay focused on their own charts. The teacher demonstration is for those who need examples. Over the next days, as students read more mentor texts and share more personal stories with their classmates, writers will add items to their charts, gathering ideas for the memoirs they will write.

When I Was Younger
Ideas Chart

People in My Immediate Family	Relatives I Remember	Friends and Classmates	Neighbors I Knew	Teachers and Professionals (i.e., doctors, dentists)
Family Activities	Holiday Traditions	Inside Games	Outside Games	Sports I Played
Pets in My Family	Special Objects	Hobbies and Crafts I Made	Favorite Foods and Meals	Favorite Toys
Places in My House(s) and Yard(s)	Parks and Playgrounds	Vacation Places	Important Events in My Life	Add Your Own Topic

Figure 13.1. Memories chart.

Neighborhood Map

Another brainstorming technique to help writers collect ideas is the neighborhood map. Teachers draw maps of their childhood neighborhoods, noting (and sharing) short memory stories. Figure 13.2 shows an example.

Students are invited to draw maps of their childhood neighborhoods or floorplans of their childhood homes and annotate with memories. Teachers may need to be sensitive in particular cases, and some students may be hesitant to share their living situations. One suggestion is that they can draw maps of one of their childhood schools or daycare facilities and mark events, people, and articles they remember. After they turn and share a story or two with their neighbors, they can add additional memories generated by the conversations.

Free Writing

A third method for generating memories is through free writing. Free writing is writing down anything the writer thinks of in response to a prompt, written in any format without regard to the formalities of writing; that is, revision and editing. There are no rules in free writing, other than to write the entire time, usually 5 to 8 minutes.

Prompts can be words, introductory phrases, quotations, short read-alouds, picture books, excerpts from fiction or nonfiction texts, objects, photographs, artwork, sounds, poems, or even headlines. Providing diverse prompts elicits a variety of responses. Some prompts that have yielded memories from students were a collection of small toys; an old-style class picture; the sound of rain; the smell of vanilla, cinnamon, or pine; and the poems

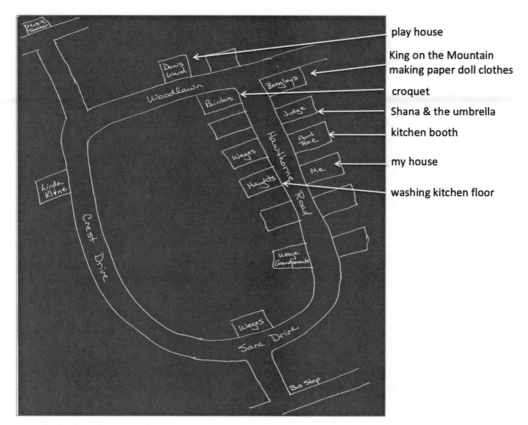

play house

King on the Mountain
making paper doll clothes

croquet

Shana & the umbrella

kitchen booth

my house

washing kitchen floor

Figure 13.2. Sample neighborhood map.

"First Day at School" and "Messy Room." Students can bring in objects or pictures from their pasts as individual free write prompts.

A 5-minute free write in response to the phrase "Looking back . . ." generated the following reflection from a high school student:

High School Student: 5-Minute Free Write

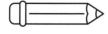

Looking back, I see a boy in the dark all alone. By himself. No one to help or guide him. Eventually he found a door to success. It was as bright as can be.

Looking forward, I see a man. He has the most amazing life. It is more than he could ever ask for.

This free write gives the writer some ideas for memoir writings: a crisis from the past; a pivotal time in his life; a person or event that has made a difference.

On one occasion, students were asked to bring in a picture from a significant moment or one that depicted a special person from the past. A 10-minute free write in response to her personal picture led Sara to reminisce about her grandmother and her grandmother's house, giving her choices of topics to expand into her drafted memoir—that is, her grandmother, family relationships, and visiting Poland.

Sara: 10-Minute Free Write

There is something special about the picture that sits in front of me. I notice that everyone was laughing. Here the eight of us were, smiling and laughing as we perched on my grandmother's bench in the back of her house in Poland.

I find her house significant because, even though I was such a young age, I remember everything that went on there. I remember not understanding a word my grandmother said, and I had to get my mother to translate. But my grandmother would let me get away with anything; when I was yelled at by my mother, she would save me, like my very own Superhero. . . .

Other prompts have elicited writings with more specific details. In this way, writers have accessed that part of the brain that stores memories.

FINDING TOPICS

Students can write memoirs about specific people, relationships, places, mementoes, grade levels or ages in their lives, events, or crises. They can base their memoirs on any of these as individual assignments. Teachers should provide short mentor memoirs—essays, poetry, picture books, storytelling videos—for students to analyze. They then will continue to brainstorm ideas or look through, and add to, their brainstorming charts, maps, or free writes, and draft these memoirs over a few days.

In some classrooms, teachers have allotted enough time for students to draft three types of memoirs—that is, an object memoir, a person memoir, and an event or crisis memoir as part of the prewriting process. In this case, each writer then chooses one rough draft to take through the writing process. Providing choice enhances intrinsic motivation, effort, task performance, and perceived competence, among other outcomes (Roessing, 2017).

FORMAT CHOICES

It is vitally important to teach the many different formats through which writers can portray their writings. This is a real-life skill for all types of writings. Information is made accessible through diverse-genre texts, such as graphics, rhyming jingles, a variety of news article formats, and picture books, to name a few; actually, very little information is imparted through essays. For example, think about how products are sold, directions are imparted, and information is passed on—jingles, rhymes or lyrics, graphics, brochures, news articles, and so on. Argument or persuasive writings, such as letters to the editors, reviews, political cartoons, and advertisements are more likely to be published than are argument essays because these formats more effectively reach the intended audiences and achieve the purpose of persuasion.

This is especially true for memoir. Memoir is an intensely personal writing, and writers should be acquainted with the possibilities so they can choose the format most fitting for the stories they want to tell. Students will observe, from reading a variety of mentor texts, that memoir can be written in diverse formats. These choices will interest and attract reluctant readers and emerging writers as prose reading and essay writing might not.

Prose Narrative

The most common form of memoir writing is prose narrative. Students can write their memoirs in essay-type formats in paragraph form, adding dialogue and other narrative techniques, which will be familiar and comfortable to many writers. But just like published authors, many student writers will want to stretch their creative wings and find the "form that fits their function" and enhances the meaning of their writing. Or they may just be ready to expand their writing possibilities.

Poetry

Poetry allows for the most diversity. Many writers prefer to begin with the most familiar poetry format—rhyming poems written in stanzas. Evan, an eighth-grade writer, began his crisis memoir about learning to ride a bicycle with the stanza:

**Evan,
Grade 8:
Poem**

*My dad walked down the stairs
A helmet in his hands.
He was set on a goal;
He was going to make a stand.*

Seven quatrains later, the poem ends with a reflection stanza:

*I'm riding now; I know that
Adventure's round every bend.
This bike that I once hated
Is now my very best friend!*

One innovative student wrote his poem about a family trip to Disneyland in limerick stanzas (Roessing, 2014). He knew from the format that he needed to write five-line stanzas following an A-A-B-B-A rhyme scheme and that his subject would need to be light and humorous.

Rhyming poetry formats include multiple options, such as narrative poetry, sonnets, limericks, and villanelle. There are also a multitude of formats that do not rhyme, the most common being free verse, odes, haiku, tanka, acrostic, and the more sophisticated sestina and pantoum. A few evolving writers have written their memoirs as list poetry after reading Nikki Giovanni's (1968) "Knoxville, Tennessee," and some have combined poetic formats within memoirs.

Graphic Formats

Some writers will wish to employ not only words but visuals to tell their stories.

Using published graphic memoirs as mentor texts, students can learn the intricacies of how images and text work together in comic or sequential art to create a story; there are a multitude of ways to play with combining words and pictures in comics. Narration can be positioned outside the panels, while dialogue is incorporated within that narration or in speech and thought balloons within the panels.

When drawing the illustrations, it is critical for writers to think about perspective and which details of the story are important to emphasize. In "Hurdles," Derek Kirk Kim (2004) employed a close-up technique to bring attention to certain features within the panels, while narration was placed beside each panel and dialogue was included in text balloons. Eighth-grade writer Kyle replicated those techniques in his memoir about his first barbershop haircut, "Snip-Snip," shown in Figure 13.3.

Less proficient writers may more clearly depict mood and action through comic art than they will be able to achieve through more traditional writing. Comic art can also lead to better writing as writers contemplate details for their illustrations. As sequential art, comics also aid with organization in writing. Teachers may wish to have writers write out their memoirs after they draft graphic versions.

Permitting students to choose their own topics or write about what matters to them results in better writing, writing that has a sense of purpose. In addition, writers can be taught to choose the format that best fits their topic and their writing styles. When students are introduced to a variety of formats it gives them choice, and with that choice they

So I get this message from the boss, and he tells me that I have to take care of some "business" for him, if you know what I mean.

I figure that I'll check the place out, see what's going on. When I arrive, I see a large man, and I don't mean that he was tall. He's got a furry rat above his lip, and he's packin' some serious heat.

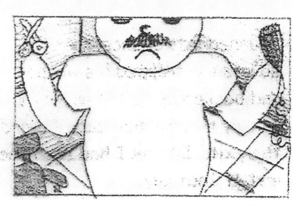

Figure 13.3.   Panels from eighth-grade writer Kyle's graphic memoir, "Snip-Snip." (From Roessing, L. (2014). *Bridging the gap: Reading critically and writing meaningfully to get to the core* (p. 509). Lanham, MD: Rowman and Littlefield; reprinted by permission.)

soar in directions that may surprise both the teacher and the writers themselves. Their voices permeate their writings. When given format choice, some students have even written their memoirs in the form of plays. One middle school student wrote a drama, "From the Midst of Act Four." The first three acts were each a memory from her past, one focusing on an event that occurred at age 2, one on a memento that was meaningful at age 8, and the third on who was important in her life at age 12. Many other students have written their memoirs as illustrated picture books to share with younger family members and relatives or their future children.

PUTTING IT ALL TOGETHER

By this time student writers have spent a lot of time in the prewriting phase: reading and analyzing a variety of mentor texts; brainstorming using one or all three of the methods outlined previously; and choosing topics and formats for the memoir(s) they will draft. In "Teach Writing as a Process, not Product" (2003), Donald Murray goes so far as to say, "Prewriting is everything that takes place before the first draft. Prewriting usually takes about 85% of the writer's time" (p. 4).

At this point writers are ready to draft a memoir about a favorite object that has become a token of their past, a person who influenced them, a crisis that changed their lives for the better or worse, a momentous event, a specific grade or age that has significant memories, or a place that has special meaning, considering different formats to ascertain which best communicates their stories.

After a few days of drafting, writers will be ready and willing to revise because this will be writing that matters. Revision is most effectively achieved when taught through daily focus lessons on such strategies as word choice, adding voice, sentence fluency, and then editing for conventions. For this writing, writers have gathered their ideas from their charts, maps, and free writes, but an Ideas lesson on adding specific details or including sensory images would be appropriate for all types of memoirs. One focus lesson especially appropriate for memoir writing would be the reflective ending; whether the memoir is written as prose, poetry, graphic, or drama, this lesson would help writers fulfill the requirement of memoir writing. The teacher's Word Choice lesson could be anything that fits their grade and discipline standards, as word choice is primary in any writing. Some lesson topics would be active verbs, substituting proper nouns for common nouns, hyphenated adjectives, or alliteration for rhythm. With choice, Voice will shine through in memoir, but a lesson on including dialogue and dialect or thinking about perspective will enhance voice. Sentence Fluency can focus on varying sentence length (even in poetry) or sentence form or adding prepositional phrases to develop short sentences.

On these days of drafting and revision, lessons can be held through a Writers' Workshop. Teachers would begin with a read-aloud of a short mentor text that illustrates the strategy or technique being taught; followed by a teacher model; then a short, guided practice, all of which should take no longer than 10–15 minutes. Next, writers would have about 30 minutes to independently work on their memoirs, applying the focus lesson, if appropriate, while the teacher confers with a few students each day. If 5–10 minutes remain, students can share how they applied the day's focus lesson to their draft or read a part of their writing to the class or a partner.

Next comes the editing process, during which the teacher teaches one conventions lesson and can refer back to conventions taught earlier in the year as students edit their revised drafts.

Last is Presentation, sometimes considered the "+1," or Seventh, Trait of Writing. Students can look over their formats to see that they follow the guidelines of the genre chosen, while allowing for creativity. For example, if they are writing rhyming poems, they should not include any free-verse stanzas unless the inclusion was deliberate and purposeful. If they change the rhyming pattern of the Shakespearean sonnet, their altered rhyme scheme should be consistent. Authors and illustrators of picture books have alternated pages of text and pages of illustrations or have included text on each illustrated page and, in most cases, have been consistent.

Some students focused on one topic in their chosen memoir. Some writers wrote about important keepsakes in the forms of odes or as list poems, such as "What's in My Drawer." A few have even written obituaries for mementoes that have "died." Paul mourned the loss of his Mickey Mouse watch, a token that was not only a constant "companion," but one that reminded him of a wonderful vacation and his childhood. This example of an object obituary is shown here.

Paul: Object Obituary

Mickey Mouse Watch, 8 years of Age, Timekeeper.

Mickey Mouse Watch, a mere eight years of age, lived in a child's wrist, keeping time with its glow-in-the-dark arms, died early this week from battery failure.

Mickey was born in Disney World, Florida, and raised in a quiet souvenir stand. Once he was sold, he moved to Pennsylvania with his new owner, Paul, to live in a yellow house. He worked for no wage, telling time on a child's wrist, for many years before retiring to a green jewelry box in the owner's room.

In his line of work Mr. Watch told time for many a stranger daily. His hobbies included moving his glow-in the-dark-arms and having his glass polished.

He is survived by his owner and his own friends, the stuffed animals Donald Duck and Goofy.

The funeral will be held in Paul's house with viewing and church services at 9 o'clock am on Saturday morning. Burial will follow the service. In lieu of flowers, donations should be made toward a new watch.

Lauren wrote about her childhood park in the form of a sonnet. Her closing couplet voices a longing as the writer shares her realization that, as an adolescent, "playtime is really almost done." The writing includes sophisticated word choice (e.g., *abode*), dialogue, and sensory images—the lack of breeze, the smell of woodchips, the hot slide that burns the child's legs. Figure 13.4 shows this example of a place sonnet.

After reading a graphic memoir and viewing professional and student graphic memoirs, Cory, a middle-school student, decided to create a graphic memoir to portray the memory of an event from his childhood. If he were to then write out the memoir, he could add the details that are included in his artwork. Figure 13.5 shows an example of an event graphic.

As do many memoirists, Cheryl included an array of topics—games, music, activities, television shows, neighborhood, and family—from her childhood in a writing based on reading and studying Lyon's "Where I'm From." In her role as poet, she employed alliteration and repetition as rhythmic devices, as well as a final stanza of reflections. Her "Where I'm From" writing is shown here.

A Walk to the Park, a Sonnet

The sun is hot as we walk down the road.
The breeze has gone, for it is summer time.
I would like to make this park my abode.
The monkey bars I just can't wait to climb.

"Come on, Mom! Hurry Up!" I beg and beg.
The smell of woodchips is calling my name.
The slide is so hot that it burns my legs
Squash the Lemon is my favorite game.

Time for the swings! Let's go high in the air.
Someone give me a push so I can start.
I just swing back and fourth without a care.
The park is like a giant work of art.

It feels like my time here has just begun,
But my playtime is really almost done.

Figure 13.4. Middle-school writer Lauren's illustrated place sonnet.

Figure 13.5. Middle-school student Cory's event graphic.

Cheryl:
Poem

Summers in the Southwest

I am from city lights and
Lightning bugs in the breezeway;
I am from braids, barretts, and ballies and
Mr. Softee stopping by on hot summer nights.

I am from Go Fish, Hi-Ho Cherry-Oh and
Barbies, blocks, and Legos;
I am from double-dutch up the street and
Playing Twister and tag and being the teacher.

*I am from **Nick at Nite** and*
***Happy Days** and **The Brady Bunch**;*
*I am from **Tom and Jerry** and*
The Disney channel and Dorothy Gale.

I am from "Over the Rainbow" and
"Sherry Baby" on dad's stereo;
I am from "Because You Loved Me" and
Dancing in the dining room to the Beach Boys.

I am from the adventures of daycare and
The sprinkler under the summer sun;

I am from picnics and park trips and
Sliding, swinging, and swimming.

I am from making mistakes and
Learned needed lessons;
I am from learning to believe and
Realizing everything happens for a reason.

While writing in the format of a chosen genre might be considered Presentation, teachers may also want writers to plan how they will publish and present to their fellow memoirists or their family or another audience, if at all. Sometimes memoirs are very private by design and are written only for the writer. One option is to summarize the memoir in a six-word memoir in the fashion of *I Can't Keep My Own Secrets: Six Word Memoirs by Teens Famous & Obscure* (Fershleiser & Smith, 2009), as did one teenager who wrote, *One parent is enough for me.*

CONCLUSION: MEMOIRS—WRITING THAT MATTERS

Memoirs almost write themselves. If teachers help their writers to think back, remember, and reflect on their pasts through reading the memoirs of others and sharing their childhood stories within the classroom writing community, after analyzing texts and brainstorming in multiple ways, stories pour out. Students have written about persons, places, mementoes, events, crises, and old photographs. Writers have published their memoirs as rhyming poems, free-verse poetry, limericks, sonnets, prose narratives, plays, and graphics. They have shared unbelievably heartbreaking personal stories, such as "The Day Daddy Left," and humorous stories, such as "Beastie."

But most importantly, writers have perceived themselves as authors as they wrote with voice, cared about their writing, and discovered meaning in their lives while they learned about themselves. When students write their lives and are given the tools to do so, they are doing writing that matters.

Fostering a Growth Mindset

Strengths-Based Superhero Stories

AMY MILLER

14

"My superhero, White Eagle, is an 8-year-old boy who wants to learn to read, but he doesn't know that he has dyslexia. If he does not succeed, he will get bullied by almost everybody in the school."

—BM, age 9

When I was a kid, I was not a big fan of superheroes. I was more into Barbies than the Justice League. That is, until I met Spiderman.

Spiderman came on television at 5:30 p.m. on weeknights, right before dinner time. It played in the background while I set the table and chatted with my mom about my day at school, until one evening, when I actually sat down to watch it.

I loved the visuals—the deep reds and black would actually end up making a frequent appearance in my dreams. But I also loved the story—it was the first time I'd heard of a superhero who was a teenager, an orphaned teenager who lived with his aunt and uncle. Aunt May and Uncle Ben were kind people. Still, they were not superheroes themselves, and Peter Parker was just a kid who had something happen to him that was totally out of his control (he got bit by a radioactive spider) and suddenly, he had a choice to make: He could use his new superpowers for good or for evil. And despite all the bad things that had happened to him, despite his insecurities, despite feeling like he wasn't good enough or smart enough or strong enough . . . he chose good. I was hooked.

Years later, I became a mom to two boys—the first was more into trains than Spiderman. The second child, though, asked for a superhero birthday party when he turned 5. He collected superhero costumes, figurines, Legos. And when he was 8 years old, he was diagnosed with dyslexia. Soon after, the Dyslexia Justice League was born.

THE DYSLEXIA JUSTICE LEAGUE

The Dyslexia Justice League (DJL) is a student-led mentorship and advocacy group founded at May Center for Learning in Santa Fe, New Mexico with the following student-articulated goals: "To help kids with dyslexia identify their strengths and be proud of who they are, and to help parents and teachers understand how to support students with dyslexia." The students chose the name Dyslexia Justice League because the organization is about advocacy and empowerment, and they quickly homed in on the notion that superheroes are stronger *because* of the challenges they face in life. They decided to make a comic book as their first project because they wanted the opportunity to more deeply understand superhero stories through a visual language that felt comfortable to them. And that is what they did.

Our group of 8- to 17-year-olds meets on Saturdays, the older students mentoring the younger ones, developing our agenda for advocacy in parallel to developing their individual comics. Our advocacy agenda culminated in DJL students choosing to endorse a new state law, SB 398, which requires screening of all first graders for dyslexia and training in the science of reading for all elementary grade teachers. Our students were proud to speak out at legislative committee hearings about their experiences in schools where educators did not understand their needs and the impact that such a law would have had on their lives. Ultimately, SB 398 became law, a lasting legacy for DJL's mission.

Dyslexia Is My Superpower, Volume 1, our first publication, is a collection of origin stories (DJL, 2018). Most of the four-panel comics in this first volume feature normal kids, or cowboys, or magicians, or dodo birds, discovering their strengths for the first time. This is just right for our group of young authors—normal kids who are discovering *their* own strengths for the very first time. They aren't all about dyslexia, but they are all, by nature, about feeling different, conquering fear and shame, and persevering in the face of the enemy, whether that's the Joker, or Señor Cactus, or Maniacal Math Teacher; not just in spite of what's challenging, but also *because* of it.

When we began creating this collection, I knew the kids would enjoy talking about and looking at comics. What I didn't anticipate was how much they would learn about composition through the process. I watched kids who normally balked at writing a couple of sentences compose entire narratives panel by panel. Students who normally struggle with a sense of time and organization naturally grasped the concept of the passage of time in a comic strip, the use of the gutter as a magic time-machine, and the power of sequencing in telling a story frame by frame. I watched kids with dyslexia think in a medium that matched the way their brains naturally think: visually.

In the midst of this process, I came to learn more about appreciative inquiry (AI), an approach to organizational growth and development that focuses on the strengths of each organization and the strengths of each member of the community (Stavros, Godwin, & Cooperrider, 2015). While AI was originally designed for work with organizations, the same principles can be applied in a school setting and to individual growth and development. Marge Schiller, Ph.D., M.Ed., a thought leader in the AI movement, co-authored a book with her grandchildren and school psychologist Shira R. Levy, NCSP, MAPP (Nationally Certified School Psychologist; Master of Applied Positive Psychology) that focuses on helping young people discover their strengths and empower others. *Stan and the Four Fantastic Powers* (Levy & Schiller, 2018) is the story of a boy who uses his strengths to bring change to his school community. Through this story, Levy and Schiller introduce young people to the four fantastic powers: ME power, SEE power, WE power, and DO Power (p. 28). This structure proved to be a clarifying framework for our focus on crafting strengths-based superhero stories. Our superheroes would go on a personal journey to discover their four powers as well. (A figure at the end of this chapter, Identifying Strengths, shows a superhero reflection based on the four fantastic powers.)

SUPERHERO ORIGIN STORIES CURRICULUM

What follows is the curriculum for the DJL's comic book project. While it was designed with students with dyslexia in mind, it can be used with any group of students, and it can easily be adapted for students ages 8 and up. Superhero origin stories are a relatable, compelling way for students to learn about sophisticated narrative structure grounded in the Hero's Journey while building an understanding of syntax and semantics in all narratives. Because superhero stories riff on the same basic pattern as the Hero's Journey, they are a logical and interesting extension to use once you have already introduced *Story Frames*. In addition, comics are, by definition, a visual medium, which allows us to engage in complex semantics without getting intimidated or stymied by spelling or grammar, which is a struggle for many students with language-based learning differences. In the same ways that picture books can make sophisticated content and concepts accessible to student readers and writers, as discussed elsewhere in *Story Frames*, so can comics.

Studying the superhero comic genre also allows students explicit practice in many executive functioning skills including sequencing, developing a sense of the sweep of time, identifying the key features of a specific thing to place it in a category, practicing cognitive flexibility, and problem solving, just to name a few. (For a broader discussion of executive function, see Chapter 11.) Perhaps most importantly, engaging in superhero storytelling allows students to authentically connect to strengths-based themes associated with "growth mindset."

The terms *fixed mindset* and *growth mindset*, coined by Carol Dweck, refer to the system of beliefs people have related to learning and intelligence. Those with a fixed mindset believe that intelligence is innate and cannot be altered by effort, while those with a growth mindset believe that effort and practice result in growth in learning and intelligence. Over 30 years of research demonstrates that those people who have a growth mindset are more successful in school and in life (see www.mindsetworks.com). Teachers can foster a growth mindset in all students by helping them discover their own fantastic powers through the narrative of a fictional superhero.

All superheroes experience tragedy of some kind; often, their superpowers are born from an experience of injustice they have no control over. These injustices resonate for all children, particularly young adolescents who often feel that the world is unfair. Superhero stories teach us that superheroes are not heroes *because* they have magical powers; superheroes have superpowers *because* they have struggled, stood up to the supervillain, and ultimately, persevered through their own, unique strengths.

The objectives of this 14-day curriculum and a brief lesson-by-lesson overview are outlined next, followed by in-depth descriptions of each lesson. Lessons are designed to take about an hour. Each lesson aligns to Dean's story elements and uses the Quick Draw and storyboarding techniques introduced in Section I of this book. Writing is a recursive process and the lessons move between prewriting and drafting activities before students revise, edit, and reflect on their work.

Curriculum Overview

Objectives

- To understand the basic structure of the Hero's Journey using *Story Frames*
- To use visual key features as a representation of a superhero's strengths

(continued)

(continued)

- To develop the structure of a superhero's story through a visual, comic format
- To empower students to understand that characters become superheroes because they face a problem and use their strengths to overcome the problem
- To connect the four fantastic powers to the student's own experience as a pathway to developing a strengths-based, growth mindset

Lessons

1. Understanding the Hero's Journey—Activating Background Knowledge
2. Storyboarding the Hero's Journey
3. Key Features of a Superhero
4. Envisioning a Superhero: ME Power
5. Four-Panel Comic
6. Envision a Villain: ME Power
7. Six-Panel Story
8. SEE Power (Plan) and WE Power (Guides/Friends)
9. Do Power (Climax)
10. Solution
11–13. Revise and Refine
14. Reflection on Four Fantastic Powers

Day One: Understanding the Hero's Journey—Activating Background Knowledge

Step 1 (15 minutes)   Ask students to define a hero. Ask, "What does it mean to be a hero? How do we know who the hero of a book or film is? Who are some heroes in stories you know?"

Write the names of the heroes and stories on the board. Choose two or three of the stories and ask students to give a brief summary of what happens in the story. Ask, "Is the hero a hero at the beginning of the story? How does the hero become a hero as the story progresses?"

Step 2 (45 minutes)   Introduce the Hero's Journey model using one of the stories that the students have identified. A good bet is to prepare to discuss *Star Wars: A New Hope* (Lucas, 1977) or the first *Harry Potter* film (Columbus, 2001), as most students are familiar with these stories. For this curriculum, we will address the following selected elements from Dean's 12-element *Story Frames* approach: 1) Ordinary World, 2) Call and Response, 3) Mentors, Guides, and Gifts, 4) Problems, Prizes, and Plans, 5) Midpoint Attempt (broken down as Attempt and Attempt in Dean's Basic Storyboard), 6) Climax, and 7) Final Reward.

Model the structure of a hero story for the students, encouraging them to contribute their thoughts as you introduce and discuss each of these elements. Many excerpts from *Star Wars, Harry Potter,* or other films are available online to illustrate some of these elements. A superhero storyboard is shown here.

Superhero Storyboard

Ordinary World	Call and Response	Mentors, Guides, and Gifts	Problems, Prizes, and Plans
Attempt	Attempt	Climax	Final Reward

Day Two: Storyboarding the Hero's Journey

Step 1 (5 minutes)   Review the characteristics of the Hero's Journey and the list of hero stories brainstormed yesterday.

Step 2 (55 minutes)   Choose a Hero's Journey story from the list of stories brainstormed yesterday. Using the *Story Frames* template, draw a sketch for each frame of the Hero's Journey. You should have one sketch that represents each of the parts of the story.

Allow students to look up a summary of the story online if that helps them identify the elements of the Hero's Journey. Students can work alone on this exercise or with a partner. In the DJL, we paired a high school student with an elementary or middle school student for this exercise.

Day Three: Key Features of a Superhero

Step 1 (10 minutes)   Ask, "What is a superhero?" As kids give their ideas about characteristics of a superhero, write them on the board.

Step 2 (10 minutes)   Ask, "What does a superhero look like?" Show students examples of various superheroes from comic books to get a sense of the common features.

Step 3 (20 minutes)   Anatomy of a superhero: Each student chooses one of the example superheroes and creates a sketch of the superhero, labeling the superhero's key features.

Again, this can be completed individually or with partners working together on one sketch. If students are reluctant to draw, an alternative would be to allow them to use magazine photos to collage together an image of a superhero. Following are two examples of a superhero collage.

Step 4 (15 minutes)   Students share their sketches and take turns talking about the key features of a superhero they identified. The teacher makes a list of the key features that the sketches have in common. Also, point out any others the students did not mention. Why are these the key features? What do these key features tell us about the superhero and his or her strengths?

Step 5, Ticket out of class (5 minutes)   Each student writes one sentence on a strip of paper to answer the following question: "What are the key features of a superhero?" Students turn in their papers on the way out the door.

Day Four: Envisioning a Superhero: ME Power

Step 1 (5 minutes)   Anonymously share a few of the responses from yesterday's final question as a way to review the key features of a superhero.

Step 2 (25 minutes)   Today, each student will have the chance to envision his or her own, original superhero.

Say, "Superheroes often have a superpower that helps them fight the bad guys. What are some superheroes' superpowers? We all face problems. What are some problems you face in your life?"

Give suggestions if students don't know what to say. For example, ask, "Are there things you aren't so good at in school? Have you ever tried a sport and it didn't go so well? Have you had a problem with a friend or your sibling?

Ask, "What is something you are good at that could help you fight the problems in your life?" Hand out notecards and ask each student to write down at least one strength he or she has. On the opposite side of the card, ask students to draw a picture that represents the strength. Above the drawing, students should write "ME Power."

Say, "These are your strengths, or 'ME Power.' We all have things that we're good at that help us reach our goals and contribute to others in our community. The same is true for superheroes."

Explain, "Today, you are going to imagine that you are a superhero who faces a problem and develops a superpower that builds on your strengths. You have three decisions to make:

- What is your superhero name?

- What is the problem that makes you stronger?

- What are your strengths, and what is the superpower that helps you fight the problem?"

Step 3 (15 minutes)   Use the superhero template that follows to have each student draw a superhero, identify the key features of the superhero's suit or physical presentation, and identify the following:

Superhero Name:

Strengths and Superpower:

I fight _____

Pass out sheets and colored pencils and circulate while they brainstorm. Encourage them to discuss with each other as they do this—it will help them develop their choices.

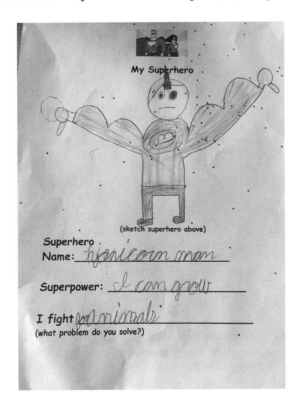

Step 4 (15 minutes)   Give students 5 minutes to brainstorm and fill in the blanks. When the timer goes off, they have 10 minutes to do a quick sketch of their superhero. Let them know they'll have plenty of time to refine this later.

Day Five: Four-Panel Comic

Step 1 (10 minutes)   Remind students of the visual key features of the superheroes they designed yesterday. Ask, "How are your superhero's strengths represented in those key features?"

Next, have students fold a piece of paper lengthwise and then into thirds. Tell students they have 5 minutes to draw a superhero in the first frame. When the 5 minutes are up, tell the students they have 3 minutes to draw a superhero in the next frame. Continue in this same fashion on the schedule detailed here:

5-minute drawing of a superhero

3-minute drawing of a superhero

2-minute drawing of a superhero

1-minute drawing of a superhero

30-second drawing of a superhero

10-second drawing of a superhero

Step 2 (10 minutes)   Have all students tape their comics to the wall, and give them the opportunity to do a walk around and view each other's drawings. Discuss how you are able to identify that the drawing is of a superhero as the artist has less time to complete the drawing. Ask, "What are the key visual features that identify the superhero figure in the most successful drawings? How might this information help us to make choices in drawing our superhero characters? What does it say about what's most important about our characters?"

Step 3 (15 minutes)   Show students some examples of four-panel comics from the newspaper or other sources. Allow students to have some time to look at various examples in small groups. Then ask students to identify the key features of the four-panel comics they looked at. Ask, "What did they have in common?" An example of a four-panel origin comic is shown here.

Introduce the format for the four-panel comic using the template that follows and show an example of a comic that fits this format.

Panel 1: Once there was a _____

Panel 2: Who _____

Panel 3: But then _____

Panel 4: And so _____

Step 4 (25 minutes)   Students will use the superhero they envisioned in the previous lesson to create a four-panel origin comic. The objective of this comic is to introduce the superhero and provide an explanation for why the person became a superhero. If the students don't identify this on their own, be sure to point out that panel 3 of the template introduces a problem into the story. Panel 4 explains the choice that the superhero made as a result of the problem, which opens up the superhero story. In future lessons, we will connect these simple panels to the Hero's Journey and *Story Frames*.

Have students fold a piece of paper into four equal quadrants. Have them sketch out each frame in pencil. The goal is not to have a perfect drawing, but instead, to focus on using visual key features to communicate what is most important in each frame. Once the drawing is complete, students can fill in the four-panel language-based framework shown previously. If it is helpful to fill out the template first and then draw the frames, students can do the work that way as well. Most students who have dyslexia choose to do the drawings first and then write the sentences afterward.

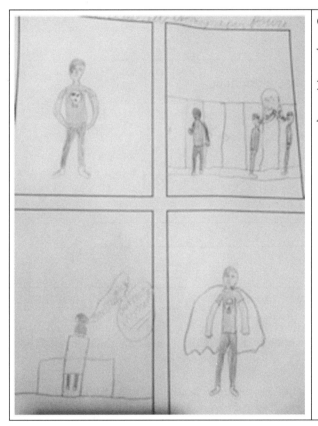

Once there was a boy

Who was bullied at school because he couldn't read

But then he found out he had dyslexia

And so he became Dyslexia Defender

Day Six: Envision a Villain: ME Power

Step 1 (15 minutes)   Remind students of the visual characteristics of the superheroes they've been working on. Have students fold a piece of paper lengthwise and then into thirds. Tell students they have 5 minutes to draw a supervillain in the first frame. When the 5 minutes are up, tell the students they have 3 minutes to draw a supervillain in the next frame. Continue in this same fashion on the schedule detailed here:

5-minute drawing of a villain

3-minute drawing of a villain

2-minute drawing of a villain

1-minute drawing of a villain

30-second drawing of a villain

10-second drawing of a villain

Step 2 (25 minutes)   Follow the same procedure for sharing and discussing the key features of a villain outlined previously for the superhero warm-up exercise in Day Five, Step 2.

Using the supervillain template shown here, have each student draw the villain for their story, identify the key features of the villain's suit or physical presentation, and identify the following:

Villain Name:

Strengths/Evil Superpower:

I hate _____

My Supervillain

(draw sketch above and label key features)

Supervillain name: _____

Evil superpower: _____

I fight against: _____

Pass out sheets and colored pencils and circulate while they brainstorm with each other. Encourage them to discuss with each other as they do this—it will help them develop their choices.

Step 3 (20 minutes)   Give students 5 minutes to brainstorm and fill in the blanks. When the timer goes off, they have 10 minutes to do a quick sketch of their supervillain. Let them know that they'll have plenty of time to refine this later.

Day Seven: Six-Panel Story

Step 1 (10 minutes)   Remind students that they now have a superhero and a villain. Explain, "We are now ready to introduce other aspects of the Hero's Journey from *Story Frames*. Today we'll be working on developing the beginning of the story: 1) Ordinary World, 2) Call and Response, 3) Mentors, Guides, and Gifts, and 4) Problems, Prizes, and Plans."

Step 2 (20 minutes)   Students will work individually or with their partner using the first four *Story Frames* elements to complete one quick sketch for each of the previous items. Ask, "Where does your superhero live when the story begins? What are the key features of this setting that you can communicate visually in your drawing? How does your superhero receive the Call to Adventure? Who is someone who serves as a Mentor or teacher for your superhero? What is the Problem that your superhero encounters and decides to help solve? How is the villain introduced to this Problem?"

Step 3 (30 minutes) Next, students fold a piece of paper into six equal sections. Students complete one panel that corresponds with each of the sentence frames in the six-panel superhero story template that follows. As with the four-panel origin comic shown in the Day Five lesson, students can choose to draw first and then write their sentences afterward or use the sentence frames first and then draw each panel.

Six-Panel Superhero Story Template

Panel 1: This is _____.
                (superhero's regular name)

Panel 2: _____ lives in _____, where everything is _____
                                    (setting)
_____. (Ordinary World)

Panel 3: _____ has a mentor named _____, who teaches him or her

_____ and helps him or her learn about his or her strengths _____ and

_____. (Mentors, Guides, and Gifts)

Panel 4: One day, _____ encounters a problem: _____,

caused by _____ (Call and Response; Problems, Prizes, and Plans)
            (villain).

Panel 5: After that, _____ discovered his or her superpower, _____, and

became _____.
            (superhero name)

Panel 6: If he or she does not succeed, _____. (what is at risk)

Day Eight: SEE Power (Plan) and WE Power (Guides/Friends)

Step 1 (20 minutes) Students share the panels they created in the previous lesson, reading their six-panel stories to the group. As they listen to their peers, have the students fill in the Key Features of Six-Panel Story Reflection template shown here, practicing identifying the elements of the Hero's Journey present in each one. The goal of this exercise is to allow the students to have lots of practice identifying the structural elements of a story.

Step 2 (5 minutes) Hand out two notecards to each student. Ask them to answer the following questions in either a drawing or a sentence on the first card: "How does your superhero plan to beat the villain and solve the problem? What might get in the way of reaching their goal?" This is their SEE power—the ability to envision a plan that will solve a problem.

Step 3 (5 minutes) Ask students to answer the following question in either a drawing or a sentence on the second card: "Who is your superhero's friend, and how does he or she help him or her with the plan?" This is their WE power—the ability to collaborate with others to solve a problem.

Step 4 (30 minutes)   Students are now ready to add more panels to their comics. The number of panels might vary depending on each student's unique story. The focus should be on adding panels that add to the "attempts" portion of the Hero's Journey story by addressing the previous questions. Emphasize that the superhero's SEE power and WE power are what should ultimately lead to the solution of the problem.

Key Features of a Six-Panel Story Reflection.

Setting/Ordinary World: _____

Mentor: _____

Strengths: _____ and _____

Problem: _____

Villain: _____

Superpower: _____

Risk: _____

Day Nine: DO Power (Climax)

Step 1 (15 minutes)   Have students share the additional panels related to SEE power and WE power with their peers. Direct their attention to the different ways that planning and collaboration are represented in each story: "What is the same in each story? What is different about some of the ways that the characters use planning and collaboration?"

Step 2 (30 minutes)   Say, "Now we are coming to the end of your superhero story. The climax is the point of the story where the superhero has to make a choice related to the problem. Usually, the climax of a superhero story is the moment when the superhero is tested in some extremely difficult way. The way they handle this test determines whether or not they succeed in their plan or fail. The climax should be related to the superhero's strengths. Maybe it is related to a strength they didn't know they had, or maybe they have to use a strength that they had doubted earlier in the story." Remind them of examples of climax moments from some of the Hero's Journey storyboards they created earlier in this unit by letting them look back at those storyboards. Discuss how allies contribute to the superhero's choice at the climax.

Put the students in small groups of four. Each student has 5 minutes to share his or her story with the small group, and together the group has an additional 10 minutes to brainstorm possible climax moments for each story. Circulate and make sure each student gets some viable suggestions, offering help if students get stuck.

Step 3 (10 minutes)   Ask students to reflect on the process of brainstorming possible climax moments. Point out that even if a character has great SEE power and WE power, sometimes DOING is challenging, even for superheroes. Ask, "What are some of the obstacles that our heroes face, and how do they overcome them?"

Step 4, Ticket Out of Class (5 minutes)   On a strip of paper, students should write an answer to the following question: "What are two reasons that DOING can be challenging, and what are two things you can do about it?"

Day Ten: Solution

Step 1 (15 minutes)   Seat students in one big circle. Say, "Today we'll be adding the climax and a solution to your comics. In order to start thinking about solutions, we're going to play a game. Here are the directions: I will say one sentence that starts a story, introduces a character, and describes their strength. For example, 'Once upon a time, there was a boy who was very good at drawing.' Then the next person in the circle will add a problem. For example, 'But one day a mean teacher tore up his drawing and said he could never draw again.' The third person in the circle will add the climax and solution. For example, 'So he told the principal, who helped him plan a special art show so that he could display his artwork there.' Let's try another one."

Go around the circle until all students get one turn contributing to a story.

Step 2 (15 minutes)   Say, "Now, you will have 15 minutes to sketch at least three different possible solutions to your own superhero story." Give each student three notecards and let the students sketch for 10 minutes. At the end of the time, ask students to volunteer to share one of their possible solutions. Then have students put a star in the corner of the solution card that they'll be using for their actual story.

Step 4 (30 minutes)   Students will now return to their comics and add frames that represent the climax and solution. Circulate and support as they work.

Days Eleven, Twelve, and Thirteen: Revise and Refine

These three days are set aside for student work time. Now that students have the entire comic sketched out, they can use these 3 days to redraw frames, add detail, revise any parts of the story they would like to, make sure they've added clarifying text, and finally, ink the comic.

Day Fourteen: Reflection on Four Fantastic Powers

This last day of the unit is focused on allowing students to reflect on the comic-creating experience and connect the narrative structure with their own personal experiences. Give each student the Superhero Reflection sheet that follows and give them the entire period to complete it. Some students will need to talk out portions of their reflection with you, and I would encourage that. This reflection should not be treated as a test, but rather as a structured way to make explicit connections between the Hero's Journey, the four fantastic powers, and each student's own unique experience with the goal of building self-knowledge and growth mindset.

Superhero Reflection

---

1. ME Power: How is your superhero like you? How is your superhero different from you?

2. ME Power: What are your strengths?

3. SEE Power: What is one goal you have for yourself? What are three things you can do to work toward achieving that goal?

4. WE Power: Who might help you reach your goal? How can you ask others for help?

5. DO Power: What is something you've tried to do that was hard? Did you stick with it or did you quit? Looking back, what's one thing you could have done when it was tough that might have helped you?

Fold a paper into four equal panels. Using the four-panel format, sketch a comic strip about yourself. The comic should tell us a strength, a problem you have faced, and what you chose to do about it.

At the end of this unit, we put everyone's comics together into a class comic book, and I hold a Superhero Ceremony, where each student receives a cape with one word on it that expresses one of his or her strengths. When I'm working with our DJL students, I ask the older students to help me identify the strengths of the younger students and vice versa. At the ceremony, I present the cape to each student, tie it around his or her neck, and use the identifying strengths template that follows to talk about each person. This is a powerful way to remind students that even when they find it difficult to identify their own strengths, others recognize and appreciate them. Often this holds a powerful influence on a student's self-concept, and it goes a long way toward developing relationships and trust within our community. It also builds self-love, which is maybe the most important gift of all.

Identifying Strengths

(*Eva's*) superpower is (*courage*). She does not let (*other people's mean words*) get to her. She shows (*courage*) when she (*reads out loud in class*). (*Eva*) you are (*Fearless Learner*).

CONCLUSION: TAPPING INTO STUDENTS' SUPERPOWERS

It has been my privilege as a teacher to witness the superpowers of my students with learning differences day after day. The fact that students who have felt unsuccessful in school, who have often felt dumb or less than their peers, who have been forced to daily face the things that are the most painful for them, still show up, still smile and say good morning, still TRY, is valiant and inspiring and, well, super. It is our job as educators to help these students recognize these great strengths in themselves. In doing so, we, like superheroes, become *our* best selves. We become lifesavers.

Advocating for Students

The Family Story

15

MARY JO O'NEILL

Section III of this book has described different ways personal narratives can empower students. In particular, they can empower students with disabilities who receive special education services. Stories allow students to receive free appropriate public education (FAPE). Unless the educators understand the child's deficits and strengths, that child will not receive FAPE. The school needs to appreciate the whole child, and the family story helps to facilitate that conversation.

My primary job as a special education advocate is to help parents tell their family story. The initial aim is to use their story to start a healthy dialogue with the school. The ultimate goal is to get their child the help he or she needs from their academic setting to ensure the appropriate, efficient, and adequate level of support required to create a level playing field with peers. These students may be dealing with academic deficits, physical needs, and/or emotional challenges. Every family is different, but whatever their issues may be, the first thing I do is actively listen and assess the family's understanding of their problems and needs. To achieve this, I ask them to tell me their story.

THE FAMILY STORY PROCESS

Different family members have different versions of the same story. Grandma may tell a very different tale from mom or dad. My job is to listen for the underlying thread and pinpoint the base of the concern, helping them to see things through each other's perspective. Then I give families the assignment of going home and creating a non-emotional timeline—an objective, factual, linear narrative. We come back together for a guided meeting to review their story as outlined on the timeline. At that second meeting, we decide if I will tell the story to the school district or if they would prefer to tell it. The purpose of this second meeting is to guide the family on how to move forward, define topics of concern, create a collaborative tone, and plan a collaborative meeting with the district. Sometimes the collaborative meeting is part of an individualized education program (IEP) meeting, a 504 plan, or an evaluation team report meeting. Often, it is a separate meeting to plan for the special education process.

The whole process goes something like this:

Step 1: Initial Meeting (face-to-face)—Parents share their story while the advocate and attorney actively listen. At this point, the attorney determines if the family needs advocacy support or legal action. If advocacy is chosen, then the following steps are taken.

Step 2: Family Exercise (at home)—The family creates a non-emotional timeline in outline form.

Step 3: Guided Meeting (phone conference)—The advocate validates the family's concerns, clarifies the educational process, and helps the family edit their story, which elevates confidence and promotes clarity.

Step 4: Collaborative Meeting (at the school)—The advocate or the family retells the family story to the district or private school.

Step 1: Initial Meeting

When parents are asked to share their story at the initial meeting, it often becomes a dumping ground for a wide range of thoughts and emotions. This first meeting is a time for parents to vent. Sometimes one parent will come in ready to pursue an eligibility for their child, eager to move forward with seeking school support, or determined to resolve a school-related issue, while the other parent doesn't even see a problem or issue. It is essential to acknowledge these different perspectives and understand that family members are all at different places in their *levels of interpretation* regarding the events of the story.

Levels of Interpretation   Imagine a story with mounting tension. Obstacles keep increasing until a character is forced to respond. Their reaction depends on their level of interpretation. Similarly, one parent may encounter challenges, such as observing his or her child's frustration with homework, receiving countless emails from teachers, dealing with homework that is finished but never turned in, or talking to an upset child about reactions from peers, teasing, or behavioral reports. Often, one parent becomes the point person who orchestrates all of the communications between the teacher, counselor, classroom aides, and so forth, while the other parent takes a vital but less visible role. As a result, even when describing the same event or situation, their versions of the same story may be quite different.

For the point person, who is receiving daily emails from school and dealing with the child's ongoing frustrations, it may appear that the story is reaching a crisis point. His or her level of frustration and rising tension may be approaching a pinnacle because of how he or she interprets or analyzes the story events, while the other parent may not sense a concern. Also, both parents may have quite different emotional reactions to the same facts or circumstances. When a situation arises, one does not see a reason to respond, while the other is calling the school office and wanting immediate support. These various emotional responses are similar to the cause and effect sequences of storytelling. One character acts and another reacts, setting up an action/reaction sequence.

One parent may feel the rising tension and come to the meeting with the advocate asking for help to manage the characters in the story. Meanwhile, the other parent may be working long hours focusing on providing financial support, and perhaps paying for services the school does not recognize are needed. This other parent may not even sense there is a story to tell. All stories center on a problem, and this parent, like the school, may not detect the same level of academic concern or the need for social-emotional supports that the point person recognizes.

Family Dynamics   As the story unfolds, the dynamics of the family appear. One person may take the lead in telling the story while the other sits by timidly listening, or both may contribute equally. Where the story starts depends on the age of the child. Parents often begin by describing where things are at the present moment. They then push backward to tell what led up to the current situation. How far back they go depends on the diagnosis in question. For students with learning disabilities, parents may go back to when the child started school and perhaps describe what life was like before that. For students on the autism spectrum, it is crucial for parents to describe their child's early years (birth to 3) because this part of the story is integral to the school qualification of autism. A deficit must be shown from birth to 3, and describing these early challenges becomes a vital part of the story.

If more than one family member is telling the story, the advocate must listen for the common threads and concerns. When outside evaluations are available, the advocate reviews the paperwork and previous testing in an effort to validate the parents' concerns. The advocate must weigh the information the parents are giving and provide clarity to them when necessary. The family may need help to interpret the test results. The advocate also looks at the school records to see if the details of the parents' story are represented in the child's school profile, looking for the common thread that connects the family story to the school story. Next, the advocate asks parents to share the same story, but in a non-emotional timeline.

Step 2: Family Exercise—Creating the Non-Emotional Timeline

The Chapter 15 Appendix presents one family's brainstorm for a non-emotional timeline. A non-emotional timeline is a story told by a family sequentially and non-emotionally. They must relay only the facts. It will be emotional going through the process. There will definitely be heated moments, especially when realizations come to light, but parents must be careful not to make the document sound emotional and not to make subjective statements. Because the timeline will be shared with the school, it needs to be objective, focused on education, and fact driven. When teachers and administrators listen to the family story told objectively and linearly, powerful changes evolve. For example, a school has decided not to provide services for a child with autism because staff observe that the child functions at grade level compared with his peers and his behavior at school is not affecting his academic performance. When the child's family presents the non-emotional timeline to the school, their story provides the ongoing evidence that although the child may seem to be well adjusted, he has actually been struggling for a very long time.

Schools are responsible for providing academic *and* social/emotional support. Sometimes schools fail to realize that a child with social-emotional challenges may qualify for services even if his or her academic grades are not suffering. Schools that only look at report cards may fail to see that a child is crying every day in the bathroom, avoiding peers at lunch, not advocating for him- or herself, or not asking for help in the classroom.

Step 3: Guided Meeting—Refining the Family Story

At the second meeting, parents share their timeline and we clarify how to present their story at the school meeting. Many parents prefer for the advocate to share the story with school personnel, while others are comfortable sharing it themselves and only want the advocate present for support. At this second meeting with the parents, it is also essential to find out who else will be attending the school meeting. Of these people, who are the ones who already believe the family story and who are the nonbelievers? The former have already seen the deficits within the school setting, and the parent story validates these teachers' concerns. It is also important to know which teachers will speak on the child's behalf, and which might not. The parents and the advocate try to determine, ahead of time, the background knowledge of the "audience" of educators regarding the student's disability. Understanding the audience helps to know how the story needs to be delivered and what precise information from outside sources is needed to support the family story. This information might include fact sheets from outside providers or disability-specific action groups such as the International Dyslexia Association or Autism Speaks.

Step 4: Collaborative Meeting—Telling the Family Story

At the school meeting, it is time for either the advocate or the family to tell the family story. The school personnel also have the opportunity to share their version of the story. Both parties typically find there was information missing on all sides. Many issues are resolved and clarified simply by sharing the different perspectives of the family and the school. Issues are typically revealed, showing difficulties with perspective-taking on both sides.

Parent Issues   Parent issues often include misunderstandings, unrealistic expectations regarding the educational process, lack of trust, and difficulty sharing concerns because of feeling intimidated by the school authorities.

Misunderstandings   Misunderstandings may include not knowing the educational process and definitions of terms used by educators, what one of my colleagues refers to as the alphabet soup of education. There are so many acronyms that it can become very confusing (e.g., IEP, BIP [behavioral intervention plan], ADA [Americans With Disabilities Act]). Not understanding the timeline of the testing and referral process is also common. This can include the sequence of requirements and how long each step will take. Another common area of misunderstanding is the difference between outside clinical diagnosis versus a school's qualifying category of eligibility. Outside evaluators have the background to give a diagnosis from the *Diagnostic and Statistical Manual (DSM-5)*, while a school bases its findings on response-to-intervention and/or the evaluation team report, which focus on state and local requirements and the child's ability to access the curriculum. The tests an outside evaluator gives may not be available in a school setting, and the impact of the child's deficits as described in the test interpretation section of the report may be viewed differently by an outside evaluator than it is by an educational team.

Unrealistic Expectations   Families may not understand the educational process and the school's need to follow federal, state, and local mandates. They may believe it is essential to have the word *dyslexia* appear on the IEP as the child's eligibility when the state only allows the term *specific learning disability*. When the school tells their side of the story, it opens the door to problem solving, such as determining where else in the IEP the term *dyslexia* could go, such as in the other information section on the first page of the IEP, the profile, or the future planning page.

Communication Breakdowns   Communication breakdowns may occur because of a lack of trust and understanding. Parents may feel intimidated by academic authorities and administrators, perhaps because of their own deficits, which go back to *their* childhood story. They may be running on fear rather than working collaboratively with teachers.

School Issues   Schools face their own challenges with perspective-taking. Their issues also include misunderstandings, unrealistic expectations, unclear demands, and communication breakdowns. There may be many team members involved, including a variety of administrators: director of special education, principal, and superintendent. A host of teachers and support staff may also have input. These may include the classroom teacher, related service providers (speech-language pathologist [SLP], occupational therapist [OT], social workers), paraprofessionals, art teachers, physical education teachers, etc.

Misunderstandings   The school might not understand the stress the child experiences. Often, kids hold their emotions together and modify their responses throughout the day and then fall apart at home. Therefore, the school feels like the outbursts after school are strictly related to home. They may even blame the parents. The school's story may center on denial. The team must clarify what behaviors the child is exhibiting at school that reflect the same stress seen at home but might be going unnoticed or be misinterpreted.

These behaviors may include making frequent excuses to leave the classroom, interrupting other students, talking excessively, and over- or under-responding.

Regarding behavior and attention, administrators often see a student's movement, but may be unable to sense their fears. Overly active students may be difficult to identify in terms of underlying causes. Our learners with attention-deficit/hyperactivity disorder (ADHD) can be extremely social, present as academically engaged, be chatty, and even be extraordinarily talented, but also be completely misunderstood. Often administrators may be unable to put the student's loud demeanor aside and recognize that how he presents himself is different from how he feels. Walking into the classroom, he may not understand the words in front of him. Looking around the school environment, he may be unable to identify helpful tools. These students may have the ability to understand the content but be unable to put words on paper or on the computer. The parents see the stress, and the administrators recognize the movement, but they don't understand the cause. The administrators may be focusing on how to get the student physically settled and not on how to settle him mentally to learn and to be academically attentive.

Our administrators play a vital role in the process, and the teachers often feel that their administrator's version of the story trumps their version of the story. When teachers are sharing their classroom observations, they need to clearly define the issues; while understanding that education involves more than just academics, also focusing on a student's social and emotional care. Teachers may feel intimidated. It's not that administrators are overpowering, but teachers (and sometimes administrators) don't understand the process.

Typically, the director of special education runs the meetings and is the voice of the school story. Often in our meetings teachers are intimidated, and sometimes the teachers are playing a delicate role, building a relationship with the parents while trying to hold their job. We want to be sensitive to the teachers. A key part of this process is understanding all of the players at the table. I often ask the families the roles of each individual who will be attending the meeting, identifying who has a strong understanding of the child's disability and needs.

Over time our educators have done a better job of relating to the child on the autism spectrum. We know more today than we did yesterday. Typically, a student on the spectrum is overwhelmed with the social curriculum and transitioning from academic classes to specials like music and art. It is vital to discuss to what extent the child is holding it together. When he arrives at home, he may either curl up in a ball or have a stress-related explosion. Sharing stories between parents and teachers allows educators to compare and contrast, while not judging or having predetermined opinions.

Communication Breakdowns   Often the emails and frequent phone calls that the teacher has made to the home are not shared in the meeting. The administrator may not realize the extent of the struggle. The administrators often see the child in the principal's office but do not know what actually occurred. They may never hear the *why*.

Parents, students, teachers, and administrators *all* play a delicate role in this process. The different versions of the story need to be shared, and while sharing, all players need to listen without judgment.

Unclear Expectations   When homework arrives home, we need to be sensitive to the deliverer, the student. The class expectations may be available on the computer, but often the student still does not see the whole picture or understand the point system. Our families only see the expectations but they do not understand the process or have a clear understanding of how points are earned. Teachers may accept homework and assign points but not review the content. Classwork may receive different points than homework. Quizzes and exams are all weighted differently. These key factors need to be identified and defined early in the school year. Students do not always understand the big picture of how percentages work or the impact of missing or incomplete assignments. Clarifying these expectations with the parents will help guide the conversation at home. Sharing class percentages and point systems in advance and defining each expectation is a useful step. Educators may assume that parents and students understand teacher's expectations and directions. It is vital to clarify instructions.

When expectations are unclear and not adequately described up front, this creates discomfort for the child involved and confusion for the families assisting the student. Clarifying what the finished product is and how it will look at the end is a key factor, especially when helping a student with an executive functioning issue. For example, if a seventh grader needs to complete an oral report and this task creates anxiety, can we be flexible regarding the outcome? Perhaps we can allow the student to present the project in front of other educators or tape it in advance. We need to remember the focus point and that the finished project is the prize. If we hope to have the student master the skill of presenting her findings, then who she presents the report to is not the identified skill.

In Summary: Sharing the Family Story With the School

Communication breakdowns, unclear expectations, and unclear academic demands create a misunderstood story. Families need to define their story and share it in a positive tone with a collaborative team. Administrators and educators all have the child's best interest in mind, but sometimes the emotions create an unclear story.

As the family story is shared, often both parents and educators have "aha" moments that begin with, "I didn't know that" or "I wish someone would have told me that." The story becomes a powerful tool for understanding, change, and advocacy.

OTHER WAYS TO SHARE FAMILY STORIES

Once families have created the family story, they may want to share it with other people besides school personnel. This may include other family members; support groups; a lawyer, if going to due process; or legislators for advocacy at the local, state, or national level. Families must consider when to share their story and with whom. Is it safe? What are the long-term implications of sharing the story for the parent, the family, and the child? Who is the audience?

Other Family Members and Support Groups

Parents may want to share the family story before large family gatherings. Sometimes parents have not told other family members their child has autism or dyslexia. Equipped with the family story, they may share their experiences with extended family for the first time. Other family members are then more aware of potentially tricky situations, like the fact that a child is sensitive to light or loud sounds or may not be able to read the assembly directions for a new toy.

Some families share their stories on blogs, at conferences, and in support groups to help other families realize they are not alone. This perspective can provide a powerful support for other parents. Still, families need to be sensitive to how much personal information they want to provide regarding their child and consider how the child may feel about that disclosure in the years to come.

Due Process and Continued Advocacy

Most families can resolve their conflicts with the school by sharing their family story. Occasionally, a student still does not receive the support needed, and the parents must go through due process to get results. At this point, they may choose to share the family story with an attorney who can then counsel the family about how to best proceed. Some parents share a family story to promote change at the local, state, and national levels. People who testify before Congress often frame their experiences in a story.

Self-Advocacy

The ultimate goal is for the student to be able to advocate for himself and tell his own story with confidence, but it is important to make sure that the audience is a safe one so that the experience is productive. It is vital for a student to be able to ask for the accommodations outlined in the IEP, ask educators clarification questions, and express concerns without fear of judgment. The goal is for a student to request the support he or she needs without apologizing for utilizing accommodations. Students benefit from recognizing that being able to tell their story and advocate for themselves is an achievement in itself and supports their other successes. When they own the power of being able to share their story, they can also own their accomplishments.

THE ONGOING STORY

The final step is adding to the story and realizing things are getting better. Reflecting on the original story and realizing there has been progress can be very beneficial. Families can see progress when comparing the new reality to the old story. As families share their stories, they can generate solutions.

CONCLUSION: THE FAMILY STORY AS A TOOL FOR ADVOCACY

Story Frames focuses on helping children learn to tell and write stories that may be fictional or personal. They need assistance to do this, but their parents sometimes need support to tell their stories as well. The process is the same. It's about describing a situation, identifying a problem, generating solutions, and dealing with consequences. The ability to tell a story effectively has powerful implications for many parts of life, including advocacy. A parent or child who can describe his or her experiences in the form of a story possesses a powerful skill that will serve him or her well in many situations and for years to come.

Family Story Example

Brainstorm for Non-Emotional Timeline

The following is an example of a brainstorm that led to a non-emotional timeline for Sam, who was diagnosed with dyslexia in early elementary school.

TIMELINE BRAINSTORM FOR SAM'S FAMILY

Directions: Complete the following brainstorm to help create a timeline of your advocacy efforts.

1. **What are your family's/child's strengths, talents, and positive attributes?**

Sam is empathetic and kind and the most understanding person I know; he is a true friend to others. Sam is what others consider to be laid back, as he honestly doesn't care about things that don't really matter in the world; he truly tries to understand the other's perspective and feels okay with who he is.

Sam NEVER GIVES UP! How about that for a strength? He works through it, all of it. And thank God for that, as he has had hurdles and disappointments that others would have thrown the towel in [about] a long time ago.

He is smart in the most unique and amazing way; he is witty and quick and a joy to be with. He can figure things out with patience and kindness; he's the boy that I say, "He's got it going on [about]."

2. **When did you first suspect there was a problem? Describe what happened.**

Sam did not talk or babble as a baby. We would brag about how quiet he was but we had concerns that he was nonverbal and seemed frustrated that he could not communicate what he wanted. As a toddler we taught him sign language to help him with his frustration. At his first birthday checkup he was written a script for speech-language therapy. Then when Sam entered preschool he seemed to be lagging behind his peers. We could see that Sam was going about learning his letters and sounds in a way that seemed unusual. He was unable to really write his name and he was just overall struggling to keep up with the pace of the room, even in preschool.

He was always friendly in other settings, but in kindergarten he pulled himself away from his friends during playtime or recess, as I believe now, he was exhausted from the learning process. Although, I asked and did meet with his kindergarten teacher every 2 weeks to review his progress, and she would assure me he was fine, at the end of kindergarten she suggested that he be held back. It was the first of many disappointments in the education system and the lack of preparedness by a general educator.

3. **Who were your helpers? Describe your support system.**

My first helper was Sam's first-grade teacher. She was amazing. I asked to speak with her prior to the school year beginning, which she happily accommodated, and I told her of my concerns. Within 2 weeks, she had enough information to go to the administration and start the process for an IEP. I owe her a debt of gratitude for her alertness and advocacy. From there, I met the school psychologist and interventionist, who, after allowing time to try and allowing me and my husband time to accept what was happening, gave me amazing advice and told me honestly, even though it hurt, what they thought I should do to best help Sam. Again, I will be forever grateful for their honesty and candor and they set us on a path to become real advocates for our son.

Then as things moved along, I ran into Mary Jo O'Neill, whom I knew but not in this capacity. Mary Jo has been my advocate and dear friend for years. She has guided me, she has encouraged me when I needed it most, and she has been my sounding board, cheer-leader, fighter, and clown (you got to laugh!), and the journey is not over. I will never forget telling Mary Jo that I was tired and she told me, "Yup, it is tiring. But you are not done, so breathe and keep going; you cannot quit." And she knows, because the beautiful part is that she never quits. I have had her with me all the way, and I could not have done it without her!

4. **Think about all of the attempts to help your child made by you and others. Consider who was involved (school, outside agency, tutors etc.). Describe your plans, attempts and the results. List these attempts in chronological order.**

    See Sam's Timeline (Figure 15.1).

5. **As clearly as possible, articulate what outcome you are seeking now. What would be a sign of success? Think in short-term, attainable objectives as well as long-term goals.**

Currently, I am starting to consider what's next for Sam after high school. I know he is interested in college and I believe he is able; I just want to be sure we provide the correct place to have success. As well, I want to be open to other options for him if that is his choice. And choice is what I am most interested in for him, to allow him the options of having choices.

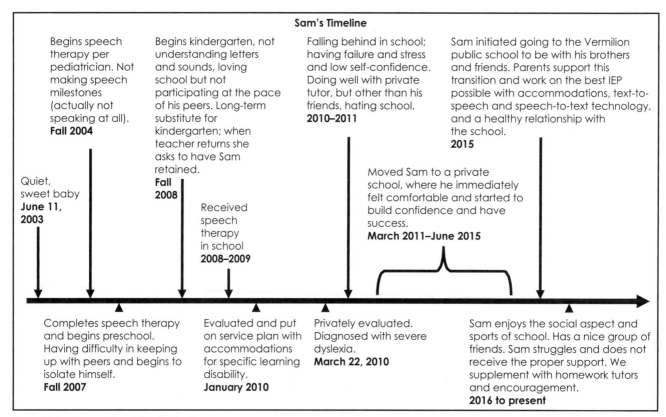

Figure 15.1. Non-emotional timeline for Sam.

The Influence of Culture on Storytelling

CAROL WESTBY

16

Many years ago, early in my career as a speech-language pathologist (SLP), I moved from the East Coast to New Mexico, taking a position on a multidisciplinary team that provided developmental assessments for children throughout the state. I had received my training in a well-known midwestern university and had several years of clinical practice and university teaching. Yet my training and experiences had not prepared me for New Mexico, a minority majority state with a large Hispanic and American Indian population. My knowledge of language development and communication was insufficient for the work I had to do. To compensate, I took linguistics, cultural psychology, and anthropology courses. I learned not only about the phonology, syntax, and semantics of Spanish and Native American languages, but also about variations in discourse organization and content, as well as cultural socialization practices for communication styles and discourse patterns. At a time when researchers were describing the organizational structure of mainstream narratives (known as story grammars), I learned of the variability of narratives across cultures.

A colleague and I applied our understanding of cultural variations in narratives in Project TALES (Talking about Life Experiences and Stories), a grant-funded program designed to teach Native American children the structure and content of mainstream narratives as a way to improve their comprehension for the state reading tests they were required to take (Westby, Moore, & Roman, 2002). Simultaneously, TALES sought to promote maintenance of Native American storytelling. Elders in the participating tribes expressed concerns about their children losing the Native American stories. Historically, children would hear stories told by elders between the first frost in the fall and the last frost in the spring. (Stories would not be told during warm summer months.) With the increased availability of technologies—televisions, iPads, and Nintendos—Native American children were less exposed to the stories of their culture. One's stories are critical for the development of a healthy self-identity. The tribes had identified storytellers who we invited to tell their stories in the schools. Among the most popular of the storytellers was Bluewater, who taught the children how to tell string stories (stories told while making figures from string to support the story).

Although I knew from my readings that string stories exist in many cultures, imagine my surprise on a recent trip to Rapa Nui (Easter Island), a remote island in the South Pacific noted for its large monolithic moai figures, when I witnessed children engaged in a string story competition. As part of maintenance of Rapa Nui culture, children are taught to tell string stories (kai-kai). In the kai-kai competition, children, dressed in traditional ancestral costumes, recite stories of legends while creating string figures. String stories are accompanied by slow and undulating body movement. Sofia Abarca, a Rapa Nui

Figure 16.1.   Teacher Isabelle Pakarati, with student Montserrat Aguirre Abaraca. (From Fariña, S.A. [n.d.]. *Kai-kai Rapa Nui: Ideogram of threads, ancestral game.* [Mixed media collection.] Chile: Author; reprinted by permission.)

involved in the maintenance of kai-kai, shared with me photos of her daughter being taught a string story by Isabel Pakarati, a Rapa Nui master of kai-kai (see Figure 16.1).

THE IMPORTANCE OF UNDERSTANDING AND APPRECIATING CULTURAL VARIATION IN NARRATIVES

Narratives have a central place in the lives of humans. Storytelling is a panhuman ability. Around the world, stories are told to teach, to pass down traditions, to entertain, to explain where people have come from and where they are going, and to reflect on our own experiences and the experiences of others. Narratives have been of particular interest to educators for several reasons:

*   Narratives are a universal genre—a primary mode of thought (Bruner, 1985).

*   Narratives are the earliest extended monologue texts produced by children (Nelson, 1989; 2004).

*   Narratives are important for establishing and maintaining social relationships.

*   Narrative comprehension and production is associated with academic success (Miller et al., 2006; Reese, Suggate, Long, & Schaughency, 2010; Suggate, Schaughency, McAnally, & Reese, 2018; Veneziano & Nicolopoulou, 2019).

*   The ability to produce coherent personal narratives is associated with the development of self-identity and psychological well-being (McAdams, 2019; McLean, 2017; Reese, Yan, Hack, & Hayne, 2010).

Potential Variations Across Cultures

Because of the importance of narratives in multiple aspects of children's development, this book and numerous other materials provide activities and strategies to promote students' abilities to comprehend and produce personal and fictional narratives. Although the ability to produce narratives is a panhuman capability, the specific nature of narrative production is dependent on cultural practices. Most of the data on narrative development is based on Euro-American, White, middle-class children, yet an increasing percentage of students are not from this background. Although storytelling is universal and stories may share many similarities across cultures, they may also differ in a variety of ways:

- Reasons for telling stories (Gee, 1989; Heath, 1986)

- Who tells stories

- How children are socialized to storytelling (Fivush, 2019; Schieffelin & Ochs, 1986)

- How stories are structured or organized (Berman & Slobin, 1994; Gee, 1989; Gee & Michaels, 1989; Kaplan, 1966; McCabe, 1996; Stromqvist & Verhoeven, 2004)

- Types and frequency of story content and themes (Chen & Westby, 2019; Wang, Leichtman, & Davies, 2000)

These differences affect both the microstructures (vocabulary, morphology, and syntax) and the macrostructures (overall content and organization) of the narratives.

Significance for Educators and Students

What is the significance of these cultural variations in storytelling?

- If educators and SLPs are unaware of cultural variations in narratives, they may evaluate students' narratives inappropriately.

- If students are unable to comprehend and produce personal and fictional stories with the expected Euro-American functions, structure, and content, they are at risk for academic difficulties (Beck, 2008; Heath, 1982; Michaels & Collins, 1984; Scollon & Scollon, 1984).

- If schools focus on Euro-American stories, students not from that cultural background do not see themselves in the educational materials used in schools, which may affect their development of a positive self-identity.

- If schools value stories from only Euro-American mainstream educational culture, mainstream students do not learn of the larger world and do not develop respect and empathy for diverse individuals that is essential for being global citizens.

In her book, *Classroom Discourse*, Cazden (1988) described some of the issues that arise when students and teachers within classrooms do not share the same structure, content, and style of storytelling. She reported that, in sharing-time activities, teachers exhibited difficulty following the stories shared by African American children. Because the teachers did not recognize the structure of the children's stories, they tended to raise questions at points that disrupted the children's thinking rather than supported their storytelling. With regard to older students, Cazden described how a story told by an African American student was perceived by both African American and White Harvard students. White graduate students called the story incoherent and judged the student as having language problems. In contrast, four of five African American graduate students reported that the story was "interesting" and "well-formed."

Seeing Oneself in Stories   Because of the importance of comprehending narratives in the school system, materials to assess and teach narrative comprehension explicitly focus on the functions, structure, and content of mainstream narratives; that is, narratives shaped by Euro-American conventions. It can be argued that explicitly teaching students from other cultural backgrounds about the structure and content of mainstream narratives can promote their academic performance (Beck, 2008; Westby, Moore, & Roman, 2002). But what is lost for these students if educators do not also recognize and support the narratives from the child's culture?

Grace Lin, the Chinese American author of *Where the Mountain Meets the Moon* (2009), a Newbery Honor book, describes her experiences growing up in a community where there were few Asians (Lin, 2016). She describes feeling alone and wanting to forget she was Asian. She suggests these feelings were related to her experience of never seeing anyone who looked like her in the books she read. Perhaps if she had seen children who looked like her, she wouldn't have felt so alone and wouldn't have wanted to forget she was Asian. She now writes books with the kinds of characters and experiences she wished she had growing up—books that serve as mirrors.

The Nigerian writer Chimamanda Adichie reports a similar experience (Adichie, 2009). She describes growing up in Nigeria where most of what she read were British and American children's books. She was an early writer and what she wrote reflected what she read. All of her characters were White and blue-eyed: "They played in the snow. They ate apples. And they talked a lot about the weather, how lovely it was that the sun had come out." Yet, she lived in Nigeria. She had never seen snow, she ate mangoes, not apples, and she never talked about the weather, because there was no need to. Adichie had become convinced that books had to have foreigners in them and had to be about things with which she could not personally identify. The unintended consequence was that she did not know that people like her could exist in literature. The discovery of African writers saved her from having a single story of what books are. Furthermore, she warns that we risk misunderstanding if we hear only a single story about another person or country. We must hear multiple stories from different cultures if we are to understand ourselves and others.

Tomi Adeyemi, the Nigerian-American author of the #1 New York Times-bestselling young adult fantasy book, *Children of Blood and Bone* (2018), voices similar concerns. Like Adichie, she began writing at a very young age, and until she was 18, all her characters were White. At that time she realized she did not think she deserved to be in her own imagination: "If you don't ever see someone who looks like you, your subconscious goes, 'Oh, I don't belong there.'" On her blog she explains her reason for writing (Adeyemi, 2015):

> It isn't fame or success; it is a burning passion to tell a story about someone who is different and to force readers to fall in love with what is different from them. It's the thought that one day a little girl might be able to walk into the library and see a protagonist that actually looks like her. It's the idea that maybe someone who grows up around people who don't look like him might like the story enough to think twice before resorting to unwavering hatred.

Students in a Global Society   These authors convey the importance of supporting children's access to stories of their culture, but they also express the need for mainstream students to become familiar with culturally diverse narratives. In the 21st century, students live in a global society. Technology is reducing the barriers between nations and people. Education must prepare students to be global citizens who can act on what they've learned and engage efficiently across boundaries and divides. That necessitates not only that culturally and linguistically diverse (CLD) students know the narratives of mainstream culture, but also that mainstream students comprehend the narratives of diverse people. McCabe (1996) maintains that people must be chameleon readers who are able to understand texts from diverse cultures so as to appreciate and relate to individuals from diverse backgrounds. She cautions that the more you focus on a narrative form preferred by one culture, the further removed you are from forms preferred by another. To match all children's sense of storytelling at least some of the time, you must, at the same time, challenge the sense of storytelling of children from other cultures. In this regard, Lin (2016) maintains that books must serve not only as mirrors, but also as windows. For children who are not from minority backgrounds, books can be windows, enabling students to see others and realize they are just like them.

Preparing students to be chameleon listeners and readers involves more than exposing them to stories that include a variety of characters and events. Educators must also realize that students learn to tell stories in different ways and that their stories vary not only in terms of what the characters look like and are doing, but also how students learn to engage in storytelling and the structure, organization, and themes of the stories. My intent with this chapter is to alert readers to potential ways in which culture may influence the structure, content, and functions of the narratives children produce so they can adjust teaching practices, when needed, for students from both mainstream backgrounds and CLD backgrounds. I do not address all the ways culture may influence narratives, nor do I intend to suggest that students from a particular culture will produce narratives that are uniquely different from mainstream narratives.

VARIATIONS IN NARRATIVE SOCIALIZATION

Children learn to tell stories and participate in storytelling in different ways. In many cultures, caregivers support children in telling stories shortly after they begin to talk, whereas in other cultures, children tell stories only after they have spent years listening to stories. Adults in mainstream North American culture encourage children to listen to and tell stories, and they scaffold children in telling these stories. Shortly after children begin to talk, these adults ask children to report on events. It is acceptable, and children are even encouraged, to relate events to others. They may be expected to "perform" stories in front of others in community, educational, or religious activities. They relate events, act in plays, and make up their own stories.

Narrative Socialization Through Reminiscing

Children in many cultures learn storytelling by reminiscing with family members, but the nature of this reminiscing varies (Fivush, 2019). Culture infiltrates family reminiscing, and family reminiscing, in turn, instantiates culture. Mainstream English-speaking families begin reminiscing with toddlers as soon as they give an indication they are remembering something that happened earlier (Reese, 2013). Mothers in mainstream cultures tend to be highly elaborative in these interactions and to support the child's autonomy by following the child's lead. For example,

Child: I talked to the balloon pilot.

Adult: You talked to the balloon pilot? What did he tell you?

Child: How to make the balloon go up.

Adult: Yes, he showed you how to pull the cord to ignite the burner. That made the air inside the balloon hot. The hot air made the balloon rise.

Child: The burner was real hot.

Adult: Yes, it was very hot so you needed to be careful not to touch it.

Child: Then the balloon went up.

Adult: I think you were a little bit scared when it left the ground.

They give voluminous descriptive information about experiences; they prompt their children to embellish on their narratives. Furthermore, they encourage children to focus on themselves and their feelings in their reminiscing. In contrast, Chinese mothers are less elaborative, paying more attention to the child's behaviors and moral standards within their community (Wang, 2013). Euro-American mothers integrate more emotion into their reminiscing and spend more reminiscing time trying to explain and resolve difficult emotions with their children than do Chinese mothers, whereas the latter devote more time to reminiscing about other people and relationships, and to emphasizing proper behavior and maintaining harmony, than do Euro-American mothers (Miller, Fung, Lin, Chen, & Bolt, 2012; Wang & Fivush, 2005).

Immigrant Chinese families in the United States have been found to blend the Chinese and United States reminiscing styles, apparently attempting to uphold the values of their culture of origin, but also to incorporate the values of the host culture (Koh & Wang, 2013). Compared to Euro-American families, they more frequently mentioned the actions of others involved and had higher expectations of proper behavior—mentioning the child's negative behaviors more, bringing up moral and social rules, and focusing on their own child's behavior rather than other children's behaviors. However, like Euro-Americans, the Chinese immigrant parents mentioned their child's internal states more than others-involved internal states (contrary to other studies of Chinese families).

Not surprisingly, the personal stories children tell reflect their experiences reminiscing. Children who experienced more elaborative reminiscing with their caregivers told stories of personal experiences that offered detailed descriptions of one or two events, with more references to themselves and more evaluations of the experiences. In contrast, children who experienced less elaborative reminiscing produced personal stories with skeletal descriptions about multiple events and with a focus on social engagement, moral correctness, and concern for authority. Generally speaking, Chinese stories are based on narratives derived from Confucian philosophy, which emphasizes virtuous activity in the service of social harmony and cultivating a communal self, whereas stories from Western European culture are based on Socratic philosophy, which emphasizes individual questioning and the ability to evaluate and judge information, attributes more strongly associated with an autonomous self (Tweed & Lehman, 2002).

Around the world, families with independent/individualistic orientations are more likely to engage in elaborative reminiscing than families with interdependent/collective orientations. The individualistic-collective cultural dimension has more of an effect on elaboration than ethnicity or language spoken (Leichtman, Wang, & Pillemer, 2003; Tulviste, Tõugu, Keller, Schroder, & De Geer, 2016). Traditionally, individualist cultures, such as those of the United States and Western Europe, emphasize personal achievement regardless of group goals, resulting in a strong sense of competition. Collectivist cultures, such as those of China, Korea, Japan, and Latin countries, emphasize family and work group goals above individual needs or desires. Within these cultures, however, there is variability regarding the degree to which people are individualist or collective. The quality of parental reminiscing with their children has been shown to be correlated with the complexity of the fictional narratives children ages 4 to 9 years of age produce when telling stories in wordless picture books (Wenner, Burch, Lynch, & Bauer, 2008).

Narrative Socialization to Storytelling Roles

In mainstream American culture, children are often the center of attention in storytelling. They are encouraged to tell stories in the presence of others. In contrast, in many cultures children are simply observers. In a number of Native American communities, public storytelling is reserved for adults. A speech-language pathology graduate student from a Pueblo Indian tribe, who was analyzing children's stories for a language development course, experienced difficulty using the assigned protocol to elicit stories from children in her village. As she thought about her experiences, she realized that although storytelling has an important place in her tribe, storytelling to others in social contexts was the prerogative of the older men. Children were expected to watch and listen to storytelling for many years before they were expected or invited to share their stories. Even then, boys were given more opportunities to tell stories publicly than girls. Watching and listening appear to be predominant means of language learning and storytelling in many cultures. Children from these cultures are likely to be hesitant or unwilling to produce a story on demand or in front of a group because they have not had the opportunity to learn what is expected.

Through narrative socialization children learn the roles the storyteller and audience have in story production. Euro-American and Latina mothers have been found to socialize children to different roles during narrative production (Carmiol & Sparks, 2014; Uccelli, 2008). When talking about past events with young children, Euro-American middle-class mothers focus on teaching the child how to produce an organized narrative by careful scaffolding, asking questions and providing comments about past experiences (Carmiol & Sparks, 2014). They are preparing their children to eventually present a coherent narrative in a monologue production, independent of assistance of others. In contrast, Latina mothers seek to have children learn to participate in a conversation rather than to produce a coherent, structured narrative. Studies found they rarely interrupted, directed, or corrected their children's narrative production. They did not question the child, but rather joined the conversation by adding information the child had not mentioned. They are preparing children to share stories in conversations—to engage listeners, pay attention to their social and informational needs, and repair breakdowns in the flow of conversation (Melzi, 2000).

In some cultural groups, the production of narratives may be a negotiated and cooperative activity with members of the audience, and the contributions of the members may overlap. Although a single individual may begin a story, other speakers and audience members contribute to its development. Cooperative storytelling is a major attribute of Hawaiian conversations called "talk story" (Boggs, 1985). In talk story, the story is constructed by more than one person, and the speech of the narrators is also overlapped by audience responses. Traditionally in schools, cooperative discourse has been viewed, at best, as disruptive, and at worst, as cheating behavior.

In some cultures, children are expected to be seen and not heard. They might not be expected to have information (Heath, 1983); they may be viewed as incapable of conversing (Scollon & Scollon, 1984). Giving a recount or account might be regarded as inappropriate showing off or attempting to appear better than others (Philips, 1983); or such a storytelling performance might be viewed as dangerous to the child's spiritual, mental, and psychological well-being (Scollon & Scollon, 1981). Children may not be encouraged to attempt to gain the floor to give a report or account and, in fact, may be actively discouraged from doing so in adult company. Yet in these same cultures, children learn a variety of appropriate strategies within their peer groups to gain the floor, share personal stories, and produce imaginative stories, which may be highly valued activities (Boggs, 1985; Brady, 1984; Heath, 1983; Labov, 1972; Shuman, 1986). Cultural groups vary in how literal these accounts must be. Some groups view any variation or elaboration on the original experience as a lie, while others value such variation as a sign of creativity and verbal skill (Heath, 1983). Understanding the types of stories to which families socialize children and the ways they socialize their children can provide insight into how children process and use stories in school.

Socialization to Narrative Types

In all cultures, stories are told for purposes—to entertain, to display knowledge and skills, to teach, to organize and plan, to warn, to gossip, etc. Each purpose represents a narrative genre. Cultures vary in the types and frequency of the genres that are privileged (Basso, 1990; Champion, 2003; Heath, 1983; Heath, 1986). In mainstream educational settings, students are frequently expected to give recounts, which involve retelling an experience or reproducing information that is known to the person asking for the recount. In science and art activities, students may be asked to event-cast, describing what they are doing as they are doing it. Particularly in elementary school, they are expected to read and produce imaginative stories, usually to entertain. In sharing time and during recess and free time, they give accounts, stories of personal experiences that are unfamiliar to listeners.

Recounts, imaginative stories, event-casts, and accounts are highly familiar narratives to children and adults in families from mainstream, middle-class backgrounds. With exposure to these narrative genres in the preschool years, these students come to school with the texts that are valued and assessed. They know how to participate in both the social and academic discourses of school. They know how to answer the types of questions teachers ask about texts, they know what types of texts are acceptable, and they know how to organize texts so they are comprehensible to the teachers. Many children, however, arrive at school with minimal experience with these genres. Knowing what genres students have been socialized to and how they have been socialized can facilitate our understanding of why students may experience difficulties participating in the social and academic texts of schools. Investigators have observed that children who have been socialized into the narrative functions, organization, and style of the school during the preschool years adapt more easily to the academic tasks of school (Beck, 2008).

VARIATIONS IN NARRATIVE ORGANIZATION

Narrative organization varies across cultures. Several aspects of organization that vary include:

- The degree to which narratives follow a clear sequence of events that are temporally or causally linked

- The ways number is used as an organizing principle

- The emphasis given to different components within a story grammar, such as setting, theme, initiating plot events, and characters' goal-directed behavior and consequences

- The extent to which narratives are topic-associated (with topics/segments linked more loosely and implicitly) or topic-centered (with more focus on one topic and explicit links between segments)

The following sections explore each of these organizational variations across a wide range of languages and cultures.

Sequence

Stories in English are likely to be organized in a very linear, temporal-causal way (Kaplan, 1966). English stories are typically direct and straightforward, with one point following logically from the preceding with minimal digressions. In Romance languages, such as French and Spanish, it is permissible for storytellers to introduce what appears to be extraneous or superfluous material. For listeners or readers unfamiliar with this style, the digressions lead them away from the main point of the story and they have difficulty following the storyline. To the writer or speaker, however, these apparent digressions are a means to elaborate on aspects of the text and to provide greater contextualization for the reader or listener. Asian texts appear indirect and circular to the English speaker. The topic develops in widening circles that turn around the topic and show it from a variety of tangential views. The topic may never be explicitly stated. Comprehension of Asian texts typically requires that the listener or reader have additional shared knowledge with the speaker or writer.

In the mainstream research literature, a basic narrative has been defined as at least two sequential independent clauses describing a single past event (Labov & Waletzky, 1967). Sequentiality or linearity, a chronological representation of events in a narrative, is considered essential in a good story. But in some cultures, events in narratives are not conveyed sequentially. Although Latino stories can present a sequence of events in stories, studies have shown that in Latino cultures there is a de-emphasis on the temporal and sequential features in stories. Actions involved in the event are not linked causally. Instead, storytellers describe single actions, preceding the description with a context and following the description with an evaluation, both of which appear tangential to the story (Carmiol & Sparks, 2014; Uccelli, 2008). Consequently, for listeners who adhere to the previous mainstream definition, these stories do not meet the minimal definition of a narrative.

To those from mainstream Anglo-American society, Native American stories may not seem like stories due to the lack of temporality or clearly sequenced events. Indeed, oral narratives of Native Americans have been described by Anglo-Americans as "unorganized" and "rambling" (Cooley & Lujan, 1982). Story plots in Native American narratives do not flow in a linear manner with clear temporal–causal relationships. L. Benally (personal communication, 1989), a Navajo educator, described the structure of Navajo narratives as being like Indian fry bread (a circular piece of dough fried in oil), "An idea bubbles up here, then another idea over there, and another idea there . . ."

Native American stories may involve selecting, combining, and recombining story chunks (blocks of story information) to relate a story (Gough, 1990). Narrators have the freedom to choose how to order the story chunks. The story chunks may be in one order in one situation, but in a completely different order or even omitted in another situation. It should be recognized that these text organizations are proposed from an American point of view. A Korean woman attending a workshop taught by the author of this chapter commented, "I thought he (Kaplan) wasn't Korean. I always thought it was we Koreans who talked in a straightforward manner and it was you Americans who talked in circles." Text structures vary, but the nature of the variation is in the eyes of the beholder. The text organization pattern a particular cultural group uses is the most logical and straightforward to them.

Number

Stories are frequently organized around numbers. Cultures vary in terms of the favored number of episodes, actions, or repetitions of behavior (Kintch & Green, 1978; McCabe, 1996; Schimmel, 1993; Scollon & Scollon, 1981). European and African cultures prefer repetitions of three, and their narratives are in three parts or three episodes. They have beginnings, middles, and ends. There are often three episodes—characters must undertake three challenges before a problem is resolved. Mainstream children's stories in American culture feature three pigs who build three houses and have three encounters with a wolf; three billy goats who have three encounters with a troll; and even Goldilocks, who engages in three activities in the home of the three bears—eating cereal, sitting on chairs, and sleeping in beds.

Narratives from Native American tribes in the Southwest often have four episodes and reference to four elements, such as the four cardinal directions. A teacher in a Native American community in the Southwest did a unit using multiple versions of "The Three Little Pigs" (a traditional version, *The Three Little Hawaiian Pigs and the Magic Shark* [Laird, 1990], and *The Three Little Javalinas* [Lowell, 1992]). The children were studying the rain forest so the teacher asked them to write a version of the story using the rain forest as a setting. The students decided the prey would be peccaries, because they were pig-like, and the jaguar would be the predator. On the board the teacher wrote the title for the story, "The Three Little Peccaries and the Big Bad Jaguar." One student began his story: "The first boy peccary went north then the second peccary went south and then the third peccary went west, the fourth went east." Narratives from Native American tribes in the Pacific Northwest may have references to sets of five.

McCabe (1996) noted that in China three and nine are lucky numbers and the number eight symbolizes riches, money, and happiness; but the number four is taboo in some regions (including Japan) because it is also the word for death. Four appears in some Western stories, but is very rare in Eastern stories. Eight rarely occurs in Western stories, but is prominent in some Eastern ones. McCabe notes that when Mahy (1990) translated the Chinese story, "Eight Gods," it became a story of seven Chinese brothers.

We come to expect certain structures in narratives. When that structure is violated, we may unconsciously reorganize the story to fit our expectations. Scollon and Scollon (1981) reported that when Athabaskan Indians retold three-part Anglo stories, they added an additional episode. In contrast, Kintch and Green (1978) reported that when Anglo students read and retold four-part Indian stories, they omitted one part or condensed two of the parts into one. A mainstream linguistic graduate student in a course I taught reported a similar personal experience. She was hired by a Native American community to interview elders, record the stories they told, and develop storybooks to be used in the tribal Head Start program. In the university course, we discussed the four-part structure of many Native American stories. She reported that the community elders had been telling her that she wasn't getting their stories right. She had responded that they just weren't used to seeing their stories in print. She reviewed her tape recordings and realized that she had been leaving out parts of their stories because they had not appeared relevant to her.

Story Grammar Organization

Variation in episode structure extends to the emphasis placed on the components of stories as reflected in their story grammars, which represent the text structures or overall organization of narratives (Stein & Glenn, 1979). According to story grammars, stories are composed of a setting or orientation that introduces the characters, place, time, and circumstances of the story and allows the rest of the story to happen. The plots of stories begin with some initiating event or complicating action that is disequilibrating, a change of state or an action which initiates a character's reaction or response. Although the theme of a story is rarely stated explicitly, the initiating event should present information necessary for the listener or reader to recognize the underlying theme. The character's reaction to the initiating events can be an internal response, such as emotional feelings and cognitions, or overt, goal-directed reactions, such as physical attempts to cope with the initiating event. The character is an agent that takes the story forward. For a story to be perceived as a "good story" by mainstream American conventions, there must be a goal and some consequence or outcome of the character's attempts to achieve the goal. In addition, there may be a resolution or reaction that relates to the character's thoughts, feelings, or actions in relation to the consequence. There may also be an ending, which may be as simple as "that's all" or "the end," or which in some way addresses the overall theme or gives a summary or a moral.

Different cultural groups vary in the emphasis they place on various components of the story structure, and the goal-directed basis of character action in the most commonly used story grammars is not applicable to stories from primarily oral and some non-Western cultures.

An analysis of Japanese folktales revealed that 80% did not have a goal structure for the main character (Matsuyama, 1983). Thus, the stories lacked attempts and consequences and consisted primarily of initiating events and resolutions. Matsuyama attributed this folktale structure to the effects of Buddhism, because Buddhism emphasizes the importance of having no desires. Furthermore, it discourages aggressiveness and usually does not encourage goal-directed behavior.

English and Vietnamese students in sixth and eleventh grade in Australia were asked to write a bedtime story for a child (Soter, 1988). English students immediately began the story and focused on the plot, producing a series of actions carried out by the characters to achieve a goal. Vietnamese students never got to the actual task, but instead produced a lengthy introductory description (a story within a story) and did not complete the actual story—for example, they spent time discussing putting the child to bed or the parents' choice of a story before beginning the actual story. They appeared intent on providing a contextual framework for their stories rather than providing a goal-directed character. The Vietnamese students placed a greater emphasis on the relationships among participants in the story and the inner states of the characters. Compared to English students, the Vietnamese students used more dialogue, but the dialogue did not include information that forwarded the action of the story; instead, the dialogue was reflective on the situation.

Native Americans are also less likely to produce goal-directed stories. When Navajos were given opportunities to produce movies, they devoted more attention to background and setting information than to the initiating events and consequences (Worth & Adair, 1972). The movie storytellers spent much of their time describing walking and the landscape they passed, talking only briefly about what, according to mainstream American conventions, are the plot lines. The emphasis in the storytelling process was on detail, rather than temporal sequence or major points (Rhodes, 1988). The stories were not necessarily goal-directed. This lack of plot or goal-directedness in stories may be related to the Native American value of living in harmony with nature. Such a worldview does not require that individuals try to change their world but, rather, that they learn to live in and with their world.

A similar pattern was observed in the narrative structure and oral storytelling strategies of Grades 1–6 Northern Ute students. When asked to retell a favorite movie, the majority of the Ute students told stories that consisted of a series of events but without an overall story direction. Some stories contained considerable detail, but there were many unconnected events and unexplained details (Lewis, 1992). In oral stories produced in response to pictures, Grades 3–5 Pueblo Indian students participating in Project TALES (mentioned in the introduction of this chapter) produced less than half the number of goal-directed stories of mainstream students in those grades (Stein & Albro, 1997; Westby, Moore, & Roman, 2002).

Developmentally, by age 8 or 9, children in mainstream American culture are expected to include all the components of a story grammar in narratives they generate (Westby, 2012). If their stories do not include goal-directed behaviors in response to an initiating event, their stories are judged as less mature, and possibly, reflective of a language impairment. The story grammar framework does not fit the structure of what are considered good stories in some cultures. Therefore, educators and SLPs should exercise caution when interpreting the results of story grammar analysis applied to stories produced by children from cultures that are less likely to produce goal-directed stories.

Topic-Associated or Topic-Centered Organization

Story organization styles have been labeled as oral and topic-associated or literate and topic-centered. Topic-associated narratives are characteristic of some cultural groups in which the members share similar background knowledge and patterns of oral language performance (Cooley, 1979; Erickson, 1984; Gee, 1985; Michaels, 1985; Michaels & Collins, 1984; Tannen, 1984). In a school context where the teacher may not share the child's background, such narratives appear incoherent. A topic-associated narrative consists of a series of segments or topics that are linked implicitly to an event or theme, but with no explicit statements of an overall theme or point. These stories lack temporal and causal conjunctions. In contrast, in a topic-centered story the child provides focused descriptions of a single event or object and makes the temporal and cause and effect links between segments explicit. The themes in topic-centered stories are developed through a linear progression of information. The themes in topic-associated stories are developed through anecdotal association rather than linear description.

Topic-centered and topic-associated narratives differ in their use of prosody, clause types, and conjunctions. Prosodically, topic-centered stories begin with a sustained rising tone. Changing tones (both rise falls and fall rises) are used to elaborate on the topic and low falling tones are used in closing. In topic-associated stories, rhythm and high hold pitches, rather than sharp rising and falling pitch contours, are used to organize information thematically. Topic-associated stories are difficult for educators to follow when they are expecting a narrative to focus on a single topic with clausal units marked off by sharp rising and falling pitches.

Many linguists have viewed topic-associated, oral narratives as having a poetic structure and have analyzed these oral narratives into verses and stanzas (Bright, 1982; Gee, 1985; Heath, 1983; Scollon & Scollon, 1981). Linguists, anthropologists, and educators have recommended that the oral stories of African American (Champion & McCabe, 2015; Gee, 2015; Urbach, 2012), Native American (Hymes, 1996), and Japanese (Minami, 2002) children may be better analyzed in terms of lines and stanzas than story grammar. Each idea unit is referred to as a line. The lines are identified by intonation patterns. Lines are grouped into stanzas—the lines have parallel syntactic structures and there is repetition within and between stanzas. Rather than building a story with a cause and effect structure, the stanzas might build the intensity of the evaluation of the event being reported, or they may link events that are similar in some way. Oral topic-associated stories do not transfer well to a written form.

VARIATIONS IN NARRATIVE CONTENT AND THEMES

In addition to organizational variations, narratives vary across cultures in terms of their content and themes. Some content and themes recur widely in narratives from many different cultures: villainy, lack or loss, trickery, and Hero's Journeys, for example. However, approaches to these themes vary somewhat. Other narrative content and themes, such as autonomy, social relationships, aggression, relationships to authority, and morality, vary even more across cultures. Narrative schemas—hierarchically organized conceptual units that describe general knowledge (Mandler, 1984)—also vary across cultures and affect how people construct and interpret narratives.

Narrative Content Themes

Because we are human, we all share certain experiences. Consequently, we would anticipate that some story content and themes would be universal. Anthropologists report that all cultures around the world have stories about villainy, lack or loss, and trickery. The earliest two themes to emerge in young children's narratives by age 4 are villainy and lack or loss (Botvin & Sutton Smith, 1977). These themes represent events that disrupt normal equilibrium. The fact that trickster tales have been reported in all cultures suggests that deception is a cultural universal (Basso, 1987; Radin, 1956). Children develop the ability to recognize deception and to deceive others intentionally and successfully between 8 to 10 years of age (Abrams & Sutton Smith, 1977; DePaulo & Jordan, 1982). Tricksters in most cultures are characters (god, goddess, spirit, human, or anthropomorphic animal) that exhibit a great degree of intellect or secret knowledge, and use it to play tricks or disobey rules and violate conventional behavior. The characteristics of tricksters vary across cultures. They may be foolish or wise; heroes or villains. In some cultures, the trickster is combined with the hero. For example, Brer Rabbit, the trickster in African American tales, as a hero demonstrates how a small, weak, but ingenious person can overcome a larger, stronger, but dull-witted power. Although in many Native American stories the coyote trickster can be malicious, he can also be a hero—teaching people how to catch fish, bringing water, changing the environment in positive ways.

Hero's Journey stories appear to be universal (Campbell, 1949, 2008). The hero goes on an adventure, wins some type of victory, and comes home changed or transformed. But the content of Hero's Journeys differs in Eastern and Western cultures. In Western stories, the hero typically acts alone; he has no special friend, and although he may lead a group of nameless others, those whom he leads do not have unique traits. Furthermore, they follow the hero out of a sense of duty, not companionship. In contrast, the hero in Eastern stories does not act alone; he works with a loyal group of supporters, each of whom has unique characteristics. In Eastern hero stories, adversaries may become companions; this rarely happens in Western hero stories. Heroes in Western stories typically achieve through their physical prowess, whereas heroes in Eastern stories typically achieve through their intelligence. The greatest Eastern fighters are typically portrayed as gurus, respected for the wisdom they have gained through martial arts, whereas the greatest Western fighters are portrayed as skilled athletes, respected for their physical abilities. If they have wisdom and intelligence, that is a bonus. Just as culture influences the components of a story grammar that are emphasized, culture influences the components of a journey that are included, as well as their content and emphasis.

High school seniors in Urbana, Illinois and Bangkok, Thailand were given an assignment to write a personal narrative on the topic, "I Succeeded, At Last" (Indrasuta, 1988). The task might be viewed as a request for a type of journey story. Thai students wrote two narratives, one in English and one in Thai. The English and Thai narratives produced from Thai speakers were more similar to each other than either was to the American English narratives. Like Soter's Vietnamese writers (Soter, 1988), Thai writers devoted more attention to background contextual information in their narratives than did the American writers. They also dealt more with internal struggles, while the narratives of the American students reported more external struggles. This could be seen in the Thai students' greater use of verbs referring to mental states and descriptions of mental states to express the writers' thoughts, as opposed to the higher use of verbs referring to action in the stories of American students.

These differences in Eastern and Western Hero's Journey stories have been attributed to the influences of Buddhism/Confucianism in the East and Socratic/Platonic/Aristotelian philosophy in the West. Buddhism emphasizes the belief that people do not have control over the events of their lives. Because of these beliefs, they cannot influence the events, but only reflect on how the events affect their lives. This contributes to the focus on internal rather than external struggles, as reflected in frequent reference to mental states and background information in the Thai students' stories. The students must adjust to and determine how to cope with or accept the events. Western philosophy emphasizes cause and effect reasoning and motivated activity. Americans perceive that they have control over their lives. Consequently, in their stories the American students emphasized settings and initiating events to which they reacted with a goal-directed plan involving a series of attempts, which led to consequences. Furthermore, in Eastern cultures, a primary use of stories is to teach; while in Western cultures, a primary role of stories is to entertain. Thai students' narratives were more likely to include a moral coda. Thai writers reported that they sought to teach, whereas American writers reported that they sought to interest readers.

I mentioned earlier the differences in how Chinese and Euro-American mothers reminisce with their children and how these differences affect children's personal narratives. Studies of Chinese and Euro-American children's fictional stories have also shown variations in the content or themes. Chinese and Euro-American children in early elementary and late elementary/middle school have been asked to complete fictional stories in response to story starters (Domino & Hannah, 1987; Wang, Leichtman, & Davies, 2000). The stories from Chinese children evidenced greater social orientation and greater concern with authority and morality. Compared to the stories by American children, the stories of the Chinese children included more people, both children and adult authorities, and more social engagement, and transgressions were discovered and punished, often severely. In the stories of American children, there were significantly more themes of aggression, and children who committed negative acts were frequently never discovered. American children exhibited greater autonomous orientation in their stories, referring more to the character's personal needs and preferences. Actions and events in the stories of the Chinese children were more often determined by forces of nature or of a quasi-spirit world, whereas the events in the stories of American children were more often determined by the characters' intentions and plans.

The Child Language Committee of the International Association of Logopedics and Phoniatrics is conducting a study of personal narratives told by children in many countries around the world. To date, themes have been coded for stories of 20 children in Taiwan and 20 children in each of four English-speaking countries (United States, Great Britain, Australia, New Zealand) in response to the prompt, "Tell me a story about a time when you had a problem and you had to fix it" (Chen & Westby, 2019). Themes for 12 of the 20 stories produced by Taiwanese children were about school problems (doing well on a test or assignment or not having something they needed or were expected to have in school). In contrast, over half of the stories produced by the English-speaking students (42 of 80) were about peer relationships (mostly aggression or being left out). The frequency of the peer relationship theme was similar in the four English-speaking countries. Only 3 of the 20 stories of the Taiwanese children were about peer relationships (helping a peer or protecting peers from bullies). Only 9 of the 80 stories of English-speaking children were about school problems.

Narrative Content Schemas

Even when narrative content and themes appear similar, people's perspectives on or interpretation of the narratives may vary because the people have different schemas for the characters and events described. Schemas are hierarchically organized conceptual units that describe general knowledge (Mandler, 1984). Schemas are structures of expectation (Chafe, 1990); they guide the story comprehension process.

With different schemas, individuals from different cultures tend to expect different kinds of behaviors in a given interaction situation and to interpret the same behaviors differently. Understanding a story requires more than understanding the words and sentences that comprise the text. If the schemas a person uses to comprehend the story do not approximate the schemas used by the producer of the story, the person will likely misinterpret the story or not be able to determine its point. Cultural differences in schema knowledge between students and teachers have the potential for affecting students' comprehension of stories and teachers' evaluation and interpretation of students' stories.

Memory for stories becomes distorted when stories contain unfamiliar schemas. University students from the United States and India read reports of an American and an Indian wedding (Steffensen, Joag-Dev, & Anderson, 1979). Students took more time to read the unfamiliar schemas. They recalled more of the familiar schema passage, added more culturally appropriate information to the familiar passages, and produced more culturally based distortions when recalling the unfamiliar texts. The groups differed on what they considered to be important in the two passages, but they remembered best what they judged as important.

A similar study was conducted with Black and White teenagers (Reynolds, Taylor, Steffensen, Shirey, & Anderson, 1981). An episode was written on "sounding," an activity that takes place primarily in Black communities in which participants try to outdo each other in an exchange of insults (Labov, 1972). Black teenagers tended to see the episode as involving a friendly give-and-take, whereas White teenagers interpreted it as an ugly confrontation, sometimes involving physical violence. A Black student wrote, "Then everybody tried to get on the person side that joke were the best." A White student wrote, "Soon there was a riot. All the kids were fighting."

A research study asking individuals to summarize a television show demonstrated how schemas affected people's memory and interpretation of a story. In the 1980s, the highly popular television series, *Dallas*, was watched around the world. The show revolved around a wealthy and feuding Texas family who owned an oil company and large cattle ranch. A researcher hosted *Dallas*-watching parties for people from five widely different subcultures; four were in Israel—Arabs, Moroccan Jews, new immigrants from Russia, and second-generation Israelis living in a kibbutz—and the other was second-generation Israeli Americans in Los Angeles (Liebes, 1988). After viewing the episode, viewers were asked, "How would you retell the episode you just saw to somebody who has not seen it?" All groups were familiar with *Dallas*. It was as though the groups had seen different shows. Arabs and Moroccan Jews retold the story primarily in a linear manner, focusing on the social roles of the characters. The Israeli American and kibbutz groups did not emphasize the sequence of events, focusing instead on selected portions of the story, discussing the characters, their motivations, and their interrelationships. The Russian immigrants generally ignored the specific story in favor of a thematic retelling concerned with the moral or message. Even though the interviewer repeatedly attempted to get the discussants beyond the thematic level, they appeared unable or unwilling to get into the details of the video.

Even when the superficial content of events in stories appears similar, the causal attribution listeners or readers give to these events because of their belief and value systems can result in markedly different story interpretations. Hispanic and Anglo students (ages 10–15 years) read brief vignettes of student behavior and were asked to choose from four possible explanations for the behavior (Albert, 1986). The vignettes involved situations such as a student not wanting to talk in class, being caught by the principal coming into school late, or not wanting to take home a slip announcing an open house. In almost all cases, the Hispanic students and teachers attributed the behavior of the students in the vignettes to their being ashamed. Anglo students and teachers rarely attributed the behaviors to being ashamed. Anglos were more likely to give personality attributions (e.g., being shy) or to object to the event in the vignette (e.g., the principal shouldn't have stopped him because he wasn't doing anything wrong). Albert suggested that the higher attribution of "shame" to the behavior by Hispanics was related to the more collectivistic culture of Hispanics, which contrasts with the more individualistic Anglo culture. Comprehension of stories students listen to or read requires that they infer the thoughts, intentions, and emotions of the story characters (Gygax & Gillioz, 2015). If they do not share the schemas of the author, they are likely to have difficulty making the inferences necessary to comprehend the story in the expected way.

CONCLUSION: IMPLICATIONS FOR STUDENTS AND EDUCATORS

Much of education is dependent on comprehending and producing narratives. Narratives around the world differ in terms of functions, structure, content, and styles of telling the stories. If students are to be successful in mainstream schools, they must be able to comprehend and produce narratives with the functions, structures, content mainstream, and style of Western culture. Therefore, it is critical that educators and SLPs explicitly teach students to comprehend and produce Western-style stories. However, educators and SLPs must be alert to how cultural differences may influence students' comprehension and production of narratives. This requires careful observation and exploration. One should not assume that students from a particular language or cultural group will demonstrate patterns mentioned in this chapter, because there is considerable diversity within cultures. While teaching mainstream narratives, educators need to be cautious so they do not denigrate the narratives of the students' home cultures.

Self-identity is developed through exposure to and production of narratives. Therefore, it is also critical that students from diverse cultures have opportunities to see themselves in stories and learn the stories of their culture. They need stories that can serve as mirrors for them. The stories and books that serve as mirrors for students from diverse cultures are important for serving as windows for students from mainstream Euro-American backgrounds. Grace Lin (2016) said, "As much as kids need books to be mirrors, kids need books to be windows. Make sure your child has books that are mirrors and books that are windows, because if you do, you're setting a path for self-worth and empathy."

References

Educational and Professional Books and Articles

Abdalla, F., Mahfoudhi, A., & Alhudhainah, S. (2020). Structural development of narratives in Arabic: Task complexity, age, and cultural factors. *Language, Speech, and Hearing Services in Schools, 51*(2), 405–415. doi:10.1044/2019_LSHSS-19-00044

Abrams, D. M., & Sutton Smith, B. (1977). The development of the trickster in children's narrative. *Journal of American Folklore, 90,* 29–47.

Adichie, C. N. (2009). *The danger of the single story* [Video file]. Retrieved from https://www.ted.com/talks/chimamanda_ngozi_adichie_the_danger_of_a_single_story?language=en

Albert, R. (1986). Communication and attributional differences between Hispanics and Anglo Americans. In Y. Y. Kim (Ed.), *Interethnic communication* (pp. 42–59). Newbury Park, CA: Sage.

American Speech-Language-Hearing Association. (2001). *Roles and responsibilities of speech-language pathologists with respect to reading and writing in children and adolescents* [Position statement]. Retrieved from www.asha.org/policy.

Anderson, L. W., & Krathwohl, D. R. (Eds.). (2001). *A taxonomy for learning, teaching, and assessing: A revision of Bloom's taxonomy of educational objectives.* New York, NY: Addison Wesley Longman, Inc.

Antonovsky, A. (1979). *Health, stress, and coping.* San Francisco, CA: Jossey-Bass.

Antonovsky, A. (1987). *Unraveling the mystery of health: How people manage stress and stay well.* San Francisco, CA: Jossey-Bass.

Applebee, A. (1978). *The child's concept of a story: Ages 2 to 17.* Chicago, IL: University of Chicago Press.

Archer, A. L., & Hughes, C. A. (2010). *Explicit instruction: Effective and efficient teaching.* New York, NY: The Guilford Press.

ARK Institute of Learning. (2015). Applying imagery to vocabulary instruction. *Perspectives on Language and Literacy, 41*(3), 45–48.

Bailet, L. L. (2004). Spelling instructional and intervention frameworks. In C. A. Stone, E. R. Sillman, B. J. Ehren, & K. Apel (Eds.), *Handbook of language and literacy* (pp. 661–678). New York, NY: The Guilford Press.

Barkley, R.A. (2012). *Executive functions: What they are, how they work, and why they evolved.* New York, NY: The Guilford Press.

Basso, E. (1987). *In favor of deceit.* Tucson: University of Arizona Press.

Basso, K. A. (1990). *Western Apache language and culture.* Tucson: University of Arizona Press.

Beck, S. W. (2008). Cultural variation in narrative competence and its implications for children's academic success. In A. McCabe, A. L. Baily, & G. Melzi (Eds.), *Spanish-language narration and literacy: Culture, cognition, and emotion* (pp. 332–350). New York, NY: Cambridge.

Becker, C. M., Glascoff, M., & Felts, M. (2010). Salutogenesis 30 years later: Where do we go from here? *International Electronic Journal of Health Education, 13,* 25–32.

Bell, N. (1991). Gestalt imagery: A critical factor in language comprehension. *Annals of Dyslexia, 41,* 246–260. https://link.springer.com/article/10.1007/BF02648089

Bell, N. (2007). *Visualizing and verbalizing: For language comprehension and thinking.* San Luis Obispo, CA: Gander Publishing.

Benson, S. E. (2009). Understanding literate language: Developmental and clinical issues. *Contemporary Issues in Communicative Science and Disorders, 36,* 174–178.

Berman, R. A., & Slobin, D. I. (1994). *Relating events in narrative: A crosslinguistic developmental study.* Mahwah, NJ: Lawrence Erlbaum.

Berninger, V., & Wolf, B. J. (2009). *Teaching students with dyslexia and dysgraphia: Lessons from teaching and science.* Baltimore, MD: Paul H. Brookes Publishing Co.

Biemiller, A. (2015). Which words are worth teaching? *Perspectives on Language and Literacy, 41*(3), 9–13.

Blachowicz, C. L. Z., & Fisher, P. (2019). Building vocabulary in remedial settings: Focus on word relatedness. *Perspectives on Language and Literacy, 45*(2), 29–37.

Boggs, S. T. (1985). *Speaking relating and learning: A study of Hawaiian children at home and school.* Norwood, NJ: Ablex.

Botvin, G. J., & Sutton Smith, B. (1977). The development of structural complexity in children's fantasy. *Developmental Psychology, 13,* 377–388. doi:10.1037/0012-1649.13.4.377

Bowles, R. P., Justice, L. M., Khan, K. S., Piasta, S. B., Skibbe, L. E., & Foster, T. D. (2020). Development of the Narrative Assessment Protocol-2: A tool for examining young children's narrative skill. *Language, Speech, and Hearing Services in Schools, 51,* 390–404. https://pubs.asha.org/doi/abs/10.1044/2019_LSHSS-19-00038

Brady, M. K. (1984). *Some kind of power: Navajo children's Skinwalker narratives.* Salt Lake City: University of Utah Press.

Bright, W. (1982). Poetic structure in oral narrative. In D. Tannen (Ed.), *Spoken and written language* (pp. 171–184). Norwood, NJ: Ablex.

Brimo, D., Apel, K., & Fountain, T. (2017). Examining the contributions of syntactic awareness and syntactic knowledge to reading comprehension. *Journal of Research in Reading, 40*(1), 57–74. (First Published April 14, 2015).

Brown, R. (1973). *A first language.* Cambridge, MA: Harvard University Press.

Bruner, J. (1985). Narrative and paradigmatic modes of thought. In E. Eisner (Ed.), *Learning and teaching: The ways of knowing* (pp. 97–115). Chicago, IL: University of Chicago Press.

Bruner, J. S. (1986). *Actual minds, possible worlds.* Cambridge, MA: Harvard University Press.

Bryant, P. E., MacLean, M., Bradley, L., & Crossland, J. (1990). Rhyme and alliteration, phoneme detection, and learning to read. *Developmental Psychology, 26*, 429–438.

Cain, K. (2016). Reading comprehension development and difficulties: An overview. *Perspectives on Language and Literacy, 42*(2), 9–16.

Callens, M., Tops, W., Stevens, M., & Brysbaert, M. (2014). An exploratory factor analysis of the cognitive functioning of first-year bachelor students with dyslexia. *Annals of Dyslexia, 64*, 91–119. doi:10.1007/s11881-013-0088-6

Campbell, J. (1949). *The hero with a thousand faces.* New York, NY: MJF Books.

Campbell, J. (2008). *The hero with a thousand faces* (3rd ed.). Novato, CA: New World Library.

Carmiol, A. M., & Sparks, A. (2014). Narrative development across cultural contexts: Finding the pragmatic in parent-child reminiscing. In D. Matthews (Ed.), *Pragmatic development in first language acquisition* (pp. 279–293). Philadelphia, PA: John Benjamín.

Cazden, C. (1988). *Classroom discourse: The language of teaching and learning.* Portsmouth, NH: Heinemann.

Chafe, W. (1990). Some things that narratives tell us about the mind. In B. K. Britton & A. D. Pellegrini (Eds.), *Narrative thought and narrative language* (pp. 79–98). Hillsdale, NJ: Erlbaum.

Champion, T. B. (2003). *Understanding storytelling among African American children.* Mahwah, NJ: Lawrence Erlbaum.

Champion, T. B., & McCabe, A. (2015). Narrative structures of African American children: Commonalities and differences. In S. Lane Hart (Ed.), *The Oxford handbook of African American language* (pp. 292–311). New York, NY: Oxford University Press.

Chen, K., & Westby, C. E. (2019). Personal narratives from 10-year-old typically developing Mandarin-speaking children. American Speech-Language-Hearing Association Convention, Orlando, FL.

Colozzo, P., Gillam, R. B., Wood, M., Schnell, R., & Johnston, J. R. (2011). Content and form in the narratives of children with specific language impairment. *Journal of Speech, Language, and Hearing Research, 54*, 1609–1627. https://pubs.asha.org/doi/abs/10.1044/1092-4388% 282011/10-0247%29?utm_source=TrendMD&utm _medium=cpc&utm_campaign=Journal_of_Speech% 252C_Language%252C_and_Hearing_Research_Trend MD_0

Connelly, V., & Dockrell, J. (2016). Writing development and instruction for students with learning disabilities: Using diagnostic categories to study writing difficulties. In C. A. MacArthur, S. Graham, & J. Fitzgerald (Eds.), *Handbook of writing research* (2nd ed., pp. 349–363).

Cooley, D., & Lujan, P. (1982). A structural analysis of speeches by Native Americans. In F. Barken, E. A. Brandt, & J. Ornstein-Garcia (Eds.), *Bilingualism and language contact: Spanish, English, and Native American languages* (pp. 80–92). New York, NY: Teachers College Press.

Cooley, R. (1979). *Spokes in a wheel: A linguistic and rhetorical analysis of Native American public discourse.* Proceedings of the Fifth Annual Meeting of the Berkeley Linguistics Society, 552–557.

Coyne, M. D., Capozzoli-Oldham, A., Cuticelli, M., & Ware, S. M. (2015). Using assessment data to make a difference in vocabulary outcomes. *Perspectives on Language and Literacy, 41*(3), 52–58.

Culatta, B., Kovarsky, D., Theadore, G., Franklin, A., & Timler, G. (2003). Quantitative and qualitative documentation of early literacy instruction. *American Journal of Speech-Language Pathology, 12*, 172–188. https://pubs .asha.org/doi/10.1044/1058-0360(2003/064

Danzak, R. L. (2011). The interface of language proficiency and identity: A profile analysis of bilingual adolescents and their writing. *Language, Speech, and Hearing Services in Schools, 42*(4), 506–519. doi:10.1044/0161 -1461(2011/10-0015)

DePaulo, B. M., & Jordan, A. (1982). Age changes in deceiving and detecting deceit. In R. S. Feldman (Ed.), *Development of nonverbal behavior in children* (pp. 151–180). New York, NY: Springer Verlag.

Dickinson, D. K., & Morse, A. B. (2019). *Connecting through talk: Nurturing children's development with language.* Baltimore, MD: Paul H. Brookes Publishing Co.

Dillon, S. (1987). *Sounds in syllables, multisensory structured language therapy.* Albuquerque, NM: S.I.S. Publishing Co.

Dobbs, C. L., & Kearns, D. (2016). Using new vocabulary in writing: Exploring how word and learner characteristics relate to the likelihood that writers use newly taught vocabulary. *Reading and Writing, 29*, 1817–1843. doi:10.1007/s11145-016-9654-8

Dodd, J. L. (2012). Adapted stories: Creating accessible stories for children with complex language problems. *Perspectives on Language Learning and Education, 19*(4), 139–146. doi:org/10.1044/lle19.4.139

Domino, G., & Hannah, M. (1987). A comparative analysis of social values in Chinese and American children. *Journal of Cross Cultural Psychology, 18*, 58–77. doi:10.1177/0022002187018001007

Duchan, J. F. (2004). The foundational role of schemas in children's language and literacy learning. In C. A. Stone, E. R. Sillman, B. J. Ehren, & K. Apel (Eds.), *Handbook of language and literacy* (pp. 380–397). New York, NY: The Guilford Press.

Dunn, D. M. (2018). *Peabody Picture Vocabulary Test, Fifth Edition (PPVT-5).* New York, NY: Pearson Education.

Dunst, C. J., Meter, D., & Hamby, D. W. (2011). Relationship between young children's nursery rhyme experiences and knowledge and phonological and print-related abilities. *CELL (Center for Early Literacy Learning) Reviews, 4*(1), 1–12.

Eberhardt, N. C. (2019). Syntax: Somewhere between words and text. *Perspectives on Language and Literacy, 45*(2), 39–45, 9–13.

Editors of the Encyclopedia Britannica. (2014). *Brer rabbit.* Retrieved from https://www.britannica.com/editor/The-Editors-of-Encyclopaedia-Britannica/4419

Ehren, B. J. (2002). Getting into the literacy game. *American Speech-Language-Hearing Association, 7*(4–5), 10.

Eisenberg, S. L., Ukrainetz, T. A., Hsu, J. R., Kaderavek, J. N., Justice, L. M., & Gillam, R. B. (2008). Noun phrase elaboration in children's spoken stories. *Language, Speech, and Hearing Services in Schools, 39,* 145–157.

Erickson, F. (1984). Rhetoric, anecdote, and rhapsody: Coherence strategies in a conversation among black American adolescents. In D. Tannen (Ed.), *Coherence in spoken and written discourse* (pp. 81–154). Norwood, NJ: Ablex.

Fisher, D., & Frey, N. (2008). *Better learning through structured teaching: A framework for the gradual release of responsibility.* Alexandria, VA: ASCD.

Fisher, D., Frey, N., & Lapp, D. (2008). Shared readings: Modeling comprehension, vocabulary, text structures, and text features for older readers. *The Reading Teacher, 61,* 548–557.

Fivush, R. (2019). *Family narratives and development of an autobiographical self.* New York, NY: Routledge.

Friend, M., & Bates, R. P. (2014). The union of narrative and executive function: Different but complementary. *Frontiers in Psychology, 5,* 469.

Frishkoff, G. A., Collins-Thompson, K., Hodges, L., & Crossley, S. (2016). Accuracy feedback improves word learning from context: Evidence from a meaning-generation task. *Reading and Writing, 29,* 609–632. doi:10.1007/s11145-015-9615-7

Gee, J. (1985). The narrativization of experience in the oral style. *Journal of Education, 167,* 9– 35. doi:10.1177/002205748516700103

Gee, J. (1989). Two styles of narrative construction and their linguistic and educational implications. *Discourse Processes, 12,* 287–307.

Gee, J., & Michaels, S. (1989). Discourse styles: Variations across speakers, situations, and tasks. *Discourse Processes, 12,* 263–265. doi:10.1080/01638538909544730

Gee, J. (2015). Discourse analysis: Stories go to school. In *Social linguistics and literacies: Ideology in discourses* (pp. 145–165). New York, NY: Routledge.

Gillam, S. L., Gillam, R., & Laing-Rogers, C. (2014). *Supporting Knowledge in Language and Literacy (SKILL).* Retrieved from https://research.usu.edu/techtransfer/skill/

Gillam, S. L., Hartzheim, D., Studenka, B., Simonsmeier, V., & Gillam, R. (2015). Narrative intervention for children with autism spectrum disorder (ASD). *Journal of Speech, Language, and Hearing Research, 58,* 920–933. https://pubs.asha.org/doi/10.1044/2015_JSLHR-L-14-0295

Gillam, S. L., Olszewski, A., Fargo, J., & Gillam, R. B. (2014). Classroom-based narrative and vocabulary instruction: Results of an early-stage, nonrandomized comparison study. *Language, Speech, and Hearing Services in Schools, 45,* 204–219. https://pubs.asha.org/doi/10.1044/2014_LSHSS-13-0008

Gillam, S. L., Olszewski, A., Squires, K., Wolfe, K., Slocum, T., & Gillam, R. B. (2018). Improving narrative production in children with language disorders: An early-stage efficacy study of a narrative intervention program. *Language, Speech, and Hearing in Schools, 49,* 197–212. https://pubs.asha.org/doi/10.1044/2017_LSHSS-17-0047

Gillam, R. B., & Pearson, N. (2004). *Test of narrative language.* Austin, TX: PRO-ED.

Gillam, R. B., & Pearson, N. A. (2017). *Test of narrative language* (2nd ed.). Austin, TX: PRO-ED.

Gorman, B. K., Fiestas, C. E., Peña, E. D., & Clark, M. R. (2011). Creative and stylistic devices employed by children during a storybook narrative task: A cross-cultural study. *Language, Speech, and Hearing Services in Schools, 42*(2), 167–181. doi:10.1044/0161-1461(2010/10-0052)

Gough, D. (1990). The principle of relevance and the production of discourse: Evidence from Xhosa fold narrative. In B. K. Brinton & A. D. Pellegrini (Eds.), *Narrative thought and narrative language* (pp. 97–127). Hillsdale, NJ: Lawrence Erlbaum.

Graesser, A. C., Singer, M., & Trabasso, T. (1994). Constructing inferences during narrative text comprehension. *Psychological Review, 101,* 371–395.

Graham, S. (Winter 2009–2010). Want to improve children's writing? Don't neglect their handwriting. *American Educator,* 20–40.

Graves, A., & Montague, M. (1991). Using story grammar cueing to improve the writing of students with learning disabilities. *Learning Disabilities Research & Practice, 6*(4), 246–251.

Graves, D. H. (1985). All children can write. *Learning Disabilities Focus, 1,* 36–43.

Gray, C. (2000). *The new social story book: Illustrated edition: Teaching social skills to children and adults with autism, Asperger's syndrome, and other autism spectrum disorders.* Arlington, TX: Future Horizons.

Gray, C. A., & Garand, J. D. (1993). Social stories: Improving responses of students with autism with accurate social information. *Focus on Autistic Behavior, 8*(1), 1–10.

Green, L. B., & Klecan-Aker, J. S. (2012). Teaching story grammar components to increase oral narrative ability: A group intervention study. *Child Language Teaching and Therapy, 28,* 263–276.

Greene, J. W. (2015). The fundamentals of academic vocabulary: Essential concepts for middle school students and their teachers. *Perspectives on Language and Literacy, 41*(3), 29–32.

Greene, V. E., & Enfield, M. L. (1997). *Framing your thoughts: Sentence structure.* Bloomington, IN: Language Circle Enterprises.

Gutierrez-Clellan, V. F., & Quinn, R. (1993). Assessing narratives of children from diverse cultural/linguistic groups. *Language, Speech, and Hearing Services in Schools, 24,* 2–9. https://pubs.asha.org/doi/abs/10.1044/0161-1461.2401.02

Gygax, P., & Gillioz, C. (2015). Emotion inferences during reading: Going beyond the tip of the iceberg. In E. J. O'Brien, A. E. Cook, & R. F. Lorch (Eds.), *Inferences during reading* (pp. 122–139). New York, NY: Cambridge University Press. doi:10.1017/CBO9781107279186.007

Halligan, F. (2013). *Movie storyboards: The art of visualizing screenplays.* San Francisco, CA: Chronical Books.

Harris, K. R., Graham, S., & Mason, L. H. (2003). Self-regulated strategy development in the classroom: Part of a balanced approach to writing instruction for students with disabilities. *Focus on Exceptional Children, 35*(7), 1–16.

Hayes, J. (1996). A new framework for understanding cognition and affect in writing. In C. M. Levy & S. Ransdell (Eds.), *The science of writing: Theories, methods, individual differences, and applications* (pp. 1–27). Mahwah, NJ: Erlbaum.

Haynes, C. W., Smith, S. L., & Laud, L. (2019). Structured literacy approaches to teaching written expression. *Perspectives on Language and Literacy, 45*(3), 22–28.

Heath, S. B. (1982). What no bedtime story means: Narrative skills at home and school. *Language in Society, 11*(2), 49–76. doi:10.1097/00011363-198612000-00010

Heath, S. B. (1983). *Ways with words.* Cambridge, MA: Cambridge University Press.

Heath, S. B. (1986). Taking a cross cultural look at narratives. *Topics in Language Disorders, 7*(1), 84–94. doi:10.1097/00011363-198612000-00010

Hebert, M., Kearns, D. M., Hayes, J. B., Basiz, P., & Cooper, S. (2018). Why children with dyslexia struggle with writing and how to help them. *Language, Speech, and Hearing Services in Schools, 49,* 843–863. https://pubs.asha.org/doi/abs/10.1044/2018_LSHSS-DYSLC-18-0024

Hedberg, N. L., & Westby, C. N. (1993). *Analyzing storytelling skills: Theory to practice.* Tucson, AZ: Communication Skill Builders.

Heggie, L., & Wade-Woolley, L. (2017). Reading longer words: Insights into multisyllabic word reading. *Perspectives of the ASHA Special Interest Groups, SIG 1, 2*(2), 86–94. https://pubs.asha.org/doi/abs/10.1044/persp2.SIG1.86

Hennessy, N. L. (2021). *The reading comprehension blueprint: Helping students make meaning from text.* Baltimore, MD: Paul H. Brookes Publishing Co.

Hochman, J. C., & MacDermott-Duffy, B. (2018). Composition: Evidence-based instruction. In J. R. Birsh & S. Carreker (Eds.), *Multisensory teaching of basic language skills* (4th ed., pp. 646–678). Baltimore, MD: Paul H. Brookes Publishing Co.

Hoffman, L. M. (2009). Narrative language intervention intensity and dosage: Telling the whole story. *Topics in Language Disorders, 29*(4), 329–343.

Hudson, N., Scheff, J., Tarsha, M., & Cutting, L. E. (2016). Reading comprehension and executive function: Neurobiological findings. *Perspectives on Language and Literacy, 43*(2), 23–29.

Hudson, R. (2016). Grammar instruction. In C. A. MacArthur, S. Graham, & J. Fitzgerald (Eds.), *Handbook of writing research* (2nd ed., pp. 288–300). New York, NY: The Guilford Press.

Hymes, D. (1996). *Ethnography, linguistics, narrative inequality: Toward an understanding of voice.* Bristol, PA: Taylor & Francis.

Indrasuta, C. (1988). Narrative styles in the writing of Thai and American students. In A. C. Purves (Ed.), *Writing across languages and cultures* (pp. 206–226). Newbury Park, CA: Sage.

Jensen, B. B., Dür, W., & Buijs, G. (2017). The application of salutogenesis in schools. In M. B. Mittelmark, S. Sagy, M. Eriksson, G. F. Bauer, J. M. Pelikan, B. Lindstrom, & G. A.

Espnes (Eds.), *The handbook of salutogenesis* (pp. 225–236). Switzerland: Springer Open Access. Retrieved from https://link.springer.com/book/10.1007/978-3-319-04600-6

Jones, S., Myhill, D., & Bailey, T. (2013). Grammar for writing? An investigation of the effects of contextualized grammar teaching on students' writing. *Reading and Writing, 26*(8), 1241–1263.

Justice, L. M. (2006). Evidence-based practice, response to intervention, and the prevention of reading difficulties. *Language, Speech, and Hearing Services in Schools, 37*(10), 284–297. https://pubs.asha.org/doi/10.1044/0161-1461(2006/033)

Justice, L. M., Bowles, R. P., Kaderavek, J. N., Ukrainetz, T. A., Eisenberg, S. L., & Gillam, R. B. (2006). The Index of Narrative Microstructure: A clinical tool for analyzing school-age children's narrative performances. *American Journal of Speech-Language Pathology, 15*(2), 177–191. doi:10.1044/ 1058-0360(2006/017)

Kaplan, R. (1966). Cultural thought patterns in intercultural education. *Language Learning, 16,* 1–20. doi:10.1111/j.1467-1770.1966.tb00804.x

Kaplan, R. (1986). Cultural thought patterns revisited. In U. Connor & R. Kaplan (Eds.), *Writing across languages: Analysis of L2 texts* (pp. 9–21). Reading, MA: Addison-Wesley.

Khan, K., Nelson, K., & Whyte, E. (2014). Children choose their own stories: The impact of choice on children's learning of new narrative skills. *Journal of Child Language, 41,* 949–962.

Khan, K. S., Gugiu, M. R., Justice, L. M., Bowles, R. P., Skibbe, L. E., & Piastaa, S. B. (2016). Age-related progressions in story structure in young children's narratives. *Journal of Speech, Language, and Hearing Research, 59,* 1395–1408.

Kim, Y. G. (2016). Direct and mediated effects of language and cognitive skills on comprehension of oral narrative texts (listening comprehension) for children. *Journal of Experimental Child Psychology, 141,* 101–120.

King, S. (2000). *On writing: A memoir of the craft.* New York, NY: Simon & Schuster.

Kintch, W., & Green, E. (1978). The role of culture-specific schemata in the comprehension and recall of stories. *Discourse Processes, 1,* 1–13. doi:10.1080/01638537809544425

Koh, J. B. K., & Wang, Q. (2013). Narrative self-making during dinnertime conversations in Chinese immigrant families. In A. McCabe & C. Chang (Eds.), *Chinese language narration: Culture, cognition, and emotion* (pp. 7–32). Philadelphia, PA: John Benjamins.

Krathwohl, D. R. (2002). A revision of Bloom's taxonomy: An overview. *Theory Into Practice, 41*(4), 212–218.

Labov, W. (1972). *Language in the inner city.* Philadelphia: University of Pennsylvania Press.

Labov, W., & Waletzky, C. (1967). Narrative analysis: Oral versions of personal experience. In J. Helm (Ed.), *Essays on the verbal and visual arts* (pp. 19–44). Washington, DC: American Ethnological Society.

Lehr, F. (1987). Story grammar. *Reading Teacher, 40*(6), 550–552.

Leichtman, M. D., Wang, Q., & Pillemer, D. B. (2003). Cultural variations in interdependence and autobiographical memory. In R. Fivush & C. A. Haden (Eds.),

Autobiographical memory and the construction of a narrative self (pp. 73–97). Mahwah, NJ: Lawrence Erlbaum.

Levy, S., & Schiller, M. (2018). *Stan and the four fantastic powers.* Chagrin Falls, OH: Taos Institute.

Lewis, J. M. (1992). The story telling strategies of Northern Ute elementary students. *Journal of Navajo Education, 9,* 24–32.

Liebes, T. (1988). Cultural differences in retelling of television fiction. *Critical Studies in Mass Communication, 5*(4), 277–292.

Lin, G. (28 Mar 2016). *The windows and mirrors of your child's bookshelf* [TEDx Talk]. Retrieved from https://www.youtube.com/watch?v=_wQ8wiV3FVo

Mäkinen, L., Soile, L., Ilana, G., & Sari, K. (2018). Are story retelling and story generation connected to reading skills? Evidence from Finnish. *Child Language Teaching and Therapy, 34*(2), 129–139.

Mandler, J. M. (1984). *Stories, scripts and scenes: Aspects of schema theory.* Hillsdale, NJ: Erlbaum.

Marks, D. (2007). *Inside story: The power of the transformational arc.* Studio City, CA: Three Mountain Press.

Marzola, E. S. (2018). Strategies to improve reading comprehension in the multisensory classroom. In J. R. Birsh & S. Carreker (Eds.), *Multisensory teaching of basic language skills* (4th ed., pp. 600–640). Baltimore, MD: Paul H. Brookes Publishing Co.

Matsuyama, U. (1983). Can story grammar speak Japanese? *The Reading Teacher, 36,* 666–669.

McAdams, D. (2019). "First we invented stories, then they changed us": The evolution of narrative identity. *Evolutionary Studies in Imaginative Culture, 3*(1), 1–18. doi:10.26613/esic/3.1.110

McCabe, A. (1996). *Chameleon readers: Teaching children to appreciate all kinds of good stories.* New York, NY: McGraw-Hill.

McKee, R. (1997). *Story: Substance, structure, style, and the principles of screenwriting.* Los Angeles, CA: Regan Books.

McLean, K. C. (2017). And the story evolves: The development of personal narratives and narrative identity. In J. Specht (Ed.), *Personality development across the lifespan* (pp. 325–338). New York, NY: Elsevier.

Melzi, G. (2000). Cultural variations in the construction of personal narratives: Central American and European American mothers' elicitation styles. *Discourse Processes, 30*(2), 153–177. doi:10.1207/S15326950DP3002_04

Michaels, S. (1985). Hearing the connections in children's oral and written discourse. *Journal of Education, 167,* 36–56. doi:10.1177/002205748516700104

Michaels, S., & Collins, J. (1984). Oral discourse styles: Classroom interaction and the acquisition of literacy. In D. Tannen (Ed.), *Coherence in spoken and written discourse* (pp. 219–244). Norwood, NJ: Ablex.

Miller, J., & Iglesias, A. (2019). *Systematic analysis of language transcripts (SALT),* Research Version 20 [Computer Software]. Madison, WI: SALT Software, LLC.

Miller, J. F., Heilmann, J., Nockerts, A., Iglesias, A., Fabiano, L., & Francis, J. F. (2006). Oral language and reading in bilingual children. *Learning Disabilities Research & Practice, 21*(1), 30–43. doi:10.1111/j.1540-5826.2006.00205.x

Miller, P. J., Fung, H., Lin, S., Chen, E. C. H., & Bolt, B. R. (2012). How socialization happens on the ground: Narrative practice as alternate socializing pathways in Taiwanese and Euro-American families. *Monograph of the Society for Research in Child Development, 77*(1), i–40.

Minami, M. (2002). *Culture-specific language styles: The development of oral narrative and literacy.* Bristol, United Kingdom: Multilingual Matters.

Mindwing Concepts, Inc. (2020). Mindwing concepts [Commercial website]. Retrieved from https://www.mindwingconcepts.com

Miner, M., & Siegel, L. S. (1992). William Butler Yeats: Dyslexic? *Journal of Learning Disabilities, 25*(6), 372–375.

Moats, L., Foorman, B., & Taylor, P. (2006). How quality of writing instruction impacts high-risk fourth graders' writing. *Reading and Writing, 19,* 363–391. doi:10.1007/s11145-005-4944-6

Montgomery, J., & Kahn, N. (2005). *What's your story? Evidence-based narrative strategies for adolescents.* Eau Claire, WI: Thinking Publications.

Montgomery, J. K. (2007). *The bridge of vocabulary: Evidence-based activities for academic success.* Minneapolis, MN: Pearson Assessments Inc.

Moojen, S. M. P., Gonçalves, H. A., Bassôa, A., Navas, A. L., de Jou, G., & Miguel, E. S. (2020). Adults with dyslexia: How can they achieve academic success despite impairments in basic reading and writing abilities? The role of text structure sensitivity as a compensatory skill. *Annals of Dyslexia, 70,* 115–140. doi:10.1007/s11881-020-00195-w

Moraine, P. A. (2012). *Helping students take control of everyday executive functions: The attention fix.* Philadelphia, PA: Jessica Kingsley Publishers.

Munro, J. (2010). Enhancing reading comprehension through explicit comprehending-strategy teaching. In C. Wyatt-Smith, J. Elkins, & S. Gunn (Eds.), *Multiple perspectives on difficulties in learning literacy and numeracy* (pp. 197–212). Dordrecht, The Netherlands: Springer.

Murray, D. M. (1972). Teach writing as a process, not product. *The Leaflet,* 11–14.

Murray, D. M. (2003). Teach writing as a process, not product. In V. Villanueva (Ed.), *Cross talk in comp theory: A reader* (2nd ed., pp. 3–6). Urbana, IL: National Council of Teachers of English.

Myhill, D., & Watson, A. (2014). The role of grammar in the writing curriculum: A review of the literature. *Child Language Teaching and Therapy, 30*(1), 41–62.

National Center for Educational Statistics. (2012). *The nation's report card: Writing 2011.* Retrieved from https://nces.ed.gov/pubsearch/pubsinfo.asp?pubid=2012470

National Center for Educational Statistics. (2015). *Highlights of performance of fourth-grade students on the 2012 NAEP computer-based pilot writing assessment.* Retrieved from https://nces.ed.gov/nationsreportcard/pubs/writing/2015119.aspx

National Governors Association Center for Best Practices & Council of Chief State School Officers. (2010). *Common Core State Standards.* Washington, DC: Authors.

Nation's Report Cards. (2019). Results from the 2019 mathematics and reading assessments. Retrieved from https://www.nationsreportcard.gov/mathematics/supportive_files/2019_infographic.pdf

Nelson, K. (Ed.). (1989). *Narratives from the crib*. Cambridge, MA: Harvard University Press.

Nelson, K. (2004). Construction of the cultural self in early narratives. In D. Daiute & C. Lightfoot (Eds.), *Narrative analysis: Studying the development of individuals in society*. Thousand Oaks, CA: Sage.

Nelson, N. W. (2013). Syntax development in the school-age years: Implications for assessment and intervention. *Perspectives on Language and Literacy, 39*(3), 9–15.

Nelson, N. W., Plante, E., Helm-Estabrooks, N., & Hotz, G. (2015). *Test of Integrated Language and Literacy Skills™ (TILLS™)*. Baltimore, MD: Paul H. Brookes Publishing Co.

Nelson, N. W., & Van Meter, A. M. (2002). Assessing curriculum-based reading and writing samples. *Topics in Language Disorders, 22*(2), 35–59.

Nippold, M. A., Duthie, J. K., & Larsen, J. (2005). Literacy as a leisure activity: Free-time preferences of older children and young adolescents. *Language, Speech, and Hearing Services in Schools, 36*, 93–102. https://pubs.asha.org/doi/10.1044/0161-1461%282005/009%29

Nippold, M. A., Ward-Lonergan, J. M., & Fanning, J. L. (2005). Persuasive writing in children, adolescents, and adults: A study of syntactic, semantic, and pragmatic development. *Language, Speech, and Hearing Services in Schools, 36*, 125–138. https://pubs.asha.org/doi/abs/10.1044/0161-1461%282005/012%29

Noden, H. R. (1999). *Image grammar: Using grammatical structures to teach writing*. Portsmouth, NH: Heinemann.

Oakhill, J. V., & Cain, K. (2012). The precursors of reading ability in young readers: Evidence from a four-year longitudinal study. *Scientific Studies of Reading, 16*(2), 91–121. doi:10.1080/10888438.2010.529219

Oakhill, J. V., & Cain, K. (2016). Supporting reading comprehension development: From research to practice. *Perspectives on Language and Literacy, 42*(2), 32–39.

Petersen, D. B., & Petersen, J. W. (2016). Re-conceptualizing expository language as narration. *Perspectives of the ASHA Special Interest Groups SIG 1, 1*(3), 109–117. https://pubs.asha.org/doi/abs/10.1044/persp1.SIG1.109

Philips, S. (1983). *The invisible culture: Communication in classroom and community on the Warm Springs Indian Reservation*. New York, NY: Longman.

Radin, P. (1956). *The trickster*. New York, NY: Schocken Books.

Reese, E. (2013). *Tell me a story: Sharing stories to enrich your child's world*. New York, NY: Oxford.

Reese, E., Suggate, S., Long, J., & Schaughency, E. (2010). Children's oral narrative and reading skills in the first 3 years of reading instruction. *Reading and Writing, 23*, 627–644. doi:10.1007/s11145-009-9175-9.

Reese, E., Yan, C., Hack, F., & Hayne, H. (2010). Emerging identities: Narrative and self from early childhood to early adolescence. In K. C. McLean & M. Pasupathi (Eds.), *Narrative development in adolescence* (pp. 23–43). New York, NY: Springer.

Reynolds, R. E., Taylor, M., Steffensen, M. S., Shirey, L. L., & Anderson, R. C. (1981). *Cultural schemata and reading comprehension* (Technical Report No. 201). Urbana: University of Illinois, Center for the Study of Reading.

Rhodes, R. W. (1988). Holistic teaching/learning for Native American students. *Journal of American Indian Education, 27*(2), 279–304.

Ritchey, K. D., Coker, D. L., & Jackson, A. F. (2015). The relationships between early elementary teachers' instructional practices and theoretical orientation and students' growth in writing. *Reading and Writing, 29*(9), 1333–1354.

Roessing, L. (2014). *Bridging the gap: Reading critically and writing meaningfully to get to the core*. Lanham, MD: Rowman & Littlefield Publishers.

Roessing, L. (2017, February). From reluctant reader to ravenous reader: How to develop lifelong readers by using choice as a motivator. *AMLE Magazine Online*.

Rollins, P. R. (2014). Narrative skills in young adults with high-functioning autism spectrum disorders. *Communication Disorders Quarterly, 36*, 21–28.

Roth, F. P. (2000). Narrative writing: Development and teaching children with writing difficulties. *Topics in Language Disorders, 20*(4), 15–28.

Russell, C. (2019, Apr 9). Tackling copyright concerns when taking storytime online. *School Library Journal*. Retrieved from https://www.slj.com/?detailStory=tackling-copyright-concerns-when-taking-storytime-online

Saddler, B. (2007). Improving sentence construction skills through sentence-combining practice. In S. Graham, C. A. MacArthur, & J. Fitzgerald (Eds.), *Solving problems in the teaching of literacy. Best practices in writing instruction* (pp. 163–178). New York, NY: The Guilford Press.

Saddler, B. (2012). *Teacher's guide to effective sentence writing*. New York, NY: The Guilford Press.

Saddler, B., & Asaro, K. (2007). Increasing story quality through planning and revising: Effects on young writers with learning abilities. *Learning Disability Quarterly, 30*, 223–234.

Santa, C. M. (1988). *Content reading including study systems: Reading, writing and studying across the curriculum*. Dubuque, IA: Kendall/Hunt.

Schieffelin, B. B., & Ochs, E. (1986). *Language socialization across cultures*. New York, NY: Cambridge University Press.

Schimmel, A. (1993). *The mystery of numbers*. New York, NY: Oxford University Press.

Scollon, R., & Scollon, S. (1981). *Narrative, literacy and face in interethnic communication*. Norwood, NJ: Ablex.

Scollon, R., & Scollon, S. (1984). Cooking it up and boiling it down: Abstracts in Athabaskan children's story retellings. In D. Tannen (Ed.), *Coherence in spoken and written discourse* (pp. 173–197). Norwood, NJ: Ablex.

Scott, C. M. (April 2009). A case for the sentence in reading comprehension. *Language, Speech, and Hearing Services in Schools, 40*, 184–191. https://pubs.asha.org/doi/10.1044/0161-1461%282008/08-0042%29

Scott, C. M., & Balthazar, C. (2013). The role of complex sentence knowledge in children with reading and writing difficulties. *Perspectives on Language and Literacy, 39*(3), 18–26.

Shanahan, T. (2006). Relations among oral language, reading, and writing development In C. A. MacArthur, S. Graham, S., & J. Fitzgerald (Eds.). *Handbook of writing research* (pp. 171–183). New York, NY: The Guilford Press.

Shanahan, T. (2015). Are you lactating? On the importance of academic language. *Perspectives on Language and Literacy, 41*(3), 14–16.

Shen, M., & Troia, G. A. (2018). Evidence-based practices to improve the expository writing performance of students with learning disabilities: Strategy instruction vs. genre study. *Perspectives on Language and Literacy, 44*(2), 10–15.

Shuman, A. (1986). *Storytelling rights: The uses of oral and written tests by urban adolescents.* New York, NY: Cambridge University Press.

Singer, R. A. (2018). Phonological awareness [glossary definition]. In J. R. Birsh & S. Carreker (Eds.), *Multisensory teaching of basic language skills* (4th ed., p. 835). Baltimore, MD: Paul H. Brookes Publishing Co.

Snyder, B. (2005). *Save the cat! The last book on screenwriting you'll ever need.* Studio City, CA: Michael Wiese Productions.

Soter, A. O. (1988). The second language learner and cultural transfer in narration. In A. C. Purves (Ed.), *Writing across languages and cultures* (pp. 177–205). Newbury Park, CA: Sage.

Spencer, M., Gilmour, A. F., Miller, A. C., Emerson, A. M., Saha, N. M., & Cutting L. E. (2019). Understanding the influence of text complexity and question type on reading outcomes. *Reading and Writing, 32*, 603–637. doi:org/10.1007/s11145-018-9883-0

Stavros, J., Godwin, L. N., & Cooperrider, D. (2015). Appreciative inquiry: Organization development and the strengths revolution. In W. J. Rothwell, J. Stavros, & R. L. Sullivan, (Eds.). *Practicing organization development: A guide to leading change and transformation* (4th ed., pp. 96–116). Wiley Online Library.

Steffensen, M. S., Joag-Dev, C., & Anderson, R. C. (1979). A cross-cultural perspective on reading comprehension. *Reading Research Quarterly, 15*, 10–29. doi:10.2307/747429

Stein, N., & Albro, E. (1997). Building complexity and coherence: Children's use of goal-structured knowledge in telling stories. In M. Bamberg (Ed.), *Narrative development: Six approaches* (pp. 5–44). Mahwah, NJ: Lawrence Erlbaum.

Stein, N., & Glenn, C. (1979). An analysis of story comprehension in elementary school children. In R. Freedle (Ed.), *New directions in discourse processing* (Vol. 2, pp. 53–120). Norwood, NJ: Ablex.

Stromqvist, S., & Verhoeven, L. (2004). *Relating events in narrative: Typological and contextual perspectives* (Vol. 2). Mahwah, NJ: Lawrence Erlbaum.

Suggate, S., Schaughency, E., McAnally, H., & Reese, E. (2018). From infancy to adolescence: The longitudinal links between vocabulary, early literacy skills, oral narrative, and reading comprehension. *Cognitive Development, 47*, 82–95. doi.org/10.1016/j.cogdev.2018.04.005

Swanson, L. A., Fey, M. E., Mills, C. E., & Hood, L. S. (2005). Use of narrative-based language intervention with children who have specific language impairment. *American Journal of Speech-Language Pathology, 14*(2), 131–141. doi:org/10.1044/1058-0360(2005/014)

Tannen, D. (Ed.). (1984). *Coherence in spoken and written discourse.* Norwood, NJ: Ablex.

Tiedt, I. (1969). A new poetry form: The diamante. *Elementary English, 46*(5), 588–589.

Troia, G. A. (2016, October.) Learning progressions for writing genres and instructional supports for students with LD/dyslexia. In G. A. Troia (Chair), *Development, assessment, and instruction of writing skills in children with and without learning disabilities.* Symposium conducted at the meeting of the International Dyslexia Association, Orlando, Florida.

Tulviste, T., Tõugu, P., Keller, H., Schröder, L., & De Geer, B. (2016). Children's and mothers' contribution to joint reminiscing in different sociocultural contexts: Who speaks and what is said. *Infant and Child Development, 25*(1), 43–63. doi:10.1002/icd.1921

Tweed, R. G., & Lehman, D. R. (2002). Learning considered within a cultural context: Confucian and Socratic approaches. *American Psychologist, 57*(2), 89. doi:10.1037//0003-066X.57.2.89

Uccelli, P. (2008). Beyond chronicity: Evaluation and temporality in Spanish-speaking children's personal narratives. In A. McCabe, A. Bailey, & G. Melzi (Eds.), *Spanish language narration and literacy development* (pp. 175–212). Cambridge, MA: Cambridge University Press.

Ukrainetz, T. (1998). Stickwriting stories: A quick and easy narrative representation strategy. *Language, Speech, and Hearing in Schools, 29*, 197–206. https://pubs.asha.org/doi/abs/10.1044/0161-1461.2904.197

Ukrainetz, T. A. (2019). Sketch and speak: An expository intervention using note-taking and oral practice for children with language-related learning disabilities. *Language, Speech, and Hearing in Schools, 50*, 53–70. https://pubs.asha.org/doi/10.1044/2018_LSHSS-18-0047

Urbach, J. (2012). Beyond grammar: Looking through cultural lenses. *Education and Urban Society, 44*(4), 392–411. doi:10.1177/0013124510392567

Vacca, R., & Vacca, J. (1996). *Content area reading.* New York, NY: HarperCollins College.

Van Cleave, W. (2014). *Writing matters: Developing sentence skills in students of all ages* (2nd ed.). Greenville, SC: W.V.C.ED.

Van Cleave, W. (2015). *Sentence sense A.* Greenville, SC: W.V.C.ED.

Van Cleave, W. (2017). *Sentence sense B.* Greenville, SC: W.V.C.ED.

Veneziano, E., & Nicolopoulou, A. (Eds.). (2019). *Narrative, literacy and other skills: Studies in intervention.* Amsterdam: John Benjamins.

Vogler, C. (1992). *The writer's journey: Mythic structure for writers* (1st ed.). Studio City, CA: Michael Wiese Productions.

Vogler, C. (2007). *The writer's journey: Mythic structure for writers* (3rd ed.). Studio City, CA: Michael Wiese Productions.

Vygotsky, L. (1978). *Mind in society.* Cambridge, MA: Harvard University Press.

Wang, Q. (2013). *The autobiographical self in time and culture.* New York, NY: Oxford. doi:10.1093/acprof:oso/9780199737833.001.0001

Wang, Q., & Fivush, R. (2005). Mother-child conversations of emotionally salient events: Exploring the functions of emotional reminiscing in European American and

Chinese American families. *Social Development, 14,* 473–495. doi:10.1111/j.1467-9507.2005.00312.x

Wang, Q., Leichtman, M. D., & Davies, K. I. (2000). Sharing memories and telling stories: American and Chinese mothers and their 3-year-olds. *Memory, 8*(3), 159–177. doi:10.1080/096582100387588

Wenner, J. A., Burch, M. M., Lynch, J. S., & Bauer, P. J. (2008). Becoming a teller of tales: Associations between children's fictional narratives and parent-child reminiscence narratives. *Journal of Experimental Child Psychology, 101,* 1–19. doi:10.1016/j.jecp.2007.10.006

Westby, C. (1985). Learning to talk-talking to learn: Oral-literate language differences. In C. S. Simon (Ed.), *Communication skills and classroom success: Assessment and therapy methodologies for language and learning disabled students* (pp. 182–213). San Diego, CA: College Hill.

Westby, C. (2001). The world of stories. *Perspectives on Language Learning and Education, 8,* 26–29.

Westby, C., & Culatta, B. (2016a). *Narrative assessment with cultural applications.* ASHA webinar.

Westby, C., & Culatta, B. (2016b). Telling tales: Personal event narratives and life stories. *Language, Speech, and Hearing Services in Schools, 47,* 260–282.

Westby, C. E. (2012). Assessing and remediating text comprehension problems. In H. Catts & A. Kamhi (Eds.), *Language and reading disabilities* (3rd ed., 1–23). Boston, MA: Pearson.

Westby, C. E., & Clauser, P. S. (1999). The right stuff for writing: Assessing and facilitating written language. In H. W. Catts & A. G. Kamhi (Eds.), *Language and reading disabilities* (pp. 259–313). Boston, MA: Allyn & Bacon.

Westby, C. E., Moore, C., & Roman, R. (2002). Reinventing the enemy's language: Developing narratives in Native American children. *Language and Linguistics, 13*(2), 235–269. doi:10.1016/S0898-5898(01)00063-8

Wiesner, K. S. (2005). *First draft in 30 days: A novel writer's system for building a complete and cohesive manuscript.* Cincinnati, OH: Writer's Digest Books.

Wiig, E. H., Semel, E., & Secord, W. A. (2013). *The Clinical Evaluation of Language Fundamentals-5 (CELF-5).* New York, NY: Pearson Education.

Wolster, J. A., DiLollo, A., & Apel, K. (2006). A narrative therapy approach to counseling: A model for working with adolescents with language-literacy deficits. *Language, Speech, and Hearing in the Schools, 37,* 168–177.

Wong, B. Y. L. (2000). Writing strategies instruction for expository essays for adolescents with and without learning disabilities. *Topics in Language Disorders, 20*(4), 29–44.

Wood, C., Schatschneider, C., & Wanzek, J. (2020). Matthew effects in writing productivity during second grade. *Reading and Writing, 33,* 1377–1398. doi:10.1007/s11145-019-10001-8

Worth, S., & Adair, J. (1972). *Through Navajo eyes.* Bloomington: University of Indiana Press.

Wright, T. S., & Neuman, S. B. (2015). The power of content-rich vocabulary instruction. *Perspectives on Language and Literacy, 41*(3), 25–28.

Zelazo, P. D., Blair, C. B., & Willoughby, M. T. (2016). *Executive function: Implications for education.* Washington, DC: National Center for Education Research, Institute of Education Sciences, U.S. Department of Education.

Poetry, Literature, and Film

Adamson, A. (Director). (2001). *Shrek* [Film]. DreamWorks Pictures.

Adeyemi, T. (2015). *Why I write: Telling a story that matters.* Retrieved from https://www.tomiadeyemi.com/blog/telling-a-story-that-matters

Adeyemi, T. (2018). *Children of blood and bone.* New York, NY: Henry & Holt.

Alexander, K. (2014). *The crossover.* Boston, MA: HMH Books for Young Readers.

Anderson, E. K., & Kenneally, M. (Eds.). (2012). *Dear teen me: Authors write letters to their teen selves.* San Francisco, CA: Zest Books.

Anderson, B. (2018). *An inconvenient alphabet: Ben Franklin & Noah Webster's spelling revolution.* New York: NY: Simon & Schuster/Paula Wiseman Books.

Anderson, H. C. (2001). *The little match girl.* New York, NY: Puffin Books Reprint.

Applegate, K. (2008). *Home of the brave.* New York, NY: Square Fish.

Avi. (2002). *Crispin: The cross of lead.* New York, NY: Little, Brown and Company Books for Young Readers.

Barnhill, K. (2016). *The girl who drank the moon.* Chapel Hill, NC: Algonquin Young Readers.

Bartynski, J. M. (2014). *Margret & H. A. Rey's Curious George goes to a bookstore.* Boston, MA: Houghton Mifflin Harcourt.

Baum, L. F. (1900). *The wonderful wizard of Oz.* Chicago, IL: George M. Hill Company.

Bay, M. (Director). (2007). *Transformers* [Film]. DreamWorks Pictures.

Becker, H. (2018). *Counting on Katherine: How Katherine Johnson saved Apollo 13.* New York, NY: Henry Holt and Co.

Bell, C. (2014). *El Deafo.* New York, NY: Harry N. Abrams.

Berg, P. (Director). (2004). *Friday night lights* [Film]. Walt Disney Pictures.

Bissinger, H. G. (1990). *Friday night lights: A town, a team, and a dream.* Boston, MA: Addison-Wesley.

Boyne, J. (2006). *The boy in the striped pajamas.* Oxford, UK: David Fickling Books.

Brooks, B. (2018). *Stories for boys who dare to be different: True tales of amazing boys who changed the world without killing dragons.* Philadelphia, PA: Running Press Kids.

Brown, M. W. (1947). *Goodnight moon.* New York, NY: Harper & Brothers.

Bryant, J. B. (2016). *Six dots: A story of young Louis Braille.* New York, NY: Knopf Books for Young Readers.

Cheney, L. (2004). *When Washington crossed the Delaware: A wintertime story for young patriots.* New York, NY: Simon & Schuster Books for Young Readers.

Collins, B. (2005). The lanyard. In *The trouble with poetry and other poems.* New York, NY: Random House.

Collins, S. (2008). *The hunger games.* New York, NY: Scholastic Trade Publisher.

Coerr, E. (1993). *Sadako.* New York, NY: Puffin Books.

Coerr, E. (1999). *Sadako and the thousand paper cranes.* New York, NY: Puffin Books; Reprint edition. (Original work published 1977)

Cook, B. (Director). (1998). *Mulan* [Film]. Walt Disney Pictures.

Columbus, C. (Director). (2001). *Harry Potter and the sorcerer's stone* [Film]. Warner Bros.

Creech, S. (2001). *Love that dog*. New York, NY: HarperCollins.

Dahl, R. (1964). *Charlie and the chocolate factory*. New York, NY: Alfred A. Knopf.

Davis, K. G. (2014). *Mr. Ferris and his wheel*. Boston, MA: HMH Books for Young Readers.

Dean, C. (2012). *Forget me not*. New York, NY: Simon Pulse.

Dean, C. (2010). *Take me there*. New York, NY: Simon Pulse.

Dean, C. (2002). *Comfort*. Boston, MA: HMH Books for Young Readers.

dePaola, T. (2002). *Adelita: A Mexican Cinderella story*. New York, NY: G. P. Putnam's Sons.

Dorling Kindersley. (2015). *World War II: Visual encyclopedia*. New York, NY: DK Children.

Dyslexia Justice League. (2018). *Dyslexia is my superpower* (Vol. 1). Santa Fe, NM: Author.

Fariña, S.A. (n.d.). *Kai-kai Rapa Nui: Ideogram of threads, ancestral game*. [Mixed media collection.] Chile: Author.

Favilli, E., & Cavallo, F. (2017). *Good night stories for rebel girls* (Vol. 2). Venice, CA: Timbuktu Labs, Inc.

Fershleiser, R., & Smith. L. (Eds.). (2009). *I can't keep my own secrets: Six-word memoirs by teens famous & obscure*. New York, NY: HarperTeen.

Fleischman, S. (1986). *The whipping boy*. New York, NY: Greenwillow Books.

Fleming, V. [Director]. (1939). *The wizard of Oz*. Culver City, CA: Metro-Goldwyn-Mayer.

Gibson, M. (Director). (1995). *Braveheart* [Film]. Paramount Pictures.

Giovanni, N. (1968). Knoxville, Tennessee. In *Black feeling, Black talk, Black judgment*. New York, NY: HarperCollins Publishers.

Golding, W. (1954). *The lord of the flies*. Boston, MA: Faber and Faber.

Henry, O. (1997). *The gift of the magi*. (L. Zwerger, Illus.). New York, NY: Aladdin Paperbacks.

Howitt, M. B. (2002). *The spider and the fly* (T. DiTerlizzi, Illus.). New York, NY: Simon & Schuster Books for Young Readers.

Hunt, L. M. (2015). *Fish in a tree*. New York, NY: Nancy Paulsen Books.

Kim, D. K. (2004). Hurdles. *Same difference and other stories*. Marietta, GA: Top Shelf Productions.

Laird, D. (1990). *The three little Hawaiian pigs and the magic shark*. Honolulu, HI: Barnaby Books.

Landis, J. (Director). (1983). *Trading places* [Film]. Paramount Pictures.

Lewis, C. S. (1950). *The lion, the witch, and the wardrobe*. London, United Kingdom: Geoffrey Bles.

Lin, G. (2009). *Where the mountain meets the moon*. Boston, MA: Little, Brown Books.

Lin, G. (2016). *The windows and mirrors of your child's bookshelf* [Video]. TEDxNatick Talk, available on YouTube. https://www.youtube.com/watch?v=_wQ8wiV3FVo

Lowell, S. (1992). *The three little javelinas*. Lanham, MD: Cooper Square Publishing.

Lucas, G. (Director). (1977). *Star wars: A new hope* [Film]. LUCASFILM.

Lyon, G. E. (1999). Where I'm from. *Where I'm from: Where poems come from*. Spring, TX: Absey & Company.

MacLachlan, P. (2015). *Sarah, plain and tall*. New York, NY: HarperCollins; Anniversary edition. (Original work published 1985)

MacLachlan, P. (2020). *Prairie days*. New York, NY: Margaret K. McElderry Books.

Mahy, M. (1990). *The seven Chinese brothers*. New York, NY: Blue Ribbon Book.

Martin, B. (1996). *Brown bear, brown bear, what do you see?* New York, NY: Henry Holt & Company. (Original work published 1967)

Martin, R. (1992). *The rough-face girl*. New York, NY: G. P. Putnam Sons Books for Young Readers.

Mattick, L. (2015). *Finding Winnie: The true story of the world's most famous bear*. New York, NY: Little, Brown and Company.

Mesiti-Miller, P. (Producer). (2019, November 1). *The garbage man*. Retrieved from https://www.wnycstudios.org/podcasts/snapjudgment/segments/garbage-man

Meyer, S. (2005). *Twilight*. New York, NY: Little, Brown and Company.

Milne, A. A. (1996). *The complete tales of Winnie the Pooh*. New York, NY: Dutton Books for Young Readers.

Nelson, G. (Director). (1976). *Freaky Friday* [Film]. Walt Disney Productions.

Nelson, V. M. (2003). *Almost to freedom*. Minneapolis, MN: Carolrhoda Books.

Nelson, V. M. (2009). *Bad news for outlaws: The remarkable life of Bass Reeves, Deputy U.S. Marshal*. Minneapolis, MN: Carolrhoda Books.

Nelson, V. M. (2019). *Let 'er buck! George Fletcher, the people's champion*. Minneapolis, MN: Carolrhoda Books.

Numeroff, L. J. (1985). *If you give a mouse a cookie*. New York, NY: Harper & Row.

O'Brien, T. (1998). *The things they carried*. New York, NY: Broadway Books.

O'Dell, S. (1960). *Island of the blue dolphins*. Boston, MA: HMH Books for Young Readers.

O'Hara, M. (1941). *My friend Flicka*. Philadelphia, PA: J.P. Lippincott Co. Reprint Edition (2008). New York, NY: HarperCollins

Parton, D. (1996). *Coat of many colors*. New York. NY: HarperCollins.

Paterson, K. (1977). *Bridge to Terabithia*. New York, NY: Thomas Y. Crowell Company.

Polacco, P. (1993). *Some birthday*. New York, NY: Simon & Schuster.

Polacco, P. (1994). *My rotten redheaded older brother*. New York, NY: Aladdin.

Polacco, P. (1996). *Meteor*. New York, NY: Puffin.

Polacco, P. (1997). *Thunder cake*. New York, NY: Puffin.

Polacco, P. (1998). *Thank you, Mr. Falker*. New York, NY: Scholastic Inc. (paperback)

Polacco, P. (1999). *My ol' man*. New York, NY: Puffin.

Polacco, P. (2001). *Betty doll*. New York, NY: Philomel.

Polacco, P. (2017, January 15). *Creating life-long readers through choice*. Retrieved from http://russonreading.blogspot.com/2017/01/creating-life-long-readers-through.html

Rey, H. A. (1969). *Curious George*. Boston, MA: HMH Books for Young Readers. (Original work published 1941)

Riordan, R. (2010). *The lightning thief: The graphic novel (Percy Jackson and the Olympians, Book 1)*. Glendale, CA: Disney-Hyperion.

Rockliff, M. (2015a). *Gingerbread for liberty! How a German baker helped win the American Revolution.* Boston, MA: Houghton Mifflin Harcourt Books for Young Readers.

Rockliff, M. (2015b). *Mesmerized: How Ben Franklin solved a mystery that baffled all of France.* Somerville, MA: Candlewick.

Rodgers, M. (2003). *Freaky Friday.* New York, NY: Harper and Row. (Original work published 1972)

Rose, C. S. (2014). *May B.* New York, NY: Yearling. (Reprint edition.)

Rose, C. S. (2019). *A race around the world: The true story of Nellie Bly and Elizabeth Bisland.* Chicago, IL: Albert Whitman & Company.

Rowling, J. K. (1997). *Harry Potter and the philosopher's stone.* London, UK: Bloomsbury Children's Books.

Ruby, L. (1994). *Steal away home.* New York, NY: Simon & Schuster Children's Publishing.

Rylant, C. (2001). *Waiting to waltz: A childhood.* New York, NY: Atheneum/Richard Jackson Books.

Sachar, L. (1998). *Holes.* New York, NY: Farrar, Straus and Giroux.

Satrapi, M. (2004). *Persepolis: The story of a childhood.* New York, NY: Pantheon.

Scieszka, J. (1994). *The frog prince, continued.* New York, NY: Puffin Books (paperback).

Scieszka, J. (1996). *The true story of the three little pigs.* New York, NY: Puffin Books; Reprint edition. (Original work published 1989)

Scott, R. (Director). (2000). *Gladiator* [Film]. DreamWorks Pictures.

Seinfeld, J. (2008). *Halloween.* New York, NY: Little, Brown Books for Young Readers.

Sendak, M. (1963). *Where the wild things are.* New York, NY: Harper & Row.

Shaw, N. (1988). *Sheep in a jeep.* Boston, MA: HMH Books for Young Readers.

Shetterly, M. (2018). *Hidden figures: The true story about four Black women and the space race.* New York, NY: Harper Collins.

Smith, C. L. (2007). *Tantalize.* Somerville, MA: Candlewick.

Smith, C. L. (2011). *Tantalize: Kieren's story.* Somerville, MA: Candlewick.

Sones, S. (2016). *Stop pretending: What happened when my big sister went crazy.* New York, NY: Harper-Teen.

Steig, W. (1969). *Sylvester and the magic pebble.* New York, NY: Windmill Books.

Stoker, B. (1897). *Dracula.* London, United Kingdom: Archibald Constable and Company.

Thompson, L. A. (2015). *Emmanuel's dream: The true story of Emmanuel Ofosu Yeboah.* New York, NY: Schwartz & Wade.

Twain, M. (1882). *The prince and the pauper.* Boston, MA: James R. Osgood and Company.

Wang, A. (2019). *Magic ramen: The story of Momofuko Ando.* New York, NY: Little Bee Books.

Warburton, T. (Director), Dorough, B. (Music director), & American Broadcasting Company (ABC). (1973). *Schoolhouse rock!* [Television series]. Burbank, CA: Buena Vista Entertainment.

White, E. B. (1952). *Charlotte's web.* New York, NY: Harper & Brothers.

Willett, J., & Rozelle, R. (2005). *Warden: Texas prison life and death from the inside out.* Houston, TX: Bright Sky Publishing.

Young, E. (1996). *Lon Po-Po: A Red Riding Hood story from China.* New York, NY: Puffin Books Reprint.

Index

Page numbers followed by *f* and *t* indicate figures and tables, respectively.